THE MIEGUNYAH PRESS

THIS IS NUMBER SEVENTY-FIVE IN THE
SECOND NUMBERED SERIES OF THE
MIEGUNYAH VOLUMES
MADE POSSIBLE BY THE
MIEGUNYAH FUND
ESTABLISHED BY BEQUESTS
UNDER THE WILLS OF
SIR RUSSELL AND LADY GRIMWADE.

'MIEGUNYAH' WAS THE HOME OF
MAB AND RUSSELL GRIMWADE
FROM 1911 TO 1955

François Péron

AN IMPETUOUS LIFE

Naturalist and Voyager

EDWARD DUYKER

THE
MIEGUNYAH
PRESS

THE MIEGUNYAH PRESS
An imprint of Melbourne University Publishing Ltd
187 Grattan Street, Carlton, Victoria 3053, Australia
mup-info@unimelb.edu.au
www.mup.com.au

First published 2006
Text © 2006 Edward Duyker
Design and typography © 2006 Melbourne University Publishing Ltd

Edited by Cathryn Game
Text and cover design by Sandra Nobes
Maps by Susan Duyker
Printed in China by Australian Book Connection

National Library of Australia Cataloguing-in-Publication entry

Duyker, Edward, 1955–.
François Péron : an impetuous life : naturalist and voyager.

   Bibliography.
   Includes index.
   ISBN 978 0522 85260 8.
   ISBN 0 522 85260 2.

   1. Péron, François, 1775–1810. 2. Péron, François, 1775–1810 Voyage de découvertes aux terres australes. 3. Naturalists—France—Biography. 4. Travellers—France—Biography. 5. Australia—Discovery and exploration—French. I. Title.

919.4042

This project has been assisted by the Commonwealth Government through the Australia Council, its arts funding and advisory body.

Australia **Council**
for the Arts

Pour

la famille Debard

Cérilly

avec mes remerciements

Contents

Contents

Illustrations

Maps

Acknowledgements

THIS book would have been impossible without the decades of meticulous scholarship undertaken by Jacqueline Bonnemains while she was Curator of the Lesueur Collection at the Muséum d'histoire naturelle in Le Havre. Jacqueline Bonnemains shared her knowledge and publications with extraordinary generosity and went to great lengths to facilitate my research when I visited Le Havre in November 2002 and March 2003. Each time I left the museum I was heavily laden with photocopies and notes, and my stomach was filled with a sumptuous Norman repast. I will never forget her help and kindness. Since Jacqueline's retirement, I have been ably assisted by her gracious young successor, Gabrielle Baglione, who has answered many reference questions with patience and diligence. I am also very grateful to Prof. Michel Jangoux, Laboratoire de Biologie Marine, Université Libre de Bruxelles in Belgium, for the many painstaking transcriptions he made in Le Havre and other archives, and for copies of his articles—in some cases even before they were published. In the category of crucial contributions, I must also acknowledge Christine Cornell Cooper for permission to quote from her elegant translations of Nicolas Baudin's journal and volume ii of Péron's *Voyage*. As co-translator of Bruny d'Entrecasteaux's journal, I know what enormous labours she has spared me!

In François Péron's birthplace, Cérilly (Allier), I owe a great debt to Dr Françoise Debard. She not only shared the fruits of her veterinary thesis dealing with the naturalist's work on seals but also gave me copies of many other useful articles and documents, guided me around the town and its environs, and introduced me to several erudite local historians, librarians and archivists. Our paths had already crossed in Sydney and would cross again in Mauritius—where she yet again assisted me with archival research. Furthermore, Françoise's charming parents, Dr Henri and Josette Debard, generously accommodated my whole family during our stay in Cérilly. I will never forget the warmth of their welcome and the fact that during two visits to Péron's *ville natale* they gave me the use of their own bed. In Cérilly, I was also assisted by the parish priest Père Michel Joussain; the mayor Olivier Filliat (who gave me access to the municipal archives in the town hall attic); the former mayor Daniel Gulon (who shared his notes and transcriptions); Alain Pétiniot, President of the Association François Péron; and historian Jacques Perchat. At times I felt that I was living in a play in which the actors comprised half the town, and everyone knew the script except me; nevertheless, I soon learned to improvise! In neighbouring Moulins and Yzeure, I thank Claude and Monique Blanchet; Bernard Trapes, Bibliothèque de la Société d'Emulation du Bourbonnais; Agnès Leca, Bibliothèque municipale, for a great deal of bibliographic precision; Jacques Desforges, Service des Archives, Evêché de Moulins, and Denis Tronchard, Directeur, Archives départementales de l'Allier, who facilitated my discovery of a treasure trove of notarial documents relating to the Péron family.

In Paris, where I undertook research for several months, I wish to thank Simone Brunau, Directeur, Cité internationale des Arts; Dr Jacqueline Goy, Institut océanographique; Martine Marin, Les Amis de Nicolas Baudin; Hélène Deleuze and Véronique Royet, Bibliothèque nationale; Caroline Picketty, Archives nationales; the marvellous Bernadette Molitor, Librarian, Bibliothèque de l'Histoire de la Médecine; Sandrine Aufray, Services d'Archives de Paris; Marie-Véronique Clin, Musée d'histoire de la Médecine; Frédéric Lions, Bibliothèque historique de la Ville de Paris; Dr Bernard Métivier, Maître de Conférences, Département Milieux et Peuplements Aquatiques, Muséum national d'histoire naturelle; Rodolphe Leroy and Pascale Heurtel, Bibliothèque centrale du Muséum national d'histoire naturelle; Bernard Chevalier, Directeur, Musée national des châteaux de Malmaison et Bois-Préau; Michèle Pierron, Bibliothèque du Musée de l'Armée; Marie-Hélène Joly, Librarian, Musée national de la Marine; Adrien Mattatia, Musée de l'Homme; Lieutenant-Colonel Bodinier, Hervé Deborre, Bernard Hamaïde, Service historique de l'Armée de Terre, Vincennes; and Magali Lacousse, Service historique de la Marine, Vincennes. Beyond Paris, I thank the late Dr Louis Dulieu,

Faculté de Médecine, Montpellier; Nicole Beziaud, Archives municipales, La Rochelle; Sylvie Barot, Archives municipales du Havre; Armelle Sentilhles, Archives départementales de la Seine-Maritime, Rouen; Dr Sylvain Chimello and Dominique Laglasse, Bibliothèque municipale de Thionvillle; and Jean-Claude Lumet, Centre Généalogique du Sud-Ouest; Dr Maurice Recq, Landerneau; and Alain Serieyx, Draguignan.

In Germany, I am deeply grateful to Dr Christiane Resch and her husband Bernd, in Saarwellingen, who were gracious and generous hosts and who took the time and trouble to drive me to the Rhineland towns and villages associated with François Péron's military service. I also thank Georg André, Saarlouis Stadtbibliothek; Dr Tobias von Elsner, Magdeburger Museen, Magdeburg; Katrin Hoptock, Stadtarchiv Speyer; Rudolf Kinscherff, Dudenoffen; and Christine Kohl-Langer, Archiv und Museum, Landau in der Pfalz. For help researching Anselme Riedlé's origins, I thank Barbara Anders and Simone Herde, archivists in Augsburg. In Spain, I thank Belém Rodríguez and Maria Jesus Martinez-Martinez, Biblioteca nacional, Madrid; and Santiago Rumeu Casares and Ana Sauri, Museo naval, Madrid. In the Canary Islands, I extend my gratitude to Lourdes Pemán and Nuria Hernández Abrante of the Biblioteca publica municipal, Puerto de la Cruz, Tenerife, for their patience with my Spanish and assistance with local sources. For help researching Nils Bergsten, Péron's Swedish colleague, I thank my very dear friend Per Tingbrand in Dalarö, and the late Tomas Anfält in Uppsala. For assistance with Péron's American acquaintances, I thank Robert C. Pembleton in Ontario, Canada, and Don Cogswell, in Sebring, Florida. For matchless hospitality and a great deal of assistance, in Mauritius, I extend my thanks to Rex and Chantal Fanchette, Ambassador Patrice Curé, Dr Madeleine Ly-Tio-Fane, Dr Huguette Ly-Tio-Fane Pineo, Dr Raymond d'Unienville, Dr Guy Rouillard and Philippe la Hausse de Lalouvière. At the University of Mauritius, I thank Prof. Vinesh Hookoomsing and Prof. Serge Rivière; and at the National Archives of Mauritius I thank Mrs U. Sohun and Dharmendra Mukool.

In Hobart, Tasmania, I extend my sincere gratitude to Louise Gilfedder, Dr Steven Smith and the late Dr Irynej Skira, Department of Primary Industries, Water and Environment; Tony Marshall, State Library of Tasmania; and Elizabeth Turner, Curator of Invertebrate Zoology, and Kathryn Medlock, Curator of Vertebrate Zoology, Tasmanian Museum and Art Gallery. In Launceston, I thank Chris Tassell, Director, Queen Victoria Museum and Art Gallery for permission to quote from the work of the late Dr Brian Plomley. On King Island I thank Donald, Bronwyn and Catherine Graham; Ingeborg Graf, Currie Library; and Ena Johnson, King Island Historical Museum. I also extend special thanks to Fred Duncan, Senior Botanist, Forest Practices Board, Tasmania, who was conducting field research on King Island at the time of my visit and provided invaluable assistance and no end of stimulating conversation. In Canberra I acknowledge an enormous scholarly debt to my dear friend, the late Dr Frank Horner and to his daughters Philippa, Harriet and Elizabeth for permission to quote from his work; I also thank Andrew Sergeant; Sylvia Carr, Teresa Donnellan, Maura O'Connor and Marika Tölgyesi, National Library of Australia; and Tom Weir and Michelle Michie, Australian National Insect Collection. In Western Australia, I thank Dr Jane Fromont, Curator of Marine Invertebrates, Department of Aquatic Zoology, Western Australian Museum; Malcolm Traill, Librarian, Albany History Collection, Albany; and Dr Phillip Playford, Geological Survey of Western Australia. I also thank Gunhild Marchant for permission to quote from the work of her late husband, Prof. Leslie Marchant. In Adelaide, South Australia, I thank Dr Jane Southwood for passing on the fruits of her work with Dr Donald Simpson on the medical scientists of Baudin's expedition, and Helen Williams, State Library of South Australia. At the University of Adelaide, I thank Prof. Maciej Henneberg, Wood Jones Professor of Anthropological and Comparative Anatomy, Dr Carl N. Stephan, Lecturer in Biological Anthropology and Anatomy, Department of Anatomical Sciences, for help comparing Péron's portraits with forensic precision, and Dr Jean Fornasiero, Senior Lecturer, French Studies, for assistance with Baudin's shipboard library. On Kangaroo Island (South Australia), I thank Dr Gabriel Bittar and his wife Jacqueline, at American River, for their kind hospitality and wise orientation; and Sharon Gullickson, Kingscote Public Library, for her help with local sources. In Melbourne, I thank Des Cowley, La Trobe Library, State Library of Victoria.

In Sydney, I thank Fiona Simpson and especially Leoné Lemmer, Australian Museum Library (who answered countless reference and taxonomic questions with extraordinary speed and precision); Dr Gregory de Moore, Western Sydney Area Health Service, for sharing his thoughts on tuberculosis and on Péron's psyche; Emeritus Prof. Ivan Barko and Prof. Margaret Sankey (McCaughey Professor of French), of the University of Sydney, for a great deal of support, constructive comment and encouragement, together with Jill Brown, Cong Tam Dao, Rod Dyson, Bruce Isaacs, Aleksandra Nikolic and Brian O'Donnell, at the Fisher Library for help with very many inter-library loans. Dr Chris Cunneen, Department of History, Macquarie University, editing the *Australian Dictionary of Biography Supplement*, was very generous with his knowledge of early Port Jackson identities. I also thank Lyn Barakat, Jacinta Crane, Ruth Ivery, Therese Kerr, Wendy Lewis, Helen McDonald, Beverley Norton, Stephen Peacock and Janet Samerski of the Sutherland Shire Library Service; and Joe Coelho, Mark Hildebrand, Edwina Rudd and Julie Wood, State Library of New South Wales, for their help with many sources and reference queries.

I am very much indebted to my wife Susan and my sons Samuel and Pierre for their understanding and assistance researching this book. Susan accompanied me on visits to many of Péron's landfalls and drafted the maps herein. My mother, Maryse Duyker, assisted me greatly in deciphering and translating numerous French sources cited in this book. My mother-in-law Betty Wade, herself a tuberculosis survivor, was also an important source of encouragement and constructive critical comment. I am very grateful to my editor Cathryn Game, to Felicity Edge and Tracy O'Shaughnessy of MUP and to designer Sandra Nobes for their respective contributions to bringing this book to fruition.

Finally, this project was assisted by the Australia Council, the Commonwealth Government's arts funding and advisory body.

EDWARD DUYKER
'Glenn Robin', Sylvania, NSW

Textual note

THE quotations from the first volume of Péron's *Voyage de découvertes aux Terres Australes* largely follow Richard Phillips's English edition of 1809. Only where the translation has wandered too far from the original French or modern English[1] have I made changes. In some places I have also revised Phillips's archaic English spelling. Regardless of whether or not the translated quotations have been revised, I have cited the page numbers from both the original French edition and the Phillips translation in my notes. However, for the second volume of Péron's *Voyage*, completed by Louis de Freycinet, I have used Christine Cornell's fine 2003 translation with her kind permission and without alteration. The page numbers for these quotations are also cited from the original French edition with bracketed page numbers for the published translation.

I have avoided translating many institutional names, but I have translated many naval ranks despite the fact that they do not always have exact English equivalents. For example, although the *aspirants* of the Baudin expedition were roughly equivalent to that of a British naval cadet and a midshipman combined, I have translated this rank as midshipman, as Frank Horner did before me. Where the rank of ensign appears in the text it is as a translation of *enseigne de vaisseau*. At the time of Baudin's expedition, this designated a sublieutenant promoted from the lower deck, who could be any age from eighteen to thirty. An *enseigne de vaisseau*, however, had more responsibility than a sublieutenant in the British navy. And where I have referred to someone as a lieutenant, this is an abbreviation of *lieutenant de vaisseau*. This should not be confused with the Ancien Régime intermediate naval rank of *lieutenant de frégate*, which was junior even to *enseigne de vaisseau*. My final authority in the translation of French nautical terms has been the classic *Dictionnaire de la marine à voile* by Pierre-Marie-Joseph de Bonnefoux, first published in 1848 and revised by E. Paris in 1856. I have also converted dates from the French Revolutionary calendar to Gregorian equivalents. Readers will find more information in my glossary of French terms.

In rendering pre-metric French measurements originally in *lieues*, *pieds*, *pouces*, *livres* and *tonneaux*, I have used feet, pounds and tons as a free translation, rather than attempting qualified equivalents. Mile in this biography usually refers to the French nautical mile (1.852 kilometres), almost the same as an English nautical mile and approximate to a minute of latitude. Péron also used some obsolete metric measurements such as *decametres*, but included *pieds* and *pouces* in brackets in his *Voyage*. I have not converted these to centimetres; instead I have retained the measurements of the published translations. I have also retained some old French spellings such as Henry with a 'y', as in Henry de Freycinet.

When citing French titles or the names of French institutions (such as museums, archives, academies and so on) I have generally attempted to follow French grammatical rules and capitalisation styles. Some variation appears in the capitalisation of the months of the revolutionary calendar; I have cited them as I found them in the titles of documents, but otherwise left them in lower case according to modern French convention. I have tried to orient my readers with reference to the old provinces of France (such as Bourbonnais, Franche Comté, Brittany, Normandy and Dauphiné), but when referring to small towns and hamlets, I have generally given the name of the surrounding present-day *département*. Although I have abandoned some archaic anglicisms, I have not forsaken familiar English equivalents such as Napoleon, without the acute accent. Similarly, modern Australian accentless versions of the place-names that originated from the Baudin voyage have also been employed, as have modern Indonesian spellings. Nevertheless, given the repeated use of several archaic toponyms in my primary sources, I have thought it best to retain them for historical ambience. These include Ile de France (modern Mauritius), New Holland (mainland Australia) and Van Diemen's Land (Tasmania). The last two date from Abel Tasman's voyage of 1642. After this explorer effectively circumnavigated the known 'south land' and established that it was an island continent, it was given the name 'Nova Hollandia' (Latin = New Holland) on the Eugene Map (*c.* 1644), which consolidated the discoveries of the early Dutch navigators. Tasman also named his southern landfall of November 1642 'Anthonie Van Diemens-land' in honour of the governor of the Dutch East Indies. He was unaware, however, that it was an island separate from New Holland. In 1854, in order to make a break with its brutal convict past, Van Diemen's Land was officially renamed Tasmania in honour of its discoverer.

Because this is the biography of a naturalist, it contains the scientific names of many plants and animals collected during the Baudin expedition. Although the extent of taxonomic discussion might be tedious for some readers, it is unavoidable for a serious discussion of Péron's life and work. Nevertheless, I have not always felt it necessary to cite the name of every zoological or botanical author after every species mentioned in the narrative. In discussing taxonomic revision, I have often inserted the generally accepted modern equivalent of an original name in parentheses. But when Péron collected a species that had already been described, and in turn revised, I have not gone to the extent of citing the author of a basionym in yet another set of parentheses. Finally, I have sought to ease the confusion of some readers with a glossary of basic scientific terms at the end of the book.

The principal French and German cities and towns associated with Péron's life

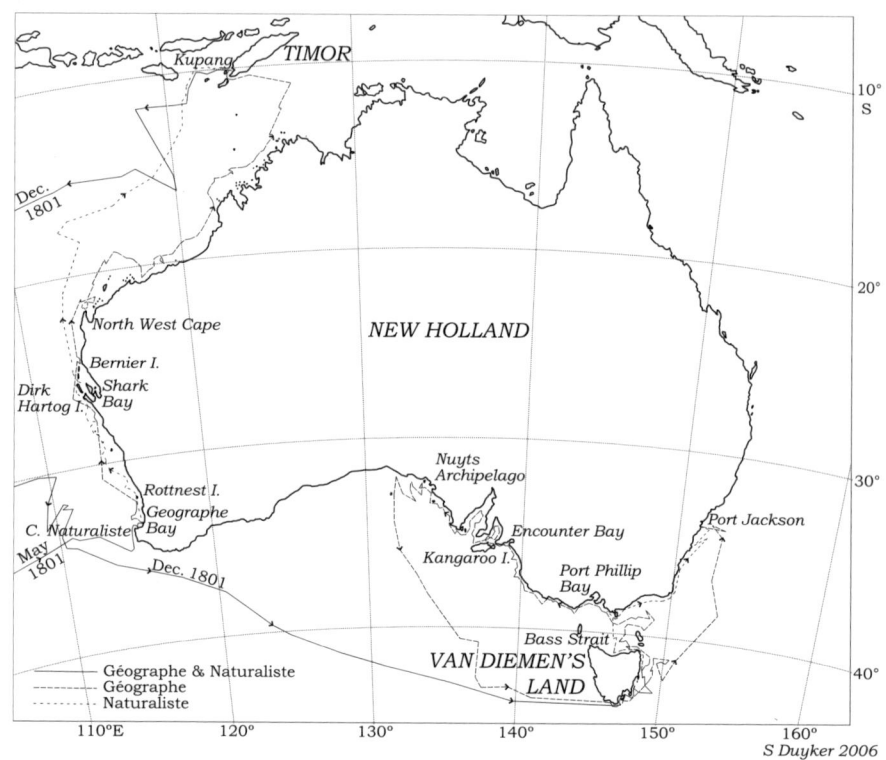

The tracks of the *Géographe* and *Naturaliste*, May 1801 to June 1802

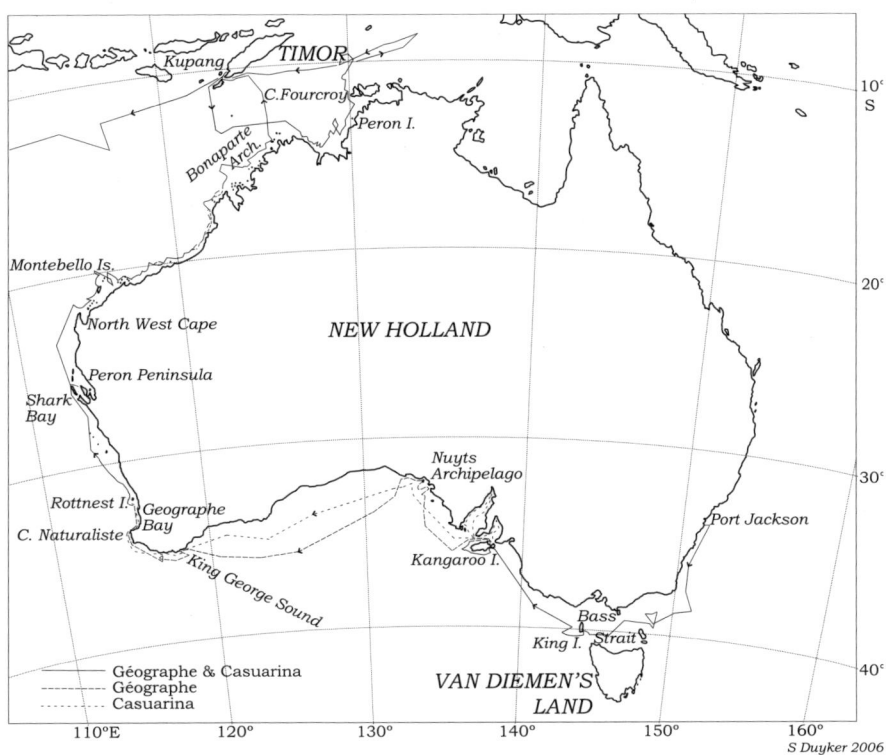

The tracks of the *Géographe* and *Casuarina*, November 1802 to July 1803

Introduction

*… possessing an impetuous imagination that never bent to authority, of
a dangerous and sometimes dishonest and imprudent frankness, too sure
of my opinions that I maintain without reserve, full of heedlessness and
inconsistency …*

FRANÇOIS PÉRON, NOVEMBER 1800

SOMEWHERE in the Atlantic aboard the French vessel of discovery
Géographe in November 1800, a young man of twenty-five stringently
reviewed his life. There was no priest to hear his 'mea culpa'. He confessed
on paper, reflecting on his studies and on the painful years of war he had
known as a soldier and as a prisoner in Germany. He declared all his failings and then surveyed his saving graces. Despite all his imperfections—
his thoughtlessness, stubbornness, indiscretion and querulousness—he felt
redeemed by the qualities he could see in his own heart. He was not without gentleness, affection or kindness. Despite the war crimes of his
compatriots, he had found love and esteem even among hapless German
civilians. He recognised his eccentricities and his discomfit with social
norms and customs, and he recognised that he had often alienated his
friends. Nevertheless he had always managed to make amends and to gain
forgiveness. The young man was François Péron, naturalist of a major
voyage of exploration to Australian waters between 1800 and 1803. It is
hard to know exactly what provoked this rigorous self-examination, found
among his papers on his death ten years later:[1] possibly self-doubt in the
wake of recent thwarted love for the daughter of a wealthy notary in his

hometown; possibly the first of what would eventually become many differences with the commander of the expedition, Nicolas Baudin. Ultimately, when he wrote the official account of the expedition, Péron would cast aside the moral scruples that appeared to concern him so much and poison the very wells of his commander's reputation. It is perhaps not surprising that the ethical and emotional tensions that Péron identified in himself should have characterised his life.

My own curiosity about Péron was first aroused, in 1983, when I consulted the report in which he took it upon himself to assess the strengths and weaknesses of the infant British colony of Port Jackson and called for its conquest with the aid of rebellious Irish convicts. Péron presented this report to Captain-General Decaen, Governor of the Ile de France (now Mauritius). This island is where my mother was born, and I had come across a microfilm of Péron's secret memoir in the course of research at the National Library. Some of my Franco-Mauritian forebears probably met Péron, if not Baudin. Others must have studied under the expedition's distinguished hydrographer, Pierre Faure,[2] the botanist Jacques Delisse and Midshipman Julien Billard,[3] all of whom taught for many years at the Collège Royal, after settling on the island. Michel Garnier, one of the original artists of the Baudin expedition, was certainly taken prisoner by the British along with one of my direct ancestors. Yet another of my forebears, taken prisoner by the Royal Navy the previous year, was one of the French naval officers finally exchanged for Matthew Flinders— another prominent figure in this story. Having searched, unsuccessfully, for Baudin's last resting place in Mauritius in 1984,[4] I was immediately drawn to Frank Horner's masterly work, *The French Reconnaissance*, when it was published in 1987. Although I did not mince words about Péron's 'calumny' in my review, I remained intrigued by the complex human chemistry of the expedition and Baudin's chequered reputation. And the more I read of Péron, the more I realised that he was deserving of more detailed scholarship.

There have already been a number of accounts of François Péron's life, beginning with the two elegies that appeared within a year of his death: one by Marie-Joseph Alard, Secretary-General of the Société médicale, the other by Joseph-Philippe-François Deleuze, librarian of the Muséum national d'histoire naturelle in Paris. Both men held Péron in high regard. Deleuze had access to some of his private papers and also sought detailed reminiscences from his close friends, including Charles-Alexandre Lesueur. Almost half a century later in 1855, when France had the misfortune to be ruled by yet another Bonaparte, a competition was held by the Société d'Emulation de l'Allier for the writing of an historical account of Péron's life. The winner of the competition was the entomologist Maurice Girard, and his glowing tribute to François Péron was published in Paris and Moulins in 1856. Girard's biography is noteworthy for the oral history he recorded from one individual who had known Péron personally in his youth and from the grandson of another. It would seem that a runner-up in this local competition was the historian Louis Audiat, who published a competing, yet equally glowing, account of Péron's life in Moulins in 1855. Audiat might have attempted to steal Girard's thunder by rushing into print first, but his work tells us little that was not already recorded in the elegies of Alard and Deleuze or in Péron's own account of his voyage with Baudin. In many respects the same can be said of the two biographies that appeared in the twentieth century: the first by Emile Guillaumin in 1937, the other by Colin Wallace in 1984. For all their valid recognition of Péron's achievements, both repeated old errors, embellished facts in the quest for an engaging narrative and avoided a critical assessment of their subject's relationship with Nicolas Baudin. The hagiographic tone of Guillaumin's work, for example, was willingly embraced by one anonymous reviewer who saw Péron ultimately 'as a prodigious worker, a firm and correct character, a hero, a kind of saint …'.[5] More recently, urologist Georges Rigondet has given us yet another hagiography, employing the techniques of a novelist, with passages of invented dialogue, even some invented characters and a great deal of romantic reconstruction and supposition.

Of English-language historians, Colin Wallace was not the first to express considerable admiration for Péron. One of Australia's most respected historians, Sir Ernest Scott, in his fine study *Terre Napoléon* published in 1910, thought Péron unreliable as an historian of the voyage, but wrote:

> One would conclude from his style of writing that he was by temperament excitable and easily subject to depression. A zealous savant, to whom fishes and birds, beetles and butterflies, were the precious things of the earth, and for whom the discovery of a new species was as great a source of joy as a glorious victory was to his imperial master, Péron appeals to us as a pathetic figure whom one would rather screen from blame than otherwise. He suffered severely, and did his final work under the difficulty of breaking health.[6]

And in his penultimate chapter, Scott declared: 'Of Péron's personal character, and of the value of his scientific work, nothing but high praise can be written. He was but a young man when he died. Had he lived, we cannot doubt that he would have filled an important place among French men of science, for his diligence was coupled with insight, and his love of research was as deep as his aptitude for it was keen.'[7]

Scott also had little time for accusations levelled against Péron as an envious and ungracious spy.[8] He recognised that the British let Péron see only what they wanted him to see during his visit to Port Jackson. Nevertheless, Scott was not blind to the injustice perpetrated by Péron and Louis de Freycinet in their treatment of Baudin in the official account of the expedition and their 'consistent suppression of his name throughout the text of the volumes'. Hence he wrote:

> Attention has to be directed to this display of animosity because, in bare justice to Baudin, we have to remember that the only story of the expedition which we have is that written by Péron and Freycinet, who were plainly at enmity with him. If the facts were as related by them, Baudin was not only an absurdly obstinate and ungenial captain, but we are left with grave doubts as to his competency as a navigator on service of this description. Yet even facts, when detailed by those who hate a man, take a different colouring from the same facts set down by the man himself, with his reasons for what he did.[9]

Scott did not have access to Baudin's journals, but he felt compelled to remark that in 'his conduct and correspondence in relation to Governor King at Port Jackson … he appears as a gentleman of agreeable manners, graceful expression, and ready tact'.[10]

The revisionist histories of the expedition, produced with access to its journals, have done much to rehabilitate Baudin.[11] But some popular histories, such as Klaus Toft's documentary film and book, *The Navigators*, have marginalised Péron as Baudin's vengeful nemesis.[12] Others have been more sympathetic. Leslie Marchant in his book *France Australe* recognised Péron's 'passionate nature' and the difficulties experienced by scientists attempting to work under rigid naval discipline. He also believed that there was a politically charged atmosphere aboard the expedition and asserted that many of its bitter differences were ideological: 'Péron was a revolutionary. Baudin was an officer of the old school. Péron had fought for the revolution and his beliefs. Baudin at the time Péron was fighting and was wounded was serving in the ships of the enemy of the French Revolution, Austria, whose armies had captured Péron. Harmony between these two was thus not readily possible.'[13]

In fact, Péron was taken prisoner by the Prussians and, as we shall see, he appears to have been more politically conservative than many historians have assumed. Frank Horner, despite his vindication of Baudin, did not seek to gloss over his faults; and while he exposed Péron's faults too, he also recognised the presence of an extraordinary young man:

> In some ways Péron was another Bory [de Saint-Vincent]: he had the same tireless passion for natural history, and the same deep patriotism rooted in service with his country's armies. But Péron's origins were as poor as Bory's were affluent; his scientific interests were even broader than Bory's: they seem to have embraced almost the whole of science, including even the new field of anthropology. His short life was lived with a prodigal expense of energy; the scientific ventures he embarked on during the expedition, whether as described by himself or others, tend to leave the reader with a sense of excess, like the style and substance of his *Voyage*; his manner of speech seems to have exhausted even himself ... It is not hard to imagine how a man like Baudin, living with such a phenomenon, could find so much zeal too much. The real tragedy of Péron's life was his failure to concentrate his superabundant energies in the channel where they would have been most rewarding to himself and the world: zoology.[14]

Most historians have given only cursory attention to Péron's achievements as a zoologist; however, a number of scientists have undertaken important studies of particular aspects of his (and his collaborator Charles-Alexandre Lesueur's) collections. They include Jacqueline Bonnemains, Jacqueline Goy and Michel Jangoux as well as Marie-Louise Bauchot, Jean-Claude Braconnot, Gérard Breton, Claire Bustarret, Claude Carré, Claude Chappuis, Jacques Daguet, Françoise Debard, Jane Fromont, Jean-Loup d'Hondt, Lipke Holthuis, Diana Jones, Charles Roux and Rolande Roux-Estève. As an historian, I have used their work as a guiding thread through the scientific labyrinth. Significantly, one of these scientists, Michel Jangoux, has also offered a convincing character assessment of Péron: 'a complex and paradoxical person. Intelligent and brilliant, impetuous and excited but also warm and loyal in friendship, without doubt pre-sumptuous, certainly ambitious, he was all these things at the same time[,] which has baffled more than one of his biographers.'[15]

Several historians have harshly criticised Péron as an anthropologist —although anthropology was not his official responsibility during the expedition—and some have misrepresented his views on race.[16] Most have ignored his significance as a philosophical traveller whose observations, particularly on the convict system in New South Wales, were surprisingly influential in France. All narratives are to some extent self-serving. Péron's *Voyage de découvertes aux Terres australes* is clearly no exception, but as a participant observer with an impressive intellect, his account remains a valuable document of Baudin's expedition—albeit one that must be read discerningly. Had Péron deserted or died, like so many of his colleagues, the glory of the expedition would have been greatly diminished. The zoo-logical specimens he gathered with his colleagues during the voyage were, at the time, the most comprehensive Australian natural history collection ever made. Soon after, kangaroos, emus and black swans graced the grounds of the Empress Joséphine's château at Malmaison. Today, many Australian species bear Péron's name as specific epithets and honour his contribution as an early zoological collector. At a time when the discovery of new species and genera was seen as the height of zoological pursuit, Péron enjoyed considerable kudos.

Nevertheless, his scientific efforts went well beyond the mere ordering of the natural world. Péron's writings suggest sympathy for the 'trans-mutationist' ideas of his contemporary Lamarck, who believed in species change through the inheritance of acquired characteristics. Péron certainly drew attention to the effects of climate and geography as forces of species modification. Although he did not argue an overt evolutionary case, based on natural selection in the modern Darwinian sense, his writings certainly had a broader systematic, morphological and biogeographical significance, upon which later evolutionary ecology was built. As we shall see, Lamarck made numerous references to Péron's work in a number of his publica-tions.[17] It is also significant that Péron was one of the authors whom Charles Darwin read (in the original French) and respected. Indeed he cited the *Voyage* in a footnote in *The Voyage of the Beagle* and made refer-ence to Péron's observations on sea-elephant polygamy in *The Descent of Man*. And in the latter work, Darwin commented on the secondary sexual characteristics of a species of leatherjacket collected by Péron and Lesueur off the north-western Australian coast and subsequently named in Péron's honour: *Monacanthus peroni* (= *Acanthaluteres peroni*).

In 1804, in his 'Mémoire sur quelques faits zoologiques applicables à la théorie du globe', Péron expressed his personal awe at the nexus between some biological and geological processes. Reflecting on the role of marine creatures in slowly laying down sedimentary deposits, such as coral reefs and limestone formations, he wrote: 'these frail animals which were ignored for so long, and which are still despised, multiply on the bottom of the sea—stupendous witnesses of a power which defies the centuries, and which our imagination itself refuses to comprehend'.[18] Despite the implicit gradualism of this statement, faced with the geological anomalies he encountered during his travels—such as the presence of marine fossils far above modern sea level—Péron adopted a 'catastrophist' position, probably rooted in the ideas of Buffon and Pallas, and viewed the geological past as a series of cataclysmic 'revolutions'. Tom Vallance asserted that these ideas gained Péron 'wide notice, the more so after [Georges] Cuvier's espousal of the doctrine'.[19] He was certainly cited by Cuvier, one of the greatest scientists of his time.[20] But it would be a mistake to think that such notions came from some desperate clinging to Genesis and a rationalisation of the Noachic flood. There was a need to explain species extinctions and sharp differences between rock strata. Furthermore, before an understanding of Ice Age glaciation, how else could geologists explain such profound changes as the movement of enormous boulders across the landscape? Nevertheless, in seeking to explain the creation of mountains, Péron's mind was open to new theories of uplift. Like such geologists as Leopold von Buch and his own expedition colleague Joseph Bailly, he initially had orthodox 'Neptunist' sympathies regarding water as the fundamental agent of geological change,[21] but soon recognised the volcanic origins of the mountainous Canary Islands and the Ile de France.[22] He also understood that the fossil record was intimately linked to the present. Indeed, during his travels he would make an important discovery of a so-called 'living fossil', the bivalve *Neotrigonia* in Tasmania. This gained the attention of Lamarck,[23] who rejected catastrophism and posited a broadly uniformitarian approach to the geological past.

Baudin, despite his avowed interest in the natural sciences, was simply intellectually ill-equipped to recognise the full importance of Péron's efforts during the expedition. Indeed Péron's work was often ridiculed in Baudin's journal—such sentiments must have sharpened the naturalist's contempt for the commander of the expedition when he eventually read his words in preparation for writing the official *Voyage*.

Even though Péron's conclusions were sometimes far-fetched, he helped to broaden the empirical foundations of the natural sciences. He was, for example, one of the founders of oceanography, and his pioneering work on seawater temperatures has particular resonance today, because ocean temperature studies have provided key baseline indicators in the debate over one of the most important issues facing humanity: global warming and climate change. As we shall see, even in his own time, this research on ocean temperatures at different depths not only overturned classical Aristotelian notions about heat generated by the agitation of sea waves but also challenged ideas about heat transfer from the core of the globe via the mantle posited by such intellectual giants as Buffon and Leibnitz.[24]

Péron's writings also offer arresting evidence of an astute ecological understanding, an appreciation of conservation issues and an analysis of human impact on the environment. Although Richard Grove did not mention him in his landmark study *Green Imperialism*, Péron certainly has a place among the select group of prescient British, Dutch and French scientists who offered an environmental critique of colonial ventures. His observations on several of Australia's offshore islands are particularly relevant, because most of these islands (with the exception of Tasmania) were uninhabited by Aborigines and only recently visited by sealers. This gave them an Edenic—albeit parched—quality in Péron's eyes as well as offering a new focus on the natural equilibrium, the finiteness of resources in restricted locations and the precious quality of unique and vulnerable species that could easily be driven to extinction by human greed or the introduction of feral animals. Péron's visits to Mauritius, before and after his visits to King Island, Nuyts Archipelago, Kangaroo Island and Bernier Island, probably also reinforced historical perceptions of species extinction (with particular reference to the dodo) and human-induced ecological change: he certainly noted local comments on the nexus between deforestation and reduced rainfall on the island.

The French Revolution gave opportunity to many men of merit, such as Baudin and Péron. Not surprisingly, some who had previously enjoyed privilege resented the new power relations. Although Baudin might have been despised by officers from such backgrounds, I personally do not believe class antagonism was the fundamental cause of his problems. His immediate subordinates, Louis and Henry de Freycinet, were both from the nobility, but if they were so governed by class prejudices, how can we explain their close friendship with François Péron, the son of a humble tailor? Some people get on well; others despise each other. Baudin, like William Bligh, had a demanding, uncharismatic and sometimes abrasive command style that made him many enemies—neither captain was ever accused of violence or brutality, but both were harsh with those they believed did not pull their weight—and, just like Bligh, Baudin's extraordinary navigational achievements are often overlooked. But, unlike Bligh, who had the good fortune to publish his own version of events and defend himself against accusations of poor management, stinginess and even fraud, Baudin died before he could return home and do so. Conversely, Péron was no Fletcher Christian. He stuck it out, even after many of his colleagues deserted, died or were sent back to France. Although a dreamy, unpunctual individualist with a tendency to speak his mind, he was always committed to his duties and lived a sobre and morally upright life, aiding his impoverished sisters and working furiously against the ticking clock of a terminal illness. Yet, when he wrote the official account of the expedition, he made few worthy references to its late commander and magnified Baudin's every fault in his text. Similarly, Péron never forgave Baudin for his seeming intention to leave him to a waterless death at Shark Bay in March 1803. A landsman, born far from the sea, Péron was prone to ill-qualified and unfair pronouncements on navigational matters. Ironically, this landsman would also gain an important place in the history of the marine sciences. Although there is little doubt that Baudin had many enemies, there is also little doubt that Péron had many friends. After his death, one of them, Pierre-François Keraudren, chief physician of the navy, wrote:

> M. Péron's physiognomy always bore an expression of gentleness and sensibility: the warmth of his intellect, the vivacity of his character were tempered by an extreme kindness that came straight from the heart; to his other attributes was added an extreme modesty. Such was his freedom from affectation, and I would add his frankness, that one could not resist his charming ways and his conversation. Academics, savants, people of rank appreciated his worth and loved him for himself. He was admitted by several important officials into their inner circle and they provided him daily with the most profound attachment. It could be said of him what does not apply to many others: his talents were many, but he had many friends.[25]

Any understanding of Baudin's and Péron's personalities, and their animosity, is limited by the sources available. Wherever possible I have returned to the original sources, but I also want my readers to draw upon their own emotional sensibilities. The late Manning Clark urged historians to nourish the 'eye of pity' in the reader. I have never forgotten his advice. Although I have not sought to write an apologia for Péron, I believe his life cannot be fully understood without recognition of the onerous conditions under which he laboured—conditions that cost the lives of many of his colleagues and probably contributed to his own premature death— in addition to the pervasive shadow of poverty, revolution, global war and the suffocating despotism of Bonaparte's *imperium*. Ultimately, even if my readers cannot forgive Péron for his ambition and bitterness towards Baudin, I believe they will still be fascinated by his impetuous, adventurous life and impressive scientific achievements.

— I —

Cérilly

*The little town spreads out among the fields, as calmly and as
comfortably as one would stretch one's elbows. In the pure country air,
along a hill, it is clean and docile, sleeping, resting. It can be seen from a
distance on a road at the end of an alley of poplars, with its roofs of tile
or slate. This perspective magnifies the importance of the small houses in
the lower quarter …*

CHARLES-LOUIS PHILIPPE,[1] *Le père Perdrix*

CÉRILLY is a small Bourbonnais town in the very heart of France.
Although some have argued that it takes its name from an ancient local
word *serre* meaning a hill, others have made reference to Gallo-Roman
sites in the vicinity and suggested an association with Ceres, the Roman
goddess of corn.[2] Whatever its etymology, there can be little doubt that
Cérilly was once a fortified hill habitation. To this day, the vestiges of a
feudal château and moat, first mentioned in 1073, can be seen in its centre.
But the town rests on still more ancient foundations of Triassic sandstone
overlaid with Pliocene soils of clay, sand and gravel. By French standards
these soils are poor, but to Australian eyes they seem bountiful and well
watered. Local farmers plant rye and potato or raise sturdy white Charolais
cattle on fields broidered with wooded thickets. The nearby vales are
gentle—for the foothills of the Massif Central are twenty kilometres to
the south—and fringe the vast arc of the forests of Tronçais and Civrais.
These rich woodlands of oak and beech, covering more than 10 000
hectares, were once the property of the Dukes of Bourbon, but were

confiscated by Francis I in 1528 and sequestered by Colbert for the use of the French navy in 1670. They remain in state hands.

François Péron was born in Cérilly, on the edge of these forests, on 22 August 1775. His mother, Françoise Bouchicot, was a local woman and descended from at least three generations of merchant drapers. His father, after whom he was named, was a 39-year-old master tailor who hailed from nearby Epineuil-le-Fleuriel (Cher) and a descendant of respectable members of the rural bourgeoisie. One of François' paternal grandfathers and his great-grandfather had been royal notaries; and a great-great grand-father, also named François Péron, had been a *procureur* in the town of Hérisson. Baptised[3] in Cérilly's eleventh-century church of Saint-Martin,[4] François was the first child of a union consecrated less than ten months. Five other children followed, but only François and two sisters—Marie-Anne (known as Rosalie) and Cécile—survived.[5]

It is not certain in which residence François Péron was born. The family did own a house, but two years after François' birth, his father leased it to one Jean Roger Gillet.[6] After Gillet's death—when François was about seven years old—this house was sold to Gillet's widow and family, payments being spread over three years. We also know that François' father, with another Cérillien named Jean-Baptiste Muguet, rented a prop-erty from a local procurator named Pierre Raby de La Lande.[7] This might well have been the house, in the embrace of the now-demolished town walls, where François Péron was raised—almost certainly the present-day Hôtel Chez Chaumat on the corner of what is now the rue François Péron and the entry to the rue Mistaudin (once a town gate, the Porte Mistaudon). In this hotel one can still see an ancient circular staircase and a vaulted passageway that leads to a small courtyard, ancient cellars and dark oak-beamed stables. Thanks to several notarial documents, we have some idea of the domestic life of the Péron family soon after François' father's death at the age of forty-five on 8 December 1783.[8] The future naturalist was then just eight-and-a-half years old.

Despite having significant assets, François senior left substantial debts, and his widow sought to protect herself with an inventory and valuation of their joint property. On 5 March 1784, two royal notaries, Pierre-Lazare Petitjean and Jean-François Bourgoing, were present when a pair of local merchants acted as expert valuers of the household effects.[9] Bourgoing also acted as trustee of young François and his sisters, who had not yet attained their majority. Walking into the living room, where the hearth was used for cooking, the widow Péron showed the officials every candlestick and lamp, pot and pan, glass and goblet, plate and piece of cutlery, that she owned—and there were many in her well-equipped kitchen.[10]

There were three beds in the first room inspected by the valuers, and this is presumably where the children slept. One was a small single bed of dark oak near the chimney. It had curtains and a mattress of straw, then floss and chicken feathers. The cover was of feathers, but there was also a woollen blanket and a quilted woollen bedspread. The other two beds were also of oak and had similar mattresses and covers, but were in the more expensive 'Duchess' style and had painted cloth bedspreads and yellow-bordered curtains of cinnamon-coloured serge. In the living room the family had several tables covered with a printed tablecloth and eleven straw-topped chairs that had seen better days. There were few ornaments in the room, save a number of utilitarian items with simple inherent beauty: copper, iron and pewter utensils, a porcelain sugar basin, a tin box, a small mirror and a shotgun that had no hammer. In eighteenth-century Cérilly—far from the sea and the mines of Alsace, Lorraine and Franche-Comté—salt was a precious condiment and the principal means of food conservation, subject to the *gabelle*, or salt tax.[11] The Péron family kept theirs under lock and key. Indeed their four pounds of salt was valued at five livres and was hence more valuable than its weight in silver. The inventory indicates that the Péron family also had a salting-tub and cover.[12]

The room next to the family living room contained two other Duchess-style beds, graced with eiderdowns and green serge curtains bordered with yellow ribbon, and a handsome two-door walnut wardrobe with two drawers. François' parents might have slept here normally, but perhaps from time to time they vacated the room for paying guests.[13] Without doubt the room had a public role, for it contained a billiard table and a dozen chairs. In another part of the room—presumably near a window with a good source of natural light—was a tailor's work-bench in oak, laden with scissors, thread, irons for pressing seams and oak candle boxes. Six iron candlesticks facilitated work at night. A pair of firedogs with yellow copper knobs appear to have stood guard in front of an iron stove. Eleven shirts—probably among the last the tailor ever made—were hung or stacked in anticipation of future customers. Eighteen plied sheets of cloth, each five ells long, were at hand for making other clothes. One can readily imagine François senior heating his irons on the stove or cutting cloth at his bench while clients bided their time around the billiard table in an acrid blue haze of tobacco smoke. Aside from François' father's work as a tailor, the Péron family appear to have run a café or tavern[14] and traded in tobacco.[15]

A tailor is a walking advertisement for his art and often for the fine product of far-off looms. François' father was partial to green and grey trousers of heavy woollen twilled *ratine* and strong Silesian linen. Aside from a sleeved jacket of Silesian cloth, he owned four vests, including one of yellow-striped calico. But in early March 1784 the tailor Péron had already reposed three months in his grave: his colourful clothes, and even his hat, clogs, shoes, buckles and stockings, were being valued by a widow anxious to pay his debts.

There were two separate attics in the house. In the first, above the billard room, the Péron family kept its larder and stored its wheat and barley and a mill to grind its grain. This attic also contained chests, trestles and lumber, and another small bed and a modest lockable oak wardrobe. A female employee might have slept here.[16] In the other attic above the living room, there was an oak chest (with what appears to have been decorative metal lockwork), a woodworking bench and several tables and trestles. In a storeroom downstairs there was a copper laundry tub and, in the cellar, a washtub linked with three 'elbow-pipes'. In the stable, the Péron family kept their horse with its saddle, bridle and an old blue blanket. Two covered horse-baskets, a pair of pack-saddles and a variety of tools and implements completed the *écurie,* along with three tonnes of hay in the loft.[17]

We do not know how good a father François senior was, but his death, at such an impressionable age for his son, represented a loss of financial security and very likely love and mentoring as well. François' enduring loyalty to his sisters suggests strong family bonds and that he assumed many paternal responsibilities thrust upon him as the senior sibling and only male of the Péron brood. This, in turn, would engender considerable self-reliance in years to come, despite a deep attachment to his resourceful mother—the dominant focus of his childhood. No one would ever replace his father, although François appears later to have been drawn affection-ately to the father of his closest friend, the artist Charles-Alexandre Lesueur, whom he addressed as 'Mon cher papa Lesueur'.[18]

When François senior died, his widow declared that she found the sum of fifty-eight livres in cash in the house. The notaries then assisted her in listing her late husband's debtors and summarising his 'titles and papers'. The widow Péron also declared that if she acquired additional knowledge of her husband's affairs she would make a further declaration. And so it was that fifteen months later, on 10 June 1785, she returned to the office of the notary Pierre-Lazare Petitjean, in the company of a merchant named Jean Clostre from Theneuille. A document dated 4 December 1780 was presented which made it clear that the late tailor and his widow owed Clostre more than 384 livres. Clostre had demanded payment, but the widow had insufficient funds. To buy time, in the face of impending litigation, she sought to divide the debt in two and technically share it with her youngest child Cécile, who clearly had no means to pay. Recognising that a court case would only amount to further financial attrition, the exasperated Clostre abandoned his law suit and agreed to an alternative proposal: that the debt be divided into instalments over the next four years and that the widow's merchant brother, Pierre Bouchicot, would act as her guarantor.[19]

Perhaps the most striking aspect of Pierre Bouchicot's rescue of his sister is that he appears to have been illiterate and was unable to sign the agreement to reschedule her debt. He was not the only one in the future naturalist's immediate family environment who was unlettered. François' godmother, Marie-Anne Péron, was also unable to sign.[20] Should it be a surprise, therefore, that the inventory of the Péron family home makes no mention whatsoever of any books? Yet, in 1811, Marie-Joseph Alard remarked that 'Péron had an extreme passion for reading' and that he was fortunate to have 'an excellent choice of books at his disposal'. His mother, however, is said to have attempted to curtail his voracious reading, fearing it was bad for his health. According to Alard, Péron would 'hide in the attics, climbing even on to the roof to read there in tranquillity'.[21] Another early biographer, Louis Audiat, would write of Péron's childhood: 'The day did not suffice for his passionate ardour; the night was also dedicated to reading. When he was refused light, for fear that the immoderate pro- longation of his wakefulness would harm his health, he was often sur- prised, at a late hour, laboriously reading the pages of a book painfully illuminated by the moon.'[22] Indeed, by his late teens, François is known to have suffered from ophthalmic problems—perhaps exacerbated by his reading habits. (According to Emile Guillaumin, this was the result of smallpox,[23] but his surviving portraits do not betray the tell-tale facial scar- ring of this disease.) We do not know which books François first pored over or where they came from, but he appears to have been steeped in the classics. The Bourbonnais, in particular Moulins, has a long history of book printing;[24] and there were books in private hands and in religious libraries in Cérilly during François' childhood and youth. But before an enquiring young man can make use of a book, he must first have learned to read.

From the beginning of the seventeenth century there had been two schools in Cérilly: one for boys and one for girls. The former carried the name of a college because it taught Latin. Some idea of François' education can be gained from what was expected of his teachers. Traditionally the choice of schoolmaster had been made in Cérilly after rallying the townsfolk with the church bells and, in the presence of local notables, submitting the candidate to an examination in reading, writing, arithmetic and Latin. The successful candidate undertook to teach three hours in the morning and three hours in the afternoon every day of the week—except all day Thursday in summer and on Thursday afternoon in winter. The schoolmaster also had to prove he was Catholic and undertake to teach the catechism every Saturday evening and conduct the children to mass every Sunday.[25]

At the time of François Péron's birth, Jean-François Bourgoing—whom we have already met in his capacity as a notary—had been rector of the school for a decade.[26] Bourgoing came from Issoudun (Indre) and, in 1766, had married one of François' cousins, Louise Péron. He had also been present at François' parents' wedding and was his sister Cécile's godfather. When the widow Péron made Bourgoing her son's trustee, she made an inspired choice. Although Bourgoing had handed over the duties of schoolmaster to Jean-Baptiste Baron in September 1775,[27] it seems inconceivable that he did not involve himself in François' primary education. A classicist whose favourite book was Plutarch's *Lives*,[28] Bourgoing seems likely to have been the teacher who first enthralled François with the lives of the great figures of ancient Greece and Rome. As he had written a manuscript on rabies, could it also be that Bourgoing first encourgaged François' scientific curiosity? There can be little doubt that he would have responded enthusiastically to a precocious child with an unquenchable thirst for knowledge. Cérilly's historian George Bodard has written of Bourgoing's dynamic personality:

> Endowed with a great facility for elocution and a great love of writing, with a depth of very serious knowledge, he does not lose an occasion to start speaking; on the contrary, he provokes it. His speech is vibrant, full of imagery, congenial, convinced … He charms his listeners; he arrests and rallies them to the cause he preaches—for it is

a sermon which is more than a discourse—and at the same time he succeeds in convincing and winning over the most indecisive and the most incredulous.[29]

But, as we shall see, Péron's relationship with Bourgoing was not always easy.

Jean-Baptiste Baron, Bourgoing's successor as rector of the Collège de Cérilly, had previously been an advocate in Bourges. He too came from Issoudun, and there seems little doubt that he was anointed by Bourgoing, who for six years held the post of town clerk in Cérilly. Baron is known to have had an important influence on François Péron's intellectual development.[30] According to Joseph Deleuze, the former advocate was enchanted by the young man's disposition and gave particular attention to his instruction. Deleuze added a personal footnote: 'We have often heard Péron recall with affection the debt he had to this respectable old man.' Deleuze also recorded that Péron's 'intelligence was announced in his early years by an extreme curiosity and by an active desire to learn'. He added that 'to satisfy a passion for reading he had recourse to all the ruses which other children employed in order to play'.[31]

Whether François Péron's interest in the natural sciences had been properly awakened in his teens is unknown. Given his future interests, it is hard to believe that the rich ecological web of the nearby Forest of Tronçais would have escaped his attention. Beneath the towering oaks, the understorey is largely composed of bracken, holly, lichen and moss as well as colourful flashes of orchid, lily (*Polygonatum*), eyebright (*Euphrasia*), pimpernel (*Anagallis*), valerian and forget-me-not (*Myosotis*) along with tangled heaths of erica and broom. It is also the domain of deer, boars, hares, badgers, martens and foxes, while the verdant canopy is commanded by a great diversity of birdlife, from orioles to eagles. And every level of the forest, be it beneath the bark or leaves of its highest branches, or amid its mossy knolls and decaying litter, is home to thousands of insect species. Moreover, Tronçais is intersected by numerous lakes and streams—teeming with frogs, snails, turtles, salamanders, eels and fish—which draw otters and waterfowl to feast among the reeds and bog bean.[32]

François' school years were characterised by great sacrifices on the part of his widowed mother to enable him to obtain an education.[33] He had only a small number of fellow students. Before the Revolution there were about thirty students at the Collège de Cérilly. Thereafter enrolments declined to about a dozen. The college itself was dilapidated. In 1791, when François was sixteen years old, it consisted of 'a kitchen, an adjacent office, a lower room, a room which served for the instruction of the young, adjacent stables, two upper rooms, an attic—all in a bad state, a cellar and a very small garden'.[34] It was in these ramshackle surroundings that the future naturalist mastered his own tongue and studied the Latin that would enable him to read the great scientific treatises of his age.

Yet at first this classical education seemed destined to support an ecclesiastic rather than a scientific career. When François completed his *rhétorique*—his final year of secondary education—he was initially encouraged to pursue a religious career by his mother and by the curate of Cérilly, Pierre Jean Marchand. According to Joseph Deleuze, Marchand 'consented to take him into his house to teach him philosophy and theology'.[35] During the Ancien Régime, a clerical career might have been a serious avenue of advancement for an intelligent young man of modest means,[36] but now the Revolution had changed everything.

— 2 —

Revolution and war

*For the husbandman weeps at blights of the fife, and blasting of
trumpets consume
The souls of mild France; the pale mother nourishes her child to the
deadly slaughter.*

WILLIAM BLAKE, *The French Revolution*, 1791

THE period immediately before the Revolution was one of great hard-
ship for ordinary Frenchmen. Drought, the coldest winter since the beginning of the century, floods, severe food shortages and soaring prices[1] cast
a dark shadow over François Péron's already insecure adolescence. He
would later write that 'the conditon of the European peasant was in many
respects more unfortunate than that of the slaves of the Ile de France'.[2]

Although the French economy continued to grow, so too did the
national debt after decades of mismanagement, royal excess and recurrent
war. As early as 20 August 1786 the Controller-General of Finances,
Charles-Alexandre de Calonne, had advised the King of an estimated
deficit of eighty million livres (later increased by another thirty-two million livres).[3] Despite France's desperate need for a more equitable taxation
system, the nobles refused to make concessions that would erode their
privileges. The fiscal crisis deepened. In exasperation, on 8 August 1788,
Louis XVI summoned the Estates General—an ancient assembly supposed
to represent the entire nation, which had not met since 1614. Although
short-term loans secured the government's immediate fiscal needs, the
King and his council had difficulty deciding the manner in which the

Third Estate (commoners) should be represented. On 27 December 1788, Jacques Necker, the Controller-General of Finances, boldly recommended that it should have double the representatives of the other estates, arguing that the King should ally himself with the majority of his subjects. When Louis XVI agreed, the balance of political power began to shift away from the nobility. In Cérilly one of the deputies chosen to draft the *cahiers de doléances* (list of grievances) for the parish to be presented to the Estates General was François Péron's trustee, Jean-François Bourgoing. Together with Pierre Raby de La Lande (from whom the Péron family rented their house) and Pierre-Lazare Petitjean, he sought the suppression of the salt and poll taxes, more equitable contribution to state revenues by the clergy (including the abolition of clerical exemption for the *corvée*),[4] reform of the criminal code, an end to the abuses associated with the purchase of offices and a cap on royal pensions, gifts and concessions.[5]

When the Estates General finally opened on 5 May 1789, arguments still raged over the manner in which representatives should vote: by estate or as individuals.[6] In the past, the estates had met separately, which had given the clergy and nobility the power of veto over the Third Estate. Now there were roughly 300 clerical and 300 noble representatives in the first two estates and 600 representatives of the Third Estate. Those who clung to a world of inequality and privilege feared any joint meeting of the estates that would provide an opportunity for progressive clerics and nobles to 'cross the floor' and bolster the votes of commoners. When, on 17 June 1789, the First Estate declared itself in favour of a vote by estate, the prospect of far-reaching national reform seemed over. But the Third Estate boldly responded by voting to constitute itself a 'national assembly'. On 20 June, excluded from its usual meeting place, the commoners held an emergency meeting in a tennis court and took an oath not to disband until France had a constitution. Although the King sided with the First Estate and threatened to dissolve the Estates General through force of arms, defections by enlightened nobles and clerics made the momentum for change unstoppable. The storming of the Bastille and a series of urban and rural uprisings confirmed the collapse of royal authority.

In an environment in which revolt had become revolution, episodes of panic were not surprising, but no one expected the 'Great Fear', which began on 20 July 1789 with a rumour that brigands financed by aristocrats were about to launch widespread attacks to restore the old order. The hysteria reached the area around Cérilly at the end of July. In the previous year, iron forges had been established in the Forest of Tronçais by Nicolas de Rambourg, with the aid of timber concessions for charcoal (to enable smelting and forging) and water from the lake of Saint-Bonnet to power a mill, hammer and bellows.[7] The local population of forest and metal workers was excited and agitated in the wake of the momentous events in Paris. The curate of Saint-Bonnet, neighbouring Cérilly, recorded what happened in his parish register:

> 30 July 1789 … a fearful panic general and universal … which lasted two days. Everybody, big and small, in the country like the towns, imagined that thieves and troops of brigands ranged the kingdom, [and] each believed that they would see them arriving in their area … all the fearful quit their houses, abandoned all that they had, hid their furniture and their money, plunged into the woods and the forests, where they rallied and withdrew to the neighbouring towns to take up arms together and prepare to fight and lay down their lives.[8]

Taking advantage of the Great Fear, on the night of 4 August 1789, the National Assembly voted to abolish feudal rights and the fiscal privileges of the nobility, clergy, towns and provinces.[9] In the following year, the clergy became dependent on the state and were required to swear an oath of loyalty to the civil constitution. There were fifty-two priests in the district of Cérilly, including François' clerical mentor Abbé Pierre Marchand, who took the oath. (Only two local priests refused and were deemed to have resigned.)[10]

The church was divested not only of its power but also of its property. In Cérilly, Jean-François Bourgoing was charged with surveying and valuing these nationalised clerical assets in 1790. He would rise rapidly in the local revolutionary administration.[11] François Péron, however, would come to resent Bourgoing's disrespect for traditional religious values,[12] but perhaps he also resented him as his trustee—as an insecure child often resents the imposed authority of a stepfather.

On 21 June 1791 the King and the royal family were arrested at Varennes while attempting to flee the country to join *émigrés* menacing the fledgling French democracy. Austria and Prussia, although long-standing rivals, were united in their fear of the missionary zeal of the French Revolution, and issued a joint declaration at Pillnitz in August 1791, which threatened force if the French royal family was not released. For many in the National Assembly (particularly the deputies from the Gironde), the Prussian menace on the Rhine and the long-standing

Austrian threat in the southern Netherlands were cause enough for war. Both sides miscalculated. The Austrian and Prussian monarchs thought France bankrupt, on the verge of administrative collapse and bereft of effective military leadership in the wake of mutiny and emigration. In contrast, the new government in Paris believed Austria and Prussia were on the verge of political upheaval with simmering popular sympathy for the values of the French Revolution. With the additional enthusiasm for potential territorial conquest on both sides, war was not long in coming.[13] France declared war on Austria on 20 April and a week later invaded Belgium.[14] Although the Austrians counter-attacked and were soon joined by the Prussians, on 20 September the French thwarted their invasion at Valmy and set the scene for protracted war. Three anxious days before the victory at Valmy, François Péron officially banished (if he had not already done so) thoughts of entering the Church and joined the 2nd Battalion of Volunteers for Allier—one of the new *départements* that replaced the old province of Bourbonnais.[15]

For the *philosophes*, with their distrust of the professional military as one of the pillars of the Ancien Régime, the notion of volunteer citizen soldiers was particularly attractive. While Jean-Jacques Rousseau believed that 'all citizens should be soldiers through duty, none should be by profession',[16] Diderot saw the citizen wearing two costumes: one for his normal daily life and the other as a willing armed defender of the state.[17] With the looming threat of Prussian and Austrian invasion, the National Assembly attempted to put in practice the ideal of citizen soldiers and form 169 volunteer battalions using the National Guard as a nucleus. Unfortunately, enough recruits stepped forward to make up only sixty battalions.

In the wake of the decree of 11 July 1792, which declared the 'fatherland in danger', the efforts to create a second battalion of volunteers for Allier were marked by a lack of local enthusiasm. The *département* of Allier was expected to create a battalion of 800 'volunteers', and Cérilly was expected to provide fifty of these men. On 6 September the town council complained that Cérilly was but a small town and would need to raise men in the countryside: 'our labourers naturally have much aversion to the profession of arms and have ideas too limited to be moved by patriotism; we ask of you to advise us positively of the regulation to follow, so that in this circumstance the regulation will be uniform'.[18] The means ultimately used appear to have been directed at the urban population 'to the exclusion of the countryside'.[19] Power relations in Cérilly had changed in the wake of the Revolution, but local politics was always destined to have subtle patterns of patronage, coercion and reciprocity. Ultimately, François Péron was among a small group of young men sent to Moulins.

Virtually all the existing summaries of François Péron's life would have us believe that he was an ardent volunteer in 1792. Marie-Joseph Alard wrote that the young man's soul was penetrated with 'noble enthusiasm' and that in such a milieu of 'boiling agitation' one could well believe that he did not listen long to Abbé Pierre Marchand, who wished him to enter the priesthood. Emile Guillaumin declared eloquently that the 'breath of new hopes filled François' meagre breast' and that he wished to 'live free and fight for a great cause'. Guillaumin even went so far as to declare that François might have enlisted in 'a moment of enthusiasm, perhaps unreflected, without informing his family'.[20] More recently Dr Georges Rigondet, in his semi-fictionalised account of Péron's life, has given free reign to notions of patriotic zeal.[21]

Although some volunteers might have made a genuinely free choice based on revolutionary commitment, many others did not. It should be remembered that François Péron did not volunteer to join the 1st Battalion of volunteers raised in Allier, as had Bourgoing's son Jean. A number of historians have contrasted the revolutionary patriotism of the volunteers of the 1st Battalion with the lack of cohesion, indiscipline and avarice of the men of the 2nd Battalion, who signed up for a pay of fifteen *sols* per day. There is also important contemporary evidence of what Lieutenant Colonel Dulac considered 'an implicit requisition'.[22] According to General Armand Biron, the latter volunteers 'were nothing but fellows bought by the communes and the majority vagrants'.[23] And one of the administrators of Moulins wrote scathingly to General Adam-Philippe Custine, commander of the Army of the Rhine: 'Rich folk daily purchase men to replace their children, notably in the 2nd Battalion of Allier which is part of your army ... we are therefore under the Ancien Régime, since the rich can exempt themselves from service in person ... Where is the decreed equality? It only exists in word and not deed.'[24] François, with neither wealth nor father, bowed to his perceived obligations and very likely the cajoling of such powerful locals as his trustee, the new town prosecutor Jean-François Bourgoing. Some idea of François' actual enthusiasm for taking up arms can be gauged from the fact that a few days after 'volunteering', he promptly requested permission to defer his departure until the following spring 'because of his feeble constitution and infirmities ... [and] impaired sight'! His request was denied by the

Procurer-General in Moulins on 1 September 1791.[25] This was more than two weeks before his official enlistment date of 17 September 1792. He is said to have departed amid the 'tears and reproaches of his mother and sisters'.[26] Four days later, France became a republic.

The volunteers wore blue (as had the National Guard), while soldiers of the line wore white. The higher daily pay of the undisciplined volunteers was a source of resentment for regular troops. They, in turn, were dismissed as servile and disdainfully called *culs-blancs* ('white arses') by the volunteers. No height was recorded for François Péron in the muster roll, although Jean-Baptiste Brugière stated that he was of medium height and very thin. Empress Joséphine was said later only to have referred to him as her *petit ami* (little friend);[27] he probably was small by modern standards, but this expression has less literal connotations of endearment in French. The other Cérilliens who joined the battalion with him were also small men: Gilbert Charretier and Claude Gellert were both only five feet tall; Pierre Retif was just an inch taller.

Initially the men were placed under the control of the officers of the National Guard, until they conducted elections for their own officers. Overall command of the battalion was conferred on François-Claude Gosse (hitherto a tax officer), who was given the rank of lieutenant colonel. François was elected corporal.[28] He could not have been well known to the other young men from surrounding areas who elected him, but perhaps they recognised the usefulness of his education and his connections with local revolutionary notables during their initial musters. Jean-Baptiste Brugière, himself elected a non-commissioned officer in the 2nd Company, recalled more than sixty years later that he recognised a 'superior intelligence' in the young man from Cérilly who would become a lifelong friend.[29]

Most of the men were billeted in barracks in the Madeleine quarter of Moulins left vacant by the Royal Guyenne Regiment.[30] The rest were lodged in the Convent of the Sisters of the Cross and the Convent of the Ursulines, which had been forcibly emptied a few days before,[31] but also (as in the case of François' 7th Company) in the homes of local residents —a heavy burden for townfolk who faced 'the continual passage of troops or volunteers from other departments returning to the front'.[32] In Moulins they received about five weeks of rudimentary training. A popular local surgeon named Justier treated the sick.[33] The equipping of the volunteers proceeded haphazardly. Two commissaires were sent to Lyon to purchase cloth for uniforms and 'other necessary furnishings', unavailable locally.[34]

But only 120 complete uniforms, 275 vests and 239 pairs of trousers had been received by the time the men set off for the front: more than 600 remained unfinished in Lyon and Moulins. Weapons were also in short supply. The men were issued with 400 or 500 'bad muskets'. Additional firearms were scoured locally 'to complete their arming'.[35]

The 2nd Battalion of Allier set off from Moulins with much patriotic fanfare on 8 November 1792. They first headed east through the Bois de Bordes, golden in its autumn mantle, then crossed the Loire at Le Fourneau. After spending the night in Bourbon-Lancy, they headed north-east to Luzy, which had few provisions to offer the weary men.[36] The volunteers spent their third night in Autun—where Talleyrand had recently been bishop. François Péron left no account of his march to the front, but Sergeant Major Allard declared in his journal that Autun was 'agreeable enough'.[37] The next day, in the heart of Burgundy, they delighted in the famous local wines.

After a week on the road, François and his comrades reached Auxonne and then struck out for the strategic town of Pesmes perched on a rock above the River Ognon. The beautiful château, belonging to the duc de Choiseul, was still standing at the time and gave a commanding view of the surrounding 'plains, forests and small mountains',[38] but four years later it was sold in the wake of the duke's emigration and demolished by a speculator hungry to profit from the resale of its stone and timbers.[39] Almost due north of Pesmes lay the town of Gray, which the men reached on the ninth day of their march. Here they appear to have spent the night in the barracks, which offered an expansive view of the magnificent plains. Allard wrote: 'One sees the Saône successively dividing and reuniting like ten or twelve schoolboys playing on the bars.'[40] After passing through the beautiful villages of Franche-Comté, which Louis XIV had wrested from the Hapsburgs little more than a century before, Péron and his comrades entered the Vosges Mountains and on 22 November reached the small town of La Marche. Sergeant Major Allard recorded nothing more than that he detested the place, but other sources give us a glimpse of the mob-like behaviour of the Allier volunteers after their arrival. About midday, with ostentatious revolutionary zeal, a local man named Planté began singing 'Ça ira, les aristocrats à la lanterne'. This caused one of the municipal officers, Benoît André, to become anxious that the volunteers might think that aristocrats were in the town when they were not. To Citizen André's horror, Planté mischievously took up his violin and began singing in front of the municipal officer's home. Sure enough, a rabble of men from Allier, believing that André's large house belonged to members of the hated aristocracy, milled about and began to 'talk of forcing the door and killing them all'. Considerable effort was required to quell their ugly bravado.[41] On other occasions, the men doubtless sang the 'Marseillaise', 'the hymn', which Péron would later write, 'was so unhappily prostituted during the Revolution, but which is nevertheless so full of enthusiasm and spirit'.[42] From La Marche the volunteers proceeded north-east to the dirty village of Lignéville in which Péron and his comrades 'were obliged to lodge in tens and twelves in the barns'.[43] On they walked, on the rough mountainous roads of the Vosges to Charmes on the River Moselle where they rested for two nights, probably in the cloisters of the Capuchin monks, who had been dispersed the previous January.[44]

After three weeks' walk in the cold winter weather, the 2nd Battalion reached the heavily fortified redoubt of Phalsbourg. All this time they had been destined for Strasbourg, but now they received orders to proceed to Landau, which was under attack. After passing through the forested Col de Saverne, they entered the province of Alsace and spent the night in Haguenau—bustling with 'a garrison and the frequent passage of troops'[45]—before resting in Wissembourg and reaching the front on 4 December 1792 'in very bad weather'. Péron, with eyes now badly inflamed by exposure, was promptly hospitalised.[46]

Landau has changed a great deal since the late-eighteenth century. Neo-classical stucco façades have replaced half-timbered medieval buildings —still so characteristic of nearby towns, such as Wissembourg. There are also few signs of its former fortifications: railways and roads have replaced the complex of multiangular walls, gates and bastions designed by Sébastien Vauban in 1687 to withstand artillery fire and to enfilade attackers.[47] On their arrival, the volunteers from Allier were sent to defensive positions on the northern outskirts of the town, but withdrew *intra muros* two days later. Thirty thousand regular French troops and volunteers faced eighty thousand Prussians. Back in hospital after his first night's sentry duty, François would soon learn of the execution of Louis XVI in early 1793.

In the winter months that followed, he and the other inexperienced volunteers from Allier were organised and trained for battle, but their contact with the enemy was at first restricted to opportunistic sorties to Edesheim, Germersheim and neighbouring Nussdorf and hasty withdrawals under artillery fire.[48] It would seem that some of the sorties, in late March, were intended to achieve more aggressive results, for one of the

2nd Battalion's inglorious retreats sparked bitter recriminations. We know from a letter written home by one of the men, a volunteer named Delageneste, that Lieutenant Colonel Gosse arrested 'the captain of the advance guard who had not shot volunteers who had retreated'.[49] Here was an attempt to enforce discipline, in the most ruthless manner, by an officer who probably had little more military training than the men under him. On the battalion's return from Nussdorf, three of its sentries had cause to fire on an enemy patrol, but Delageneste recognised their good fortune compared to another battalion, which, two days later, lost forty men.[50] Their real baptism of fire had yet to come.

Despite General Custine's efforts to keep the Austro-Prussian forces at bay between Landau and Wissembourg, the enemy noose began to tighten. Péron's comrade, Delageneste, gives us an idea of what it was like inside Landau in early April: 'The town here is full of troops; in every corner, one pitches tents, in all the forts and on all the places ... the generals, commandants and a part of the population swear to sooner die than to speak of surrender, but I believe that the siege will not last long if there is fire in the town.'[51] By April the troops 'touched no money' and were now paid in *assignats* (promissory notes). Inevitably prices soared and shops closed rather than accept seemingly worthless paper.[52] By May, bottles of mediocre wine cost more than two days' wages.[53] Patrols by the 2nd Battalion and firefights with the enemy were now a frequent occurrence. Jean Tullat, another volunteer in François Péron's company, wrote to his mother on 7 May that they were involved in combat every day and often took prisoners, but his principal complaint was that he and his comrades slept on straw and 'more often outside'. Tullat also informed his mother that an arsenal had gone up in flames with the loss of 3000 muskets and an unknown number of lives.[54] Six of François' comrades died in a significant engagement on 22 July.[55] Although the volunteers from Allier received praise for their bravery, there were at least eleven desertions from the battalion during this period. Their mettle would be tested further when 55 000 Austrians under General Dagobert Würmser, together with 2500 émigrés under the Prince de Condé,[56] captured Wissembourg and blockaded Landau on 27 July.

Even earlier, the setbacks experienced by the over-extended French army had had internal political repercussions: the relatively moderate Girondins deputies in the National Convention (which replaced the National Assembly when France became a republic on 21 September 1792) were overthrown in early June 1793, and sweeping powers were granted to a twelve-member executive known as the Committee for Public Safety. Dominated by Maximilien Robespierre and the 'Mountain'[57] faction of the Jacobin leadership, the committee met the counter-revolutionary crisis with ruthless efficiency. In August 1793, on the advice of Danton and then Lazare Carnot, it ordered universal conscription, which raised the largest army Europe had ever seen and permanently changed the face of modern warfare.[58] On 5 September 1793, a 'Reign of Terror' was initiated to crush all domestic opposition (by the end of July 1794, 16 594 people had been guillotined and between 18 000 and 23 000 others had died in prison or as a result of summary mass executions during bloody counter-insurgency operations in the west and in the cities).[59]

In besieged Landau, discipline was also ruthlessly enforced; at least twenty-nine executions took place on the orders of the military tribunal, and there were summary executions for those who spoke of surrender.[60] For François it must have been a savage contrast to the life he had enjoyed in Cérilly (for all its difficulties and privations). Furthermore, denunciations and bitter feuding also occurred between Landau's own militant revolutionaries, led by Georg-Friedrich Dentzel,[61] and the tenacious French garrison commander, Joseph-Marie Tenet de Laubadère.[62] A career soldier who had joined the army at nineteen, Laubadère had spent fifteen years as a captain in the corps of engineers. Although from a noble family, he did not flee the country as did many other army officers during the Revolution. For his loyalty and ability he received swift promotion. By May 1793 he held the rank of *général de division*, and so too did his brother Germain.[63]

After the withdrawal of the majority of the French troops from Landau under Custine, Laubadère took charge of 4200 townsfolk and 5000 troops in the town.[64] Surrounded after the fall of Wissembourg, he had enough bread and biscuits for only 137 days. Recognising that strict rationing of these food stocks was crucial to the survival of his besieged garrison, but not knowing how long the ordeal would last, he came into conflict with his civilian counterparts, whom he accused of 'impolitic consumption at different stages of the siege'. Ultimately Laubadère managed to hold out for 150 days[65] by further dividing his meagre resources, ordering foraging sorties and slaughtering 171 horses for meat.[66] In the charged atmosphere of political recriminations relating to conduct during the siege, a hundred volunteers overtly supported Labaudère and (in March 1794) signed a declaration condemning Dentzel's administration. Despite assertions that Labaudère had even more supporters, they appear to have been confined to the lower ranks; only one corporal was among the signatories. Corporal Péron did not sign, but his fellow Cérillien, Pierre Retif, did.[67]

Many of the volunteers were members of revolutionary 'sociétés populaires' in Allier. Lieutenant Colonel Gosse was secretary in Moulins, and he established close links with Dentzel and his like-minded democrats in Landau when the 2nd Battalion arrived. Those who knew François Péron recorded that 'he spoke many times' of Landau's société populaire.[68] One can assume that many of the volunteer NCOs were both committed revolutionaries and distrustful of career army officers—especially nobles with Ancien Régime credentials—but we cannot assume that Péron held such views. Rumours of spies and traitors were rife. Volunteers such as Jean Tullat, for example, were fully aware that General Dumouriez, commander of the Army of the North, had abandoned his men and sought refuge with the Austrians in April 1793.[69] He was also aware of the French reverses at Mainz and no doubt soon learned of General Custine's recall and execution on 27 August. (Previously a marquis, Custine had already incurred the hatred of many volunteers for ordering the execution of French looters in Speyer in October 1792.) Many must also have been aware that General Würmser, who led the enemy they faced, was born in Strasbourg and had once served in the French army. On one occasion, when Landau's defences were almost overwhelmed, one volunteer from Indre later declared that the traitors had been fortuitously exposed thanks to the timely intercession of the 'supreme being'![70]

The 2nd Battalion made thirteen sorties during August 1793—mainly in search of food. The volunteers came under artillery fire during one sortie to the Infling Heights on 12 August without loss of life, but some days later one of their number was shot dead while leaving a hay loft.[71] One wonders with what meagre provisions François celebrated his eighteenth birthday on 22 August. Despite dwindling rations, Laubadère ordered only three sorties in September and October 1793 respectively;[72] but, as we shall see, these might have been associated with tactical reinforcement of the outlying fortifications rather than predatory foraging in Landau's hinterland—for hunger was not the only problem the volunteers had to contend with. Laubadère estimated that '35,000 bullets, bombs and incendiaries fell on the town, ramparts and houses' during the siege.[73] Not surprisingly, there were casualties during the bombardment. In October a sergeant of the 2nd Battalion lost both his legs, and a volunteer's arm was smashed while he lay in hospital. Several historians have declared that

François lost his right eye during the siege,[74] but other sources suggest that this is an exaggeration and that he simply lost the sight in this eye after his pre-existing ophthalmic condition was exacerbated by cold and exposure. Despite his handicap and twice being hospitalised in Landau, Péron is known to have participated in numerous sorties and good-humouredly assumed the sobriquet 'Horatius Cocles', after the half-blind Roman hero immortalised by Livy and Virgil for single-handedly holding off the Etrurians on a bridge over the Tiber.[75] Later Péron would write to a friend: 'I have lived in the camps and in the tumult of arms; I have learned, do not doubt, to defy and to scorn an ever present death. Accustomed to face it without fear, I have also learned to mete it out.'[76]

For some six weeks after the incarceration of their battalion commander Lieutenant Colonel Gosse—who was suspended on 28 September because of his support for Dentzel—the men of the 2nd Battalion were camped in the 'Cornichon' part of a complex of earthwork fortifications south of the main walls. While Gosse's star plummeted, several young lieutenants were promoted to captain, and François Péron was made sergeant.[77] Between 10 November and 7 December, Sergeant Péron and his comrades withdrew to the inner ramparts of Landau, but then reoccupied the Cornichon for a fortnight before Christmas. The plight of the defenders was now desperate. On 27 November, General Laubadère drafted an anguished appeal to his compatriots, which he entrusted to a courier who slipped through the Austrian lines. 'We are threatened with imminent capitulation', he wrote, 'if you do not come to our rescue soon.' And he added: 'Each moment is precious; do not waste time. You know, as we do, the importance of this place; save the Republic and at the same time let us not see the name of France dishonoured.'[78] Yet it would be another month before General Lazare Hoche, the son of a royal stableman, attacked and outflanked the Austrians at Geisberg and forced Würmser to evacuate Wissembourg amid falling Christmas snow.[79] On 28 December 1793, the siege of Landau was finally lifted. Although the Austrians still occupied one of the adjoining Vauban bastions (outside the town proper), the besiegers had now become the besieged.

A degree of normality returned to Landau's muddied streets,[80] but there were further executions: a captain accused of royalist sympathies and a sublieutenant convicted of defeatism during the siege were both put to death.[81] France was still in the grip of the Terror. On 16 February 1794 the 2nd Battalion of Allier received a further 200 conscripts and was reviewed by a *commissaire de guerre*, who judged it to be 'adequately instructed' and to have had 'sufficiently good discipline'.[82] Yet for all its abilities and achievements, the battalion appears to have remained haphazardly dressed: two officers were sent to Moulins in an attempt to speed up the arrival of their still undelivered uniforms. Finally, on 21 February, the men were ordered to pull out of Landau and to move into winter quarters in Lingenfeld, just north of Germersheim. Here, as part of the Army of the Rhine, Péron and his comrades busied themselves training their raw replacements until posted to the small village of Dudenhofen, on the outskirts of the magnificent episcopal town of Speyer, in early April 1794.[83]

From Dudenhofen, one of the Allier volunteers wrote home: 'We have just arrived in a new cantonment and we will not delay in measuring up to the slaves of despots.'[84] François Péron, however, was soon in no position to measure up to anyone, for he fell ill. His constitution was weak; he had endured exposure and lean rations for months; he had lost the use of his right eye; and, although he was unaware of it, he had already lived more than half of his life. Yet for years to come, he remembered with affection the kindness of the respectable head of a Rhineland family who nursed him in his home in Dudenhofen during his illness. Six and a half years later (in November 1800), Péron asserted that this family was named 'Kiner'.[85] His memory could been flawed—he often got names wrong[86]—since no such a family appears in the records of the village of Dudenhofen in the late eighteenth century. However, the 1789 tax roll for hearths in the village does list a family named Kinscherff,[87] which ultimately had a great deal to do with the occupying French. The head of the family, Leonard Kinscherff, was born in Birckenau and moved to Dudenhofen in 1774 at the age of twenty to manage an estate owned by the Bishop of Speyer. There he married, had five sons[88] and leased a mill on the Woogbach.[89] Well respected by his fellow villagers, Kinscherff served as mayor of Dudenhofen between 1789 and 1790. As a Catholic, it is doubtful that he was involved in the iconoclastic rage of the local *sans culottes*, who, emboldened by the occupying French, smashed religious images in the village and tore down the great cross of Dudenhofen on the road to Speyer.[90]

Although Rhineland Lutherans generally opposed the French and Calvinists largely supported them, Catholics were split in their revolutionary sympathies.[91] Many locals welcomed the abolition of tithe and seigneurial dues, and some even enriched themselves through the purchase of nationalised ecclesiastical land, but they bitterly resented the heavy demands made on them by the French army. Between late 1793 and May 1794, poor Kinscherff had to deliver 20 *malter* (equal to 20 x 125.7 litres) of corn (still the principal crop of the village), 60 pigs, 6 cows and 4 horses to the French! In the month François Péron arrived, the French advanced on Neustadt from Dudenhofen and were shadowed by imperial troops who camped on the banks of the Woogbach, which fed Kinscherff's mill. The French were mainly positioned on the parallel Speyerbach. In October 1794 the unfortunate Kinscherff was forced to mill corn for the French without payment, then for six weeks he could not mill at all because they diverted his water source.[92] Although Kinscherff had reason to resent the French, in wartime human relations are rarely black and white: it seems very possible that the ailing young Sergeant François Péron, who had only recently contemplated taking Holy Orders, struck up a genuine friendship with the pragmatic Catholic miller while billeted in his home. 'Respectable Kiner [*sic*]!' he wrote. 'I remember with pleasure the care you lavished on me while I was sick in your house.'[93] Politically adroit, Kinscherff again served the French as mayor of Dudenhofen during the Napoleonic administrations: from 1802 until shortly before his death in March 1808.[94]

During the idle hours of illness and lulls between battles, books remained Péron's greatest solace. Marie-Joseph Alard noted that Péron had the habit of visiting the closest monastic library, with one or two friends, and asking 'permission to make a choice of good books'. With sack filled, he would make his way back to the lines with the aid of the baggage train, read the books and (he would have us believe) either return the volumes to the same monastery or give them to the next one he encountered. There he would make a fresh selection, which would be just as rapidly read and exchanged. Accounts of the pitiless French looting of Speyer during the winter of 1793–94 can only make us wonder how easily the cloistered residents (if they were not already dispersed) could have refused 'borrowers' who came with muskets rather than library cards.[95] Péron's bemused eulogist asked his readers whether this new form of *bibliothèque* was not an 'uncommon usage of the terrible right of war'.[96] There is no doubt that some of the books Péron devoured came from the episcopal library in Speyer, for Sergeant Major Jean-Baptiste Brugière recalled, as a very old man, that he had gathered sixty volumes of the most remarkable French authors, which had been looted from the bishop and 'abandoned in the houses of diverse villages' where they had been quartered: 'Péron could not help notice and asked me for them.' At the time Brugière had been responsible for distributing newspapers among the battalion; he normally received them at night and distributed them in the morning, but Péron was so 'eager to read, to learn' that he called personally on his friend in the evenings and demanded the papers that had arrived for his company.[97] Of the looting, which he himself witnessed, Péron declared in a personal memoir: 'Oh! What excesses and plunder have soiled the glorious trophies of our soldiers! How many times has my heart grieved! Unable to stop them, at least I will never join them.'[98]

On 9 May the 2nd Battalion of Allier was detached from the Army of the Rhine, placed under the command of General Jean-Jacques Ambert[99] of the Army of the Moselle, and deployed on the right flank of the Kaiserslautern defences. Although the battalion was now 1034 strong, Ambert's division totalled only 5000 men with just 250 cavalry and a few cannons sprinkled through the neighbouring Pfälzwald villages. Sergeant Péron and his comrades were camped in Hochspeyer, a red-sandstone village of 176 families[100] nestled in a valley among the rugged forested hills west of Frankenstein. It was late spring, and the forest had many ecological lessons to offer a future naturalist. But although the splendours of the natural world were never far away, neither was the war. At 3.00 a.m. on 23 May the sound of artillery fire shattered the tranquillity of the woods; and two and a half hours later, Ambert's division was under attack from all sides. Péron never forgot that the head of the unfortunate family in Hochspeyer, in whose 'peaceful home' he had been billeted, warned him tearfully of the first shots, declaring: 'Run, good Frenchman … your army is already completely surrounded by Prussian troops; hear the rumbling of the cannon coming closer every moment, run with me, hurry and do not fear.'[101] But he did not flee with the German family with whom he had shared his meagre ration of bread. 'Duty bound', he later wrote, 'I took my arms and joined the fight.'[102]

While General Ambert withdrew towards Tripstadt and Schopp to the south in two columns, the 2nd Battalion served as the rear guard on the heights above Hochspeyer. The volunteers stopped the enemy long enough to allow the division to escape but were soon surrounded. Despite the loss of most of their baggage train and virtually all of their artillery, they were rallied by their officers and fought off a cavalry charge with the aid of a single cannon loaded with grapeshot. In such desperate circumstances it is not surprising that there were casualties. François Péron was slashed on the arm with a sabre while attempting to rescue a comrade pinned on his back under a fallen Prussian horse.[103] He was taken prisoner during a second Prussian charge. Five of his comrades were killed by enemy infantry at a nearby abandoned farm, but many of his fellow volunteers were among those who were captured by the encircling Prussians that day. Sergeant Major Jean-Baptiste Brugière, Sergeant Pierre Labry and Corporal Jean Baudoin, of the 2nd Company, together with the little Corporal Augustin Dupont (he was only four feet ten inches tall!), of the 8th Company, all fell into enemy hands.[104]

The wounded *Kriegsgefangener* (prisoner of war) François Péron was sent north—presumably by boat down the Rhine—to Mainz and then Wessel, near the border with the Netherlands, before being taken to Saxony by his Prussian captors.[105] In 1856 Maurice Girard, on the basis of the testimony of Péron's fellow prisoner Jean-Baptiste Brugière, recorded: 'During the course of this sad journey in Prussia ... the fatigues and the misery of captivity did not stifle in him the taste for study; he took note of all which might be of interest on the report of customs, of the habits of different populations he visited, as well as the productions of diverse provinces. It was the curiosity of the savant which had already revealed itself.'[106]

His route during the second part of this journey is unclear. The *Allgemeine Weltbegebenheiten* carried a report of 30 July from Wesel recording the 'transport' of 500 sick French prisoners of war to Magdeburg. It is not certain when François Péron actually reached the Prussian fortress, but nine days later the *Magdeburgische Zeitung* reported the arrival of sixty-six French infantry and cavalry officers, who were allowed to lodge in the town, and 1481 non-commissioned officers who were placed in barracks. Similar arrangements were made for another two groups (totaling 126 officers and 2290 NCOs), which arrived on 21 August, and for a much smaller group of a few hundred, which arrived on 14 October.[107] Péron is said to have been imprisoned in the 'citadel' of Magdeburg.[108] Until its demolition for housing in 1927, Magdeburg did indeed have a specific, heavily fortified area known as the 'citadel' located on an island in the middle of the River Elbe.[109] An elongated pentagon, with forbidding ramparts and bastions at each point, it contained magazines, an armoury, a parade ground and barracks.[110] The latter barracks might very well have been those in which François and the other non-commissioned French prisoners of war were held. Although the officers—lodged in private houses—had limited freedom on parole, the lower ranks (in much greater numbers) were more closely confined and released individually in the town only every 24 days to buy necessities.

Perhaps the most famous modern prisoner in the citadel was Marshal Jósef Pilsudski, later president of Poland. In 1929 he offered a potent insight to the psychology and suffering of the prisoner, based on his own experience in Magdeburg between 1917 and 1918:

> This suffering consists firstly of the limitation of material liberty to the minimum, of the freedom of movement to the tiniest space destined as a cell for the prisoner, that is to say, a door more or less large and a window eternally grilled. Here is a prison. In the second place, it is an incontestable fact that the prisoner is submitted to observation at all hours, at every moment. His life, his conduct, no longer depends on free will …[111]

A decade after his own confinement, when writing of the convicts of New South Wales, Péron also referred to prisoners as 'incessantly subjected to an inspection as inflexible as it is active'.[112] For Pilsudski, the psychological necessity of the prisoner, faced with long periods of reflection, was to 'find a life outside the conditions of the prison'.[113] Péron chose to transcend his incarceration through the printed word. Marie-Joseph Alard asserted that while other prisoners traded clothes and food, Péron 'sacrificed everything' to obtain the 'nourishment of the mind', for in reading and meditation he could forget the suffering occasioned by his 'loss of liberty'. In Alard's opinion it was a 'fortunate captivity' because it profoundly influenced his intellectual development.[114] Joseph Deleuze also affirmed the formative significance of this period of imprisonment because the future naturalist bought and borrowed books from many people to study 'historians and voyagers' and was distracted only by the 'need to sleep'.[115] Magdeburg, the birthplace of the physicist Otto von Guericke and the composer Georg Philipp Telemann, has a rich scientific and cultural heritage. Although François probably did not have access to the town's municipal library—founded on a monastic collection in 1524 and one of the oldest in Germany[116]—Magdeburg's significant educated population offered a promising intellectual catchment in which to borrow books, and we know that when free in the town he regularly visited a bookshop. We do not know exactly which books he read during this period, but there can be no doubt that he eventually became very familiar with the classic works of travel and natural history.[117]

Considered unfit for further military service because of the loss of sight in his right eye, within a couple of months Péron was included in a prisoner-of-war exchange by the Prussians and repatriated to Thionville, in Lorraine (via Wesel), in the spring of 1795.[118] Although his former comrades had only recently been stationed among the garrison of Thionville, he did not rejoin the 2nd Allier Battalion of Volunteers. Instead, he convalesced and assisted his old sergeant-major now working as a doctor in the military hospital. Strategically located on the Moselle, Thionville's intricate fortifications (now largely demolished) straddled the river and protected a population of 5000 civilians and 5400 soldiers. Like Landau, the town had recently endured a heavy siege.[119] Like Landau, Thionville had also had its share of executions during the Terror.[120] Although François Péron arrived many months after the fall of Robespierre and the end of the Terror (on 27 July 1794), Thionville, post-thermidor, was a far from happy place. Local herds were ravaged by disease and wolves; and although General Hoche might have found enough food and drink to celebrate marriage to his sixteen-year-old bride in Thionville in March,[121] meat, oil, soap and salt were now impossible to find after repeated requisitions. Furthermore, the town was rife with venereal disease thanks to the size of its garrison and the energetic enterprise of its prostitutes.[122] And it was still a place of suspicion and distrust. On one occasion, Péron was set upon by three townsfolk as he walked unarmed along the banks of the Moselle gathering his thoughts. He was dragged physically before the commandant, accused of planning to steal drying linen, but soon freed. By now he was determined to quit the army and, with the aid of his friends in the hospital, managed to secure a medical discharge on 9 August 1795.[123] It must have been a blessed relief after almost three years of military service, captivity in Germany and prolonged sickness. He arrived back in Cérilly and the embrace of his family three weeks later.[124]

Medical student

*What a frightful sight an anatomy theatre is, stinking cadavers, slimy
and livid flesh, blood, disgusting entrails, frightening skeletons, pestilential
vapours! It's not there, believe me, that Jean-Jacques will go looking
for amusements.*

JEAN-JACQUES ROUSSEAU, *Rêveries du promeneur solitaire*,
SEPTIÈME PROMENADE, *c.* 1778

CITIZEN François Péron returned home to Cérilly with a certificate
from the hospital in Thionville, dated 24 thermidor an III (11 August
1795), which declared that although he was unfit for military service, 'he
had received an education which could give him the means to serve the
Republic in the civil administration, where he wished to be preferred
because of the painful torments he had suffered during his sojourn in
Magdebourg as a prisoner of war'. He also bore a testimonial signed by
the officers, under-officers and volunteers of the 2nd Battalion.[1] Such
recommendations must have been hard to ignore, for Péron soon gained
employment as 'secrétaire de la mairie', a position that probably approxi-
mated that of a town clerk.[2] As such he participated in a number of
republican festivities, including the 'Fête de la Liberté' organised by Jean-
François Bourgoing on the orders of the Directory on the second anniversary of the fall of Robespierre. Bourgoing even composed a hymn set to
music from *The Marriage of Figaro*.[3] Ten days later, during further celebrations, Péron was also noted among a group of three veterans who sang a
song entitled 'La chute de la tyrannie' set to the tune of 'La Marseillaise'.[4]

But the two men were no longer close. Péron—who appears to have had a conservative religious streak—had grown discreetly critical of Bourgoing for what he considered immoral (perhaps even sacrilegious) references to the supposed 'Immaculate Conception' of the Virgin Mary and was moved to compose private verse satirising him for 'Disgusting obscenities and inept absurdities'.[5] And for all his ostentatious republican ardour and participation in Bourgoing's celebrations, one of Péron's first actions, just over a month after his return to Cérilly, had been to request six shirts in replacement for the same number given to the local military commission by his mother after he enrolled as a volunteer.[6] Péron might serve the Republic, but it would not get the shirt off his back (or the five others in his backpack) without paying for them. He remained in the employ of the commune of Cérilly for one year, ten months and sixteen days. Although his departure was a direct consequence of the war and the upheaval in French medical institutions during the Revolution, it was also very much to his advantage.

On 8 August 1793, with purported democratic zeal, the National Convention had abolished eighteen medical faculties, fifteen surgical colleges and both the Royal Society of Medicine and the Royal Academy of Surgery.[7] The aim was to destroy privilege and elitism, but the result left France virtually without medical schools when there was a desperate need for doctors, particularly in the army.[8] Although a law had also been enacted to make all physicians, surgeons and pharmacists eligible for military service, by the spring of 1794 the French army had lost almost a thousand medical officers since the beginning of the war. Debate raged on how new medical personnel should be trained. Jean-Gabriel Gallot, a physician from Saint-Maurice-le-Girard in the Vendée and a deputy to the National Convention, had already advocated the creation of centralised medical schools in Paris, Montpellier and elsewhere, but—most importantly—the teaching of general medicine, surgery and *materia medica* 'together in the same schools'.[9] Surgeons and physicians had hitherto belonged to two distinct and rival professions. In July 1794 the Committee of Public Safety commissioned Antoine-François de Fourcroy and François Chaussier to advise on the structure of a new system of medical education. Their report echoed many of Gallot's ideas, especially the establishment of a central *Ecole de santé* in Paris that combined medical and surgical training as well as providing a program of clinical instruction.

The term 'clinical' is derived from the Greek word *kliné*, for a couch or bed, and alludes to a patient lying down or 'reclining'. Clinical medicine is bedside medicine, and it pertains to sick people and their diseases. Thus a clinician is a healer. Today we take 'clinical instruction' for granted. Certainly doctors, from Hippocrates to Hermann Boerhaave, observed and learned from their patients,[10] but the use of empirical examination techniques in the advancement of medical science and the instruction of new doctors through clinical cases studied in hospitals was a relatively new concept in the late eighteenth century. In the last years of the Ancien Régime six new hospitals had been constructed in Paris, while during the early years of the Revolution the Hôtel Dieu was renovated, the bed capacity of the Charité was more than doubled and three former monasteries were converted to create the hospital of Saint-Antoine, the Maison royale de Santé and the Maternité.[11] Yet medical thought was still emerging from philosophical notions of illness that harked back to the ancient Greeks. Hippocratic and Galenic ideas, such as the belief that disease was a result of a disequilibrium of the four 'humours'—blood, phlegm, bile and melancholy—were still widely held. Nevertheless, the profound scientific discoveries of the previous century had helped to engender a growing use of empirical scientific methods in the study of the body, the causes of diseases and the treatment of illnesses. Between 1757 and 1766, Albrecht von Haller had published his seminal work of modern experimental physiology, *Elementa physiologicae*. René-Antoine Ferchault de Réaumur had shown in 1752 that digestion was the result of the chemical action of gastric juices, and the experiments of Lavoisier, Priestly, Laplace and Lagrange revealed the role of oxygen and chemical processes in respiration. In 1761, Giovanni-Battista Morgagni's work *De Sedibus et Causis Morborum* had made a major leap in pathology through a careful comparison of 700 postmortem findings with the clinical histories of the same individuals when still alive. Those who sought to reform French medical education took up the mantle of Morgagni in order to place an emphasis on diagnostic accuracy founded on direct and meticulous observation of pathological processes in individual patients.

On 4 December 1794, after five months of debate, the National Convention voted to adopt Fourcroy and Chaussier's proposal, but extended it to create three medical schools—in Paris, Montpellier and Strasbourg—rather than just one in the national capital. Regional committees were established to select prospective medical students. The ideal candidate, they were told, should be 'capable of clear thought, quick and accurate judgment, keen analytical observation, able to understand at a glance the relationship of complex facts and to draw valid conclusions ... filled with dedication to science and eager to devote himself unreservedly to his medical studies.'[12] When news reached Cérilly that 550 *élèves de la patrie* (students of the nation) were to be trained as doctors each year without charge, François saw a golden opportunity to advance his intellectual horizons and forge a career that would otherwise have been impossible for someone of his modest means. Before the Revolution, to qualify as a doctor in Paris cost a student without a scholarship as much as 7000 livres, and even the provincial universities charged a third to a quarter of this sum.[13] It would seem that Péron gained a recommendation for his candidature from the notary Pierre-Lazare Petitjean. Maurice Girard offers a melodramatic portrayal of the events leading up to Péron's acceptance by the Ministry of the Interior in July 1797, which is based on the testimony of Petitjean's grandson, Emile de Rochefort, who clearly wanted to give his ancestor a pivotal role as a prescient promoter of brilliance: 'After submitting Péron to a deep examination, he [Petitjean] judged that he was capable of following the professors of the higher sciences and that there was nothing but Paris for this vast intelligence. Péron, whose heart was as highly placed as his desire to learn was ardent, fell into the arms of his benefactor on learning of his fortunate news, calling him his second father.'

The decision, of course, could not have been up to Petitjean alone. It is hard to imagine that Jean-François Bourgoing was absent from the story at this stage. As has already been mentioned, he had an interest in medical matters. Article 24 of the *Cahiers de doléances* for Cérilly, which he had drafted with Petitjean in 1789 for the Estates General, made specific reference to the need to reform the hitherto lax training and accreditation of surgeons: 'They should never be admitted but after the most serious examination and the most authentic certificates.'[14] Cérilly had two surgeons at the time. One was Pierre Simonnet; the other was Sébastien Trimouille, originally from Montluçon. In the revolutionary period, Trimouille was the official *officier de santé* for the municipality[15] and presumably also had something to do with examining François Péron as a candidate. But regardless of the probable role of Trimouille and Bourgoing in selecting Péron, it appears that Petitjean rendered the future naturalist important financial assistance for his studies, particularly after scholarships for chosen medical students were discontinued in May 1798. But as we will see, this might simply have been to keep him away from Cérilly.

Paris in the late eighteenth century was a medieval labyrinth of around half a million people, and Péron moved into lodgings in one of its thirteen hundred narrow, dirty, unpaved streets: no. 367 rue du Cloître Saint-Benoît.[16] François Boucher had once lived and painted his sensuous rococo nymphs in a third-floor apartment in the same street,[17] later obliterated when Baron Haussman created the Boulevard Saint-Germain.[18] A surviving watercolour shows no footpath, just surprisingly wild and unkempt grassy banks beneath the narrow five-storey tenements leaning cheek by jowl over the street.[19] Running from the rue des Mathurins, it gave access to the cloister of the now demolished gothic church of Saint-Benoît, which fronted the rue Saint-Jacques. A well was located in the centre of the cloister, and a nearby passage enabled access to the rue de Sorbonne (later obliterated by the rue des Ecoles). From these lodgings it was only a few minutes walk to the Ecole de Santé located in the recently requisitioned buildings of the Académie de Chirurgie.

Péron's fellow students came from all over France. They included Sébastien Guyetand, the future author of a flora of the Jura; Jean-Baptiste Fleury, discoverer of the venous canals of the cranial bones; Georges Cuvier's nephew Georges Duvernoy, later professor of natural history at Strasbourg; Antoine Varéliaud, future surgeon to Napoleon; and several men who would distinguish themselves as military surgeons in a host of European campaigns.[20] Some of Péron's fellow students came from abroad. One was the Belgian Pierre Nysten, later famous as an epidemiologist and paediatrician; another was the colourful Irishman Patrick MacMahon, who later became librarian of the medical school.[21]

In his first semester, Péron attended courses by the leading luminaries of the new Ecole de Santé. He was, for example, one of 814 students who attended Antoine Fourcroy's course in chemistry and pharmacology. A strong supporter of Lavoisier who rejected the phlogiston theory, Fourcroy was already famous for his book *Philosophie chimique* (1792)—translated into twelve European languages—his reform of chemical nomenclature, and his pioneering studies on the composition of urine, urea, bone and plant and animal tissue. Although he would later be an important patron, the extent of his intellectual influence on François Péron is difficult to determine, but it is worth noting that Fourcroy was also a naturalist who believed in an interdisciplinary approach to the study of natural history, chemistry and pharmacology. His *Leçons élémentaires* [later simply *Elémens*] *d'histoire naturelle et de chimie* (1782) had been published in at least five editions before François Péron began his medical studies. Fourcroy was also the author of a major work on the insects of Paris: *Entomologia parisiensis* (1785) and a member of the Société linnéenne de Paris and later the Société d'histoire naturelle. Furthermore, he drafted instructions for chemical and medical experiments to be conducted during La Pérouse's voyage.[22]

In his first semester, Péron also studied anatomy and physiology under François Chaussier, who had worked as a doctor in the hospitals and prisons of Dijon before being recruited by Fourcroy;[23] operative medicine under Raphaël Sabatier, formerly surgeon major at Les Invalides; external pathology under Pierre Lassus, formerly physician to Louis XVI's daughters Sophie and Victoire;[24] and internal medicine under Jean-Nicolas Corvisart des Marets, whom Péron himself declared (after the naming of Corvisart Bay in South Australia) was 'the celebrated doctor who, through the establishment of the first practical clinic in France and through his fine research into organic illnesses, has deserved so well of medical science and the nation'.[25] In his second semester, Péron studied clinical surgery under Philippe Pelletan, the former surgeon major of the National Guard; materia medica under Bernard Peyrilhe; internal pathology under Philippe Pinel, chief physician at the Salpêtrière and one of the great pioneers of psychiatry; and obstetrics under Alphonse Leroy, who was capable of outdoing Hamlet with five human skulls during his lectures.[26]

War still raged in Europe, and the conflict had broadened during Péron's first year in Paris when Bonaparte departed for Egypt with an army and a large scientific complement.[27] Despite initial victories against the Mamelukes, the French were soon cut off after the destruction of their fleet at Aboukir by Nelson.[28] Disease, pestilence and stubborn resistance then ground the stranded troops to a halt before the impregnable walls of Acre. Abandoning his floundering army, Bonaparte returned to France to overthrow the Directory in the *coup d'état* of 18 brumaire (9 November 1799). While Bonaparte consolidated his dictatorship with a host of administrative and judicial changes, Péron once more attended courses by Chaussier, Corvisart, Fourcroy, Lassus, Leroy, Pinel and Sabatier, in addition to physical medicine and hygiene under Jean-Noël Halle.[29] Yet, regardless of what appears to have been a ferocious dedication to his studies, he would neither complete his course nor submit a dissertation.

— 4 —

Savant

Alas! You know how such a voyage was far from my tastes, how it is
contrary to my inclinations, my manner of living and feeling ... Scarcely
a few days have passed and all our projects, all our joint life plans have
disappeared. Ready to leave you for so long, perhaps for ever, with such
profound bitterness, I remember dear, we dreamt together of happiness,
you alone will enjoy it ...

FRANÇOIS PÉRON, LETTER TO A FRIEND
(PROBABLY ANNE-SOPHIE PETITJEAN), 1800

DESPITE the breadth of his intellectual interests, François Péron was
unable to ignore more fundamental human concerns. He fell in love. An
anonymous biographical manuscript drafted in Cérilly, possibly by the
naturalist's childhood friend Jean Bonnet, recorded that Péron 'was on the
point of becoming a doctor when an unhappy love affair made him abandon this brilliant career and, out of resentment more than relish, he sought
to join the vessels destined for an expedition to the South Lands'.[1] He had
known Anne-Sophie Petitjean, the daughter of his family friend and benefactor, the notary Pierre-Lazare Petitjean, from childhood. The Petitjean
family lived in a substantial stone house on the wide expanse of the Grande
Rue.[2] The rear garden of the Petitjean family home in the very heart
of the ancient walled town backed on to the south-western remnants of
Cérilly's ancient château. François must have passed it often during the
course of his life in the town and particularly on market days. He appears
to have been a familiar-enough visitor in 1796 to inscribe a witty epigram

on the fireplace of one of the rooms in the Petitjean home, mocking Henri Dufour, a young artist visiting Cérilly from Moulins and a rival suitor for Sophie's hand. After Péron's apology, the two young men became firm friends.[3]

It is uncertain when his feelings for Sophie blossomed as they did. The notary's daughter must have been one of the few relatively well-educated young women in Cérilly. In his teens he might have contemplated the celibate life of Holy Orders but, as we have seen, revolution and war had offered him other possibilities. There are grounds to believe that Péron's relationship with Sophie was both passionate and physical. He was undoubtedly writing from personal experience, in Tasmanian waters on 22 February 1802, when he declared: 'The kiss on the mouth is much more tender and much more delicate [than on the cheek]; and that which a happy lover savours rapturously on the palpitating bosom of his mistress is undeniably one of the most profound sensations and the most voluptuous which one can experience.'[4] During his medical studies he visited his family in Cérilly a number of times. We know, for example, that on 20 October 1799 he and Sophie Petitjean respectively became godfather and godmother to Péron's niece, Sophie-Anaïs Coupery.[5] This would suggest that their presence as a couple had the approval of the Péron family if not the Petitjeans.[6] We know François was back in Cérilly in February 1800, for he witnessed the curate of Cérilly, Pierre-Jean Marchand, take the oath of allegiance to the new constitution of Bonaparte's Consulate.[7]

Although the notary's daughter stood by the baptismal font as the spiritual partner of the talented young medical student, she was never to stand with him in front of the altar as his partner in marriage. It might have been a case of a change of heart. But, more likely, such a marriage was seen as a *mésalliance* by the Petitjean family. Brilliant he might have been, but Péron was also frail, half-blind[8] and the penniless son of an impoverished widow. Could it be that Pierre-Lazare Petitjean gave him financial assistance to continue his studies in the hope of keeping him away from Cérilly and his daughter? If so, it only put matters off for two years. The firm rejection, when it came, was very painful for Péron, and it appears to have precipitated his desire to leave France. In a draft letter, almost certainly to Sophie, he agonised:

When this one [letter] will reach you, without doubt [I will be] already far from you, oh my friend, far from my family, far from all those who are dear to me, everything that holds me to my life. The mighty Ocean will have enveloped me … Why are you not here, how much shall I need your counsel, you would sustain my courage, you would agree with my hopes. Alas! You know how such a voyage was far from my tastes, how it is contrary to my inclinations, my manner of living and feeling … Scarcely a few days have passed and all our projects, all our joint life plans have disappeared. Ready to leave you for so long, perhaps for ever, with such profound bitterness, I remember dear, we dreamt together of happiness, you alone will enjoy it …[9]

Two and a half years later, the notary's daughter married the son of Péron's landlord (Pierre Raby de La Lande) rather than the widow's gifted son.[10] Sadly, the marriage lasted a mere eighteen months, ending with Anne-Sophie's premature death on 30 August 1804.[11]

It could be that enlistment in a major voyage of exploration was a young man's desperate means of distraction from emotional pain or perhaps a way to prove himself worthy of his beloved's hand in marriage, but it seems unlikely that a young man like François Péron would have joined such a venture without some previous thought of, and underlying attraction to, such an expedition. Although he purchased a French translation of Linnaeus's *Systema vegetablium* (with a concordance for Jussieu's natural system)[12] on 19 July 1798, it was only in the second semester of the third year of his course that Péron formally studied botany under Louis Richard[13]— a course that might very well have precipitated Péron's metamorphosis from a bookish dreamer into a young savant determined to make his name through a voyage of exploration.

Unlike virtually all the other professors who taught François Péron, Louis Richard was neither a doctor nor a pharmacist. From a family of royal gardeners at Trianon and Auteuil—his father had been gardener to Madame de Pompadour, and his grandfather had corresponded with Linnaeus—Richard had initially been destined for the Church, but with his imagination fired by accounts of exploration, he decided to devote himself to natural history instead. He achieved a measure of fame between 1781 and 1789 as a plant collector in Guyana, Brazil and the Antilles. Unfortunately, on returning to France in the midst of Revolution, he found that past promises of reimbursement and patronage had disappeared like straw in the political wind—a source of bitterness for the rest of his life. Richard brought back three thousand plant specimens, together with a large number of quadrupeds, birds, insects, shells, rocks and minerals. He became an influential figure after Fourcroy recruited him as a professor in the medical school in 1795. Indeed Richard's efforts as a zoologist were particularly admired by Georges Cuvier, who wrote: 'His work on shell-fish was of the greatest importance. No collection of this kind was better organised, more exactly named than his.'[14] Richard is also said to have 'maintained that his method of classification had influenced the ideas of several authors justly celebrated in this branch of natural history'.[15] Very possibly Cuvier was alluding to François Péron as among the 'several excellent students' Richard had trained;[16] he too would achieve fame in the study of marine species.

Richard was a charismatic teacher whose lessons were theoretical, analytical and practical. Every Sunday he botanised in the country fol-lowed by two to three hundred pressing students. Noticing an interesting plant, Richard would forget his infirmities and be 'the first in the swamps, jumping hedges and ditches, tracing a route across the scrub'.[17] In 1800 Péron would almost certainly have taken part in these excursions as part of his studies. Significantly Richard also drafted a memoir giving instruc-tions to the naturalists of d'Entrecasteaux's expedition in search of La Pérouse.[18] It is hard to imagine that he and his collections were not a source of inspiration for Péron. Although Péron had by this time moved to new lodgings at no. 17 Place de Cambrai,[19] now part of the place Marcelin Berthelot in front of the Collège de France,[20] he ultimately settled in rue Copeau, the same street that Richard lived in with his wife and six children.[21]

At some stage during his medical studies Péron began frequenting the Jardin des plantes (formerly the Jardin du roi), which became home to the new Muséum national d'histoire naturelle in 1793. Here Georges Cuvier, whose 'advice and instructions' Péron asserted served him as a 'rule in his investigations',[22] was assistant to the professor of comparative anatomy (and would gain a professorial chair of his own in 1802). Here too the zoologist Bernard de Lacépède, whom Péron described as 'one of my earliest and dearest teachers',[23] held a chair as professor of fish and reptile natural history.

It is hardly surprising that there was an intimate nexus between natural history and medicine during this period. The earliest botanic gardens in Europe—such as those of the universities of Pisa, Florence, Padua, Leiden, Montpellier and Heidelberg—had their origins in physic gardens attached to medical faculties in the sixteenth century. Many famous traveller naturalists began their careers as doctors,[24] and François Péron was about to make the same transition.

The commander of the expedition Péron sought to join was Nicolas Thomas Baudin. Born on the Ile de Ré near La Rochelle in 1754, Baudin was the son of a merchant. In his youth he had served as an apprentice on merchant vessels and as a volunteer cadet in the local naval depot. In his early twenties, he joined the French East India Company's Pondicherry Regiment, but failed to gain a commission and returned to France in 1777. Although his naval record is sketchy, during the American War of Independence Baudin appears to have served on the frigate *Minerve* and then gained command of the forty-four-gun *Apollon* engaged in humdrum convoy escort duties. When his hopes of commanding a vessel bound for India were dashed by his humble status as a non-noble *officier bleu*, he quit the navy and returned to merchant service.[25] By chance he gained employment as a chartered botanical collector–voyager in the service of Emperor Joseph II of Austria. Although his first voyage was a great success and he was eventually commissioned as a post-captain in the Austrian navy, his three subsequent voyages ended in shipwreck and failure.[26] With the outbreak of war with France in 1792, the Austrians questioned Baudin's loyalty, and he was also accused of improprieties. In late 1795, however, he returned to France determined to recover collections he had left in Trinidad. After tantalising the Muséum and the government with details of their contents, he was given command of the flute *Belle-Angélique* (but no official naval rank) and departed Le Havre on 30 September 1796.[27]

On 18 October she was struck by a violent storm between the Azores and Madeira. Holed fore and aft, and without a rudder and some of her masts, Baudin made slowly for Tenerife in the Canary Islands. There the *Belle-Angélique* was condemned and replaced with an American brig, the *Fanny* (which was rechristened *Belle-Angélique*). During the expedition's four-month sojourn in the Canaries, the naturalists worked diligently collecting specimens on the islands. The expedition set sail on 15 March 1797 with a greatly reduced crew and reached Port-of-Spain in Trinidad on 17 April. Unfortunately the island had been captured by the British two months before and the new governor, Thomas Picton, refused to accept Baudin's scientific passport or allow him to load his collection. Eluding a British vessel ordered to escort him to Martinique, Baudin made for the neutral Danish island of St Thomas. There he and his scientists collected specimens and living plants for two and a half months and replaced the *Fanny* with yet another vessel: the *Triomphe* (recently captured from the British by a French frigate and also rechristened *Belle-Angélique*). Baudin then made for Puerto Rico where, despite serious illness among the naturalists, another rich harvest of living plants was made before returning to France on 7 June 1798.[28] He soon had other ambitious plans.

Baudin, like Charles-Pierre Claret, comte de Fleurieu (who had previously drafted instructions for La Pérouse[29] and Bruny d'Entrecasteaux[30]), recognised an historic opportunity to fill in numerous gaps in cartographic knowledge of the coast of New Holland. Despite his record of shipwreck and questionable enemy service, Baudin had the enthusiastic support of Antoine-Laurent de Jussieu at the Muséum, who lobbied the Minister of Marine, Pierre-Alexandre Forfait, in support of his proposal and recommended his leadership on 20 July 1798.[31] Within two weeks, the ministry promoted Baudin to the rank of *capitaine de vaisseau*, and—in a submission to the Directory—officially endorsed and budgeted an expedition to southern waters under his leadership. However, financial constraints, Bonaparte's *coup d'état* and then the First Consul's preoccupations in Italy left plans for the expedition in limbo for almost two years. Anxious to secure final approval, Baudin had addressed a combined session of three classes of the Institut national (France's peak scientific and academic body) at the end of the first week of March 1800, and declared that, in New Holland,

> ... all the sciences claim the care and attention of the voyager. Astronomy and geography still have many points to fix, coasts to delineate, harbours to identify. History and political economy demand comprehensive ideas on the races which inhabit these regions, on their population, their manners and practices, their form of government, and on the kind of commercial relations which might be established with them. Agriculture desires cultivated products of these places, and above all that which under the name of New Holland flax furnishes the clothing of the inhabitants. Natural history, which has only found new objects in the collections of animals and dried plants gathered on the coasts, desires that the same objects be transported alive to populate its gardens and menageries. It hopes as well that new researches will produce more discoveries.[32]

The members of the Institut thought Baudin's proposal—which at this stage also included surveys of the South American coast, California, the Hawaiian Islands and Tonga—worthy of further consideration, so they referred it to a commission that included, among others, the geographer Fleurieu, the explorer Louis-Antoine de Bougainville, the zoologist Lacépède and the botanist Jussieu. When the commission reported back favourably on 16 March, its members were ordered to make representations to the First Consul, who was also a member of the Institut national. Baudin joined them when they had a receptive audience with Bonaparte on 25 March 1800. Two weeks later France's young dictator gave his final approval after receiving a detailed report from the Minister of Marine. Bonaparte also asked the commissioners of the Institut to assist the navy in nominating scientific personnel for the expedition and charged them with directing the different areas of scientific endeavour for the voyage.[33] Baudin's orders, when he finally received them from the Minister of Marine, excluded mention of South America and stated that he was to undertake a 'detailed reconnaissance of the south-west, the west and the north of New Holland, parts of which are still entirely unknown, while others are only known imperfectly'. The intention was to consolidate the work of previous 'English navigators on the east coast and that of d'Entrecasteaux in Van Diemen's Land' and to chart parts of the east coast of New Guinea. 'All these countries more or less new to us', the minister stated (using words drafted by Fleurieu), 'present a vast field for geographical operations and for research of all kinds which can combine to perfect the natural sciences and augment the mass of human knowledge.'[34]

Baudin arrived in Le Havre on 14 June 1800 and was unimpressed by the state of the two vessels nominated for his expedition. Within two weeks he had gained the approval of the minister for their replacement with the corvette *Galathée*, later renamed *Géographe*, and the storeship *Menaçante*, later renamed *Naturaliste*.[35] Baudin had less influence over the choice of the members of the expedition. He would sail with 118 men on the *Géographe* and 120 on the *Naturaliste,* and find himself with another two passengers and eleven stowaways. The overwhelming majority were from Normandy (including the commander of the *Naturaliste*, Emmanuel Hamelin), but there were also numerous Bretons, Girondins and Parisians, together with a handful of individuals from the Low Countries, Germany, Sweden, Russia, India, Guadeloupe and the Ile de France (Mauritius). Aboard the *Naturaliste* there was also a Chinese passenger named A-Sam, who had been captured aboard an English East India Company vessel and had become something of a celebrity in Paris after his release from the hospital of Val-de-Grace; treated like one of the officers, he was destined for his native Canton via the Ile de France with the blessing of the First Consul. Although Baudin had requested none, there were fifteen midshipmen (including Bougainville's eighteen-year-old son, Hyacinthe), and there were twenty-two scientists, although he expected only sixteen. Ultimately Baudin was faced with feeding and disciplining thirty-seven souls more than he thought necessary. This was mainly because the Institut and the navy were determined to make the most of the scientific and training opportunities offered by the voyage and because so many requests had been made on behalf of well-connected young men. The midshipmen would bear the weight of Baudin's resentment throughout the voyage. And the savants (most of whom were not subject to naval discipline) would also chafe under the restrictions of shipboard life and the frustrations of undertaking scientific research perceived to be ancillary to the broader hydrographic ambitions of the expedition.

The scientists of the expedition were a very mixed group. The most famous was André Michaux, celebrated for his botanical collecting and travels in England, Spain, the Middle East, North America and the Caribbean.[36] The other botanist of the expedition was Louis Leschenault de La Tour, from Châlons-sur-Marne, who had studied medicine in Paris in the student intake the year before Péron. He is remembered through the Australian genus *Lechenaultia*, named in his honour (despite the lack of an 's' in the spelling) by the Scottish botanist Robert Brown.[37] Yet another botanist, André-Pierre Ledru, who had sailed with Baudin to the West Indies on the *Belle-Angélique*,[38] volunteered for the expedition but then withdrew after the entreaties of his widowed mother. Two of the zoologists of the expedition, René Maugé,[39] from Cély-en-Bière (Seine-et-Marne), and Stanislas Levillain,[40] one of the founders of the museum in Le Havre, had also sailed with Baudin on the *Belle-Angélique*, as had the gardener Anselm Riedlé[41] from Irsee near Augsburg in Germany; all three now rejoined him on the *Géographe*. Two other zoologists sailed on the corvette *Naturaliste*: Désiré Dumont and Jean-Baptiste Bory de Saint-Vincent, who would prove to be one of Baudin's most bitter critics.[42] Born in Agen (Lot), Bory began to collect plants and animals as a boy while he and his family took refuge in the countryside during the Terror. One of the most colourful characters of the expedition, Bory later rose to the rank of lieutenant colonel in the Grande Armée and was decorated with the Légion d'Honneur.[43]

There were two astronomers: Frédéric de Bissy, on the *Géographe*—born in London to an English mother and a French father, he served for a time in the French Consulate in Boston and then the French army and the National Guard before being imprisoned during the Terror as an English subject!—and Pierre-François Bernier,[44] on the *Naturaliste*, who was originally from La Rochelle but had grown up in Montauban and had drawn the attention of Joseph Jerôme Lalande when his work on the movements of the planet Mercury was published in the *Connaissance des Temps* at the age of only seventeen. There were two hydrographers: Charles Pierre Boulanger from Paris and Pierre Faure from Nantes, who would carry out important coastal surveys in Australian waters.[45] On the recommendation of the Ecole des Mines, two mineralogists were appointed to the expedition: Louis Depuch Monbuton from Jonzac in the Gironde, who had been a student of the founder of modern crystallography, René-Just-Häuy, and Joseph-Charles Bailly[46] from Nancy, who had previously studied at the Ecole polytechnique.

There were also several official artists: the landscape painter Jacques Gerard Milbert, who worked as a professor of art at the Ecole des Mines and had some experience as a travel artist, having accompanied Picot de Lapeyrouse on his journey in the Pyrenees;[47] the genre painter Michel Garnier, the son of a floor polisher at the Château de Saint-Cloud, who had studied under Jean-Baptiste Pierre and was expected to record ethnographic details during the voyage and assist with botanical illustrations;[48] and Pierre-Louis Le Brun, from Douai, an experienced nautical and portrait painter—whom the celebrated botanical artist Pierre Redouté reported was a man of 'much talent' and 'probity'[49]—who seems to have been expected to assist with animal drawings. But there were also two unofficial artists on board the expedition who appear to have been engaged by Baudin to illustrate his private journal. One was Nicolas Martin Petit, from a family of Parisian fan-makers and colourists; the other was Charles-Alexandre Lesueur, from Le Havre, who would become François Péron's lifelong friend. Both Petit and Lesueur were enrolled as assistant gunners (fourth class). As we shall see, the presence of the two 'assistant gunners' would prove particularly fortuitous.

To gain a place among the expedition's complement of savants, Péron had to persuade the Institut that he could fill a special role. Although

Péron later asserted that the expedition was already full at the time and that it was just about to leave, in fact there had already been resignations (such as by Ledru) and the vessels did not sail for another two months. Deleuze tells us that Péron sought the support of Antoine-Laurent de Jussieu for his candidature, and there is evidence for this in Péron's correspondence. To gain the support of other influential figures he chose to present his case in a fifteen-page pamphlet, *Observations sur l'anthropologie, ou l'Histoire naturelle de l'homme* …, which he had printed and sent with a covering letter to the professors of the Ecole de Médecine on 29 messidor an 8 (18 July 1800) and two days later to the Commission of the Institut. In his pamphlet he declared:

> An important expedition is being prepared. Scientists of every kind will be sailing beyond the Tropic of Capricorn, in climates still relatively unknown, to reap a vast array of useful observations. Every branch of science is represented … Only medicine has been denied its share of the dangers and successes of so noble an enterprise … Would it be less noble, would it be less useful to society to attach to the group of naturalists leading this research, a few young physicians who specialise in the study of man, who could gather interesting information about the lives of various tribes, how their physical and moral behaviour can be influenced by the climate in which they live, as well as how their customs, their habits, their internal and external illnesses might be related, and how they could be alleviated …?[50]

To reinforce his argument, Péron made reference to several physicians who had made major discoveries during their travels; and—appealing to national honour—he remarked that none had been French. They included the German physician Andreas Cleyer, author of *Specimen Medicinae sinicae* (1682), the first illustrated European work on Chinese medicine, which contained discussion of Chinese theories on the pulse and the first acupuncture chart published in the West; the Dutch physician Jacob Bondt (Bontius), author of a pioneering book on tropical medicine, *De Medicina Indorum* (1642); Willem Pison, the Dutch physician who discovered the ipecacuanha tree in Brazil and popularised its medicinal use as a purgative in his treatise 'De Medicinae Brasiliensi';[51] the German traveller Georg Marggraf, who commented on Brazilian and Chilean constitutions and languages;[52] and the Italian physician Prosper Alpinus, author of

De Medicina Egyptiorum (Venice, 1591), which contained the first European account of the coffee plant. With the hope of other important ethno-botanical discoveries, such as quinine, and comparative medical and anthropological knowledge, he asserted:

> It is said that the fleet will sojourn a long time at New Holland, Van Diemen's Land and New Zealand. What better theatre for new and interesting observations than these immense countries, from which voyagers and historians have so far mentioned very little, and physicians not yet a thing? To determine the physical nature of the climate, to research and state its influence on the organic constitution of the people who inhabit them, as well as its influence on their moral and physical development; to study their dominant passions, as well as their source; describe their occupations, their work, how they exercise; and detail finally everything concerning their hygiene; such should be the first part of this interesting work. The second part of their study would be no less useful: it would be to observe with care everything concerning medicine itself, to study carefully all internal illnesses, either general or sporadic, most of all those that are endemic; it would be to describe scrupulously all the symptoms, independently of all theory and hypothesis, noting their progress and their end; applying themselves above all to distinguish the particular phenomena relating either to the climate or the physical or moral temperament, of habit, mode of living, and the kind of food of these people; it would be important to make use of the enlightenment of physics, chemistry, geography, natural history; I believe it would be important to research the source of these endemic maladies, and the means to prevent them.[53]

Although Péron might have been the first to use the term 'anthropologist',[54] the expedition had already drawn the attention of the Société des Observateurs de l'Homme founded by Louis-François Jauffret the previous year, and in August one of its members, the young philosopher Jean-Marie Degérando, delivered a paper that considered 'the diverse methods to follow in the observation of savage peoples'.[55] Ultimately Georges Cuvier provided the expedition with detailed anthropological instructions.[56] François Péron was not appointed as 'anthropologist' to the expedition; instead he gained a place last on the list of zoologists as an *élève* (student) 'specially charged with comparative anatomy'.[57]

— 5 —

To the shoals of Capricorn

*... those captains who have scientists, or who may some day have them
aboard their ships, must, upon departure, take a good supply of patience.
I admit that although I have no lack of it, the scientists have frequently
driven me to the end of my tether and forced me to retire testily to my
cabin. However, since they are not familiar with our practices, their
conduct must be excusable.*

NICOLAS BAUDIN, *Journal*, 2 NOVEMBER 1800

PÉRON appears to have arrived at his port of embarkation, Le Havre, in
early October 1800. As he waited ashore, he had an opportunity to
become familiar with the officers and other savants well before the expedition set sail. Their departure had already been delayed by the installation
of cooking stoves that doubled as desalination boilers—unfortunately their
flues proved too narrow and the hold offered insufficient draught for them
to yield more than four pints every twelve hours—then the late arrival of
ancillary victuals, from Paris, caused a further postponement. Wines, liquor,
syrups, sweetmeats, soups, Italian pastas and powdered lemonade were
among the provisions that drew Péron's attention. He also remarked on
the astronomical, surgical, meteorological and navigational instruments
made by the 'most celebrated artists of the capital' and added: 'Everything
necessary for chemists, painters, and draughtsmen, was carefully selected; a
numerous library, composed of the best works on marine subjects, astronomy, geography, natural history, botany and voyages, was collected for
each ship.'[1] Bory de Saint-Vincent, however, thought that 'the library of

the corvettes was truly contemptible' except for works by Linnaeus, Jussieu, Ventenat and Lacépède.[2]

With a band playing and an enormous crowd of spectators on the shore, the *Naturaliste* and *Géographe* finally weighed their anchors on the morning of 19 October 1800. In the company of a neutral American vessel, the two French ships faced their first challenge: a British frigate. Although the Peace of Amiens had not yet been concluded, Baudin was armed with passports from a number of European nations, including Great Britain. His initial reception was surly, but the scientific status of the expedition was duly recognised by the commander of HMS *Proselyte*, and Baudin was allowed to sail unhindered into the misty waters of the English Channel. The weather warmed and the fog dissipated as they traversed the Bay of Biscay and sailed south along the coasts of Spain, Portugal and North Africa. Early on the evening of 1 November they sighted the island of Tenerife and Pico de Teide—its base enveloped in clouds and its summit, in Péron's words, 'illuminated by the last rays of the setting sun'. According to Baudin, the sight of land unleashed pandemonium on board:

> all the scientists and even most of the officers were so overjoyed that they behaved like madmen ... If a stranger had witnessed what went on and had not known when we had left Europe, it would have been impossible for him not to think that we had just completed a voyage lasting at least six months and that we had been without all essential provisions. Towards evening, when the general curiosity had been satisfied somewhat, everyone went off to get his portfolio and his pencils and, to fore and aft of the ship, there was not a soul to be seen who was not busy sketching.[3]

Péron, viewing his first landfall, appears to have been swept up in this same hysteria. Although he was well aware that Teide, at 3718 metres, was dwarfed by Mont Blanc and a number of other European and South American peaks, he was clearly entranced by its volcanic history, isolation and the brooding manner in which it announced the Canary Islands from afar. With grandiose authority, he declared that it was a mountain whose importance was 'above all others on the globe'.[4]

On 2 November 1800 the *Géographe* and *Naturaliste* anchored in Santa Cruz harbour. Baudin's principal reason for visiting Tenerife was to purchase wine for the voyage. The Canaries are famous for their Malmsey grown from vines originally introduced from Greece. Unfortunately, when he made enquiries through the French consul, Pierre-Marie-Auguste Broussonet, he found that it would cost almost three times more to satisfy the expedition's needs than he had allocations for. Hoping to find cheaper wine at the Ile de France, he purchased only three months' supply in addition to forty hogsheads of beer. The expedition's departure was further delayed by the late arrival of fresh provisions from Grand Canary.

The expedition members resided aboard ship, although an observatory was established at the governor's residence by the astronomer Frédéric Bissy[5] and his colleague Pierre Bernier verified the expedition's chronometers at the Tenerife observatory of Joseph Rodriguez Orta.[6] The savants were ferried ashore and back thrice a day. With little sympathy for their scientific curiosity, which he later declared 'a pretext for teaching themselves about a well-known country',[7] Baudin complained: 'I could no doubt have cut out one of these three trips, but as the scientists do not yet realise fully enough the inconvenience of having boats continually coming and going, I want to wait until experience has convinced them of the results which will soon follow from their useless excursions.'[8]

Baudin had already spent four tedious months in Tenerife in 1796 after his then command, the *Belle-Angélique*, was severely storm-damaged. Lacking further personal curiosity about the Canary Islands and expecting to depart at short notice, Baudin was reluctant to permit other 'useless excursions' beyond Santa Cruz; hence a group of savants and officers who had resolved to climb Pico de Teide was denied permission to ascend the peak, despite the favourable weather and lack of snow.[9] By now Bory de Saint-Vincent felt contempt for Baudin. In his account of a visit they made to the French consul, who possessed a fine insect collection, Bory portrayed Baudin as scientifically comic. He tells his readers that Baudin was transfixed 'with all the enthusiasm of a connoisseur' by a white *Argia* butterfly—presumably the widely distributed *Nepheronia argia* of Africa—and that he naïvely exclaimed: 'It is the butterfly of the orange!'[10]

Although the consul Broussonet is mentioned in several of the expedition journals and gave specimens to other naturalists, such as the mineralogist Depuch, it is surprising that Péron makes no mention of him. Broussonet was not simply a diplomat who dabbled in natural history. He was a graduate of the medical faculty of Montpellier, a friend of Sir Joseph Banks, a Fellow of the Royal Society of London, author of a major work on fishes, a foundation member of the Société linnéenne de Paris and, after the Revolution, a member of the National Assembly. During the Terror, however, he was forced to flee to Spain, where the enmity of *émigré* royalists forced him to flee again to Portugal and then Morocco, where he became physician to the American consul. After the fall of Robespierre he was appointed French Consul in the Canary Islands. Broussonet eventually returned to France and was appointed Professor of Botany at Montpellier, but died soon after—in 1807.[11]

Given Broussonet's medical training, he might very well have been the source of at least some of Péron's epidemiological information on the Canary Islands. There is no doubt that Péron was aware of Broussonet's significance as an icthyologist, because in Australian waters when a specimen of the then undescribed school shark was caught, he initially intended to name it *Squalus broussonet*. Later, however, he crossed out Broussonet's name and replaced it with *rhinophanes*. Ultimately, not even this name was published by Péron, and eighty years later William John Macleay, founder of the Macleay Museum at the University of Sydney, published the name *Galeorhinus australis*.[12]

Baudin's lack of scientific sophistication was not the only source of friction with the better-educated members of his expedition. He also came into conflict with the officers and savants when he denied them fresh victuals during their stay in Tenerife. Baudin himself declared that he refused their request on the grounds that he had already spent more on provisions than he had been allocated and asserted that he diffused the protests by threatening to 'make over everything on board to them' such that 'henceforth they could do themselves as well as they pleased'.[13] (They were not entirely without fresh greens, since the gardener Riedlé cultivated a regular supply of lettuce, radish and watercress for their table.)[14] With hindsight—given that the expedition ultimately stayed eleven days at Tenerife—it is a pity Baudin did not let the scientists reside ashore, at their own expense, with the freedom to pursue their scientific interests as they saw fit for an agreed period. Instead, the restrictions he imposed on highly educated men used to civilian scientific freedoms only generated further antagonism.

Close company bred other problems. Baudin was forced to deal with an unseemly altercation between the artist Pierre-Louis Le Brun and the ship's surgeon François Lharidon: they scuffled and would have come to blows had they not been separated. The witnesses sided with Lharidon, so Le Brun was ordered ashore. When he refused, he was placed under arrest in his cabin. There is little doubt that Le Brun had a difficult personality; on Christmas Eve, he would respond to Milbert's mild teasing by throwing a glass of water in the face of his fellow artist. For this he faced renewed threats of arrest and expulsion from the expedition. Lharidon was also a difficult, troubled individual with intellectual ambitions well above his station as surgeon, and it would not be long before both Baudin and Péron had their own separate confrontations with him.[15] (In July 1807, after a night of heavy drinking, Lharidon would hail a boat and put an end to his recurrent depression by jumping into the Penfeld River near Brest with his pockets full of stones.)

Ironically, Péron shared Baudin's desire to depart Tenerife as soon as possible: 'I had yet to complete too great a voyage', the young naturalist wrote, 'to remain long at the Canaries.' And echoing Baudin, he added: 'The situation of these islands, in the midst of the Atlantic Ocean, has submitted them to the observations of a great number of modern travellers.'[16] Although he clearly felt there were more important scientific enquiries to be conducted in southern waters, Péron appears to have been disappointed by the 'Fortunate Isles' of Horace and other classical authors.[17] While still aboard the *Géographe* he had thought the approaching shores 'inhospitable', the mountainous scenery 'barren and wild' and the habitations of Santa Cruz 'miserable'. Nevertheless, once ashore he reflected on the island's volcanic origins, strategic location, climate and maladies. His manuscript notes—free of sanctimonious moral airs and any hint of bitterness towards Baudin—are imbued with immediacy and curiosity and begin with military rather than scientific musings. In reviewing the island's fortifications, he was inevitably reminded of Nelson's failed attack on Tenerife in 1796, when the British admiral lost his arm. Expanding his notes for publication, Péron also recorded local admiration of recent French victories in Italy. Less than six months after the Battle of Marengo, it did not take much for the soldier and ardent patriot to surface in him: 'Ah!' he wrote. 'If it is ever permitted for an honest man to be proud of his country, it doubtlessly should be in such circumstances, when far from his fellow-citizens, he sees among strangers that every idea of greatness, glory and power is attached to the very name of his country.' But in reading the works of the naturalist and historian José de Viera y Clavijo, he also found time to admire the stubborn valour of the indigenous Guanche 'who, armed only with clubs and staves, fought during almost a whole century, against the French, Portuguese and Spanish … making them purchase the possession of these then wretched isles, with more battles and more blood, than the conquest of a new world has since cost them'.[18]

Although Péron did not climb Pico de Teide, he did make a number of botanical excursions with Bory de Saint-Vincent and other naturalists.

On one such excursion, Riedlé lost his foothold on a rock ledge and fell twelve metres; although he escaped fatal injury, he was brought back to the ship, badly bruised and pale with shock.[19] While on Tenerife, Péron met a number of prominent local residents. These included the duc de Betancourt, a colonel in the Ultonia (Ulster) Regiment of the Spanish army; Alejandro Saviñón, government physician in San Cristóbal de La Laguna,[20] who showed the naturalists his shell collection; and Bernardo Cólogan Fallon, a merchant of Irish Jacobite descent, who had studied in France, England, Holland and Spain and had hosted Alexander von Humboldt en route to the Americas the year before.[21] Cólogan, the author of an account of the eruption of Pico Viejo in 1798, loaned Bory de Saint-Vincent a coloured sketch of the eruption of Cahorra that, to Péron's disgust, was later published without acknowledgement. Péron also met Alonso Nava y Grimón, marquis de Villanoeva del Prado, a swarthy nobleman with a near-aquiline nose, dark penetrating eyes and sharp intelligence, who in 1790 had established a Jardín de Aclimatación outside the charming, basalt-cobbled highland town of La Orotava.[22] This beautiful botanic garden now contains numerous Australian species and striking examples of endemic Canary Islands flora, in addition to a herbarium of 30 000 specimens.[23] Baudin contributed to the marquis's collection by sending him more than thirty plant species (including ten pineapple plants and China tea), together with the seeds of another 120 species the expedition had transported from the Jardin des plantes, Val-de-Grâce and the garden of Jacques Martin Cels.[24] The marquis reciprocated with seven mule-loads of bananas and other fresh fruit. Affable and talkative, Péron also befriended more humble local residents, including a Milan-born innkeeper who had settled in Tenerife on a return voyage from China. According to Bory, Péron and Bernier knew enough Italian to 'passably flay' the fat innkeeper's language and ask him many questions.[25]

The expedition finally set sail from the Canary Islands on the afternoon of 14 November. Although Baudin had disembarked a number of sailors who were sick or incompetent, he gained three men left behind by the French corsair *Mouche* and several deserters from the Ultonia Regiment who stowed away on the *Naturaliste*. The next leg of the voyage took just over four months. It was a very long passage to the Ile de France because of seventeen days of calms near the equator and six weeks of contrary winds approaching the Cape and traversing waters south of the Mozambique Channel and Madagascar. When Péron came to write the official account of the voyage, he used Baudin's sea route to the Ile de

France as a stick to beat him with: 'The obstinacy of our commander in ranging the coast of Africa', he wrote, 'was the chief cause of this delay.' And in Péron's opinion it was a delay that had 'the most fatal influence' on the expedition's plans.[26] In support of his assertions, he made laboured reference to the works of William Dampier, Louis Granpré and others. But as Frank Horner has cogently argued, such fine navigators as James Cook (on his second voyage to the Pacific), Bruny d'Entrecasteaux and Matthew Flinders, all took similar routes and, if we omit stops, only Flinders was faster than Baudin (although not to the equator) and only by ten days.[27]

Ironically the long calms were days of halcyon stillness for Péron and provided him with several valuable scientific interludes. Determined to use his time aboard the *Géographe* to the fullest, he had not only recorded the gradual rise in the surface temperature of the sea since their departure from France but also (at the suggestion of Fourcroy, Laplace and others) sought to compare the temperature of the sea at different depths. Péron was not the first to conduct such experiments. Charles Blagden, James Cook and Benjamin Franklin had all measured surface seawater temperatures between 1775 and 1777. Franklin's work enabled him to identify the Gulf Stream for the first time. Deeper measurements had been undertaken by Luigi Marsigli and Horace-Bénédicte de Saussure, in the Mediterranean, and Vitaliano Donati, in the Adriatic—recording relatively constant temperatures of around 10° Réaumur, even at depths of up to 300 fathoms. In January 1751, Henry Ellis, captain of the slave ship *Earl of Halifax*, had reported using a bucket sea gauge with a system of valves (designed by Stephen Hales) to bring up seawater from as far down as 891 fathoms for temperature measurement on the deck.[28] Johann Reinhold Forster had appropriated the results of similar sampling experiments conducted by William Wales[29] during Cook's second Pacific voyage in 1772–73.[30] And Charles Irving had carried out other observations at 780 and 673 fathoms on Constantine Phipps' voyage to the Arctic in 1773.[31]

Péron, who sent a mercury thermometer down (rather than bringing water samples up for measurement), concurred with the findings of Ellis, Wales and Irving: temperatures fell with depth. This led him to speculate that in polar regions the sea was frozen to its greatest limits and to challenge Buffon's ideas on the terrestrial formation of polar ice. Nevertheless, Péron also rejected Irving's and Phipps' assertions, actually Aristotelian notions, that the sea grew warmer during a storm because of the agitation of the waves. While Péron found that mean sea temperatures were higher than that of the air, he astutely argued that this was because air cooled more rapidly than water and hence the surface temperature of the sea was relatively warmer than the air.

For all of Péron's criticisms of Baudin for the periods becalmed, they were crucial to the success of his experiments. If the ship had been moving, the instrument would not have settled vertically beneath the ship; instead it would have been dragged towards the surface and thus prevented temperature readings at any significant depth. Indeed, when the expedition vessels were under sail, it seems that Baudin begrudged Péron any more than five minutes to haul up his thermometer, even though it took more than twice this time to bring the instrument up from just 500 feet.

Despite the calms, accurate readings were not easy to achieve. During one early experiment, at just 300 feet, water pressure flattened the external tin cylinder and broke the thermometer in its charcoal-filled wooden case. Even when Péron successfully reached 2144 feet and waited an hour and a quarter before commencing the recovery of his instrument, it took another forty-five minutes to haul it to the surface because of what he calls the 'ill-will' of the crew. When finally recovered, the thermometer was found to have fallen 19° below surface temperature.[32]

Although Baudin did not find Péron's observations 'anything very extraordinary', they would later become the subject of an important oceanographic memoir published in the *Annales du Muséum national d'histoire naturelle* in 1804 and republished in English in the *American Journal of Science* in 1830. Péron's work also gained the official approbation of the Institut national and the praise of Lamarck and Guyton Morveau. Furthermore, Jean-Claude Delamétherie, editor of the *Journal de Physique*, which also republished Péron's memoir, recognised that it offered a significant challenge to the theories of Leibnitz and Buffon, who—relying on Marsigli's Mediterranean observations reported in Jean-Jacques de Mairan's *Dissertation sur les glaces* (1749)—argued that the geothermal heat of the earth's molten core heated the sea floor and thence uniformly warmed the sea from the bottom to top; only the shallow surface zone being influenced by atmospheric conditions.[33] As we shall see, later in Péron's life he would seek to understand the seemingly anomalous temperature profile of the much shallower Mediterranean.

Aside from measuring the temperature of the sea, Péron took meticulous humidity readings during the voyage in the vain hope of proving theories that harked back to Herman Boerhaave: that humidity and heat were the 'principal if not the exclusive cause of scurvy', rather than, as we now know, Vitamin C deficiency. Every ten days, at midday and midnight,

he descended from the poop to the quarterdeck, then from the gun deck
to the hold where he locked himself down for a half an hour to take
measurements. His research on applications of meteorological observation
to naval hygiene was eventually published in the *Journal de physique, de
chimie, d'histoire naturelle et des arts*, but during the voyage itself, Péron's pronouncements and advice to Baudin on sleeping arrangements for the
sailors, the storage of provisions and the purification of the air in the hold
inevitably strained their relationship.[34] Hence when a mishap befell Péron
during his readings on 17 November 1800, Baudin described the incident
gleefully in his journal:

> Towards midday he [Péron] was in the port head taking readings on
> a thermometer. A wave washed right over him and carried away his
> observation book as well as his thermometer. This accident, caused by
> the very heavy seas, did him no apparent harm, but he thought he was
> drowned beyond hope. So when the water which had entered the
> head ran out again, he was quite amazed not only to find himself
> alive, but still in the same place, for he had thought himself washed
> right out to sea.[35]

Although his journal contains many references to Péron's observations, it seems that Baudin sometimes found it hard to take such empirical obsession seriously. According to the young naturalist, Baudin also
opposed his proposal to evaporate seawater in alembics in order to compare the residual salts collected at different latitudes. Although the salts in
seawater are fairly constant, there are variations—Australian waters, for
example, are low in phosphorus; furthermore salinity levels can also vary
with evaporation or dilution of surface water through large amounts of
monsoonal rain and discharges from large rivers. It was yet another example
of an intense young man determined to use every spare moment of the
voyage productively. This was often in marked contrast to the rest of the
crew—sapped of energy and purpose by the breezeless heat and humidity.
The landscape artist Milbert was plunged into deep depression for lack of
terrestrial subjects and contrasting praise for young Lesueur's masterly
marine natural history paintings—gleaned from illicit readings of Baudin's
private correspondence.[36]

In the stillness of 27 November a large shark was caught. Even
when it thrashed dangerously on the deck, Péron's scientific ardour was
not dampened, and he challenged Surgeon Lharidon for the 'glory of

dissecting it'. Baudin recounts, with almost fatherly good humour, that he was pacing the quarterdeck when Péron came up to him

> dripping all over with blood, to complain that Mr Lharidon had snatched the shark's heart from him. He would not go on dissecting after such behaviour. I did my best not to laugh at the complaint, which Doctor Péron considered very grave. But to console him I promised him that the next one we caught should be his alone and that he could depend upon it and Surgeon Lharidon was left the undisturbed possessor of the shark's heart.[37]

But instead of sharks, Péron would make a major contribution to scientific knowledge of medusae, or jellyfish. In 1558 Guillaume Rondelet had described two species in his *Histoire des Poissons.*[38] Another three species were described in the sixteenth century by Pietro Andrea Matthioli, Ferrante Imperato and Ulisse Aldrovandi respectively. In the seventeenth century there were few original contributors to their study except for the Dutch naturalist Willem Pison and the English traveller Richard Ligon, who both observed and described the genus *Physalia* or Portuguese man-of-war. Although another forty-two species of jellyfish were haphazardly described by some of the most important naturalists of the eighteenth century, including Linnaeus—who was himself the first to coin the generic name *Medusa* in the fourth edition of the *Systema naturae* in 1744[39]—their study was still in its infancy.[40]

Péron's own jellyfish studies began in the equatorial waters of the Atlantic. Before departure, Cuvier and Lamarck had encouraged him to study 'mollusca',[41] a term that had a far wider meaning at the time. As Michel Jangoux has pointed out, Péron would have understood mollusca to include not only nudibranchia and cephalapoda but also medusae, starfish, holothuroids, polychaete worms and sea anemones.[42] Péron does not mention lowering a boat while the expedition was becalmed, but his colleagues Stanislas Levillain and Maugé 'invented a kind of small pocket of fine mesh ensleeved on a piece of very long wood', which enabled them to net what passed along the side. 'Often', Levillain recorded, they were able to present to 'Commandant Baudin some new individuals of the family of molluscs and other gelatinous [species] which he then had sketched'.[43] Perhaps Levillain and Maugé shared their specimens with Péron for study, or he trawled his own net. We do know that Péron described four species of medusae collected in the equatorial waters of the

Atlantic and two in the south Atlantic, which were illustrated on vellum by Charles-Alexandre Lesueur.[44] These included an entirely new species, *Pegasia dodecagona*, later included in the genus *Pegantha* by the Danish zoologist Paul Lessenius Kramp.[45] Péron's description of this 40mm-wide cap-shaped jellyfish, with twelve tentacles, would not be published for another decade, but in his account of the voyage he offers us a vivid word portrait of the genus *Physalia* spreading 'on the surface of the waves its sinewy snares or nets, several feet in length, and of a pure and lively ultramarine blue'. One can almost feel the burning pain he and Lesueur must have felt when they handled this species for study and illustration, perhaps transferring them into a glass jar or tank: 'Woe to the hand which attempts to seize them!' he wrote. 'This sensation is attended with an intolerable smarting in the whole limb ... the almost instantaneous effects of the slightest touch of *physalia*.'[46] Péron's work on jellyfish would ultimately include pioneering observations of their anatomy and physiology, and the collection of many previously undescribed species.

Péron's attention was also drawn to other pelagic genera. At 34°S 13°W, three species of fish were caught that he could not identify but which Lesueur illustrated.[47] Péron's descriptions of other marine species in these waters reveal a man deeply touched by the beauties of nature. Of beroes (ctenophores commonly known as comb jellies or sea gooseberries), he wrote: 'Their substance, more transparent than the purest crystal, is generally of fine rose colour, opal, or azure ... all the longitudinal sides become so many living prisms, which seem to enclose the animal in eight or ten animated undulating rainbows, of which language, or even painting, can give but a very imperfect idea.'[48] 'Vellelas', he informed his readers, were creatures in which 'the transparency of the sail, the beautiful azure blue colour with which it is adorned, all unite to make it one of the most beautiful species of the class to which it belongs', and he added that in calm weather he observed 'thousands of these zoophytes manoeuvring on the surface of the seas ... like so many beautiful flotillas in miniature, directed according to the principles of our naval tactics'.[49] Some of these species appeared as illustrations in the *Atlas du Voyage de découvertes aux Terres Australes*. According to Jacqueline Bonnemains and Claude Carré: 'Péron was one of the first authors to have observed, not only the essential morphological characteristics of these animals, but also their behaviour: floating on the surface, role of the sail in the displacement, bending movements of the tentacles and their possible autonomy, grouping by innumerable swarms evolving in response to the direction of the wind.'[50]

Furthermore, Péron's account contains tantalising references to *Porpita* (circular raft-like medusozoa with club-shaped tentacles that drift on the ocean surface)[51] and Thaliaceans, such as salps.[52] Patrick Brown had first used the term 'Thalia' in his landmark *Civil and Natural History of Jamaica* (1756), and Pehr Forsskål had later coined the term 'Salpa'. They had been little studied in the half-century since, so Georges Cuvier had 'particularly recommended to M. Péron ... to observe and to study as much as he could of these animals'.[53] He would not be disappointed. Péron and Lesueur conducted 'minute dissections' in order to better understand the internal structure of these organisms. These dissections were particularly difficult, not just because of the small size of these creatures but also because they 'altered very quickly out of their milieu'. Important details are evident not only in Lesueur's beautiful studies but also in small elevations drafted by Péron himself.[54] Later Péron attempted to divide salps into two large families; ultimately he would study more than fifty identifiable species.[55]

In his official narrative, Péron did not intimidate his readers with the results of his morphological and physiological researches, but he was certainly prepared to offer them lyrical prose they could all understand. One of Péron's most striking descriptions is his account of bioluminescence at sea:

> Here the surface of the ocean sparkles and shines as far as the eye can reach like a sheet of silver, when electrified in the dark—there it unfolds its waters in immense sheets of sulphur and flaming bitumen; in another place it resembles a sea of milk, the extremities of which are not to be perceived. The minutiae of these great phenomena are not less to be admired than the grandeur of the whole ... Others have made mention of those masses of fire which roll on the waves like so many enormous red balls, and of which we ourselves saw some that did not appear to be less than twenty feet in diameter. Many seamen have observed fiery parallelograms, cones of light inverted, whirling about on their points, shining garland and luminous serpents. In some places of the seas are to be perceived sparks of fire springing from the surface; in another part bodies of light and phosphorous are seen moving on the waves in the midst of darkness. Sometimes the ocean appears as if ornamented by an immense steep of moving light, whose undulating action seems to reach the edge of the horizon.[56]

This phenomenon had been recorded by both Aristotle and Pliny the Elder. Some years before Baudin's expedition, Benjamin Franklin had erroneously speculated that luminescence at sea was a result of an electrolytic discharge between salt and water. Others attributed luminescence to the presence of phosphorus or the influence of hydrogen. In the same year that Franklin made his speculations, luminescence had been observed in the Adriatic among single-celled zooplankton known as *Noctiluca*, so naturalists increasingly began to suppose that they were observing a biological rather than a purely physical phenomenon. This was certainly the conclusion Péron came to after careful observation: 'All the phenomena of the phosphorescence of the waters of the sea, however multiplied, however singular they may appear, may be nevertheless deduced from one single principle—the phosphorescence peculiar to marine animals.'[57] It remains to be said that there are many kinds of bioluminescence, but among the Coelenterates, to which the Medusae belong, it appears to be chemical rather than caused by light-emitting bacteria or organs (photophores). Whether it is a sexual attracter, a lure for food, a warning to predators of stinging cells or a sophisticated camouflage against background surface light is not clear.

Although this leg of the voyage facilitated pioneering contributions to marine biology and oceanography, it also encouraged introspection and continued yearning for Sophie Petitjean: 'Our vessel … moves with more certainty … the tired sailors weary with work will surrender their still wet limbs to the sweetness of sleep. Everything is already still around me … I alone am still awake … but I am soon taken over by fatigue … my heavy eyelids close, but they open however once more. They turn to you my friend and my heart turns with them to farewell you Sophie … adieu.'[58]

Although Baudin demonstrated great pride in the marine zoological discoveries of his scientists and the impressive achievements of the young (unofficial) artists illustrating his personal journal, his relationship with several of his junior officers continued to deteriorate. At Tenerife he had been at odds with Captain Henry de Freycinet, who invited a local resident, allegedly of ill-repute, to dine with the officers without consulting the commander. On 23 November, Baudin accused Henry's brother Louis of discourtesy after the elder Freycinet accompanied a boat from the becalmed *Naturaliste* and went straight to his sibling's cabin (apparently to borrow clothes)[59] before calling on Baudin—who not only refused to see him but also wrote to Hamelin to have him put under arrest for two days in his cabin as a lesson.[60] The day after Christmas, dissatisfied with

Lieutenant François Baudin's[61] performance and familiarity with the midshipmen, he humiliated him by taking over his subordinate's watch. In the journal of Lieutenant Pierre-Guillaume Gicquel Destouches one sees a growing hatred for Baudin. Born in Dinard, Brittany, he had entered the merchant marine in 1784 and then joined the navy as a volunteer in 1788. Three years later he joined the *Recherche* under d'Entrecasteaux in search of La Pérouse and was promoted to ensign. Gicquel could have been a valuable addition to the expedition, having visited Van Diemen's Land (twice), New Holland, New Ireland, the Admiralty Islands, Tongatabu, New Caledonia and the Dutch East Indies. He had also served with distinction in the French naval squadron based at the Ile de France. At the suggestion of the hydrographer Charles Beautemps-Beaupré, he had joined Baudin's expedition with the hope of further promotion but, as Frank Horner put it, he was 'one of those awkward subordinates—a volunteer who has changed his mind, too late'.[62] In his journal Gicquel chronicled Baudin's failings and apparent spitefulness with almost methodical relish; nevertheless, his criticisms of Baudin's style of command were not without justification. Even Frank Horner conceded that 'Baudin's methods of discipline must bear some of the blame for the feeling that must have spread in the ship: that one never knew where one stood with him'.[63]

Confronted with growing bickering among the savants and officers, Baudin summoned them all to the great cabin, expressed his dissatisfaction and declared that he had the authority 'to get rid of them at the next port if they did not mend their ways'.[64] To bolster his authority, he even forged additions to the written instructions he had received from the Minister of Marine, Pierre Forfait. They included a sentence requiring officers to instruct midshipmen in rigging and ship-handling; a sentence authorising whatever form of discipline the expedition commander thought fit— where there had actually been a sentence requiring strict adherence to the laws and regulations of the navy; and another sentence giving Baudin authority to replace any officer who was disruptive or whose performance was poor. These illicitly altered instructions were then read out to those assembled and were inserted in the ship's log.[65] What Baudin had not realised is that many members of the expedition were about to quit the expedition at the Ile de France—their next port of call.

— 6 —

Ile de France

*... one finds everywhere simple customs, a generous hospitality, a careful
education, a warm-hearted freedom and, above all, an ease of
communication which alone can give all its value to society; the character
seems to have received the imprint of gentleness and of the charm of
agricultural occupations ...*

FRANÇOIS PÉRON, MANUSCRIPT NOTES ON THE ILE DE FRANCE[1]

ON the morning of 14 March 1801 a large number of sea birds heralded
approaching land. Late in the afternoon, the Ile de France and two tiny
offshore islands—Ile Ronde and Coin de Mire—were sighted to the west.
Unfortunately, currents and overnight squalls drove the expedition vessels
south, and it was another day before they negotiated the reef-lined passage
around the northern tip of the island and attempted to enter Port Nord-
Ouest (Port Louis). When they failed, they spent yet another night at sea,
anchored off Baie du Tombeau. The next day, with the aid of a pilot, they
finally entered the principal port of the island and learned that their arrival
had precipitated a mobilisation of the garrison and the National Guard.
Although they had anchored with every mast illuminated and responded
to every signal, they were treated with suspicion. As we shall see, even
if they were not British, it was thought possible that they might bear
unwelcome visitors from France.

The Ile de France had no indigenous inhabitants. France had claimed
the island five years after it was abandoned by the Dutch in 1710. Settlers
from France's coastal provinces had then turned the island into a powerful

naval and trading base. With the labour of slaves from Africa and Madagascar, the French had established the town and harbour of Port Louis (named in honour of King Louis XV), begun a shipbuilding industry, built sturdy hospitals, barracks, storehouses, offices, aqueducts and fortifications of local blue-grey basalt, and constructed a network of roads that fanned out into the interior and facilitated the development of agriculture. In the rich brown soil, between the weathered volcanic craters and plugs, the colonists cultivated fields of sugar cane, cotton, coffee, fruit trees and indigo. By the time François Péron arrived, probably more than 70 000 people were living on the island and who had an emerging créole cultural identity.[2] As Péron himself acknowledged: 'there are the real créoles, that is to say, the real descendants of the first French colonists. It is for them alone truly a native land—it is for them alone that it represents all the titles that remain dear—it is there where the bones of their ancestors lie ...'[3] A decade of revolutionary change had also left its mark. Port Louis was renamed Port Nord-Ouest; a colonial assembly was established; National Guard detachments were raised; and local representatives were elected and dispatched to Paris.[4]

The colonists, however, did not welcome all revolutionary reforms, especially the National Convention's vote, on 4 February 1794, to abolish slavery in French colonies. Opposition to emancipation hardened among colonists in September 1795 when news arrived of the massacre of French planters by their slaves on the island of Saint-Domingue. Given the level of opposition, Governor Maurès de Malartic and his successor Magallon de la Morlière made little effort to challenge the local colonial assembly and enforce the emancipation order. The government in Paris, preoccupied with internal problems and international conflict from 1793, also had little ability to impose its will. Two representatives of the Directory, René Baco and Etienne Burnel, were even forcibly expelled from the colony in 1796 and were lucky to escape with their lives. It is perhaps not surprising that one of the first questions asked of Baudin was whether he had 'any secret agent on board entrusted with putting into execution the decree concerning the liberty of the natives [sic]'.[5]

Yet, despite the island's rebellious semi-independent status, the colonists had actively supported France in her war with Britain. As privateers under the tricolore, they raided British commerce with spectacular success. Between 1793 and 1802, more than 176 prizes would be taken by just eighteen armed merchantmen and the local naval squadron during daring combat operations launched from the island. But this brash nest of privateers, planters, merchants and ruthless slave traders—fighting for survival on an isolated Indian Ocean island with limited resources—had little sympathy for the needs of an ill-provisioned scientific expedition sent from metropolitan France.

Baudin, who had himself once been involved in the odious slave trade, managed to allay local concerns about emancipation, but faced insurmountable difficulties securing provisions from the local administration—let alone fresh victuals while in port. Even his attempts to insinuate secret political objectives for his expedition, in a letter to the Governor, failed to gain him any special consideration and served only to generate a complaint to the minister and then an anxious report to First Consul Bonaparte regarding his compromise of the expedition's scientific neutrality.[6] Furthermore, Baudin had old enemies in the colony and experienced the indignity of insulting placards posted on some streets that read: 'The Expedition that Failed'. Refusing to accept defeat, Baudin made arrangements for provisions from private purveyors and his friend the Danish Consul, Pelgrom. He paid for these provisions with cash obtained from a Danish captain accorded bills of exchange promising 33.3 per cent interest on redemption in Europe. Clearly, such an arrangement was not without its risks and, if we are to believe Lieutenant Gicquel, Baudin had already made enemies in the colony after unpaid provisioning debts going back to his service with the Emperor of Austria in 1790.[7]

Baudin's problems, however, had only just begun, for his expedition began to haemorrhage officers, scientists and sailors. As Péron put it, 'it shall suffice to say, that … we could not procure any of the most necessary provisions; that we lost forty excellent seamen, who here deserted, and that a great number of officers, naturalists, and artists belonging to our ships, already tired and disgusted with the ill usage they had experienced from our commander, or justly alarmed for the future, chose to remain on the island'.[8] Many sailors, as Péron states, quite simply deserted—seduced by recruiting agents for privateers. They included the commandant's secretary Louis Petitain; the assistant second master, Jean-Noël Moutié; the second chief helmsman, Charles Prosper Fiquet; three assistant helmsmen, Pierre Cohars, Louis Tocqueville and Jean-Baptiste Avice; and the cooks, Jean-Louis Lepine and Nicolas Coulon.[9] The savants who left included the artists Garnier, Le Brun and Milbert, the astronomer Bissy, the botanists Michaux and Delisse, the gardeners Cagnet and Merlot, and the zoologists Bory de Saint-Vincent and Dumont.[10] The officers who departed included Lieutenants Bonnié and Gicquel,[11] the Russian-born Ensign Capmartin and six midshipmen: Peureux, Morin, Montgéry, Billard, Bottard and Isabelle.

André Michaux left mainly because he did not want his plant specimens to be transferred to government ownership; he would die of fever in Madagascar in October 1803.[12] However, illness was the excuse most gave to justify their decision to quit at the Ile de France. Some appear to have been genuinely ill, but most appear to have feigned their maladies. Indeed, when Baudin visited the hospital, none of his men could be found. Although the commander of the expedition made strenuous efforts to apprehend the deserters from the lower ranks—trapping many at a public execution!—he did not pursue disciplinary action against his officers. In Frank Horner's opinion, 'It was as though Baudin, happy to allow the malcontents and the useless ones to find a way out of the expedition via the hospital, still wanted to assure himself that they were not really ill—perhaps in case they tried later on to blame him for their illnesses.'[13]

Péron's published account of the Ile de France—largely made up of historical, botanical, geological and meteorological summaries—provides sparse personal detail of his visit to the colony. Fortunately, his private manuscripts are more revealing. There can be little doubt that he found the island agreeable and picturesque. On 20 March 1801 he wrote: 'Long points of rock rise into the air in a thousand forms as singular as [they are] bizarre ... The vast fertile plains are intersected by a great number of small rivers which descend in torrents and discharge into the sea. All are covered in plantations of sugar cane, of rice, in a word, all here announces the fertility of a land new and fecund.'[14]

Bory de Saint-Vincent tells us that he landed 'near the hospital with Péron, Bernier and Deslisses'.[15] According to his account, Péron was hospitalised with Milius, Bernier and Faure. He does not tell us for how long, only that Péron recovered.[16] According to Baudin, 'most of the naturalists disembarked their belongings and took lodgings in various parts of the town' on 17 March.[17] We know that Péron visited the Pamplemousses district in the north-west of the island and that he met Jean-Nicolas Céré, director of the famous botanical gardens there.[18] Because of the strategic location of the Ile de France—close to Africa and on the sea routes between Europe and Asia—the Pamplemousses gardens comprised a major reference collection of tropical species from many parts of the world and served as an important nursery for economically valuable species introduced to local plantations and to other French colonies.[19] Péron's extensive description in his published account and his manuscript plant list[20] are evidence of the deep impression the splendid gardens made on him.

> M. Céré has skillfully naturalised, in the space of thirty years, a prodigious number of trees and shrubs, some from the ardent climates of Africa, other from the humid shores of Madagascar; some from China and Pegu [*sic*; Péru?], and again, others are natives of the banks of the Indus and the Ganges; several are the produce of the summits of the Gháts, others flourished originally in the rich valleys of Kashmir; and in the isles of the great archipelago of Asia, Java, Sumatra, Ceylon, Bouro, the Moluccas, and the Philippines: Tahiti itself has contributed to the richness and beauty of this garden. The Canaries, the Azores, the orchards and groves of Europe, and the forests of America, are there combined, and we may there also find several plants of Arabia, Persia, Brazil, of the coast of Guinea, Cafraria, &c. and we ourselves added to the collection numerous specimens of the curious vegetables of the south.[21]

Céré was a man in his early sixties, with receding hair, a prominent nose, pointed chin and a small, thinly lined mouth.[22] Born on the Ile de France but educated in Brittany and Paris, he was acclaimed for successfully propagating the clove and nutmeg seedlings that Pierre Poivre had smuggled out of the Dutch East Indies thirty years before. So great was Céré's fame that he was even asked by the Hapsburg emperor Joseph II to assist in expanding the Gardens of Schönbrunn. And, in 1787, the emperor's head gardener and botanist, Franz Boos, was conveyed to the Ile de France on *La Pipita* by none other than the future explorer Nicolas Baudin.[23] Céré also had a wide correspondence with many notable French scientists known to Péron.[24]

Another impressive friendship Péron made was with Jean–Baptiste Lislet Geoffroy, born on the neighbouring island of Réunion, the son of a slave woman and an East India Company engineer. Lislet was taught mathematics and drawing by his father and studied physics and astronomy with the aid of books loaned to him by the Chevalier de Tromelin. He rose to prominence as an able hydrographer after drafting charts in Madagascar, the Seychelles, the Ile de France and Réunion. Both Péron and Lislet shared an interest in meteorological observation, and Lislet gave his new friend a Saussure thermometer, which had been given to him by

Jacques-Julien Houtou de Labillardière when he called at the island in 1795.[25] For Péron, Lislet exemplified 'all the injustice and the absurdity of our [racial] theories and our prejudices'.[26]

Yet despite his enormous admiration for a man who had risen from slavery to become a corresponding member of the Académie des Sciences in 1786, Péron held conservative views on emancipation essentially because of the prospect of disorder and violence. 'Blacks', he wrote in one of his unpublished manuscripts, 'are very numerous on the island and such is their proportion to the whites that it suffices to sojourn [here] very briefly to sense all the folly of the innovators who wish to give them their liberty and all the justice of the alarm of the owners in this regard.'[27] After reviewing medical facilities available to the slaves, he added: 'I am convinced by my own eyes that nothing which is necessary for the sick is refused them.'[28] Indeed for Péron, who hailed from the heart of rural France and had witnessed the terrible hardships of peasant life leading up to the Revolution, the choice between the supposedly benign paternalism of slave life on the Ile de France and the free life of a peasant was one that he thought would perhaps leave a wise man indecisive 'after weighing the advantages and the inconveniences of one and the other'.[29] Although he recognised that slaves 'were not equally well treated everywhere' and that there were 'barbarous masters',[30] he made no mention of the Code Noir (the legal code for slaves) and the brutal (often mortal) punishments that could be meted out under the law. Nor did he write of the sexual exploitation of slave women and the agony of families separated on the auction block.

While Céré and Lislet are prominently mentioned in Péron's published account of the voyage, he made a list of eighty-five individuals (and their families) whom he got to know at the Ile de France. Some of these individuals he could not have met until his return to the island in 1803, but aside from the Governor, General Magallon de la Morlière, it is clear that he met many naval officers, engineers, teachers, merchants, surgeons, physicians and pharmacists during his first visit. Fourth on his list was Léonard Clair Laborde, a graduate of the Montpellier medical school who arrived at the Ile de France in 1786 and had several times been elected as a deputy for Port Louis in the Colonial Assembly. With his medical background he maintained a strong interest in public health and epidemiological issues, particularly relating to smallpox and leprosy.[31] And it was in Laborde's company that Péron visited a number of men afflicted with leprosy, recording that he himself 'thrust a large pin into the face without any of them having given the slightest indication of pain or of feeling'.[32]

Péron also met a number of naturalists who almost certainly assisted him in his researches. They included the impressive Swedish polymath Nils Bergsten, a graduate of the University of Uppsala who had arrived in the colony three years before and established a medical practice on the island;[33] the ailing, near-destitute naturalist Louis Aubert du Petit-Thouars, described by Péron as an 'excellent man of the most gentle and the most honest character' who would soon publish several major works on the botany of the region; and Johann Frederich Stadtmann, a native of Wissembourg (a town Péron knew well from his military service), a graduate of the medical faculty of Strasbourg and a passionate botanist and botanical artist in whose honour Lamarck named the genus *Stadtmannia*.[34]

Péron continued his research into the medusae at the Ile de France, collecting a species of 'upside down' jellyfish that he provisionally included under a new generic name *Neptunia* in his manuscript, but which he and Lesueur published as *Cassiopeia* in 1810.[35] This jellyfish contains zooxanthella (single-celled algae) in the protruding bladders of its mouth-arms. Its sedentary posture better facilitates a remarkable symbiotic relationship by enhancing algal access to sunlight and hence photosynthesis and nutrient production. Nevertheless the pulsating bell of the jellyfish also draws food and oxygen from the surrounding waters of its habitat—usually shallow, sandy-bottomed lagoons.[36]

François Péron's visit to the Ile de France also offers a window on his broader ecological imagination. Most significantly, the notes he made on the great size of European leeches introduced to the Ile de France indicate that he did not believe in the immutability of species and that he held Lamarckian evolutionary beliefs.[37] To a modern reader, his discussion of deforestation at the Ile de France and presumed associations with significantly diminished rainfall[38] also seems marked by a prescient ecological consciousness. He was, however, reporting local opinion and must already have been aware of pioneering conservation legislation that had been introduced to the Ile de France as early as 1769, making it obligatory to retain trees on 25 per cent of all landholdings, particularly mountain slopes, and protecting forests within 200 feet of water. And in 1804, the year after he returned to the island, the top two-thirds of mountain vegetation was formally protected with even tougher legislation.[39] Although Péron accepted the possible veracity of the link between clearing and diminished rainfall, he also questioned local assumptions and asked whether the rainfall might be the same, but evaporation increased as a result of the clearing! Athough Péron was often wrong, his mind seems always to have been active at the behest of fertile empirical urges.

While Péron got to know the Ile de France and many of its prominent inhabitants (human, animal[40] and vegetable), Baudin continued his preparations for the next stage of the expedition and also unloaded numerous mysterious crates, labelled 'B.' (apparently containing the latest Paris fashions!), which he had transported to the colony despite the strict naval prohibition against *pacotillage* (private trade).[41] To reprovision his vessels, the naval intendant had provided him with the services of thirty slaves, requisitioned from local residents under the *corvée* system—the obligation to provide unpaid labour to the state. Given the desertions from his crew and the unenthusiastic assistance of the local administration in finding his missing sailors, Baudin refused to return the *corvée* labourers until his men were returned. He relented, however, when the intendant sent him a dozen sailors from a prison hulk, two of whom escaped the same night. Finally, on 24 April, Baudin called on the Governor and requested permission to take six Malays who were also languishing in the hulk and awaiting repatriation. The Governor agreed when Baudin promised to return them to Batavia.[42] With a hundred men on the *Géographe*, eighty-five on the *Naturaliste*, improvised rations and a small herd of cattle given by the intendant, Baudin felt able to depart the Ile de France and continue his expedition.

At no time does Péron's commitment to the expedition appear to have waivered at the Ile de France, although he too must have had some concerns for the future course of the voyage given the limited provisions on offer. Baudin secured no biscuits, but managed to load 7500 kilograms of wheat and was able to secure only forty hogsheads of wine, which he planned to ration to one meal every ten days—a severe restriction for Frenchmen![43] Péron was certainly shrewd enough to know that the greater the number of erudite savants to leave the ranks of the expedition, the greater were his prospects of shining in the pool that remained. And as Michel Jangoux has pointed out, regardless of the opinions he later expressed in the official account of the voyage, even after leaving the Ile de France for New Holland, Péron was satisfied with his prospects and Baudin's leadership, declaring: 'Oh! With what pride I am pleased to repeat daily: "I am of this expedition … truly destined to the progress of the sciences" … The character of our chief, those of our good friends, of our companions and finally my own, all answer sufficiently that my hopes will not be deceived.'[44]

— 7 —

A course for New Holland

During a long crossing, it is prudent seldom to confide and never to argue. The sea has a tendency to sharpen tempers naturally. The slightest disagreement thither degenerates into a quarrel.

JACQUES-HENRI BERNARDIN DE SAINT-PIERRE, 'OBSERVATIONS SUR LES MŒURS DES GENS DE MER' IN *Voyage à L'île de France*

ON the morning of 25 April 1801, the expedition set sail from Port Nord-Ouest (soon to be renamed Port Napoléon). As they rounded the south-west tip of the Ile de France, their final view of the island was the rugged natural redoubt of Le Morne Brabant, where runaway slaves are said once to have jumped to their deaths rather than face recapture and retribution.[1] They had put to sea more than two months after the latest date Baudin had orders to leave the island.[2] Although he had instructions to proceed directly to Van Diemen's Land, his accumulated delays now meant he faced the prospect of surveying the D'Entrecasteaux Channel and the treacherous waters of Bass Strait in winter. Without even advising his superiors in case of mishap (indeed his last letter from the Ile de France affirmed his intention to fulfil his original orders), Baudin decided to head for Cape Leeuwin and then survey the north-west coast of New Holland. In his published account, Péron unfairly suggested that Baudin 'feared to be driven towards Van Diemen's Land'.[3] Although he had grounds to assert that the 'season, though advanced, was not so much so as to prevent us from doubling the South Cape',[4] as a landsman, he could not have known how long Baudin required for the surveys in Tasmanian waters and how 'prudent' adherence to the original instructions actually was. How-ever, Péron hissed: 'We shall see in the end the consequences produced by this first deviation from our orders.'[5]

Péron's retrospective account of Baudin's expedition rationalised numerous responses to unforeseen circumstances as errors in command with malignant consequences. Earlier, he had blamed Baudin's route 'ranging the coast of Africa' for having 'the most fatal influence' on the expedition's plans.[6] Now he blamed the provisions as the 'chief cause of all the miseries we in the end experienced'.[7] There is no doubt that the victuals were limited and in many respects of poor quality—they had set out in time of war—but as Frank Horner bluntly put it: 'Péron's story ran far from the truth.' Fresh bread was available only once every ten days, yet wine was not entirely replaced by cheap rum from the Ile de France. (Péron does not mention the daily allowance of beer.) Furthermore, 'biscuit and salt provisions' had not become their 'general food'. As Horner points out, 'peas and rice were served regularly as well—rice every day on the *Géographe*. It is even possible that fresh meat was enjoyed from time to time, at least on the staff tables.'[8]

During his traverse of the Indian Ocean, Péron continued his meteorological observations (musing, as they approached the coast of New Holland, on continental influences reducing humidity at sea) and still puzzling over the temperature of seawater, which was higher than the surrounding atmosphere. A bemused Baudin wrote: 'At the time of his departure from Europe, Citizen Péron could not imagine the temperature of the sea-water to be greater than that of the atmosphere. But he is at last beginning to believe it, for all his observations and experiments have con-sistently given results that contradict his earlier opinions.'[9] The fact that his opinions could change in the wake of raw data collection exemplifies the empirical manner in which he helped to lay the foundations of modern oceanography.

At dawn on 27 May 1801 New Holland became visible for the first time. That evening, hove to in coastal waters, Péron collected his first Australian natural history specimens after he, Maugé and (it would seem) Baudin trawled for half an hour with a dragnet on a 150-fathom line. Their efforts yielded a tubful of small potato-shaped sponges, broken coral and two species of worms, but no shellfish except for two white Neritas and a goose barnacle.[10] Baudin was clearly excited by the exercise and wrote: 'this first attempt in deep water [the bottom was at 72 fathoms] was so satisfying, that I promised myself that whenever the opportunity offered we would put to good use the time that we would lose in making no progress.'[11]

Ironically, although Baudin uses the word 'we' in describing the 'dredging', he makes no mention of those who were specifically involved. Péron, on the other hand, refers only to his colleague Maugé, who was now the senior zoologist,[12] and to his friend Lesueur; the latter helping him to draw and describe the new specimens for the rest of the night and after the subsequent night's trawling. Ultimately it was Lamarck, citing Péron and Lesueur, who published a description of one of the sponges collected in the 'seas of New Holland along the coasts of Leeuwin' and named it *Spongia tabula*.[13] In 1930 it was placed in the genus *Ectyoplasia* by Emile Topsent, but it still retains Lamarck's specific epithet: *tabula*.[14]

Three days after their initial sighting of the Western Australian coast, the expedition rounded a large cape and made its first important geographical discovery: the sweeping arc of Geographe Bay. A boat under the command of Ensign Picquet was dispatched to plot the exact location of the cape and to make a landing. Unfortunately, Ensign Picquet failed to fulfil his orders because of the currents, winds and breaking seas.[15] On his return, he was unfairly castigated for alleged disobedience; and in seeming recognition of the young ensign's unhappiness Baudin sarcastically named the jutting promontory 'Cap des Mécontents'. Today the cape honours the *Naturaliste* and a nearby point honours the unhappy Picquet.

A second boat under the more experienced command of Henry de Freycinet had more success, but the naturalists were disappointed when only the mineralogist Depuch and the gardener Riedlé were allowed to accompany it because of limited space. They set off before dawn on 31 May. Riedlé returned with many new plants, and Depuch drafted a report on the geology of the area and offered a number of preliminary remarks on its natural history. Their waiting colleagues must have been tantalised.[16] Poor Péron had to occupy himself for another three days before he was able to go ashore. It was perhaps during this frustrating period at anchor that he studied a number of fish caught in Geographe Bay. These included a species of hussar commonly known as Chinaman fish in Australia[17] and a Port Jackson shark, *Heterodontus portus jacksoni*.[18]

Péron finally set off for his first landing on Australian soil at 5.00 a.m. on 4 June 1801. He was accompanied by the botanist Leschenault in a small boat commanded by Midshipman Breton. In his published account, Péron wrote:

As soon as we landed I ran towards the interior in search of the natives, with whom I had a strong desire to be acquainted. In vain I explored the forests, following the print of their footsteps, of which I saw here and there the recent traces. All my endeavours were useless, and after three hours' fatiguing walk to no purpose, I returned towards the sea shore where I found my companions waiting for me, and rather alarmed at my absence.[19]

Péron could not have had much time ashore. According to Baudin, Breton had orders to return to the ship by 9.00 a.m., and by that time the inexperienced midshipman had departed the shore and was already (inadvertently) far to leeward of the *Géographe*. Given that they were far out to sea by 9.00 a.m., it is unlikely that Péron delayed Leschenault and Midshipman Breton's departure, as Frank Horner has suggested.[20] Nevertheless, there remains the possibility that Péron was lost for part of the time or overestimated the time required to return to his companions after deciding to terminate his solitary foray. After weeks at sea, he would not have been used to walking. According to Péron, their boat did not manage to return to the ship until 6.00 p.m. (that is, after another nine hours!) mainly because of the contrary currents and lack of wind. Baudin, observing from the *Géographe*, believed that Breton had mishandled the boat, but when he himself ventured forth with a landing party to make lunar observations in order to fix the longitude of the coast and double-check the accuracy of his chronometers, he too faced a very strong south-westerly current, which he thought the result of an ebb tide.[21]

In the meantime, at another part of the bay, Depuch had a brief encounter with an elderly Aboriginal man. Unfortunately, no dialogue was established, and the anxious man disappeared swiftly into the bush. Another group of about five or six local men approached the longboat, but they too fled at the fearful cries of the lone sailor on guard. The gardener Riedlé had a more productive time: collecting plant specimens and sowing wheat, maize, barley and oats, and planting pear, apple, apricot, peach and olive trees.[22]

The following day Péron joined a much larger landing party in a longboat commanded by *Capitaine de Frégate* Le Bas de Sainte-Croix. They were joined by two smaller boats from the *Naturaliste*. The object was to reconnoitre a lake reported the previous day by Ensign Heyrisson, which was thought to be an estuary. All the expedition's scientists, with the exception of the zoologist René Maugé, the astronomer Pierre Bernier and the hydrographer Pierre Faure, joined the landing party. They took weapons and supplies for two days. On reaching the shore, it was decided that the draught of the longboat was too large to explore the inlet, so it was left at anchor in the charge of two sailors. Since it was low tide, Péron first decided to 'pursue the shore'. One of his first finds was a so-called 'Orbulite', which he thought was a living fossil belonging to a genus only recently distinguished from cretaceous nummulites by Lamarck. Although it is hard to know exactly which species of foraminifer Péron had in mind, his terminology in discussing this specimen and the fossil record of its antecedents—particularly in the context of the 'proofs of the great catastrophes of nature'[23]—provides unequivocal evidence of his adherence to 'catastrophist' notions of the geological past punctuated by major cataclysms.

After his initial exploration of the shore, Péron turned inland, once more in hope of encountering the indigenous inhabitants. Beyond the coastal dunes, he found the salt marsh fringed with *Salicornia* (perhaps a species of *Sarcocornia* or *Atriplex*)[24] and graced by 'several companies of black swans'. Soon after he met his fellow zoologist Stanislas Levillain, recently transferred to the *Naturaliste*, and the mineralogist Joseph Charles Bailly. They were hunting and declined to join Péron in search of the local Aborigines. Indeed they attempted to dissuade him from searching. Unperturbed, Péron stripped off, crossed the marsh and entered the forest on the opposite bank. The forest was largely made up of a white-barked *Melaleuca*. In his published account, Péron considered it a new species, but it was very likely the same salt paperbark, *Melaleuca cuticularis*, collected by Labillardière at Esperance Bay in December 1793 and published by him in 1806.[25] In a sandy clearing near the water's edge, he found cut reeds arranged by human hands in a manner he thought rune-like. 'I much regretted', he wrote, 'that I could not discover in the characters before me, the ideas and sentiments of the rude race who had formed them.' Péron was deeply moved by the beauty of the trees and water that framed the scene, but his romantic imagination—fired by the recent discoveries made by Napoleon's campaign in the Levant—appears to have got the better of him:

Oh! With what pleasure I gave myself up for a few moments to the reflections such a scene naturally inspired. 'This charming place', I repeated to myself, 'is probably dedicated to some public or private mystery. The worship of the gods may be the particular object. It is from this river and the marshes adjoining, that the inhabitants of these shores in a great measure derive the food for their sustenance. A new race of Egyptians, who probably like the ancient inhabitants of the Nile, have consecrated by their gratitude the stream which supplies their wants. Perhaps on particular solemn occasions, they assemble on its shore to pay the debt of gratitude, and offer up their thanksgivings![26]

Making his way through the open, lightly grassed forest (which showed signs of recent fires), he was disappointed by his failure to make human contact and by the paucity of the fauna—collecting only a few ant species. It was now late in the afternoon, and he decided to turn back. Once more he stripped to cross the water, but found the adjoining marshes so deep in one place that he feared for his life. This would suggest that the tide (which had been low when he arrived) had now turned and that he had difficulty keeping his clothes out of the water. On reaching the beach his anxiety rose again when he could not find the longboat. It was now about five o'clock and, given the fact that the southern winter solstice was only two weeks off, sunset must have been fast approaching. The wind had also turned and now beat strongly against the shore. Fortunately Péron found Lesueur and the engineering officer Ronsard, who it seems were aware that Le Bas had earlier ordered the longboat to set off for the mouth of the inlet two leagues off.

As they walked along the shore in the gathering dark, Lesueur and Ronsard informed Péron of their surprise meeting during the day with a heavily pregnant Aboriginal woman who had become completely paralysed with fear on their approach. Lesueur showed Péron the place of their encounter. The 'miserable child of nature' had now fled, but without taking any of the trinkets they had attempted to give her. With forensic precision Péron wrote that she had also 'left behind her the most unequivocal proofs of her great trepidation, and which, as it appears, is manifested among savages in the same manner as among more civilised people, by the same spontaneous evacuations'.[27]

Although extremely cold in his wet clothes, Péron was still curious enough to examine empty Aboriginal bark huts and the remnants of fish, kangaroo and black swan among the extinguished cooking fires they passed along the way. After continuing their 'forced march', they finally met up with Hamelin and most of the boat crews and savants. Here they learned that in approaching the inlet in heavy seas, the longboat (manned by two sailors under the influence of brandy!) had been thrown abeam by a wave, swamped and then embayed on a lee shore. The longer it remained in this position, the more the boiling surf filled it with sand, yet there was little prospect of salvaging it that evening. They would have to try the following morning.

From Depuch and Louis de Freycinet, Péron learned that the river they had attempted to explore had proved little more than a marshy lagoon. Despite his previously grand Nilotic imagery, Péron now asserted that this report had confirmed the opinion he had 'previously formed of the river'.[28] In fact, several rivers—the Vasse, Sabina, Abba and Ludlow—do flow into a large complex of shallow coastal wetlands north-east of present-day Busselton, but the Wonnerup Inlet remains essentially unnavigable. Although the explorers made little progress in the shallow marshes, they had encountered some of the local people. Unfortunately, they remained very wary and unimpressed by the mixture of French, Polynesian and southern Indian tongues that the French used in an attempt to communicate with them from afar.

That night Péron and his fellow castaways huddled by a fire behind the dunes in an improvised shelter fashioned from the longboat sail. In the meantime Hamelin set off in an attempt to get help. Aboard the *Géographe*, Baudin, waiting anxiously for word of the longboat, allowed his prejudices towards the naturalists to come to the fore: 'The only likely explanation', he wrote in his journal, was that Le Bas de Sainte-Croix 'had allowed himself to be swayed by the fine talk of the naturalists with him'.[29] The following night, 6 June, he would learn that the naturalists were not to blame. After twenty-two hours of rowing their small boat with four other men, Hamelin and Freycinet had managed to reach the *Géographe*, seven miles off, and report on the events that had taken place.

Ashore, there was little food or water for twenty men to share. Their few biscuits were sodden when the longboat was deluged, and no fresh water had been found in the vicinity. The next morning attempts were made to catch fish, shoot game and find water. A solitary seagull was bagged, some brackish water was found and the botanists harvested some 'wild celery' (presumably *Apium prostratum* Labill.) and '*Salicornia*' (possibly *Atriplex*). The latter was placed in a pot and cooked with rice and brackish water. Members of the Chenopodiaceae family are often edible, but as halophytes they usually need to be boiled in fresh (rather than brackish) water to render their very salty leaves palatable. Of course we cannot be certain that Péron and his colleagues actually ate an edible species. Péron tells us he suffered violent colic and stomach pain throughout the night. As he was wet from crossing the lagoon and with a delicate constitution, the cold offshore wind probably took an added toll on him. Leschenault, who as a botanist must have been one of the principal gatherers of the ingredients, was also 'so much affected by the sad effects of the food' that he was unable to walk and suffered 'extreme agony'.

In the morning Baudin dispatched a boat, which Péron and his companions guided to the shore with a beacon on top of a sand dune and with shirts and handkerchiefs flown from the top of a long pole. The ailing Péron was the only man Le Bas allowed to return to the mother ship; he still hoped to salvage the longboat and wanted as many hands as possible to haul it clear. Péron's evacuation, however, was no simple matter, and this could explain why Leschenault did not leave at the same time: he was dragged by rope through the waves to the boat because it could not make land in the heavy seas. The long haul back to the ship—they reached the *Géographe* at 10.00 p.m.—must have been yet another cold and miserable trial for Péron. In Baudin's words, he was 'more dead than alive'.[30] Péron himself acknowledged: 'I was then in such a state of debility, and so extremely ill, that my friends scarcely knew me, so much had I suffered from the want of sleep, fatigue, and the colic, occasioned by the unwholesome food.'[31] An anxious Baudin angrily insisted on the evacuation of all the men ashore, but sent the master carpenter to assess the prospects of saving the longboat. (He concluded that such an exercise would have to wait until a spring tide.)[32]

Although the men were retrieved, all the naturalists' specimens, more than thirty firearms, several sabres, a barrel of gunpowder, the sails of the longboat and the carpenter's salvage equipment had to be left on the beach.[33] The withdrawal was fraught with danger. When Lieutenant Milius sought to recover some of the tools and equipment with a boat from the *Naturaliste*, it overturned and stranded him with still more men on the beach. They and the overturned boat were ultimately rescued, thanks to the efforts of a brave sailor on another boat who swam ashore with a rope. But an assistant helmsman, Timothée Vasse,[34] could not hold on and disappeared beneath the waves after three failed attempts to climb aboard. This could easily have been Péron's fate the day before. Although his shipmates never saw Vasse again, later rumours circulated in Paris and in Western Australia that he had made it ashore and had survived for a time among the Aborigines.[35] Péron would later investigate and discount these rumours. To this day, however, the Vasse River honours his name.

On 9 June 1801, with the barometer plunging, Baudin decided to clear Geographe Bay before the wind robbed him of the possibility and presented other dangers. He succeeded in what he described as the 'worst weather we had had since leaving France',[36] but soon faced the danger of the Naturaliste Reef. To avoid the danger, Baudin changed tack and made the *Géographe* 'carry all her courses, her topsails close reefed, her mizzen topsail and her fore-topmast staysail'.[37] Péron captured the urgency of the night. 'Never were manoeuvres performed with more expedition; never was the zeal of every individual manifested in a more striking manner. And indeed it required the united exertions of every individual to evade the dangers that threatened us during this dreadful night.'[38] In the enveloping gale the *Géographe* was blown south and became separated from the *Naturaliste*. It was another five days before Baudin redoubled his tracks and re-entered the bay. The *Naturaliste* was still nowhere to be seen. Continuing north, Baudin failed to sight her at their appointed rendezvous point: Rottnest Island. Yet she was there—at anchor between the island and the mouth of the Swan River. Baudin, however, kept to the west of the island and, to Péron's surprise, decided not to search. The *Géographe* and *Naturaliste* would remain separated for another three months.

— 8 —

Shark Bay

... the sea abounds almost beyond conception, from the whale down to the microscopic polypus.

FRANÇOIS PÉRON, Voyage

SHORTLY after his arduous landfall, Péron wrote a courteous letter to Baudin proposing that each time they anchored and went ashore, he should submit 'a small notice of works and researches' undertaken. With this proposal he attached notes on the soil and vegetation of Geographe Bay[1] but no zoological observations.[2] Clearly Péron wanted to be useful, but perhaps he also wanted to ensure an enhanced place in the Citizen Commander's narrative of the expedition. He would already have been aware that his friend Depuch's mineralogical report on the bay had been incorporated into Baudin's journal. We know from Bory de Saint-Vincent's account that this journal could be 'examined without indiscretion, since Riedlay [*sic*] and Maugé not only handled it freely themselves, but also showed it to strangers'.[3] Whether Péron deliberately sought to rival the official botanist Leschenault is unclear. All the plant names he mentioned in his 'Observations sur la Baie du Géographe' are those of Linnean genera: *Gnaphalium, Juncus, Salicornia, Casuarina* etc. Péron did not have a sufficient grasp of botany to recognise entirely new genera as Labillardière had when he visited western New Holland and Van Diemen's Land a decade before.[4]

The *Géographe* continued to sail north, but well to the west of the Houtman Abrolhos for fear of sharing the fate of the Dutch East Indiaman

Batavia, which had come to grief in these waters in 1629.[5] On the after-noon of 16 June 1801, when there was little wind, Baudin recorded the use of the dragnet in the relatively shallow coastal waters. This yielded several sponges, jellyfish, starfish, sea slugs and thousands of what Baudin thought was a dwarf bivalve belonging to the genus *Avicula*.[6] Péron does not record this trawling of the sea bottom in his official account, but it is clear that many of the species collected were new to science and that several appear later to have been described by Lamarck. In 1984 Michel Jangoux identified three Western Australian starfish species among numerous sketches and watercolours of Asteroidea by Charles-Alexandre Lesueur. These included Lamarck's *Asterias obtusangula* (= *Pseudoreaster obtusangula*), a yellowish-orange starfish that is the only known member of its genus; the beautiful bluish-coloured *Coscinasterias calamaria*; and *Archaster angulatus*, white with rose, red or blue peg-like paxillae.[7] The shellfish mentioned by Baudin was possibly the pearl shell that Lamarck named *Avicula virens* (= *Pinctada virens*), sourced to Péron and recorded as 'inhabiting the seas of New Holland on the coast of Eendracht's Land'.[8]

The reference to 'Eendracht's Land' is telling. The first European to reach this part of the Australian coast was Dirk Hartog in command of the Dutch East India Company vessel *Eendracht* (Concord) on 25 October 1616. He and his crew landed at the northern end of what is now known as Dirk Hartog Island.[9] Péron, who sighted this island with his com-panions on 23 June 1801, described it as 'yet more barren and inhospitable than the space of which it seemed to form a part: with the same natural characters, it did not appear less inaccessible, and the surf broke furiously the length of the coast westward'.[10] No landing was attempted, but five days later, after rounding another island to the north (which Louis de Freycinet would ultimately name in honour of the astronomer Bernier),[11] the *Géographe* anchored in Shark Bay,[12] where William Dampier and his men had feasted on shark in 1699. Péron was filled with excitement:

> To this dismal sterility of the continent and the isles, may be pleasantly contrasted the productions of the sea, which are astonishingly numer-ous and in very great variety. We were everywhere surrounded by shoals of Salpa, Doris, Medusae, Beroes, and Porpita; different kinds of Testaceous animals, and zoophytes … The amazing number of these animals, their strange and whimsical forms, the beauty of their colours, the facility of their motions, and the agility of their evolutions, furnished an agreeable spectacle to all our ship's crew, and to myself,

and my friends Lesueur and Maugé; their number and diversity afforded an inexhaustible fund of pleasure, and were the subject of philosophical enthusiasm.[13]

There were also brightly marked sea-snakes and suddenly 'a vast shoal of whales', which rapidly approached them. 'Never had we seen so extraordinary a spectacle,' wrote Péron, and added,

> The amazing number of these cetacea, their gigantic size, their quick evolutions, and their spouting up the water, all appeared to me to be surprising, but still less so than to see these mighty Colossi springing perpendicularly above the waves, and standing, if I may be allowed the expression, on the extremity of their tails, spreading vast fins, and then falling again on the bosom of the waters and thus sinking beneath the waves in the midst of torrents of foam and eddies.[14]

Péron was convinced that Shark Bay would soon become a lucrative whaling centre and later urged the merchants of the Ile de France to become involved in the industry despite the apparent lack of fresh water.[15] Whaling was eventually attempted in the bay, but lack of fresh water was indeed the main reason why the industry did not prosper in the area.[16] It was, for example, more successful in Geographe Bay, where a whaling station, Port Vasse, was named after the *Géographe*'s unfortunate assistant helmsman Timothée Vasse.

Péron did not land on Bernier Island until 29 June. He landed in the company of Baudin and several of his scientific colleagues. In puzzling over the island's 'brownish calcareous stone'—Tamala limestone formed from enormous wind-blown dunes of the glacial periods of the Pleistocene[17]— and the many gastropod fossils impacted in it,[18] he concluded that they had 'doubtless been in this state of petrifaction for many centuries'. But even if the rocks aged in mere centuries rather than millennia in his mind's eye, the dense strata had still more surprises with which to erode biblical certainties and nourish his catastrophist ideas: the sight of fossil (actually terrestrial gastropod) shells '150 feet above the actual level of the sea'.[19] To this day, except for a small ruined hospital, which dates from the early twentieth century, Bernier Island is little changed.

Péron found the teeming shore of the island an engaging location for research and collection. The sea, he wrote, 'abounds almost beyond conception, from the whale down to the microscopic polypus'. There were oysters,[20] trochus, volutes and cones aplenty and, although he freely gave names to many of them in his *Voyage*, the lack of matching published descriptions made the names taxonomically meaningless. Because Péron did not live long enough to study and publish all his collections, many of the mollusca he collected at Shark Bay were eventually published by Lamarck with acknowedgements to him. These included Lamarck's *Venus crassisulca*[21] (= *Paphia crassisulca*)[22] and *Ostrea trapezina*[23] (= *Dendostrea trape-zina*). In some cases, such as with Lamarck's still valid *Cardita aviculina*, reference was made to the 'seas of New Holland, Shark Bay and King Island' but with no mention of Péron.[24]

Péron tells us that although crustaceans in general were not plentiful on the shore, there were 'great numbers' of two species of *Portunus* crabs, which belong to a family with distinctive rear swimming legs. This determination post-dated the expedition, because Pierre Latreille's new genus and the order Decapoda were not established until 1803. In his notebooks Péron used the designation *Cancer* for actual members of this genus and closely related genera.[25] His interest in these species was not purely scientific. Péron tells his readers: 'Some of these crabs are 4 or 5 inches in breadth; and the meat being excellent, they might in times of necessity supply an inexhaustible store of wholesome food.'[26]

Aside from sea urchins, which were so difficult to remove that they seemed to be 'encrusted', Péron collected a number of starfish in the 'midst of the rugged rocks'. He promptly thought he recognised two new species belonging to the Linnean genus *Ophiura* (from Greek *ophis* = snake). The Ophiuroidea (the class to which the genus belongs) is the largest non-fossil echinoderm class, comprising 1800 species. They are sometimes called snake-stars because of the sinuous serpent-like movement of their arms, but more often they are known as brittle-stars because they have a tendency to break off pieces (sometimes the whole arm) at the slightest disturbance. This is not just a defensive mechanism: the separation can produce another, non-sexually reproduced individual. One of the species Péron observed had arms 'from 8 to 10 inches in length'. Brittle-stars filter mud and sand for food (largely decaying animal and vegetable matter) but also graze on algae. Péron incorrectly asserted that hidden in the 'fissures of the rocks, this animal spreads out its long arms, and with much address seizes and drags the prey to the bottom of its little cavern'. More credible is his description of one of the species shining during the night 'like a bright star'.[27]

Péron did indeed spend time on the island at night. With several of his scientific colleagues he had left the rocky shore and made his way through the spinifex and the distinctive local hammock grass (*Triodia plurinervata*) first mentioned by William Dampier[28]—which the gardener Riedlé thought might be useful to bind the advancing dunes of Cadiz and Bordeaux—and mulga scrub. On the way he noted gnarled and stunted Mimosa (= *Acacias*),[29] 'a sort of fig' (almost certainly the rock fig, *Ficus platypoda*), 'a small Melaleuca' (possibly the dense prickly *M. cardiophylla*)[30] and 'a kind of Cyperus'.[31] Then, with the aim of traversing the island alone, Péron parted company with the other naturalists—something that Riedlé later justly termed an 'indiscretion'.[32] Péron met no Aborigines, and the only observable mammal was the banded hare-wallaby, which is now extinct on the mainland. This beautiful marsupial was first mentioned by William Dampier as a 'raccoon' in 1699,[33] but Péron drafted the first scientific description and Lesueur executed an exquisite watercolour.[34] Although it is no longer known as *Kangurus fasciatus* (John Gould placed it in the genus *Lagorchestes* in 1842, and Oldfield Thomas included it in its present genus, *Lagostrophus*, in 1887), it still bears Péron's original specific epithet *fasciatus*. Péron found this wallaby 'mild and timid' and added: 'Like the hare of our climates, the slightest noise alarms them—sometimes even the whistling of the wind will put them to flight.'[35] And when he eventually tasted its flesh, he thought it reminiscent of wild rabbit but 'more aromatic' on account of its diet. Baudin also hoped to return to France with several joeys captured when their mothers were shot, but none survived beyond Timor.[36]

In his official account, Péron devoted one short paragraph to the birds of Bernier Island and wrote in general terms about petrels, gulls, cormorants, sea eagles, flycatchers, magpies and a 'beautiful species of tom-tit, with a blue ring round the neck'[37] (probably the variegated fairy-wren *Malarus lamberti*). In his notebook, however, he recorded only a pelican, a booby and the garganey (*Anas querquedula*),[38] the latter being a rare visitor to Australia. And he refers to just three reptile species on Bernier Island: a large skink 'with such a short thick tail, that at first sight, the animal appears to have two heads' (probably the bobtail lizard *Tilqua rugosa*); a gecko 'about four or five inches long' (probably the knob-tailed gecko *Nephrurus levis*); and almost certainly the beautiful Gould's monitor (*Varanus gouldii*) 'four or five feet in length', which he thought related to the Tegu of South America and christened *Tupinambis eendrachtensis*.[39]

None are listed in Rolande Roux-Estève's catalogue of the reptile specimens preserved in Lesueur's collection,[40] and the artist does not appear to have sketched any of them.[41]

Long separated from his companions and engrossed in his collecting, Péron lost track of time. According to Baudin, everyone 'had orders to be back on the beach by five o'clock at the latest for a meal [of crabs, oysters and fresh fish netted by the boat crews off the island] before returning to the ship'.[42] Unfortunately Péron, surprised by the rapidly setting midwinter sun, became lost in the scrub. Heavily laden with specimens, he kept walking in the dark and, at 8.00 p.m., reached the sea only to realise that he was on the wrong side of the island: the west coast battered by the full force of the Indian Ocean. According to his account, having walked since the morning without food or drink, he was exhausted. Fear and adrenalin, however, roused him to further exertion, and he trudged across the northern tip of the island and headed south in the moonlight (presumably along the east coast) until 11.00 p.m. Once again he collapsed with exhaustion. This time he slept for four hours—only to wake with his sweat-soaked body benumbed by the cold night air. Rising stiffly from the ground, he pressed on. Just before dawn, his spirits soared when he heard the sound of a gunshot in the distance. Not long after, he sighted bonfires that had been lit for his benefit as beacons on the dunes and on the shore. And according to his own account, at 6.00 a.m., twelve hours after Baudin had left the island, Péron reached the shore camp.[43]

Before leaving, Baudin had dispatched some of the men to search for the missing naturalist; but when they returned unsuccessful, he ordered Ensign Picquet to remain with the small boat and crew and quit the island with the rising of the moon (ostensibly because the weather appeared to be changing). Picquet, however, disobeyed his orders and refused to leave the island until Péron was found. Even then, it took more than a whole morning of tacking in the contrary winds to reach the *Géographe* by one o'clock in the afternoon. Of Péron's arrival aboard, Baudin wrote:

> … he presented himself to me in the most pitiable state. He had not eaten for twenty-four hours and was quite worn out … Since he is to make me a report on his adventure, I shall refrain here from saying what I could say. However, I firmly promised him that when we went ashore again, I would send someone with him who would keep him constantly in sight and be responsible to me for getting him back to the place of departure at the specified time.[44]

In his observations on the islands, Baudin made no mention of Péron's scientific achievements during their sojourn, but noted that Riedlé had found 'seventy specimens of plants' and that Maugé 'collected ten kinds of insects, most of which belong to the dorbeetle class'.[45] It was now too late for the *Géographe* to get underway again that day, so she remained at anchor until sunrise the following morning. Progress on 30 June was slow, but Péron was deeply impressed by the fact that they were 'sailing all the while in midst of great shoals of fish'. He added: 'all the different kinds were new to us, and belonged to the genera Labrus, Balistes ... Ostracions, Chaetodons, &c.'[46] On 28 June Baudin recorded that his men had caught 'more than six hundred pounds of good fish' on a line. Some of these fish were studied by Péron and sketched by Lesueur. They included the three-lined spinecheek *Scolopsis trilineatus* (Kner, 1868), the gummy shark *Emissola antarctica* (Günther 1870)[47] and the spotted swell shark *Cephaloscyllium laticeps* (Duméril 1853).[48] None was published by Péron, but it would appear that he and Lesueur originally intended to name the latter shark in honour of Lacépède. However, as we shall see, Péron would ultimately name the broadnose 'seven gilled' shark, *Notorhynchus cepedianus* (collected in Tasmanian waters) in honour of the great French ichthyologist, and this name remains valid to this day.[49]

Although the *Géographe* left her anchorage off Bernier Island, she returned a few days later—battered by squalls and thwarted in an attempt to find a safe landing place on the Peron Peninsula, which at the time was thought to be another island. On the morning of 5 July, Baudin and all of the scientists once again landed on Bernier Island. This time a camp was set up with two tents. Although Baudin still hoped for a rendezvous with the *Naturaliste*, his principal objectives were to conduct astronomical observations in order to plot the island's location more accurately and to check the rate of his chronometers. Henry de Freycinet was ordered to undertake similar observations on the southern tip of neighbouring Dorre Island, but the weather, inadequate provisions and the distractions of wallaby hunting combined to make this officer yet again a disappointment in Baudin's eyes. His opinion of Péron's reckless individualism was also confirmed when the young naturalist set off on yet another solo excursion.[50]

Péron's intention was to find a more productive stretch of shoreline for collecting purposes. In his account he suggests that the molluscs where they landed were few in number and either dead or shrunken. Baudin's account, however, suggests that the naturalist once again traversed the island and, finding little of interest, descended to the beach on the harsh wind-blown western shore in the hope of at least collecting some shells.[51] In his *Voyage*, Péron wrote: 'I resolved to go beyond a dangerous reef which projected some distance out into the sea, and in the clefts of which, I hoped to find some of these shells that were alive.'[52] He was delighted to discover great numbers, but while working to detach these shellfish under-estimated the capricious power of the sea and his own hold on the rocks.

> ... a strong surge broke over the top of the breaks, that I was driven against the neighbouring rocks, and over these frightful reefs; all my clothes were in a moment torn to pieces, and I was in an instant covered with wounds and weltering in blood: I recovered myself, how-ever, and exerting all my strength to escape from the surge, which, as it retreated, would have carried me back against the reefs, I clung to the point of a rock, and thus succeeded in avoiding this last misfortune, which doubtless would have been my destruction. Having thus got clear of the waves, I with great difficulty reached the shore, where I sank fainting, with pain and loss of blood.[53]

Péron tells his readers that he remained there battered, wounded and immobilised until nightfall. His right knee was badly lacerated and at first he found it impossible to walk but, forcing himself to move, the pain became more bearable. 'I again took courage', he wrote, 'a great fire on the summit of a sand-bank directed my footsteps, and about midnight I was once more among my companions.'[54] However, Baudin's journal record (presumably based on a personal report by Péron) casts doubt on the account the naturalist eventually published. According to Baudin, 'instead of orienting himself to go from West to East, he took a North–South course, so that for the second time he became completely lost'.[55] Baudin also asserted that the naturalist returned by 9.00 p.m. (not midnight), which makes one wonder whether Péron really did remain prostrate on the rocky foreshore for as long as he claimed. Baudin certainly had no doubt about Péron's injuries, but his journal extract is a portrait of almost comical failure. The romantic image of all of Péron's clothes 'in a moment torn to pieces' is undermined when we read in Baudin's account that in amusing himself before his mishap Péron had already taken off his shirt and tied up about fifty crabs in it. Baudin had not witnessed Péron's undoubtedly nasty spill on the reef when he was 'knocked head over heels by a wave which carried off most of the beautiful shells that he claims to have found'.

Nevertheless, he did witness Péron's return 'worn out with weariness and exhaustion, having had to abandon on the way his tin box, his shirt and his crabs'.[56]

For his part, Péron sought more pathos in recounting the return of his prodigal self: 'On seeing me thus covered with wounds and contusions, and weltering in blood, several of my friends even shed tears, and the commander himself seemed touched with my deplorable situation.'[57] Ultimately, Péron's injuries were superficial (as he himself acknowledged). Although he at first suffered from a violent fever, which might have been a symptom of other chronic ailments, he was soon infusing meaning into his second sojourn on Bernier Island by hobbling about with a thermometer comparing the temperature of 'the atmosphere and the interior of the soil'.[58] On 10 July, in the company of the astronomer Bernier, Péron went back aboard the *Géographe* to have his wounds dressed.

By 12 July, with firewood replenished, some additional surveys completed and the men treated to a further week of fresh seafood and game (including dugong), the *Géographe* began to manoeuvre to make her way out of Shark Bay. Péron clearly approved of their impending departure despite the continued division of the expedition: 'Nothing, therefore, now detained us on these shores, but the expectation of being joined by the *Naturaliste*, and she did not appear.' Departure, however, proved to be no simple matter. Baudin later recalled: 'A strong gale from the north-west struck us. The continual rain which accompanied it obliged us to tack all night, lead in hand, and it was only after thirty-six hours of misery and fatigue that we managed to leave the bay without any sight of the coast.'[59]

A few days later, on 16 July, the *Naturaliste* rounded Dirk Hartog Island and entered the strait (now known as the Naturaliste Channel) that separates it from Dorre Island. Hamelin was disappointed not to find the *Géographe* in the bay, and his anxiety over her fate was in marked contrast to Baudin's lack of concern for the safety of the *Naturaliste*. In seven weeks of waiting, Hamelin and his officers virtually completed the charting of Shark Bay, including Dirk Hartog Island and the east and west coasts of the Peron Peninsula (including the Hamelin Pool with its remarkable Stromatolites), before they too set sail for Timor.

— 9 —

Timor

O what an endlesse worke have I in hand,
To count the seas abundant progeny,
Whose fruitful seede farre passeth those in land,
And also those which wonne in th' azure sky!
For much more eath to tell the starres on hy,

EDMUND SPENCER, *The Faerie Queene*

OVER the next five weeks the *Géographe* continued to sail cautiously up the Western Australian seaboard. Wary of the enormous tidal range on the coast, Baudin did not land at North West Cape and estimated the location of the westernmost point of the Australian mainland from about four miles out to sea. Although his latitude was out by a mere eleven minutes, his longitude was one and a half degrees too far to the west, because both his chronometers were fast.[1] The *Géographe* failed to survey Exmouth Gulf, but her initial reconnaissance of the north-western coast resulted in the discovery of the Rivoli Islands, L'Hermite Island, Depuch Island, the Forestier Islands, the Geographe Shoals, the Lacepede Islands and much of the Bonaparte Archipelago, which still bear the names of a host of French scientific luminaries. Baudin's journal entry for 12 August 1801 exemplified his attitude to landings for scientific purposes:

I should think, as Dampier points out, that one could land on some parts of these islands when there is high tide and that one could beach one's boat, while waiting until the tide returned before setting off again. The naturalists would very much like me to do just that, but apart from my not having a boat to endanger, this island, as well as all those that we have passed in the last several days, did not look suitable to me for research in Natural History and especially not in the field of Botany. We could see nothing but a few trees dotted here and there. They were of middling height with very little foliage.[2]

Although Péron continued to study pelagic marine organisms when-ever he could, even he found the coastal islands a disappointing prospect: 'In the midst of these numerous islands', he wrote, 'there is not any thing to delight the mind. The soil is naked, the ardent sky seems always clear and without clouds. The waves are scarcely agitated.'[3] A week later, with less than three weeks of fresh water remaining aboard, only a few days of firewood left and the naturalists complaining after more than a month without fresh provisions, Baudin decided to break off his coasting and set a north-westerly course for Timor. At 3.00 p.m. on the afternoon of 20 August 'through the fog that enveloped the land' the expedition sighted 'the lofty peaks of the island of Timor'.[4]

Baudin's objective was the sheltered port of Kupang on the south-western tip of the island, which had been established by the Dutch in 1613. The following day, Henry de Freycinet, in the company of a Dutch and a Malay crew member as interpreters, was dispatched by boat with a letter for the Governor at Fort Concordia advising him that the expedi-tion carried a Dutch passport and was in need of a pilot to guide them to anchorage. Freycinet did not return until the next day because of initial suspicions that the expedition was British. This far-flung outpost of the Dutch colonial empire had been captured and briefly occupied by the British the previous year. Harried by the locals, the British had withdrawn, but not before putting the town to the torch and blowing up the fortress.[5] Ironically the pilot dispatched by the Dutch was a Frenchman (a native of Bayonne, according to Baudin, and from the environs of Bordeaux, according to Péron) who had lived in Timor for fifteen years.[6]

On 23 August, the day after the *Géographe* anchored in Kupang roads, Baudin called on Governor Lofstett to present his passports, outline his victualling needs and request assistance to build a new longboat. Péron was part of a delegation that accompanied him. After dining, the Governor showed his French guests several houses that had been placed at their dis-posal for a modest rental. The first, a graceful dwelling that Baudin would occupy in the company of the astronomer Bissy, the geographer Boulanger and the artists Petit and Lesueur, belonged to a Madame van Esten née Tilleman, the wealthy Ambonese widow of a former governor. The second, 'not so elegant but just as spacious', soon accommodated Péron and his fellow naturalists. The third, a warehouse belonging to the Dutch East India Company and damaged during the British occupation, was hastily made ready as a hospital for the *Géographe's* sick cases.

Péron's first scientific excursion was to the beach on the morning of 25 August, and he was not disappointed. 'Never until that moment', he wrote, 'had I ever seen such a picture of fecundity; fish, molluscs, testaceous and crustaceous animals, &c. &c. all seemed to multiply by thousands on these shores.'[7] From Lesueur's sketches we have some idea of the riches Péron observed on this and other days on the shores of Timor: the starfish *Archaster typicus*,[8] the crab *Carpilius maculates*[9] and numerous fish, many of which were new to science, including *Paratrigla papilio*, which was first described from Péron's specimen by Georges Cuvier in 1829.[10] Similarly, from Lamarck's *Histoire naturelle des animaux sans vertèbres*, we know that in Timor Péron collected the type specimens of several new molluscs, including *Cyclas australis* (= *Lasaea australis*),[11] *Ostrea tuberculata* (= *Pustulostrea tuberculata*)[12] and very likely *Arca pistachia* (= *Barbatia pistachia*).[13]

Péron was also deeply impressed by the corals he found in the bay, but even more so by their presence as fossils deep inland. Although he could see that they had been 'raised' by nature, he had no coherent geological theory of uplift to explain them: 'In the midst of the mountain in the interior of Timor, in the very heart of deep valleys and torrents, we everywhere find the remains of these astonishing animals, although it is utterly impossible for the mind to conceive how or by what means nature has raised these large madreporic plots to such heights above the present level of the seas.'[14] Furthermore, Péron's concept of geological time was distorted by his notions of rapid petrifaction and fossilisation:

That which is the most surprising in the singular work of nature, is the quickness with which this kind of metamorphosis operates. I have reason to believe in effect, after my observations, that one month after being cast on the beach, a shell would not be recognisable. The force of the sun's rays, the strength of the light reflected by the white sands of the shore, suffice with some days of sea water to remove all colour and to so confound, that in the middle of the calcareous bed which has already seized it, the most experienced eye would mistake it and arrange it in the class of the most ancient petrified shells.[15]

In fact the raised reef limestones of Timor's 'Viqueque Formation'—comprising beach sands, fringing coral and shell banks—are relatively recent (from a modern geological perspective) and date from the Upper Miocene to the Upper Pliocene. Thus they appear to have been uplifted 2500 metres within a mere six million years.[16]

On 26 August, Péron, together with Depuch, Bernier and Lesueur, travelled to the outskirts of Kupang. He soon began to survey the ethnic mix of the island in very subjective terms. One can detect a degree of sympathy and even respect for the indigenous inhabitants of Timor, in his words: 'driven into the interior of the lands ... living exclusively on the fruits of the earth, and the produce of the hunt, always in arms, always at war'. Similarly, in the Malays he recognised a character of 'independence, boldness and ferocity' and later even admirable frankness and generosity. But in the 'indefatigable' Chinese he saw only weakness and pusillanimity. Those of mixed race he described uncharitably as 'a few mongrel Portuguese, the miserable witnesses of the vicissitudes of nations, and the revolutions of empires!' He dismissed the Dutch as 'sustaining with difficulty the former glory of the Batavian name, and only preserving by their policy or by the favour of the people, the dominion which was in former times purchased by so much heroism and courage'.[17]

The group's first attempt to visit a Malay house, which was set 'like a small antique temple, at the end of a long avenue of orange trees, bananas, pomegranates, and other aromatic and beautiful trees', was met with a defiant snub. This was probably in the neighbouring hamlet of Oba east of Kupang. Later, when Baudin and many of his shipmates were entertained there in lavish style, Péron learned that this enchanting residence belonged to Madame van Esten. Further inland they met with a warmer reception; nevertheless, the presence of the French seems frequently to have rekindled memories of recent British depredations.

Two days later, Péron tells us that he and Depuch were visited by Amadima, the middle-aged Rajah of the neighbouring island of Savu. Unfortunately for them, the honour of the visit was soured by the thefts perpetrated by the Rajah's courtiers, who 'nearly stripped the apartment of all it contained'. But even these thefts became an excuse for philosophising on Péron's part and heralded an erosion of his Rousseauist sympathies. Thus he declared: 'They have this vice in common with all savage nations, and those who are but little civilised; which sufficiently proves, that it is not without reason that legislators have determined the right of property to be the foundation of all social and civilised institutions.'[18] For his part the Rajah became obsessed with acquiring a bottle of phosphorus. It had been used by Péron, like a flamboyant alchemist, to demonstrate spontaneous combustion to his visitors. Restrained by fears of the injuries the volatile element might cause the Rajah and his retinue, Péron refused offers of pigs, chickens, sheep and even (he tells us with suppressed mirth) a Spanish dollar in exchange. Finally, however, he relented and gave the avaricious princeling a two-inch strip wrapped in wet linen. The consequences had almost the air of an operatic farce. Despite Péron's caution, Amadima was soon seen in 'a state of utter consternation; the phosphorus had taken fire ... the king's betel bag had been consumed, and several of the most officious courtiers had burnt their fingers'.[19] Making amends with their handkerchiefs, the cycle of reciprocity continued when Depuch and Péron were repaid with a pig. This they cooked *à la mode française* and shared with the Rajah the next day. Other common meals would follow, and Péron tells us that he even exchanged names with Amadima in the Polynesian fashion on 11 September.

Péron made other, perhaps more genuine friends among the Timorese population in the course of his collecting. In particular he mentions a man named Néâs (later described as a rajah) and his family. Péron tells us that he offered to take Néâs's son Cornelis back to France with him, but the young man's fear that he might find himself sold into slavery made him decline—despite Péron's assurances that slavery did not exist in metropolitan France.

Just as at the Ile de France, pre-existing tensions aboard the *Géographe* resulted in the loss of more capable men from the expedition. The first of these was Ensign Antoine Picquet, who had incurred the ire of Baudin for failing to acknowledge a signalman's depth sounding calls one morning in early August.[20] When Piquet challenged Baudin for his reprimand in his cabin, the young officer was relieved of his command of the watch. Then, on arrival in Timor, Baudin dismissed him from his staff and ordered him to find lodgings ashore until the *Naturaliste* arrived. Picquet took great offence at the humiliating tone of Baudin's letter of dismissal and once more rushed to Baudin's cabin to protest. Baudin ordered Picquet out of his presence and closed the door on him. The following day, when Picquet requested permission to go ashore as he had previously been ordered, Baudin paid him no heed. The day after, however, he came ashore in full uniform and demanded an explanation for his treatment from Baudin. Once again the expedition commander rebuffed him with complete silence—for a full two minutes, according to his own account—but called for four Dutch fusiliers to arrest his insolent junior officer when the enraged Picquet threatened to use his sword if Baudin came near him. Ultimately, although Picquet was placed in the fortress, he was not stripped of his rank or escorted there under guard. This was mainly because Baudin had to contend with the entreaties of several officers who were angered by Picquet's treatment.[21]

François Péron described Picquet as 'one of our most deserving officers … arrested by order of our commander, whom he had the misfortune to offend'.[22] Picquet spent six weeks confined in the fortress before being sent to Batavia in a brigantine. By this time the *Naturaliste* had been joyfully reunited with the *Géographe* at Kupang and, according to Péron, 'the principal officer of both ships gave M. Picquet the most flattering testimonies of their friendship and esteem'. Péron added: 'Every day one of our officers, with one of the *Naturaliste*'s, went to keep him company, and to partake with him such dinner as we were able to send him. At the moment of his departure, everyone was eager to give him letters and proper attestations to refute the calumnies which might be repeated to his prejudice.'[23]

In a postscript to the episode, Péron informed his readers that, despite Baudin's orders, Picquet was given his liberty by the Regency Council in Batavia and on his return to France was promoted to lieutenant. In the meantime, when Baudin heard of the role of Le Bas de Sainte-Croix (his second-in-command on the *Géographe*) in rallying support for Picquet and his insinuations that victualling funds had been misappropriated at the Ile de France, he resolved to remove Le Bas from the expedition with the connivance of Surgeon Lharidon. Le Bas had long complained of pain in his legs, and Baudin suggested that the surgeon diagnose them as symptomatic of a condition 'incurable at sea'. Le Bas, however, rejected Lharidon's diagnosis and suggestions that his illness was contagious. He retorted by insisting on the opinion of four doctors, including Péron. Baudin then abandoned pretence, threatened Le Bas with dire consequences if he repeated his assertions about misappropriation and made it clear that he wanted to get rid of him. Le Bas, probably recognising that a good working relationship with Baudin would now be impossible at sea, agreed to quit the expedition contingent on guarantees of food and lodging. A week later Le Bas was wounded in the left arm after a duel with Ronsard (the engineering officer hard at work building a new longboat for the *Géographe*), whom he blamed for reporting his conversations to Baudin. Surprisingly, just before the expedition left Timor, Ronsard (soon promoted lieutenant) and Le Bas would shake hands before going their separate ways.[24]

Throughout this period Baudin was seriously ill with what appears to have been a falciparum malarial fever. Péron tells us that Baudin 'experienced successively three such violent attacks that for some hours he was thought to be dead'. He also recounted his own involvement in Baudin's treatment:

> ... there was not a moment to lose in giving him the [quinine-rich cinchona] bark, in large doses; but as that belonging to our ships was of a very inferior quality, I shared with him the small quantity which I had brought from Europe for my own use. This medicine operated in a manner that seemed almost miraculous. It stopped this terrible fever, and in all appearance saved the life of our commander.[25]

Lesueur also fell seriously ill after being bitten on his heel by a reptile. Surgeon Lharidon cauterised the wound and dosed him with ammoniac, the resin from the umbelliferous *Dorema ammoniacum*. The artist's heel went green, his whole leg swelled to the thigh, and he experienced a violent fever. However, the diaphoretic qualities of the ammoniac (which contains salicylic acid) might have helped, for Lesueur survived the bite.[26] By 15 September, although the scurvy cases had recovered, eighteen men were ravaged by severe dysentery. They included Péron's 'amiable friend' the mineralogist Depuch, his 'colleague' the zoologist Maugé and the 'good and active' gardener Anselm Riedlé. On 27 September 1801 Riedlé had written to André Thouin at the Jardin des Plantes:

> I have no fever, but I have been tormented by a bloody flux for close to three weeks. I would be cured already if I did not leave every day to rove the countryside; but it is impossible for me to remain in the house, when one is surrounded everywhere by precious plants. What pain I had to see so often the land of New Holland without the power to land! It is this that gives me the strength to bear my illness and the fatigues of my excursions.[27]

Riedlé did not blame Baudin for their infrequent landings; rather he blamed the loss of the longboat and hoped that with its replacement, the naturalists would 'land more often'. Nevertheless, in seeking to make up for the lost opportunities on the coast of Western Australia—rising daily at dawn to collect specimens beyond Kupang—he gave himself no rest, his condition soon worsened, and he died on 21 October. He was only in his mid-thirties. In his personal journal Baudin declared: 'It will suffice me to say that I lost one of my best friends and that the painful state his death has reduced me to will not be quickly erased from my memory.'[28] At Baudin's request, the warm-hearted German, who had left a wife and young daughter in Paris,[29] was buried the next day with full honours: the Dutch Governor and his officers appeared in mourning; four Dutch soldiers bore his coffin escorted by two of the naturalists and two French officers; the ships' colours were lowered to half-mast and the guns were fired sombrely every quarter of an hour.[30] Several volleys were also fired over Riedlé's grave—beside that of David Nelson (veteran of Cook's third voyage and gardener on the *Bounty*, who, twelve years before, had died in Kupang after William Bligh's epic 3600-mile open-boat voyage).

Péron asserted that he gained Baudin's permission to search for Nelson's tomb, but in his personal journal the expedition's commander makes no reference to his young zoologist as the source of the suggestion. Rather he tells us that he wanted Riedlé buried under the most beautiful tree in the environs of Kupang, but ultimately agreed to the confines of the European cemetery when fears were raised that the gardener's remains might be disturbed by grave robbers.[31] Péron tells us that Riedlé was buried with Nelson's monument 'made to preserve the memory of the two naturalists united in the same tomb'.[32] And in Paris André Thouin would later name in Riedlé's honour a greenhouse where his Australian, Timorése and earlier Caribbean plants were grown.[33]

Sadly, Riedlé was not the only member of the expedition to die in Timor. Five others succumbed to dysentery. They, like Geoffroy Frantz, a humble assistant gunner from Alsace, were also buried with a volley of musket fire—not in deference to their rank, but according to local Dutch custom, simply because they were Europeans. Péron tells us that he attempted to assist the expedition's surgeons in finding ways to stem the epidemic (even performing autopsies on several of the victims in search of clues), but without success. 'It pursued us to the extremity of the globe', he wrote, 'and strewed the seas with our dead bodies.'[34]

Soon after his return to France, François Péron published an article in the *Journal de physique, de chimie, d'histoire naturelle et des arts* based on his clinical observations in Timor.[35] In it he saw the cause of dysentery in terms of the effects of heat and humidity on the skin in the tropics, rather than from protozoan (or viral or bacterial) infection. And although he recognised the severity of symptomatic dehydration in dysentery cases, he could not have understood its physiological consequences—otherwise he would have recognised the need to counter it with fluids. Instead he suggested topical treatments such as cold baths and argued that the immunity of those native to tropical climes was a consequence of the use of betel. Here too was an attempt to offer an ethno-pharmacological 'discovery' to Western medicine. Péron would further expound his notions on temperature and humidity in another article on naval hygiene published in 1808;[36] alas, betel was not destined to become another cinchona.

The week Riedlé died was also the week a British frigate, the *Virginia*, appeared off Kupang eyeing the *Géographe* and *Naturaliste* as potential prizes —that is, until Midshipman Bonnefoy de Montbazin went out by boat to present the expedition's passports in place of Baudin, who was still ill. Her captain graciously withdrew, but not before offering Bonnefoy 'some bottles of excellent wine' for his ailing commander. Baudin was probably disappointed to learn that the young officer declined because he 'did not think himself authorised to accept'.[37] On 6 November Ronsard launched the *Géographe*'s new longboat and restored the operational flexibility of the expedition.[38] In the days that followed, the fresh stores of rice already loaded were augmented with a veritable farmyard of livestock, all paid for with bills of exchange: 350 chickens, 42 goats, 40 pigs and more than 30 sheep. Finally on 12 November the officers and savants took their leave of Governor Lofstett, and the next morning the now reunited French vessels set sail again. Few of the many still ailing men aboard could have imagined that they were destined to return to these 'destructive shores' before the expedition's end.

— 10 —

Van Diemen's Land

Nature does not reveal all her secrets at once. We imagine we are
initiated in her mysteries: we are as yet but hanging around her
outer courts.

SENECA, *De Cometis*

BAUDIN now determined to resume his course for Van Diemen's Land
as outlined in his original orders. The voyage south along the Western
Australian coast was very slow. It took fifty-two days just to reach Cape
Leeuwin because, as Péron put it, they were 'long opposed by the calms
and winds'.[1] Once they rounded Cape Leeuwin, however, their passage
east was powered by the westerlies and, after crowding extra sail, they
reached South West Cape in Van Diemen's Land in a remarkable eight
days. During this passage another eleven men died from dysentery or fever
(or both) contracted in Timor. In addition to the deaths of a number
of petty officers, sailors and gunners, the dead included Riedlé's young
assistant gardener Antoine Sautier and the 'mild and amiable' zoologist
Stanislas Levillain. Furthermore, by late November, there were twenty-five
sick cases, including the zoologist Maugé and the mineralogist Depuch.

From their second day out from Timor, Baudin had ordered that water
be rationed to avoid the shortages they had experienced towards the end
of the previous leg of their voyage.[2] In his published account Péron made
the startling (uncorroborated) assertion that by 19 November 'water was so
short, that some of our unhappy men were seen to drink their own urine!'

and added, 'Every remonstrance of our doctor, to increase our allowance of water for the present, and to diminish it the more when in cooler latitudes, was in vain.' Furthermore, Péron asserted (on the basis of the supposed authority of Cook, La Pérouse and Vancouver) 'that the want of water was the chief cause of the scurvy in long voyages'.[3] In suggesting that the recurrence of this disease during their voyage was directly attributable to the rationing régime Baudin instituted, Péron was not only unfair but also completely wrong. Although ascorbic acid (essential to the formation of collagen in connective tissue) was not isolated until 1932, the link between scurvy and a lack of fresh fruit and vegetables had been suggested as early as 1753 when James Lind published *A Treatise of the Scurvy*; on the basis of empirical dietetic studies of presumed anti-scorbutics, he recommended the use of dehydrated citrus juices on long sea voyages.

Unlike his published account, Péron's shipboard manuscripts for this part of the voyage give no hint of personal animosity towards the expedition's commander. Indeed, in his report of January 1802 to Baudin on the animals observed during the traverse from Timor to Van Diemen's Land, he was not only polite and respectful but also willingly informative.[4] Yet in Baudin's own historical journal there is an account of one encounter between the two, on 2 December 1801, which appears to have begun with good humour but ended with a sour reclamation. According to Baudin:

> Between five and six in the evening, while we were all talking on the quarter-deck, the conversation turned on the great humidity that there was at night. I then asked Citizen Péron, who was in charge of this part of our observations, if he were continuing to take them from his bed (since he was talking about the humidity) or whether he had observed it on deck or in some other part of the ship. From the beginning of our stay in Timor, this scientist had plunged headlong, furiously even, into collecting shells, although he had no knowledge in that field. A periwinkle, a nerita, etc., was a treasure to him, so in order to collect great quantities of shells, he spent all his time on them and thus neglected other work that he would have done much better than this. However, in accordance with his principles he will no doubt continue with this new interest. Whatever may occur in the future (as I am writing here of what took place yesterday), it so happens that I was just teasing him. But to get out of the difficulty, he told me that as his mother was no longer producing children and he was the family's sole hope, he did not want to kill himself taking observations

at night. He added that in any case he had taken enough in this field on the way to Timor. I remarked to him that, despite the excellence of his observations, the sun was not in this part of the hemisphere when we sailed along the coast of New Holland and that consequently it was a good thing to have observations taken at different periods. For a scientist, his replies were disjointed and inappropriate, and I was astonished by them. So in order that the conversation should stop, I contented myself with saying: 'You are certainly the one to decide whether you will work or not, but don't you at least find something wrong in my getting others to continue the task that formerly you would not have wanted to let them do?' I then asked him to give me back the hygrometer that I had put in his charge.[5]

It is not hard to imagine a source of anger in Péron's mind when he eventually consulted his dead commander's historical journal in preparation for the official account of the voyage and read such comments as those that defined him personally as knowing nothing of mollusca and making disjointed and inappropriate replies for a scientist. In his official account, however, Péron remains a sure and self-confident naturalist. He delights in informing his readers of the sighting of the white dolphin that Bernard Lacépède would soon name *Delphinus peroni* (= *Lissodelphis peroni*, Gloger, 1841) in his honour,[6] yet it is perhaps the thrilled still-boyish Péron who recounts the capture of a ten-foot shark that continues its violent death throes on the deck for hours—even after being decapitated, gutted and washed out at the pump. Nevertheless, the language of the serious scientist is always evident. Aside from pelagic marine life, Péron kept a detailed record of seabirds observed along the Western Australian coast. The sight of his first tropicbird provoked a lyrical quotation from Buffon, while petrels, albatrosses, pelicans, terns and gulls all engendered references to earlier navigators and naturalists and distracted him from the roll-call of deaths aboard the *Géographe* and *Naturaliste*.

In stormy seas on 13 January, two months after leaving Timor, Péron gained his first sight of Van Diemen's Land shrouded in thick cloud. He was clearly touched by the grandeur before him:

... we admired those lofty mountains, which nature has placed like so many ramparts of granite to oppose the rage of the stormy sea ... We observed with admiration those large plains in the interior of the island, which rise in amphitheatres over the whole surface, and are covered with immense forests … long clouds of vapour gathered round the grey sides of the woods and mountains. This fog was succeeded by heavy rains, hail, and hoar frost, innumerable flights of boobies, gulls, cormorants, swallows, &c. flew from the neighbouring rocks and encircled our ships, mingling their piercing cries with the noise of the angry waves; a long rank of white muzzled dolphins, with several large whales, played around us; in a word, every thing seemed to unite in giving a sort of solemnity to our arrival off these shores, and all proclaimed that we touched the extreme boundaries of the southern world.[7]

Entering the D'Entrecasteaux Channel, the expedition coasted the Labillardière Peninsula and then anchored off Partridge Island. Péron was inevitably reminded of their predecessors in these waters: the Dutchman Abel Tasman, who first ushered Van Diemen's Land (later renamed in his honour) into the European imagination in 1642;[8] Marc-Joseph Marion Dufresne, who made the first contact with the indigenous inhabitants in 1772;[9] Bruny d'Entrecasteaux, who discovered the channel named in his honour in 1792 and returned in 1793;[10] and the British navigators Furneaux, Cook, Cox, Bligh and Hunter.

Baudin's immediate objective was to obtain fresh water, and the next morning he dispatched several boats to search for a watering place. Henry de Freycinet was put in command of one of these boats and ordered to go north to Port Cygnet and to the Huon estuary. Péron and Lesueur accompanied him. For Péron, Port Cygnet, wedged within a mountainous arc, was the 'most picturesque and pleasant' place he had visited during the voyage so far. As he and his companions 'sailed along a number of small well-rounded capes and romantic little coves',[11] they were charmed by calm waters covered with elegant black swans and by lofty trees growing to the edge of the seashore. This dense woodland was also alive with exquisite blue wrens and multicoloured parrots and, as they would soon discover, a number of indigenous inhabitants.

Two men, one of whom was carrying a firebrand of lighted bark, were sighted on the shore, but quickly plunged back into the forest when the longboat came closer. Yet, when Péron and his companions landed, two Aboriginal men—perhaps the two they had seen earlier—appeared on top of a hill and 'in the twinkling of an eye' one was in their midst. According to Péron: 'His physiognomy had nothing fierce or austere, his eyes were lively and expressive, and his manner displayed at once both pleasure and surprise.' Péron added, 'What appeared at first to interest him most, was the whiteness of our skin, and doubtless, wishing to ascertain whether the rest of our bodies was of the same colour, he successively opened our jackets and shirts, and expressed his astonishment by loud exclamations of surprise, and by very quick motions of his feet.'[12]

Their new acquaintance was captivated by the longboat and its construction, yet was seemingly oblivious to the sailors still sitting in it. One of the crew, however, presented him with a bottle of arrack. At first the shining unfamiliar glass provoked profound surprise, but just as quickly it was thrown into the sea. 'Neither the exclamation of the seaman, who was vexed at the loss of his bottle of arrack', wrote Péron, 'nor the haste with which one of his comrades threw himself into the water to fish it up again, seemed to give him any concern.'[13] Péron and Freycinet then walked up the hill to meet the second man, who was more than fifty years old and had greying hair and beard. He too drew aside their shirts and jackets to examine their skin, then hailed two women some way off. After some initial hesitation, they approached the French: one, about forty years old, leading her companion of about twenty-eight. Both were completely naked except that the younger woman gently suckled an infant girl under a kangaroo skin. While Freycinet went in search of fresh water and Lesueur left in search of animals, Péron remained behind with the indigenous inhabitants in the hope of studying their language and customs.[14]

This was Péron's first genuine ethnographic opportunity in Australia, other than the traces of human occupation he had witnessed in Western Australia. At Geographe Bay he had only been able to report the observations of others. Hence he had described the Aboriginal woman who had been frozen with fear on the beach as 'horribly ugly and disgusting'[15] even though he had never seen her. But now, surveying the naked young woman before him, his prejudices seem to have evaporated: her breasts were already a little sunk, but 'otherwise well formed'; her countenance was 'very interesting'; 'her eyes had an expression and fire which astonished us' and her maternal behaviour was 'kind and affectionate'. Later, when a large fire had been lit with the aid of an Aboriginal firebrand[16] and one of the sailors took off his fur gloves to warm his hands, Péron was amused at the young woman's alarming scream: 'she had taken the gloves for real hands, or at least for a sort of live skin, which he could thus take off and put into his pocket or replace at pleasure.'[17]

Péron has been criticised by a number of scholars for his failure to adhere to the suggestions of Joseph-Marie Degérando of the Société des

Observateurs de l'Homme on 'diverse methods to follow in the observation of savage peoples'. This was an ambitious program of anthropological research on such subjects as language, clothing, kinship, family relations, sex, marriage, divorce, law, education, politics, war, cannibalism and illness (including insanity). John J. Honigmann, for example, was scathing of Péron: 'the topics of inquiry and the counsels helped the Australian expedition hardly at all', he wrote. 'The inept ethnographer on board carried out only the most superficial observations and totally ignored the instructions of Degérando and of other experienced travelers.'[18] Degérando's English translator, F. C. T. Moore, was equally critical and unfairly suggested that Péron's appointment as 'anatomiste des animaux' was 'perhaps merely an administrative slip';[19] in other words, that Péron should still be judged as an anthropologist despite his consuming duties as a zoologist. Although Moore acknowledges that 'occasional passages' in Péron's official account show 'the capacity for a form of encounter extremely valuable to the anthropologist', he cannot resist criticising him for treating such encounters as 'a luxury that took him away from his real work'.[20] Yet this was the case. Although Péron's anthropological observations might have been inferior to those of other travellers of the period, it is hard to accept Moore's opinion that he failed to exhibit any sign of the 'philosophical traveller'.[21]

One of Péron's most significant anthropological findings was the recognition of strong physical and cultural differences between the inhabitants of Van Diemen's Land and New Holland (on the basis of which he designated two separate races). These differences, and the absence of the dingo in Van Diemen's Land, led Péron to conclude, in an article he published on his return to France, that the separation of the two regions must date from 'an époque very much more ancient than one could suspect at first'.[22] Unfortunately, this statement was mistranslated or mistakenly represented by the American anthropologist George W. Stocking Jr as 'before the epoch of the population of these countries'. Stocking also seized on Péron's questions about existing theories on 'the communications of peoples, on their transmigrations and on the influence of climates on man' to suggest that he believed in polygenism (separate human creations)![23] Unlike the polygenists, Péron placed great stress on the influence of environmental forces. And like Montesquieu—and before him John Arbuthnot[24]—he expended a great deal of effort proposing cultural differences as a result of climate. Nowhere did he divide humanity into separate species or propose separate 'Adams', although he did see plant and animal species largely confined to 'distinct' areas. Forty years later, Stocking's ill-founded speculations about Péron's beliefs emboldened Jean Fornasiero, Peter Monteath and John West-Sooby to damn the naturalist as a racist.[25] Yet nowhere did Péron propose an immutable intellectual inferiority simply on the basis of race, even if he considered the people of New Holland to be technologically superior to those of Van Diemen's Land.

Péron also had his anthropological admirers. In the nineteenth century, Jean Louis Armand de Quatrefages de Bréau wrote:

This excellent observer had numerous encounters with the Diemenlanders and profited from them. His accounts are certainly the most complete original documents, which have been published on this population, at a time when they still appeared to be untouched by Europeans. The details which he gives on their manner of life, the customs which one encounters among them, as among all savages—indeed among all men—leaves little essential to desire.[26]

Rhys Jones identified Péron's 'progressionist' notions of cultural difference and described him as the 'first self-consciously defined anthropologist ever to set forth on an empirical field programme', adding that he was 'firmly within the objectivist, natural-history and medical tradition of the dawning nineteenth century'.[27] Margaret Sankey, reviewing Péron's loss of Rousseauist notions in the course of the voyage, has rightly observed that his writings are marked by a contest between 'a pre-revolutionary vision of savage man and a post-revolutionary vision where savage man, demystified, begins to become the object of science'.[28] More recently Colin Dyer has asserted that in Van Diemen's Land Péron was a 'more analytical … less generous' and 'more precise' anthropological observer than his fellow expeditioners.[29]

Péron's anthropological detractors tend to forget the fact that ultimately —despite his initial lobbying—he was not appointed as an 'anthropologist' to the expedition. As has already been mentioned, he was last on the list of zoologists and had specific responsibilities for 'comparative anatomy'.[30] Degérando's approach was wholistic and quite sensibly dependent on learning the subject group's language, but Péron had very limited opportunities to study the language of the indigenous Tasmanians. In an astute and modest report to Baudin, he would review the problems as he saw them:

The lack of time and favourable circumstances, the prejudices of the natives, their suspicions, their fears, their threats, even the dangers, all combine against the observer. Obstacles throng around him … Although I am strongly convinced of a deep feeling of my inferiority, which was for me so certain a guarantee of the hopelessness of my efforts, I have been very careful until today not to attempt to undertake too lightly so difficult a study. I therefore did not seek to establish with the natives that multiplicity of contacts and that continuity of communication indispensable to obtain coherent and interesting results. Furthermore, I must tell you frankly that I have always been strongly convinced that an enterprise of this nature was so difficult that it must absorb all the faculties and all the time of he who wishes to devote himself to it in a special way, and that this was the only means of rendering it useful … Today, Citizen Commander, imbued like me with the importance of the study of man and equally distressed to see it so neglected in your expedition, you have imposed upon me the obligation to occupy myself with it in a more special manner. You wish me to devote all my attention to establish a complex rapport with the natives, to occupy myself with their language, to record their customs, their ways and their habits, all of which deserve to hold the attention and researches of the philosopher.[31]

Yet, as his scientific colleagues continued to die, the expedition's zoological responsibilities also weighed more and more on his shoulders. There was nothing dishonourable in Péron's attempt to wear two hats, but it could be that we do not have a full picture of his efforts. Brian Plomley, who patiently extracted a wealth of important Tasmanian ethnographic information from Péron's manuscripts and his official account, declared: 'It is much to be regretted that both the collection at the Archives Nationales and that at Le Havre are incomplete. The most important papers which are known to be missing are various reports by Péron which were received into the official series but are not there now.'[32]

At Port Cygnet, Péron returned to his zoological duties when his initial ethnological investigations were cut short by the departure of the Aboriginal family group. It was low tide, and he spent two hours collecting 'more than forty new species' of molluscs, crustaceans and other shellfish. It is hard to know, from Péron's notes, exactly what species were collected at Cygnet on that day, but a number of species published by Lamarck in his *Histoire naturelle des animaux sans vertèbres* are known to be based on type specimens collected in mainland Tasmanian waters and off-shore islands by Péron.[33] These include the commercially significant scallop *Pecten asperrimus* (= *Mimachlamys asperrimus*) and the nutshell *Nucula obliqua* (= *Ennucula obliqua*).[34] Other molluscs first published by Lamarck are also found in the D'Entrecasteaux Channel.[35] They include his cockle *Cardium tenuicostatum* (= *Fulvia tenuicostata*),[36] borer *Corbula australis* (= *Hiatella australis*),[37] wedge shell *Crassatella cycladea* (= *Anapella cycladea*),[38] *Venus anomala* (= *Irus anomala*)[39] and razor shell *Solen vaginoides*.[40]

Returning to the longboat for a meal with the sailors, Péron learned that Lesueur had brought back a dozen bird specimens, including a blue wren and three parrot species. Henry de Freycinet, however, had not found water so, after eating, the party made a landing on another part of the coast in order to continue their search. On the shore they found an Aboriginal bark shelter and a foul-smelling midden of oyster and abalone shells. There were also two bark canoes of very simple construction, which were sketched by Lesueur. Soon after, a family group—including the individuals they had only just met—was seen approaching on the beach. 'As soon as they observed us', wrote Péron, 'they shouted for joy, and mended their pace to join us.'[41] Kindling a fire, they roasted their abalone catch on the coals and shared them with their French visitors. The explorers reciprocated with a stirring rendition of what appears to have been the 'Marseillaise', which generated great excitement and pleasure among their hosts. Péron's attention was particularly drawn to a young woman of sixteen or seventeen named Ouré-Ouré. He wrote that she was 'entirely naked, and did not seem at all to be aware that any person could imagine there was any indecency or immodesty in this absolute nudity. Of a constitution and form more delicate than her sister and brother, she was also more lively and animated.' And Péron added, with almost a hint of jealousy, 'M. Freycinet, who sat next to her, seemed to be more particularly the object of her regards, and it was easy to perceive in the manners of this innocent pupil of nature, that delicate shade, which gives to the most simple playfulness, a character of serious preference: coquetry itself seemed to be called in to the assistance of the natural attractions of the sex.'[42]

Péron recorded details of Aboriginal implements and exchanged a handkerchief, a hatchet and a hammer for Ouré-Ouré's rush bag. This, he tells us, was bestowed with 'an obliging smile and some tender expressions'. By this time, Péron and his companions were ready to move further into the bay with the intention of making camp for the night. However, Ouré-Ouré and several members of her family decided to accompany them back to the longboat, seemingly oblivious to the scratches their naked bodies received from the scrub and more troubled by their inability to communicate effectively with the French. As Péron and his companions approached their objective, they were surprised by gunshots, which caused great fear among their Aboriginal companions. These shots were from a landing party from the *Naturaliste*, comprising Louis de Freycinet, the hydrographer Pierre Faure, the mineralogist Joseph Bailly and Midshipman François Breton. They too had failed to find fresh water. Both landing parties departed together, but not before bestowing more presents on their friends. Most appreciated by Ouré-Ouré was a long red feather presented by the young Guadeloupe-born Breton. 'She actually jumped for joy', wrote Péron; 'she called to her father and brothers; she cried; she laughed; in a word she seemed quite intoxicated with delight and pleasure.'[43]

Péron departed Port Cygnet convinced of the 'kindest and most interesting affection and friendship' with the indigenous inhabitants. At this stage of the voyage, he appears to have still been a Rousseauist:[44] 'I realised with inexpressible pleasure, those charming descriptions of the happiness and simplicity of a state of nature, of which I had so often read, and enjoyed in idea.' This view would change, for Péron admitted in his official account: 'I was at the time far from conjecturing the many privations and miseries to which such a state is liable.'[45] He would also be shocked to discover that, during their absence, one of the assistant-helmsmen—Jean-Marie Maurouard, a native of Caen—received a serious spear wound between the neck and shoulder after he apparently shamed one of the Aborigines in a wrestling match. And some days later Baudin, Hamelin, Leschenault and Petit were attacked with a shower of stones after Petit refused to part with a portrait he had sketched of an Aboriginal man. Nevertheless, although his idealised Rousseauist view of primitive man might have been affected, Péron retained a strong Rousseauist celebration of the ecological balance of primaeval nature in his portrait of the Tasmanian coastal forests:

> The immense forests of trees that seem coeval with nature itself, and where the sound of the axe was never heard, present an extraordinary spectacle to the eye of the traveller. Here vegetation is continually enriched with its own spontaneous productions, and everywhere expands without control; and where at the extremities of the globe, such forests are exclusively formed of trees totally unknown to the European world, and vegetable productions that are extraordinary both in their organisation and their great variety, the scene becomes

still more interesting. Here a mysterious and perpetual shade obscures the light of the day, an extreme coolness, a penetrating humidity is constantly felt. These large trees sinking into the earth with age, again produce many healthy suckers: the aged trunks now decomposed by the united effects of time and humidity, are covered with different kinds of moss and adhesive herbage; the interior harbouring numerous reptiles and swarms of insects: these fallen trunks obstruct every avenue of the forest, crossing each other in a thousand different directions; they oppose the passage like so many protectors of the boundaries, and multiply the obstacles and dangers which surround the footsteps of the traveller: often they sink under the weight of his body, and thus he falls among the perishing remains, and still more frequently the moist and putrid bark slips from under his feet: sometimes their heaps form natural banks from 25 to 30 feet in height; in other places they have fallen over the bed of the torrents, and across the depths of the valleys, thus forming so many natural bridges, on which it is dangerous to step without great caution. This picture of disorder and the ravages of time, these scenes presenting devastation and destruction, are counter balanced, if I may be allowed the expression, by the beauties of nature; all that its creative power can display that is most majestic and beautiful, here delights the eye and the contemplative mind.[46]

Péron went on to provide a survey of the littoral flora of Van Diemen's Land, employing a host of established, but sometimes superceded, generic names.[47]

Returning to the shore, he joined his companions in hunting swans from the longboats. Then, after a welcome lunch of roasted game, Péron went off exploring and discovered a rivulet. Although its waters were sweet and alive with fish, it proved impractical for refilling the expedition's casks because of its deep fringe of marshland. So, with the rays of the late-afternoon sun dancing upon the waves and with their bellies filled further with a feast of mussels boiled in seawater, the landing party set off to rejoin the *Naturaliste* and *Géographe*. On 17 January the two vessels proceeded further up D'Entrecasteaux Channel, but were unable to tack past Kinghorne Point on North Bruny Island. Baudin therefore decided to anchor off Green Island and await more favourable winds. This gave Péron an opportunity to land on Bruny Island with Henry de Freycinet and Midshipman Bonnefoy de Montbazin. Although Baudin declared that 'Citizen Péron brought back little from his excursion' and that the 'shores offered few shells or marine animals',[48] the young zoologist himself gushed with excitement at collecting beetles (two of which he thought belonged to a new genus), lizards, mollusca and one quadruped—probably an Australian water-rat, *Hydromys chrysogaster*, since the specimen Etienne Geoffroy Saint-Hilaire described in 1804 is known to have come from Bruny Island[49]—in addition to 'beautiful samples' of the island's 'granite', which at that time meant any manifestly crystalline rock. On 20 January Péron accompanied a fishing expedition off Bruny Island and 'collected about twenty new kinds of fish' and twelve to fifteen species of shellfish. On seeing this collection, Péron tells us that his colleague Maugé 'absolutely wept, and notwithstanding his consumptive weak state of health he determined himself to go on shore on the morrow'.[50] Alas, poor Maugé collapsed shortly after landing the next day and had to be carried back aboard. Of Péron's specimens, arguably the most important was a species of bivalve that had hitherto been thought to exist only in fossil form. Péron christened it *Trigonia antarctica* in his *Voyage*, but it was Lamarck who first published the name *Trigonia margaritacea* (= *Neotrigonia margaritacea*)[51] using this specimen in 1804.

Baudin's instructions for the D'Entrecasteaux Channel were to follow up on Charles-François Beautemps-Beaupré's impressive charts drafted a decade earlier during d'Entrecasteaux's expedition. This particularly meant the exploration of rivers and the poorly charted coast north-east of the channel. When Henry de Freycinet was ordered to survey the estuary of the Rivière du Nord (now the Derwent), Péron seized the opportunity to accompany him. They departed at 3.00 a.m. on 24 January, but made slow progress because of 'calms, the currents and the winds'.[52] There were compensations, for the excursion offered opportunities to hunt fresh game, and the survey party shot more than a dozen black swans before running firmly aground on a large mudbank. Faced with this obstruction, Freycinet decided to continue his survey of the river on foot the following morning. According to Péron, the effects of fire made the riparian woodlands far less dense, and thus more accessible, than the forests along the channel.

Although Péron at first remained with Freycinet's armed party, he soon decided to head off alone—as appears to have been his habit—to explore the interior. Near a deep ravine he encountered fourteen Aboriginal bark huts. Fires were still burning, and Péron believed that the occupants had only just fled because of the sound of French gunshots. Kangaroo and bird bones were also in evidence, as were flat stones 'warm and greasy' on which he assumed the Aborigines broiled their food. Péron also tells us that he 'picked up some of the hatchets and knives used by the natives; which were simply fragments of a sort of granite'.[53] Unarmed and worried by 'piercing cries' at the bottom of a nearby valley, Péron left hurriedly and by 4.30 p.m. managed to return to the longboat guarded by several sailors and Joseph Brue, the young midshipman who had joined the expedition at the Ile de France. Freycinet and his party arrived three hours later, having surveyed four leagues into the interior and gained further knowledge of the course of the river from the summit of a mountain.

On their return journey down the river the next day, Freycinet and Péron decided to make numerous landfalls to collect specimens and ethnographic information. Baudin wrote that Péron 'was disappointed in his search for objects of Natural History and brought back so few things, that they are not worth mentioning'.[54] However, in his *Voyage* Péron was at pains to record the birds he observed and to mention the geological specimens and several species of vascular plants, moss, fungi and lichen he collected.[55] He also wrote that he had found fossil shells 600 to 700 feet above sea level and mused: 'From these circumstances it appears, that in this extremity of the eastern world, the terrestrial globe has experienced its revolutions and catastrophes; and there have been, as in other places, ravages by the devastating fires of volcanoes, and lands swallowed up by the seas!'[56] He could only guess at the awesome expanse of geological time.[57]

Over the next three weeks in Van Diemen's Land, Péron made many other similar landings, but in his *Voyage* he focused on a visit to Bruny Island on 31 January. Joining a large fishing and wood-gathering party, made up of men from both the *Naturaliste* and the *Géographe*, he reached the island at low tide. 'I immediately left', he wrote, 'to follow the circumference of the coast.'[58] It is hardly likely that Péron could have achieved this ambitious plan in the brief time at his disposal. Bruny Island is fifty-five kilometres long from north to south, and its deeply indented coast is very much longer. Furthermore, in the south-east there are sheer cliffs of reddish-brown dolerite that rise almost 300 metres above the sea. According to his account, Péron turned back not because of the topographical obstacles but because he was unnerved by a group of twenty indigenous inhabitants coming towards him. No doubt he was also mindful of the recent incident in which his compatriots had been stoned by the Aborigines of the same island. On retreating, he encountered Ensign François Heyrisson and Surgeon Jérôme Bellefin[59] from the *Naturaliste*, who were hunting on the edge of the coastal forest. Emboldened by their firearms and their company, he accepted Heyrisson and Bellefin's proposal to seek contact with the Aborigines.

Surprisingly, the indigenous group proved to be entirely female. Quickly at ease and seated in the presence of the French, they fell silent when Surgeon Bellefin began to sing, but the oldest women applauded enthusiastically after every verse. Almost all the women were entirely naked except for a few who had kangaroo skins over their shoulders. All had covered their skin with seal fat and crushed charcoal, and powdered their hair with red ochre. Péron admitted that he found their 'natural constitution ... in the highest degree disgusting'—except for a few firm-breasted teenage girls with 'agreeable form and pleasant features'. Yet with some sensitivity, he added:

> These young girls had also something ingenuous in the expression of the countenance, something soft and tender in their manners, as if the most amiable qualities of the mind were always, even among the most savage hordes of the human species, the most particular appendages of youth and beauty. Among the most aged of these females, some were ill-formed and clumsy; others, but these were few, looked sulky and ferocious; but in general we observed in them all something unhappy and depressed on the countenance, which misery and servitude always print on the faces of those who are compelled to bear the yoke. They were, besides, almost all of them covered with sores, the sad consequences of the ill treatment they had received from their ferocious husbands: one only, among all her companions, had preserved any degree of confidence with a lively and merry temper ...[60]

One of the Tasmanian women followed Bellefin's singing with a song of her own. Although Péron tells us that 'it would be very difficult to give any idea of music, such as it was, so different from the general principles of any European music', his account is not entirely without significant detail. 'Their tunes', he added, 'seem entirely to accord with their language.'[61] This suggests a one-note tune with the natural inflection of the rise and fall of the speaking voice perhaps accompanied by monotone percussion. Given the paucity of knowledge we have of the island's indigenous languages, Péron's linguistic comments are both tantalising and frustrating: 'it is impossible ... to distinguish their pronunciation with any degree of precision: it is a sort of rolling sound, for which our European languages do not furnish any expression of comparison or analogy.'[62]

Péron and Heyrisson, their faces now blackened with charcoal thanks to the obliging attentions of their new friends, decided to return to their boats with Surgeon Bellefin. Although they attempted to take their leave of the women after bestowing numerous gifts, all appeared intent on walking in the same direction. However, the women—heavily burdened with broiled crustaceans and shellfish—insisted on taking a parallel and presumably more arduous course in the sandhills while the French remained on the beach. Péron tells us that from the vantage of the higher ground the women 'played many tricks, and practised many drolleries'.[63]

This joyful flirting ended suddenly with the sight of the longboat parties on the shore. All but one of the women—Arra-Maïda handsomely rendered in a sketch by Nicolas Petit[64]—fled in terror, but were gradually coaxed back by the entreaties of the bravest of their number. On reaching the boats, however, the women were further surprised to find their menfolk had arrived just a few minutes before. Péron's account suggests that the Aboriginal men deeply resented the fact that their women had kept company with the French: 'their savage husbands gave them such looks of rage and anger, as were not at all likely to reassure them'.[65] After depositing the food they had brought at the feet of their disconsolate male kin and receiving no share for themselves, they positioned themselves meekly in the background and 'did not dare to speak, or smile, or even lift up their eyes from the ground'.[66]

On 3 February, when next Péron landed on Bruny Island in the company of Henry de Freycinet and Louis Bonnefoy de Montbazin, two women fled on their approach.[67] Clearly this was not the same kind of joyous interracial contact that Labillardière had recorded during d'Entrecasteaux's visit a decade before, but perhaps these Aborigines had already become wary of Europeans after contact with rough and lawless sealers—many of whom were former convicts.

By 18 February the crews of the *Naturaliste* and *Géographe* had replenished their firewood and taken on water (regrettably somewhat brackish) in the difficult estuarine conditions of North West Bay River. After clearing D'Entrecasteaux Channel, traversing the Derwent Estuary and rounding the great basalt redoubt of Cape Pillar, they anchored in Mercury Passage four kilometres off Point Mauge on Maria Island. The following day, 19 February, Baudin ordered Charles Boulanger to survey the island in the company of Péron and Jean-Marie Maurouard. Tasman had named this island in honour of Maria van Diemen, wife of the Governor of the Dutch East Indies. Its first French visitors were Marc-Joseph Marion Dufresne and his men in 1772, but the most recent survey had been undertaken in July 1789 by John Henry Cox, a British merchant shipowner who sailed with Lieutenant George Mortimer on the *Mercury*.[68] Aside from a study of the natural history and anthropology of the island, Baudin was intent on a verification of Cox's chart. During his anti-clockwise survey of the island, beginning with the west coast, Boulanger did in fact find numerous errors. Ultimately, many parts of the island would be named in honour of members of the expedition, and these names survive to this day: Cape Peron, Cape Maurouard, Cape Boulanger, Point Lesueur, Point Mauge and Riedle Bay.

Although Péron's manuscript *Fasciculus Zoologicae Hollandiae-novae* is now missing, three drafts of his natural history of Maria Island have survived.[69] His final definitive account, *Histoire naturelle. Topographie générale de l'île Maria sur la côte orientale de la Terre de Diemen*, is a pioneering work of ecological writing on Tasmania because of the author's comprehension of the relationship between living organisms and their environment. His observations on gannets, which he found far less plentiful on Maria Island than in the D'Entrecasteaux Channel, provide a good example:

> The reason for this difference seems to me to be easily understood. It obviously resulted from the comparison of this bird's habits with the nature of the seabed and that of the shore. The gannet is especially at home in the midst of more peaceful waters: it seeks out shallower, muddier areas. These were the principal reasons for its seeming to be relegated to the part of the Channel near Port Cygnet. The sea in this area appeared to be covered with gannets, and when they flew up, the sky seemed (as it were) to be obscured by them. But also, how many powerful attractions must have drawn them thither and established them upon these shores! There are waters perpetually calm and pure, an entirely muddy bottom and numerous shoals of all kinds of fish. On Maria Island everything is different. The bottom of Oyster [now Shoal] Bay is too sandy and rocky … and so discourages them; the shore and the eastern bay, constantly battered as they are by stormy seas, would be even more uncomfortable for them, and so they shun them.[70]

And when writing of crustacea, he also writes of the 'striking proof of the influence of nature on the seabed' upon the existence of a particular species, 'in preference to others'. This was writing on the cusp of modern evolutionary biology. Although many of Péron's geological and geomor-phological observations on Maria Island are astute (such as the alluvial formation of Shoal Bay), his manuscripts appear to be rooted in the Wernerian 'Neptunist' orthodoxy that so-called primitive rocks (including even granite) were chemical precipitates from a universal ocean.[71] Thus Péron wrote:

> The island was formerly submerged. In an undoubtedly very far off era, lost in the mists of time, all the highest peaks of this island were still hidden away at the bottom of the ocean. Everything was covered by the waves. Over the centuries the mass of water diminished, and (this dimunition being too gradual for us to perceive, but not passing unnoticed by Nature) the ground must have risen imperceptibly towards the surface of the sea ... By and by, the first peaks appeared. Coming forth from Nature's flank in the earliest days of the world, they were necessarily formed of primitive rock, and indeed all of them are very beautiful granite ... Thus we have seen no other agents, in the midst of so many upheavals, than the waves themselves and the primitive rocks entirely hidden away in their depths ... We have seen our granite peaks, isolated at first, gradually become joined to one another, form chains of reefs, extend their ramifications and give birth to deep valleys protected from the fury of storms, and we have seen the formation in these underwater valleys of the first deposits and the first secondary rocks.[72]

Ironically, in an earlier draft, Péron noted examples of supposedly primitive 'granite' (in fact Jurassic dolerite) on the east coast of Maria Island that was clearly younger than underlying sedimentary formations, which are now known to be Permian.[73] How long such anomalies took to undermine his Neptunist notions is unclear. He must eventually have become aware of the work of the 'plutonist' James Hutton, who, in 1794, had pointed to similar geological 'intrusions' to those on Maria Island to argue that granites were in fact created by the cooling of molten rock injected into earlier (more primitive) formations. In the same year Péron visited Maria Island, Leopold von Buch visited the craters of the Auvergne close to Péron's native Cérilly and had his Neptunist faith shattered by the abundant evidence of volcanic forces, which had thrust basalt through a great underlying plain of granite—without any sign of vast burning beds of subterranean coal suggested by Werner as an explaination of volcanism.[74] Ultimately von Buch would review the geological specimens and observations made during Baudin's expedition.[75]

Although Péron's unpublished manuscripts in many respects exhibit less advanced geological ideas than in his published *Voyage*, they do reveal an appreciation of volcanism[76] and a sense of evolutionary progression among plant and animal species, for he wrote of the 'first shellfish' and the 'first marine plants'.[77] It was once said of Werner that, like Linnaeus, he had disciples 'who covered the earth' and that 'from one pole to another' nature had been 'interrogated in the name of one individual man'.[78] Péron should perhaps be seen as one of these 'interrogators' who, like von Buch, was ultimately made uneasy by the answers he received.

During his visit to Maria Island, Péron collected important specimens of two Australian mammals. The first of these appears to have been the Tasmanian marsupial mouse. He provisionally named it *Didelphis muroides*, but shortly after his return to France Geoffroy-Saint-Hilaire (himself recently returned from Bonaparte's Egyptian expedition) included it among the quolls and used Péron's alcohol-preserved specimen to publish the name *Dasyrus minimus*.[79] However, since 1963, this species has been included in the genus *Antechinus*.[80] The second mammal Péron collected on Maria Island appears to have been yet another specimen of the Australian water-rat. Péron skinned his specimen (it has a dense otter-like fur with a golden belly and white-tipped tail) and gave it the manuscript name *Mus insule maria*, but this was little more than a *nomen nudum*. In 1804 his thunder was once again stolen by Geoffroy-Saint-Hilaire, who described and published it as *Hydromys leucogaster* along with *H. chrysogaster* for the water-rat from Bruny Island.[81] The two specimens, however, actually belong to the same species, and *H. leucogaster* is now considered a senior synonym.

It was on the coast of Maria Island that Péron collected the type specimen of a beautiful pink and white jellyfish to which he gave the provisional manuscript name *Medusa rosea*,[82] then *M. hexachremona*, but ultimately published as *Chrysaora hexastome*, as part of an entirely new genus he named in 1809 after the warrior Chrysaor, born of the blood of Medusa.[83] Péron wrote that he had also noted between thirty-five and forty species of molluscs and observed that with only 'two or three exceptions' they were among the more than a hundred species he had seen in the D'Entrecasteaux Channel. Surprisingly, despite his excitement at having previously found the 'living fossil' *Neotrigonia* on Bruny Island, Péron does not mention this genus on Maria Island; yet they are so bountiful that the southern end of Riedle Bay is to this day known as Trigonia Corner. Birds, too, were largely the same as those he had seen and collected on the D'Entrecasteaux Channel, but his manuscript suggests he might also have observed the fire-tail finch (*Emblema bella*) and the yellow-throated honey-eater (*Lichenostomus flasicollis*) on the island. Although seals were plentiful, he found it 'impossible' to obtain a single specimen. The remains of whales, however, 'littered' the entire shore 'at the head of the eastern bay'.[84]

In addition to his natural history observations, which contained several ethnographic references to Aboriginal food and material culture, Péron drafted a formal account of his anthropological observations on Maria Island. This was after another landing on the island in the company of the artist Nicolas Petit on 22 February 1802, during which he met the indigenous inhabitants by the remains of a campfire. Far from seeing these people as his intellectual inferiors—as Fornasiero, Monteath and West-Sooby have asserted—he declared: 'In general, they seemed to me to be very intelligent and they easily grasped the meaning of all my gestures and seemed to understand both their object and their purpose. They repeated willingly the words which I had not been able to grasp readily on the first attempt, and they laughed heartily when, attempting to repeat them myself, I made mistakes or pronounced them very badly.'[85]

Parts of Péron's report offer an amusing read, for he rationalised numerous erogenous characteristics of civilised society and contrasted them with what he thought to be the reduced libido of the uncivilised Tasmanians. This was after indigenous surprise at the apparently robust and fulsome genitalia of just one of the sailors of the *Géographe*: the slightly built Jean-Baptiste Martin. According to Péron, several of the Aborigines 'showed with a sort of scorn their soft and flaccid organs and shook them briskly with an expression of regret and desire which seemed to indicate that they did not experience it as often as we did'. Péron went on to suggest that 'natural man … is placed in a situation where everything combines to reduce the keenness of his desires, to deaden them, and to quench them promptly in the midst of the rigours of winter, and sometimes also the anxieties of lean times'.[86]

Once again Péron submitted to a charcoal face-powdering. As he put it: 'Soon, through the care and briskness of my Diemenese, I found myself of a colour little different from sienna, a result upon which all seemed to congratulate me.'[87] He also recorded words from the local Aboriginal language—indeed at least two dozen in excess of those collected by Labillardière during the previous French expedition. Unfortunately, this vocabulary appears to have disappeared—perhaps along with the eleven missing pages of his manuscript anthropological observations. These missing pages might have formed the basis for that part of his official account in which he describes how he was menaced by a man with a spear, who wanted his jacket, and how one of the large gold rings was pulled violently from his ear—fortuitously opening the lock rather than tearing his lobe. Péron was convinced that only the threat of muskets among his party prevented him and the artist Petit from becoming the 'victims of these fierce people'.[88]

Yet 'although tired of all the unpleasant manners of the savages of Maria Island', Péron still wanted to 'repeat some experiments' he had commenced among the inhabitants of the D'Entrecasteaux Channel. These involved testing their physical strength with a Régnier dynamometer. This instrument was designed by the engineer Edmé Régnier as a portable device—weighing around a kilogram—to measure the strength of men of different ages and states of health. Its central, almost elliptical, steel spring could be clasped and compressed to record the strength of the hands, or a T-shaped handle and a foot piece could be fitted to test the strength of the back and arm muscles through traction. The results were read from an arrow on a graduated semicircular brass disc, with each degree on the scale equivalent to 500 grams pressure. It was not long before it was suggested that Régnier's instrument be used to test the strength of different races and to test Rousseau's proposition that civilised man 'living a softer life' was weaker than natural man having lost something of his 'strength and ferocity'.[89]

Péron's full results were published in the second volume of his *Voyage* in 1816, but in his first volume he provided a summary (chapter xxi) and reported that his experiments on Maria Island created a sense of shame and irritation among the Aborigines, who thought themselves wanting in strength compared with himself. In 1817 Régnier would declare with satisfaction that Péron had 'observed that savage peoples were less strong than civilised men' and added that he had 'demonstrated in an obvious manner that the perfection of the social order did not destroy our physical strengths as some people have pretended'.[90] This represented yet another argument against Rousseau's notions of the physical superiority of savage man.

Péron's tests, as Quartrefages cautioned in 1884, were probably biased against subjects unfamiliar with the operation and purpose of the dynamometer. Nevertheless, Rhys Jones observed that his measurements amounted to 'the first quantitative ergonometric research experiment to be carried out in an ethnographic context'.[91] Ultimately, the humiliation engendered by these tests forced Péron to extricate himself once more with the threat of muskets. As he and his companions retreated warily to their longboat, Péron reflected despondently on the 'many difficulties and dangers' experienced by voyagers attempting to communicate with 'people belonging to these savage nations, and how impossible it is to conquer the natural ferocity of their character, and their prejudice to us'.[92] He appears not to have considered that his own interpersonal skills might have been found wanting compared to Labillardière's a decade earlier.

Péron also had precise instructions from Georges Cuvier to collect human anatomical specimens and portraits to advance the work of the German comparative anatomist J. F. Blumenbach, who had distinguished physical differences between Caucasians, Mongols and Ethiopians and sought further to isolate differences or potential affinities among the inhabitants of Lapland, the Americas, the South Seas and New Holland. For Cuvier, the 'principal and the most necessary' human specimens to obtain were skulls, which he wanted boiled in a solution of sodium or potassium hydroxide. Aware that this might appear barbarous to sailors, he asserted that the leaders of an expedition aimed at the advancement of science had to be guided by reason. Each head, once removed of its flesh, was to be enveloped in cloth (for fear that loose bones might become separated) and labelled.[93] Péron attempted to fulfil his macabre orders by excavating an ossuary at an Aboriginal cremation site he discovered on Maria Island. In his book he tells his readers that he shuddered with horror on drawing forth 'the jaw-bone of a man, to which there yet adhered some remains of flesh'.[94] Lesueur even captured the subsequent moment in a pencil sketch: Péron kneeling with a broad-brimmed hat on his head and (it would seem) a femur in his left hand.[95] To this day the site is known as Cape des Tombeaux, and Péron acknowledged in his official account that, like the 'monument' he had seen on the Vasse River on the western coast of New Holland, it was 'consecrated by affection'.[96] In both his book and his anthropological notes, Péron wrote that the action of fire had rendered the bones excessively friable,[97] so it seems unlikely that he took any remains with him.

Surprisingly, on the basis of Lesueur's sketch, Jean Fornasiero, Peter Monteath and John West-Sooby have collectively proposed Péron as the herald of genocide and master of a landscape devoid of humanity.[98] Yet Péron is actually portrayed kneeling—hardly a symbol of dominance. Furthermore, with human empathy, rather than arrogant racism, this same image by Lesueur appears in copper bas-relief on Péron's own tomb in Cérilly.[99]

The expedition would bury one of its own on Maria Island, for René Maugé died late on the evening of 20 February 1802. He was laid to rest between two casuarinas and two eucalypts on the point that now bears his name. With Maugé's death, like Riedlé before him, Baudin lost 'the only two genuine friends' he had on board. Péron, however, is unlikely to have agreed with Baudin's assessment that Maugé 'alone did more than all the scientists put together'.[100] Although Péron certainly acknowledged Maugé's 'zeal and courage'[101] and declared that he was 'universally regretted by all on board', he would ultimately act dishonourably to his memory. Michel Jangoux has demonstrated this through a careful study of two versions of Péron's report on more than ninety largely new species observed during the traverse from Timor to Van Diemen's Land.[102]

Péron's original report, politely addressed to Baudin (presumably around January 1802), is twenty-four pages long and largely consists of descriptions of birds and marine animals based on daily notes. Michel Jangoux, however, has drawn attention to the fact that some time after Baudin's death, Péron not only changed some of his proposed species names but also crossed out his introductory address to Baudin, the concluding salutation and respects and—most shamefully—substituted his and his friend Lesueur's name for Maugé's as collectors of a number of specimens. In one case Péron denied Maugé credit for collecting a species of *Janthina*, a gastropod that floats on the surface of the open sea with the aid of a bubble to which its eggs are attached. He also took personal credit for collecting a species of pelagic crab living symbiotically with one of these aforementioned *Janthina* when he had previously recorded Maugé as the collector. Finally he substituted 'my friend Lesueur' for 'my colleague Maugé' and 'Citizen Maugé' when recording the identity of the collector of a *Sepia* squid and of yet another crab (*Portunidae*) found on a piece of kelp. To be fair, Péron's official account suggests he was probably present on deck when these various species were taken. However, Jangoux argues that the unamended original draft of the memoir demonstrates that Péron, when still a modest student zoologist, 'respected' Baudin and 'appreciated' Maugé. But he argues that this was when he was 'far from the grandiloquent Péron, sure of himself, of his knowledge and of his judgments that one recognises a few years later'.[103]

During Péron's field research in the D'Entrecasteaux Channel and on Bruny and Maria islands, the expedition's indefatigable hydrographer Pierre Faure had carried out important surveys of Frederick Henry Bay, Tasman Peninsula (proving that it was not an island, as d'Entrecasteaux thought), Norfolk Bay, North Bay, Oyster Bay, Freycinet Peninsula and the coast of Tasmania to 42° latitude south. The *Géographe* and *Naturaliste* would revisit much of this coast after commencing a running survey north on 6 March. Off Cape Tourville, however, Baudin dispatched the hydrographer Boulanger with a boat crew of six under the command of Jean-Marie Maurouard (recently promoted from assistant helmsman to midshipman) to make a closer survey of the Van Diemen's Land coast. Unfortunately, the boat was soon out of sight of the mother ship. Péron blamed Baudin for inexplicably standing 'further out to sea';[104] but it seems likely that he simply tacked to maintain his northerly course in the face of a north-easterly wind.

That night, Baudin ordered rockets fired from the *Géographe* in an attempt to draw the attention of the missing boat, which had only two days' rations. Instead, he drew the attention of the *Naturaliste* and, during a clumsy attempt to pass close astern in the dark to hail for an explanation, her foremast rigging clipped the *Géographe*'s spritsail yard and tore it down. Fortunately the hulls did not collide. All efforts to find the survey boat— including requesting the assistance of a passing British sealing schooner, the *Endeavour*—came to naught in the following weeks. In formulating his search pattern, an anguished Baudin repeatedly sought the opinions of his officers and Péron, before lack of success led him to resume his northerly survey. During this period Baudin was twice laid up in his cabin with severe intestinal pain—perhaps related to his psychological state—and Henry de Freycinet had to take temporary command. It would be more than four months before the missing men would be reunited with the *Géographe*. But by then Baudin had had the added anxiety of four months' unplanned separation from the *Naturaliste*, which also disappeared from sight on the evening of 8 March.[105]

On 17 March, Baudin, having recovered from his severe colic, decided to make for Banks Strait (which separates the Kent Group from the Tasmanian mainland) and to sail to Waterhouse Island, the appointed rendezvous point in case of separation. On arrival, he was disappointed to find no sign of the *Naturaliste*. Then, thwarted in his attempts to reach Port Dalrymple because of storms and contrary currents in Bass Strait, he was driven north and then east before seeking shelter on the east coast of Flinders Island. When the weather improved, Baudin ordered a course for Wilson's Promontory before commencing his survey of the uncharted southern coast of New Holland.

— II —

Uncharted waters

What were it now to toss upon the waves,
The madden'd waves, and know no succour near;
The howling of the storm alone to hear.

ROBERT SOUTHEY, *O God! Have Mercy*
in This Dreadful Hour

ALTHOUGH numerous explorers and cartographers had suspected that Van Diemen's Land and New Holland were two separate land masses, the existence of an intervening strait was not confirmed until Surgeon George Bass sailed through it in 1798. Four years later, when the *Géographe* entered Bass Strait, its northern and southern boundaries and its gale-swept, island-strewn gateways were still not completely surveyed. Pierre Faure, hydrographer on the now-separated *Naturaliste*, would help fill in some of the gaps with his chart of Westernport, but it seems that François Péron falsely asserted, when he came to write his *Voyage*, that the expedition had sighted the entrance to Port Phillip Bay and revised the nomenclature on its charts only after learning that it had 'been already more particularly reconnoitred by the English brig, the *Lady Nelson*'.[1] Baudin did later amend his working chart with reference to 'Port Philipe' (*sic*; almost certainly during his visit to the British colony of Port Jackson), but his journal includes no mention whatsoever of the sighting of any such opening on that part of the coast.[2]

Baudin was aware neither of James Grant's west–east traverse on the sixty-ton *Lady Nelson* fifteen months earlier nor of his follow-up voyage of 1801 from Port Jackson—aided by the *émigré* French engineer and surveyor 'Francis' Barrallier. Although Baudin mistakenly thought his chart from Wilson's Promontory onwards was entirely new, he was able to make a more careful survey of many parts of the rugged Victorian coast first discovered by Grant. Indeed Baudin's expedition would bestow such names as Cape Reaumur (near Port Fairy) and Cape Duquesne and Descartes Bay (west of Portland) that remain to this day. It was only when the *Géographe* reached 140° 44′ E and sighted the inland peak of Mount Schank[3]—close to the present Victorian–South Australian border—on 2 April 1802 that Baudin truly began to explore waters previously uncharted by any other European. This coast filled Péron with dread. The reefs were 'like the teeth of a saw', and immense waves broke the length of the shore with 'dreadful noise'. The coast also appeared to offer Péron little comfort: 'the most hideous sterility is seen in every direction, and there is not the least appearance of there being even the smallest stream of fresh water.' He added: 'We may judge of the wretched situation of navigators who are so unfortunate as to be lost on these frightful shores.'[4]

As the *Géographe* traced the great arc of the bay that would be named in honour of the French icthyologist Bernard Lacépède and sailed along the narrow dune-robed neck of the Coorong, Péron was surprised that a shore which seemed to be characterised by the 'inhospitable appearance of monotony and sterility' was also well populated—judging by the number of Aboriginal fires he could see. Had he been able to land and cross the dunes, he would have found a teeming lagoon 145 kilometres long, 200 bird species—including an enormous colony of Australian pelicans—and a highly adapted arid-land coastal flora. Although the breakers and dunes masked these littoral treasures, the open sea still offered Péron a scientific bounty, and on 6 April he collected specimens of a portunid crab, salps and beroes; while at night, beneath a dark and brooding sky, he marvelled at the sea glowing with the phosphorescent bodies of many of these pelagic creatures.

On 8 April, shortly after harpooning nine large dolphins to restock their diminishing food supplies, the men of the *Géographe* sighted a ship. At first the approaching vessel was thought to be the missing *Naturaliste*, but it was soon learned that she was HMS *Investigator* and that her captain was the brilliant young navigator Matthew Flinders, whose survey of Banks Strait Baudin knew of and respected. A little more than a year older than François Péron, Flinders was born in Donington, Lincolnshire, the son of a surgeon. He joined the navy in 1789 and in 1791 sailed with William Bligh to Tahiti. While Péron had languished as a prisoner of war of the Prussians in June 1794, Flinders had seen victorious action under Lord Howe on HMS *Bellerophon* against the French Atlantic fleet of Villaret de Joyeuse. The following year he made his first voyage to Port Jackson with Surgeon Bass on HMS *Reliance* and then undertook surveys of the Georges River, Botany Bay and the coast of the Illawarra. Promoted lieutenant, he fulfilled surveys of the Furneaux Islands, a circumnavigation of Van Diemen's Land and hydrographic work on the Queensland coast between 1798 and 1799. In 1800, Flinders returned to England. Promoted commander, he was given command of HMS *Investigator* in 1801 and, like Baudin, was ordered to explore the still-unknown part of the southern coast of New Holland. Thus, when the *Géographe* met the *Investigator* in what would become known as Encounter Bay, the last remaining gap in the outline of the coast of New Holland had been filled in through their combined efforts from east and west.[5]

When Flinders sighted the *Géographe* he had cleared for action. Even when he ascertained the identity of the French vessel, he kept the *Investigator's* broadside trained on her. Ironically, France and Britain were not then at war, for the preliminaries of the brief Peace of Amiens had been signed six months before and the final treaty less than a fortnight earlier, but news travelled slowly in the early nineteenth century. Around 6.00 p.m., Flinders went aboard with the Scottish naturalist Robert Brown as a translator, although the conversation appears to have been largely in English. According to Brown, they stayed three-quarters of an hour. Flinders inspected Baudin's passport, but when Flinders extended his own, Baudin graciously returned it unopened. According to Robert Brown, Baudin provided Flinders with details of his work on the west coast of New Holland and the corrections he had made to the charts of Van Diemen's Land. He also spoke of the losses his expedition had suffered from desertion at the Ile de France and from disease at Timor. Furthermore, Baudin showed his guests many of the ethnographic sketches executed by the expedition's artists.[6]

Péron wrote that 'Captain Flinders showed great reserve on the subject of his particular operations',[7] but he does not appear to have actually been present in the great cabin during the meeting and presumably either repeated Baudin's assessment or embellished it. We do know that Baudin found Flinders reserved. Brown does not mention Péron in his notes, but recorded that Baudin spoke of a hundred boxes of natural history specimens aboard. He did not see any of them, and even the pots in Baudin's cabin contained only earth.[8]

Flinders returned the following morning to give Baudin 'various pieces of information concerning the coast that he had examined from Cape Leeuwin as far as here'.[9] They breakfasted together: Flinders in full uniform; Baudin, according to an uncharitable Midshipman Bougainville, 'looking like a robber'.[10] Baudin found Flinders 'much less reserved on his second visit than before', and the Englishman presented him with a number of charts published by Aaron Arrowsmith after their departure from Europe.[11] Baudin informed Flinders of his missing boat crew and asked the captain of the *Investigator* 'to give it all the help he could if he should chance to meet it'.[12] At no time does Flinders appear to have invited Baudin and his officers aboard the *Investigator*. Although Flinders summarised his cartographic achievements, to a considerable degree he appears to have spoken in generalities and was far less forthcoming than Baudin. The latter would soon complain, when looking for a port on Kangaroo Island that Flinders had only recently discovered: 'So far, it looks as if I misunderstood or misheard the latitude he gave me, for the land does not yet appear to run as far North as I thought I heard him say.'[13]

Twenty months later it was Flinders' turn to languish as a prisoner of war on the Ile de France. Although he would be released shortly before Péron's death, his account of his voyage was not published until he himself was on his deathbed in 1814. Péron's official account of the residual western part of the southern Australian coast was peppered with French toponyms where one might have expected an acknowledgement of the British navigator's priority. Although he died before seeing Flinders' published charts, Péron must have had some knowledge of Flinders' toponyms—such as Kangaroo Island—after the *Géographe*'s encounter with the *Investigator*, and he was apparently present when Flinders showed Baudin a draft chart at Port Jackson. Flinders, however, refused to think ill of Péron, whom he came to know personally; he was more inclined to blame the Napoleonic régime:

> How then came M. Péron to advance what was so contrary to truth? Was he a man destitute of all principle? My answer is, that I believe his candour to have been equal to his acknowledged abilities and that what he wrote was from over-ruling authority, and smote him to the heart … The motive for this aggression I do not pretend to explain. It may have originated in the desire to rival the British nation in the

honour of completing the discovery of the globe; or be intended as
the fore runner of a claim to possession of the countries so said to
have first been discovered by French navigators.[14]

Imperial pressure, or sycophancy, or both, as we shall see, might explain
Péron's failure to acknowledge Flinders' priority, but it is possible that
Péron, as a zoologist, simply adhered to the conventions of the natural
sciences. Regardless of whether a scientist is the first to discover, collect or
describe in manuscript form a plant or animal species, if he or she is delayed
in publishing, someone else has an opportunity. Even today, belatedly
published manuscript names are still regarded as mere synonyms.

For example, in 1792 and 1793, Labillardière collected numerous plant
species in Van Diemen's Land that belonged to entirely new genera and
to which he gave manuscript names. Unfortunately, he was delayed in
publishing his results because his specimens were taken from him—and
were not returned until the intervention of Sir Joseph Banks in 1796—
and because he needed time and money to complete the task. Indeed he
took between eight and fourteen years to publish his names and descriptions. Not surprisingly, in some cases he was pre-empted by botanists
working independently, such as Antonio José Cavanilles and Henry
Andrews.[15] No modern taxonomist would accuse Cavanilles or Andrews
of any moral infringement. Indeed the natural sciences would be thrown
into chaos if such publishing rules were not observed. Péron had to accept
similar pre-emption when Lamarck, Cuvier and Geoffroy Saint-Hilaire
published different names for species he had collected and already provisionally named in Van Diemen's Land and New Holland. As a zoologist
it is very possible that Péron believed toponymy and cartography should
be bound by the same rules and that Flinders, because of his internment
on the Ile de France, was simply too late.

The British hardly had the right to cast the first stone. Governor
King, clearly anxious that the French might establish a colony on the
D'Entrecasteaux Channel, persisted in referring to the waterway as 'Storm
Bay Passage', even in a letter to Baudin.[16] And in a letter to Lord Hobart,
of 24 June 1803, he acknowledged that it was called by 'the French
"Le Canal D'Entrecasteaux" to whom they attribute the discovery of
that passage'.[17]

After parting with Flinders, the *Géographe* anchored briefly off
Kangaroo Island and undertook surveys of the Gulf of St Vincent and the
gale-swept Spencer Gulf (respectively, Péron's 'Ile Decrès', 'Golfe Joséphine'

and 'Golfe Bonaparte'), before sailing on to Nuyts Archipelago. With most of the helmsmen ill, Henry de Freycinet asked Baudin to order the master carpenter and second caulker to serve at the helm. Instead, he ordered each of the midshipmen to spend an hour and a half at the wheel each day. When, with the exception of Charles Baudin (no relation to his superior), they refused because they considered it beneath their dignity, the expedition commander prohibited them from undertaking any duties on board.[18] Clearly a different kind of leadership was called for. Although the dutiful Midshipman Baudin was promoted,[19] the expedition commander willingly deprived himself of the services of all the other young trainee officers.

Friendless, isolated and ill with tuberculosis and the effects of malaria, Baudin appears to have compounded his estrangement from his men by withdrawing further into himself. After the winds thrice thwarted his attempt at a closer examination of the islands of St Peter and St Francis, Baudin sailed on to Cape Adieu, where lack of water had forced d'Entrecasteaux to end his survey of the southern coast. With growing numbers of scurvy cases (Péron wrote that 'already more than half our seamen were incapable of service'),[20] shortening daylight hours, little more than old planks and casks for firewood, and fresh water and food reserves seriously compromised, Baudin decided to break off his own survey of what Péron or his superiors would call 'Terre Napoléon'. Of their hardships at the time, Péron wrote unsparingly:

> Three quarters of a bottle of stinking water was our daily allowance: for more than a year we had not tasted wine; we had not even a single drop of brandy ... the biscuit served out to us was full of insects; all our salt provisions were putrid and rotten; and both the smell and taste were so offensive, that the almost famished seamen, sometimes preferred suffering all the extremities of want itself, to eating these unwholesome provisions, and even in the presence of the commander they often threw their allowance into the sea.[21]

Given his want of provisions, and with only thirty men fit enough to handle the vessel, by his own admission Baudin decided to make for Port Jackson, where he also hoped he might find his missing boat crew[22] and perhaps even the *Naturaliste*. Péron, however, would have us believe that Baudin's decision to sail via Van Diemen's Land, rather than directly through Bass Strait, 'spread a general consternation'.[23] Péron ignored the fact that desperately needed water and firewood could be had with certainty in Van Diemen's Land and that the open more southerly route to Port Jackson was safer and perhaps even faster than the unpredictable waters of Bass Strait. Yet Péron had grounds to question Baudin's rationale when the latter insisted on resuming his running survey of the coast of Van Diemen's Land, cut short by the disappearance of Boulanger's boat. Indeed Baudin later admitted the real reasons for his course in a letter written to the Minister of Marine from Port Jackson.[24]

After a cold, wet and squally passage, the *Géographe* altered course on 8 May and sighted the Tasmanian coast on the morning of 19 May. Baudin originally intended to enter the D'Entrecasteaux Channel, but the contrary winds forced him to round Fluted Cape—which Péron described as an 'enormous causeway of basaltic prisms'[25]—and anchor in Adventure Bay[26] on 20 May. Péron promptly went ashore with the first watering and wood-gathering party, accompanied by his friend the astronomer Pierre-François Bernier, and began to explore the bay. He made no contact with the indigenous inhabitants, but found 'numerous streams … besides several ponds and marshes, large enough to support several sorts of freshwater fish, which are found in great plenty'.[27] Péron must have reported this to the expedition commander, for Baudin wrote dismissively in his journal:

> Citizen Péron (who makes fresh discoveries, or always thinks he does) claimed to have found a river that no one had seen before, since none of the explorers who have examined this area better than we have mentioned it. However that may be, water was abundant there, and in all the ravines there was no lack of it. It seems that rain had already fallen heavily along this part of the coast.[28]

Péron went ashore again the next day but, as on his previous landing, was unable to make contact with the Aborigines, whom he suspected had moved to the mainland. Aside from fresh water and firewood, fish were plentiful at Adventure Bay. Unfortunately, after such a lean diet, a number of the men over-ate and suffered stomach pains and a relapse of dysentery. (Baudin's own cook would die from the recurrence of his illness.) Given the good fishing, it is perhaps not surprising that Péron's most significant achievement at Adventure Bay was ichthyological. He collected and described the perlon, or seven-gilled shark, which he named *Notorhynchus cepedianus*[29] in honour of Bernard Lacépède, author of *Histoire naturelle des poissons*.

Because his crew was so tired from its exertions ashore, Baudin decided not to set sail that night. Instead, he waited until the following morning and even excused the men their watches. Despite the exhausted state of his men, Baudin stubbornly resolved to continue his running survey of the east coast of Van Diemen's Land with all the extra shiphandling this required. Unfortunately for Baudin, his vain attempts to find Cape Tourville exposed him to further censure and ridicule. Louis de Freycinet would later write in volume iii of the official account: 'The *Géographe* remained on the coast for thirteen days, vainly occupied in verifying some geographical positions already fixed by our earlier operations.'[30] There is no doubt that men were now suffering aboard the *Géographe* for no scientific gain, but there are no grounds to accept Péron's exaggerated assertion that 'every day the sea consumed one of our unfortunate companions'.[31] In fact only three men died between Adventure Bay and Port Jackson and, of these, only Baudin's cook died in Tasmanian waters; the others died off the New South Wales coast.[32] Nevertheless, the weather once more turned bad and created a special purgatory for the scurvy-ridden crew of the *Géographe*. Péron's account of life aboard at the time (omitted from the English translation of 1809) deserves to be quoted at length:

On June 2 and 3 the weather became very bad. Showers of rain succeeded each other incessantly, and squalls blew with a violence that we had never experienced before. On the 4th, during the whole day, the weather was so frightful that, accustomed as we had become to the fury of tempests, this last made us forget all that had preceded. Never before had the squalls followed each other with such rapidity; never had the billows been so tumultuous. Our ship, smitten by them, at every instant seemed about to break asunder under the shock of the impact. In the twinkling of an eye our foremast snapped and fell overboard, and all the barricading that we had erected to break the force of the wind was smashed. Even our anchors were lifted from the catheads despite the strength of the ropes which held them. It was necessary to make them more secure, and the ten men, who were all that were left us to work the ship, were engaged in this work during a great part of the day. During the night the tempest was prolonged by furious gales. The rain fell in torrents; the sea rose even higher; and enormous waves swept over our decks. The black darkness did not permit the simplest work to be done without extreme difficulty, and the whole of the interior of the vessel was flooded by sea-water. Four men were compelled to enter the sick bay, leaving only six in a condition to carry out the orders of the officer on the bridge, and these unfortunates themselves dropped from sheer exhaustion and fatigue. Between decks, the sick men lay about, and the air was filled with their groans. A picture more harrowing never presented itself to the imagination. The general consternation added to the horror of it. We had nearly reached the point of being unable to control the movements of the ship amidst the fury of the waves; parts of the rigging were broken with every manoeuvre; and despite all our efforts we could scarcely shift our sails. For a long time our commandant had had no rest. It was absolutely necessary to get out of these stormy seas at the extremity of the southern continent, and hasten on our course for Port Jackson.[33]

Baudin responded to the anger of his scurvy-ridden men and 'the lamentations of the scientists, whose fear of dying had made them lose their heads'[34] with repeated recriminations against his officers, whom he accused of past negligence that necessitated renewed surveys and delays. But for all Péron's past hyperbole, there can be no doubt of the parlous state of the *Géographe*. By 4 June, even Baudin, struggling to retain effective command, was forced to admit that 'there were only four men able to remain on deck, including the officer of the watch'. He added: 'That decided me to sail off the wind and make for Port Jackson, for we were no longer in a position to keep the sea.'[35]

— 12 —

Port Jackson

Here she a while may make her safe abode,
Till she repaired have her tackles spent,
And wants supplide; and then againe abroad
On the long voiage whereto she is bent:
Well may she speede, and fairely finish her intent.

EDMUND SPENCER, The Faerie Queene

THE *Géographe*, with a skeleton crew for each watch, managed to reach the weathered sandstone heads of Port Jackson, New South Wales, on 17 June 1802. From a departing whaler, Baudin learned of the signing of the peace between Britain and France, that the *Naturaliste* had visited Port Jackson briefly and that she had Boulanger's boat crew with her. His spirits must have soared at this news. Péron, however, would have us believe that this was the nadir of the expedition and that the *Géographe* was incapable of entering port until a large English longboat came to her rescue on the orders of Governor Philip Gidley King: '… having correctly judged by our manoeuvres that we had need of most urgent assistance … a pilot and men necessary to bring us into port.'[1] Matthew Flinders also wrote that 'Captain Baudin arrived on the 20th and a boat was sent from the *Investigator* to assist in towing the ship up to the Cove'.[2]

Péron's ignominious portrait of the expedition—requiring British rescue at the Heads—was rightly questioned by Frank Horner, who asserted that it often took an arriving vessel a number of days to enter the Heads when faced with unfavourable winds and that it was also a common occurrence for a pilot to assist those unfamiliar with the port. More pointedly, Horner argued that the assistance rendered by a boat from the *Investigator* refers 'not to the entry from the heads, but to the events of the following morning, when the *Géographe* shifted her anchorage'.[3] Furthermore, Horner demonstrated that the ship was actually 'towed only the short distance to the fairway, where it continued under sail' and concluded that neither the *Géographe*'s logbook nor Engineer Ronsard's journal 'suggests a ship so disabled as to need assistance in coming to anchor or shifting its anchorage'.[4]

Although the *Naturaliste* had departed Port Jackson on 17 May, Hamelin had left Lieutenant Pierre Milius behind because of ill-health. From him, Baudin learned of Hamelin's efforts to find the *Géographe*, of the *Naturaliste*'s surveys in Bass Strait (including Pierre Faure's thorough charting of Westernport) and of the reunion with Boulanger's boat crew shortly after it had been rescued by the English brig *Harrington*. Hamelin waited more than three weeks for the *Géographe* to arrive in Port Jackson; when she failed to appear, he made a seemingly desperate decision to sail to the Ile de France. However, the slowness of the *Naturaliste* and her meagre stores—which soon reduced her crew to a pathetic and fast-diminishing diet of boiled wheat—forced Hamelin to reconsider. Despite having sailed 'several hundred leagues', the *Géographe*'s rat-infested consort returned to Port Jackson on 26 June.[5] The reunion with the *Géographe* at Neutral Bay was joyous and surprisingly free of recriminations.

Péron was surprised that the arrival of the French at Port Jackson 'did not excite so much surprise amongst the colonists' as might have been expected.[6] Yet he and his companions were 'completely astonished' at the flourishing state of the far-flung British colony and the beauty of the harbour. Nascent Sydney was located beneath two hills with a rivulet (the Tank Stream) flowing between them. Péron found 'this infant town … at once agreeable and picturesque'. The former soldier and the veteran of the siege of Landau cast his eyes over the colony's defensive batteries, which had recently been upgraded by the Toulon-born *émigré* engineer Francis Barrallier. And not surprisingly, for a product of the Paris medical school, Péron also surveyed the hospital buildings, where twenty-three scurvy cases from the *Géographe* were soon transferred with the permission of Governor King.[7]

Péron was impressed by the fine warehouse at the quay and the private docks where a local ship-building industry, which used indigenous timbers, had taken root.[8] There were also large storehouses, an observatory, two fine windmills, an imposing walled prison and an armoury in front of which the 'numerous and well-composed' members of the New South Wales Corps paraded each morning. Although the garrison no doubt reminded him of his days in military service, the coffee-house 'maintained by subscription' and frequented by the 'principal civil and military officers' must also have reminded him of his parents' café in Cérilly, for he noted that it offered billiards 'at which any person may play, free of expense'.[9]

On the western end of the garrison's parade ground was the Lieutenant Governor's residence and adjoining it 'a vast garden', which Péron declared was 'worth the attention both of the philosopher and the naturalist, on account of the great number of useful vegetables which are cultivated in it, and which have been procured from every part of the world'.[10] This was the domain of Lieutenant Colonel William Paterson, a Scot who became Péron's firm friend. In his youth Paterson had visited South Africa and made four journeys into the interior that not only heightened his early interest in botany but also became the subject of a well-regarded travel book, which had been translated into French.[11] He had served in the army in India and had arrived in Sydney as a captain in the newly formed New South Wales Corps in October 1791. As commander of the garrison on Norfolk Island, Paterson had collected botanical, geological and entomo-logical specimens and maintained his long-standing correspondence with Sir Joseph Banks. Back in Britain he had been promoted to lieutenant colonel and elected a fellow of the Royal Society, before returning to Sydney in late 1799 with orders to investigate the rum trade among the New South Wales Corps.[12]

This trade in spirits briefly embroiled members of Baudin's expedition. The scandal broke after accusations were made by Captain Anthony Fenn Kemp that the French had resold brandy Governor King had allowed them to purchase from the recently arrived *Atlas*, whose unwelcome cargo the Governor had forbidden from landing in an attempt to restrict the liquor trade among his officers. Kemp appears to have been motivated by a desire to discredit the Governor and re-establish the trading right of his fellow officers. The truth was that Ensigns Joseph Saint-Cricq and Louis de Freycinet had merely exchanged rum from their daily ration for fresh vegetables from an ex-convict named Chapman, a legitimate transaction given the dearth of coinage in the colony and the use of spirits as the *de facto* local currency. Kemp was forced to apologise, but was subsequently mercilessly lampooned in a caricature probably executed by Nicolas Petit.[13] Nevertheless, he enjoyed good relations with a number of officers from the *Naturaliste* who were freemasons and with whom he is believed to have convoked the first Masonic meeting in Australia.

Earlier there had been yet another storm in a tea cup when the French were accused of flying the British ensign discourteously on their yard-arm (in fact the place of honour for the French national flag), in response to a salute extended to the *Géographe* by other vessels in the harbour on the occasion of the French republican new year's day. None of this was recorded in Baudin's journal, for he did not make any entries during his sojourn in Sydney, but lengthy correspondence over the matter survives.[14] Péron and his companions were fortunate that Governor King, a gracious francophile, usually wrote to Baudin in French and avoided further misunderstandings. The French were also fortunate that King offered 'every assistance'[15] to fulfil Baudin's request to revictual the expedition with 'biscuits, flour, salt meat, spiritous liquors, fresh meat, vegetables ... from the Government or private stores'.[16] The men were also able to buy new clothes, make repairs and carry their arms during their excursions. Furthermore, Governor King furnished interpreters and guides (who appear to have kept Government House well informed of French activities) and a guard to protect the French observatory tents, erected near those of the *Investigator*, on the 'north point of the eastern bank of Sydney Cove'. Little wonder Péron declared that 'the English government behaved to us with such generosity, that they acquired our warmest gratitude'.[17]

However, the arrival of Alexandre Josselin Lecorre on yet another French ship, the *Entreprise*,[18] on 9 September 1802, began to try Governor King's patience and generosity—especially when he realised that the ninety-ton vessel's cargo was largely made up of spirits and wine. Lecorre arrived with a crew of twelve men and an American supercargo named Nathaniel Cogswell.[19] Because his ship had been savaged by a violent storm and much damage had been done to her sails and bulwarks, Lecorre was grudgingly given permission to sell as much of his cargo in Port Jackson as was necessary to pay for repairs. This amounted to about a third of his cargo of spirits and half of his lading of wine. He then asked for permission to go sealing in Bass Strait. Governor King, ever suspicious of French ambitions, flatly refused him. Apparently facing financial disaster, Lecorre managed to secure the intercession of Baudin. King finally relented on the condition that permission would not be given again and that the sealing would be confined to the Two Sisters in the Furneaux Group, which offered no permanent anchorage.

Lecorre sailed south, on 4 October, to try his luck in these inhospitable waters. On 27 October 1802, after a week off the Sisters, he was surprised by a storm and the *Entreprise* was wrecked,[20] apparently 'while anchored in the foul bay on the east side of these islands'.[21] Lecorre and five other members of the crew drowned. Although Péron was later angered by the territorial claims and restrictive trading régime of the British, for the moment he remained positively disposed to Governor King's administration. His admiration for what he saw as a valuable British social experiment in the antipodes was also partly engendered by a number of important penological observations he made at Port Jackson. Reflecting on the convicts, he wrote:

> The population of the colony was to us a new subject of astonishment and contemplation. Perhaps there never was a more worthy object of study presented to the philosopher;—never was the influence of social institutions proved in a manner more striking and honourable to the distant country in question. Here we found united, like one family, those banditti, who had so long been the terror of their mother country: repelled from European society, and sent off to the extremity of the globe; placed from the very hour of their exile, in a state between the certainty of chastisement, and the hope of a better fate; incessantly subjected to an inspection, as inflexible as it is active, they have been compelled to abandon their anti-social manners; and the majority of them, having expiated their crimes, by a hard period of slavery, have been restored to the rank which they held amongst their fellow-men. Obliged to interest themselves in the maintenance of order and justice, for the purpose of preserving the property which they have acquired; while they behold themselves in the situation of husbands and fathers, they have the most interesting and powerful motives for becoming good members of the community in which they exist.[22]

Péron's observations on the redemptive qualities of the British penal colony would have a resonance for many years to come in France, because French perceptions of Britain's transport of convicts to her Australian colonies shaped arguments for and against the establishment of a French 'Botany Bay'. Colin Forster has written that Péron's glowing notes on the convict system in New South Wales, which 'remained the only important observations by a Frenchman until the 1820s[,] ... were of particular importance in influencing early French opinion'.[23] Thus Péron stands at the head of a procession of French thinkers who saw the Australian example as a moral and economic triumph and paved the way for the transportation of French convicts to Guiana from 1852 and New Caledonia from 1864.

Marnie Bassett, in her biography of Anna King, the wife of Governor Philip Gidley King, declared that Péron's report on the colony, written from 'a political or would-be conqueror's point of view ... checked against other contemporary accounts, gives a much too glowing picture of the state of the settlement at the time—it was seen with the eyes of envy, looking through rose-coloured spectacles'.[24] Péron did eventually draft a preliminary politico-military memoir on Port Jackson more than four months after arriving back at the Ile de France[25] and then a more substantial version en route (or shortly after returning) to France addressed to his former teacher at the Ecole de Santé, Antoine de Fourcroy.[26] Furthermore, part of this memoir was published in his *Voyage*.[27] Yet, when he was actually in Port Jackson, France and Britain were at peace. There is no evidence that he believed that renewed hostilities were imminent. Nevertheless, he, Hamelin and apparently also Louis de Freycinet,[28] did appraise the weaknesses and strengths of the colony's fortifications—almost an involuntary reflex for anyone with a military background—but they saw only what the British allowed them to see. And it is a telling fact that some limits were placed on him. For example, when Péron sought to accompany Francis Barrallier during his attempt to cross the Blue Mountains,[29] he was refused permission by Governor King.[30] Although the outbreak of war ultimately influenced the recommendations Péron offered for any future campaign in the region, it seems likely that, regardless, he would have drafted a detailed account on the colony after spending five months in residence there.

In her criticisms of Péron, Marnie Bassett does not allow for his personal experience of poverty and crime in Europe. Furthermore, it should be remembered that Péron had spent enough time in garrison towns and in Paris to know something of the unfortunate life of prostitutes and to see that the example of New South Wales offered some hope for such women. Hence he wrote:

> ... those who were wretched prostitutes, have imperceptibly been brought to a regular mode of life, and now form intelligent and laborious mothers of families. But it is not merely in the moral character of the women, that these important alterations are discoverable,

but also in their physical condition, the results of which are worthy the consideration, both of the legislator and the philosopher. For example, everyone knows that the common women of great capitals, are in general unfruitful … though we are unable to assign any other cause, than a sort of insusceptibility of conception … After residing a year or two at Port Jackson, most of the English prostitutes become remarkably fruitful.[31]

This led Péron to draw a strange physiological conclusion: 'that an excess of sexual intercourse destroys the sensibility of the female organs, to such a degree, as to render them incapable of conception; while to restore the frame to its pristine activity, nothing is necessary but to renounce those fatal excesses.'[32] Regardless of the fact that Paris, then a city of 700 000, still had 4000 foundling births reported annually during the revolutionary period (a good proportion of which must have been produced by prostitutes),[33] Péron neither suspected that malnourished and abused prostitutes might cease to menstruate or be more prone to miscarriage, nor guessed that the very nature of contractual sexual relations might not be entirely conducive to conception. Nor does he appear to have reflected on the age—and thus the relative infertility—of many prostitutes, let alone haphazard contraception and the deleterious effects of venereal disease on the reproductive system.

Although Péron was not allowed to accompany Barrallier on his attempted crossing of the Blue Mountains, he was able to range widely. His first major excursion was south to the northern shore of Botany Bay. Péron's attention was also drawn to the area's remarkable flora: 'Various species of *Hakea, Styphelia, Eucalyptus, Banksia, Embothryum* and *Casuarina*, grow amdist these sands, and large spaces are occupied entirely with the *Xanthorea* [sic].' He appears to have turned back when he encountered the extensive marshes 'formed by the brackish waters of Cook's River, towards the north, and of George[s] River to the south'. Nevertheless, the banks were resplendent with 'a thousand species of trees and shrubs'.

Péron's contact with the indigenous inhabitants during this excursion appears to have been fleeting. He wrote: 'In the distance may be perceived the smoke of a few huts, belonging to the unfortunate hordes of natives who exist on these desolate shores.'[34] Yet his account is significant for his acknowledgement of the indigenous name for Botany Bay, *Gwea*, and his implicit belief that the Gwea Gal inhabited both shores of the bay rather than just the southern shore, as has been asserted by some ethno-historians.

His assertion that Bennilong was a Gwea Gal[35] also lends weight to those, such as Norman Tindale, who placed them among the Eora language group, rather than the northernmost horde of the Dharawal-speaking people, as Peter Turbet and others have asserted.[36] Péron also noted the presence of a kiln 'for the preparation of lime, which is made from the shells that abound on this part of the coasts', but did not speculate on the source of these shells, almost certainly vast Aboriginal middens—the archaeological heritage of Sydney—burned and crushed for mortar.

Péron tells us that, in the company of Jérôme Bellefin, the surgeon of the *Naturaliste*, he 'took the earliest opportunity' to visit Parramatta.[37] The two were guided by a sergeant of the New South Wales Corps. Péron conjures a romantic image of the unsealed Parramatta Road: '... opened through vast forests, that were never before assailed by the axe, this grand road appears at a distance, like an immense avenue of foliage and verdure. A charming freshness, and an agreeable shade always prevail in this continuous bower, the silence of which is interrupted only, by the singing and chirping of the richly plumed parakeets and other birds which inhabit it.'[38] As the road is now a vast expanse of asphalt unceasingly choked with automotive traffic and devoid of any natural canopy, one would require more than an hallucinant to imagine it thus!

At Rose Hill, which neighbours Parramatta, Péron was deeply impressed by the already highly productive merino wool industry and the success of other domesticated European agricultural animals. Named by Arthur Phillip in honour of Sir George Rose, then Secretary of the Treasury, Rose Hill in turn gave its name to the Rosella (*Platycercus* sp.)—almost certainly 'the richly plumed parakeets' Péron had seen—for they were originally known as 'Rose Hillers'.[39]

In the area around Parramatta, Péron added 'more than 150 new species of insects to his collections',[40] including forty species of butterflies and moths, and an emerald-coloured 'Cetonia' with a golden lyre-shaped pattern on its back. The latter was probably a fiddler beetle, *Eupoecila australasiae,* common in heaths and woodlands in south-eastern Australia, which the British naturalist Edward Donovan first published as *Cetonia australasiae* in 1805.[41] Péron also collected numerous reptiles, including the type specimen of the bearded dragon lizard to which he gave the name *Stellio discosomus*, now a *nomen nudum* because it was accompanied by insufficient descriptive detail in his *Voyage*. Ultimately it was Georges Cuvier who published a new name and a more detailed description in 1829—

Agama barbata (= *Pogona barbata*)[42]—based on the specimen preserved in alcohol by Péron and Lesueur.[43] The environs of Parramatta were also the source of several tree-frogs. In his *Voyage* he proposed names for several species of what he considered to be the genus *Hyla*, including one with striking lemon-coloured markings, which he named *H. citripoda*.[44] Once again, because of inadequate descriptive detail, his *H. citripoda* is regarded as a *nomen nudum*.[45] However, Péron's specimen does have type significance, because forty years later the French herpetologists André Duméril and Gabriel Bibron used it as the basis for the description of their *Hyla lesueurii* (= *Litoria lesueurii*).[46] He also collected the green tree-frog, which had already been described by Surgeon John White of the First Fleet as *Rana caerulea*[47] (= *Litoria caerulea*)[48] and a specimen of the green and golden bell frog considered a syntype for René Lesson's *Hyla aurea* (= *Litoria aurea*),[49] described and published in 1829.[50] And it was very probably in Parramatta that he collected the Péron's marsh frog, *Lymnodynastes peroni*, named in his honour by Duméril and Bibron in 1841.[51] Light brown or grey, with dark brown stipes, it is still found in the Lower Blue Mountains.

While in Parramatta Péron met a Frenchman named 'James' Larra who had been transported for life for the theft of a silver tankard from a tavern and had arrived in Sydney on the Second Fleet in June 1790. He was fortunate: sixty-eight of his fellow convicts on the *Scarborough* died during the voyage. Born in 1749, Larra was a Jew (probably from a Sephardic family who fled the Spanish Inquisition and settled in Bayonne). He might have gone to Britain, where he was convicted, through his employment as a cargo shipping agent. Gracious and well behaved, he received a conditional pardon a little more than four years after arriving in New South Wales. By the time Péron met him, he had already received a full and final pardon and had become the first publican in Parramatta.[52] For Péron, Larra was an example of the reformative power of the British convict system. According to Péron, he

> directed his industry to other objects, and engaged in commercial speculations; which succeeded beyond his hopes. In short, by the most honourable means, he gradually acquired a fortune; and he is now generally considered as one of the richest landholders in New South Wales; while the regularity of his conduct, and the honesty of his character, have caused him to be respected by the principal civil and military officers of the colony.[53]

Péron also noted that Larra had two other Frenchmen among his employees who were 'overcome with melancholy and remorse'.

In Larra's Parramatta establishment, Péron enjoyed exquisite food prepared by 'an excellent French cook, a native of Paris' and served on fine plates with the best Bordeaux and wines of Portugal, Madeira and the Cape in the purest flint glasses. Péron, nevertheless, expected warmer and more generous hospitality, for he was surprised that his countrymen charged him and his guide, despite a letter of introduction from the Lieutenant Governor. Although Colonel Paterson would show resentment at this apparent lack of graciousness, Péron conceded that the sum did 'not appear too much, considering the sumptuous manner in which we were entertained'.[54]

Péron's visit to Larra's tavern might have been significant for another reason. It was the favourite drinking place of the Irish nationalist leader 'General' Joseph Holt, whom Péron might have met.[55] And was it perhaps at Parramatta that Péron saw Irish rebels with 'their eyes bathed in tears, pouring out curses against England, imploring Bonaparte and calling for the moment of vengeance upon their oppressors'?[56] Given the number of Irish deportees in the colony, it is little wonder that Péron would consider them potential allies when his thoughts turned to possible military action in the Pacific after war resumed between France and Britain. Holt was later suspected of involvement in the Irish convict rising of 1804 and was moved to Norfolk Island.

Departing Larra's establishment, Péron and Bellefin embarked on a packet boat in front of the barracks and began a leisurely return to Sydney Town via the Parramatta River at a cost of a shilling each. The river was the main conduit for shipping timber and agricultural produce down to Sydney. With its limited catchment, tidal rhythms and deep saline reach, the Parramatta River did not remind Péron of the Allier in his native Bourbonnais. Nevertheless, he was impressed by the rural idyll presented before him:

> Here the European has already shown that he exists, by his habitation and the extensive portions of soil which he has cultivated. Here, at the verdant entrance of a stream, is discovered the humble cabin of a new colonist; while the distant sound of the hatchet announces his efforts and activity: farther on, the eye is attracted by a natural meadow, in which wander the oxen, cows, and horses, of a newly established farm; and the picture is completed by the ripening harvest of newly

cultivated fields. Often on the summit of a picturesque hillock, may be discerned a large and elegant mansion, surrounded by more considerable cultivated lands, and covered by greater numbers of flocks and labourers—all indicating it to be the property of a rich and industrious owner.[57]

On their way down to Long Nose Point and the flooded estuary of Sydney Harbour they passed a prosperous property belonging to the paymaster William Cox,[58] whom Péron had already met through Colonel Paterson. When Cox became aware that Péron and Bellefin were aboard the packet boat, he rowed out to invite them both to dine with him and to spend the night. Péron tells us they could not 'resist his friendly solicitation'.

Because of the duration of the expedition and the substantial number of specimens so far collected, Baudin decided to send them back to France in the *Naturaliste* in the care of Captain Hamelin along with all his ailing crew members and the midshipmen Bougainville, Maurouard and Brue, who had incurred their commander's wrath.[59] The return of the *Naturaliste* would also enable a full report of his geographical achievements so far. Consequently, Péron tells us that he and Lesueur

> suspended all our intended researches and for three weeks employed ourselves day and night in this delicate and difficult branch of our duty. It may be imagined what we had to undergo, when it is known that we arranged in the most methodical manner more than 40,000 animals of all sorts and descriptions, collected in various parts during a period of two years. Thirty-three large packing cases were filled with these collections, which were more valuable and numerous than any voyagers had ever sent to Europe, and which, when only partially displayed in the house which I occupied with M. Bellefin, excited the admiration of all the learned Englishmen in the colony ...[60]

To replace the *Naturaliste*, Baudin decided to purchase 'a little vessel of thirty tons', which he named *Casuarina* after the timber from which it was largely constructed.[61]

After arranging the natural history collections aboard the *Naturaliste*, Péron once again travelled up to Parramatta. This time he was accompanied by Colonel Paterson and Lieutenant Thomas Laycock, son of the colony's quartermaster, and was met by Mrs Paterson and her carriage before heading north to Castle Hill. There he visited yet another property belonging to William Cox and once more devoted himself to collecting beetles and reptiles. Ironically, he found insect life 'much more scarce' in the uncleared forest and speculated that this was because of Aborginal fires, which destroyed 'an enormous quantity of eggs, as well as larvae and perfect insects'.[62] Nevertheless, there were fires aplenty in the area around Castle Hill, the colony's youngest settlement. As Péron put it: 'Six hundred convicts were continually employed in felling trees, to open roads through the forests; and in twenty quarters immense volumes of flame and smoke may be seen rising, produced by the burning of new concessions.'[63] And there were men, too, who burned inside with the idea of freedom. 'These were the same workers', Péron wrote in a footnote, 'the majority Irish, deported as revolutionaries, who, a short time after our departure, the English papers stated to have revolted spontaneously, and joined other bodies of their countrymen.'[64]

Péron was referring to the Battle of Vinegar Hill, named after a battle fought in Ireland during the rebellion of 1798. During the night of 4 March 1804, two hundred convicts overpowered their guards at the Castle Hill Government Farm with the intention of marching on Windsor in order to liberate other convicts, capture additional arms and ammunition, then attack Sydney Town. Their ultimate aim was to capture vessels in Port Jackson and sail to freedom. Unfortunately for these brave Irish patriots, the alarm was raised in Parramatta. Major George Johnston mobilised the garrison and sought to parley with the rebel leaders under a flag of truce only to clap pistols to their heads, before routing their followers at Rouse Hill near the existing Castlebrook Lawn Cemetery.[65] Ten of the rebel leaders were executed, and their bodies were left hanging from the gibbet for several months as a grim warning to their compatriots. Others were flogged mercilessly with up to 150 lashes.

It was at Castle Hill that Colonel Paterson introduced Péron to a mysterious Frenchman whom he referred to as 'M. De La Clampe'. He was, in fact, Pierre Lalouette de Vernicourt, a former French army officer who had served on the Ile de France and in Pondicherry, but—with the advent of Revolution—surrendered to British forces under John Floyd, then joined the military service of one or more Indian princes before growing vines at Chingleput near Madras and seeking asylum in England as an *émigré*. According to Paterson, as reported by Péron, Vernicourt refused to 'bear arms against his nation', but 'disgusted with a life of indolence, so little congenial with his inclination and former habits, he solicited permission to establish himself in this distant climate'.[66] Vernicourt arrived in New South Wales on the *Minorca* in December 1801 under the name 'Chevalier de Clambe', although he was never invested in the order of Saint-Louis.[67] In February 1802 he was granted 100 acres of land at Castle Hill by Governor King and assigned six convicts whom, Péron tells us, were 'almost naked', like their French master. There he built what Péron described variously as a 'modest habitation' and a 'rustic manor', the interior of which was an 'agreeable union of extreme simplicity and a sort of elegance, which proved the delicate taste of its owner, at the same time that he was an utter stranger to every sort of luxury'.[68] Just five feet two inches tall, with black eyes, very dark complexion and a greatly protruding underlip, Vernicourt lived an isolated and frugal existence. Although Vernicourt is said to have largely shunned colonial society, Matthew Flinders encountered him in August 1803, as did the visiting French merchant Louis Charles Ruault Coutance.[69] At Castle Hill Vernicourt set about raising cattle, sheep and pigs and planting wheat, maize, coffee and cotton.

Péron, in many respects a conservative repulsed by the excesses of the Revolution, was drawn to this *émigré* soldier. When Vernicourt asked for news of France, Péron roundly sang the praises of Bonaparte and would have us believe that his hermetic compatriot heard his recital 'with ecstasy' and 'offered up his vows to heaven for the happiness and preservation of the First Consul'.[70] This is surprising since, when Vernicourt sought permission from the Duke of Portland to settle in New Holland in July 1800, he described France as being 'in the hands of an infamous Corsican'.[71] But by mid-1802, he might have learned of the Concordat with Pope Pius VII signed on 10 September 1801 and perhaps changed his opinion.[72] Indeed the Concordat with the Church might also have laid the foundations for Péron's own Bonapartist sympathies.

Yet Vernicourt does not appear to have given away much of his true identity. He was in fact the son of Pierre Lalouette, regent of the Paris medical faculty for fifty years, famous for his description of the anatomy of the thyroid gland and for his highly successful method of treating syphilis with mercury vapour.[73] Péron would very likely have heard of this distinguished doctor, but made no mention of him. Poor Vernicourt would never see his family again and died of apoplexy on the night of 4 June 1804. Ironically, he was on his way to a dance at Government House—

one of the very few social invitations he appears to have accepted in the colony and one that fate prevented him from keeping. A number of eligible young ladies might have been disappointed, but they might have been less so had they known that he already had a wife and children abandoned on the shores of the Indian Ocean. And although he assumed the title of chevalier and the rank of lieutenant colonel, he had never been promoted beyond captain.[74]

On returning to Parramatta, Péron met the remarkable, but temperamental, Yorkshire-born plant collector and explorer George Caley. Largely self-educated, Caley had worked as a gardener in Manchester, Chelsea and Kew. After repeatedly cajoling Sir Joseph Banks, he had gained official employment as a plant collector in New South Wales and had arrived in the colony on the *Speedy*, along with Francis Barrallier, in April 1800. Caley was provided with a house at Parramatta where he kept his herbarium and tended the government garden established by Colonel Paterson in the domain of Government House. This garden was used to naturalise useful plants imported from other parts of the world and for Caley to nurture seedlings before transporting them to Kew Gardens in England. Nearby Government House was a recently completed two-storey, stuccoed-brick residence where Caley was permitted to dry his herbarium specimens. The building, with faux-marble floors and fireplaces, which Péron visited, still stands, albeit with Francis Greenway's neo-classical portico and John Watts' extensions.

Parramatta was also Caley's base for many exploratory journeys in New South Wales, which enabled him to make a significant contribution to geographical knowledge and send vast numbers of plants and seeds to Britain. In 1798 he had declared: 'What few talents I am possessed of are not to be known by seeing me upon a carpet, under the roof of a conservatory, nor upon a fine gravel walk in a garden. Let me be tried upon the lofty mountain, the dark and intricate wood, the wide-extended plain, the marsh and peaty bog.'[75] It is not surprising, therefore, that Péron was attracted to the company of this remarkable energetic naturalist as a local guide; together they set out, along with William Paterson, to collect natural history specimens on the outskirts of Parramatta. Péron tells us that his 'philosophic colleagues' also gave him numerous other specimens he had not been able to find himself.

It was also through Colonel Paterson that Péron met the Reverend Samuel Marsden, sometimes referred to as the 'flogging parson', at Parramatta. Later, in his secret report to Captain-General Decaen at the Ile de

France, he would describe him as a cultivator 'as rich as [he is] vigilant' and one of those who furnished him with 'precious information'.[76]

On his second visit to Parramatta, Péron met still more French residents: two vignerons (or purported vignerons), Antoine Landrien and François Duriault or du Riveau. They were former prisoners of war in Portsmouth who arrived in Port Jackson on 21 November 1800 on the *Royal Admiral*. Although British sources indicate that they were from Nantes,[77] Péron wrote that they were from Bordeaux. And although their wine-making efforts at Parramatta were unimpressive (despite planting 12 000 vines), Péron wrote prophetically: 'it is certain that the English government will not abandon the culture of the vine, till the last extremity, and that it will make every sacrifice to ensure success, which would soon be of the greatest advantage to its country.'[78] Landrien left the colony after planting another thirty acres at Castle Hill, and Governor King expelled Duriault for his involvement with the Irish convicts of the Parramatta area.[79]

Yet another Frenchman Péron recorded meeting in the colony was a 'Monsieur Morand', who with 'extravagant fanaticism' attempted to clothe his counterfeiting crimes in patriotism, asserting that he had attempted to destroy Britain through 'finances' rather than 'arms' along with an Irish accomplice, likewise influenced by a supposedly 'noble patriotism'. Probably closer to the mark was his admitted desire 'to be a partner in the Bank of England, without putting in any stock'.[80] 'Morand' was almost certainly Ferdinand Meurant, who hailed originally from the Champagne region before his conviction in Ireland. When Péron met him, he had already received a conditional pardon and owned land on the Hawkesbury. Meurant received a full pardon in June 1803 and married in Parramatta in May 1811. There can be little doubt of his Bonapartist sympathies, for he gave his son Ferdinand the middle name 'Napoleon'.[81]

During Péron's Parramatta and Castle Hill excursions, his 'worthy friend' Lesueur made a rich zoological collection of two hundred bird and quadruped specimens and 'a great number of sketches and paintings'.[82] Similarly, the mineralogists Depuch and Bailly conducted wide-ranging geological studies that gave them an understanding of the strata underlying Sydney and Parramatta, including the fossiliferous Narrabean shale formation. But Depuch was now ailing, and Baudin transferred him to the *Naturaliste* so that he could return to France early. He was joined by Surgeon James Thomson and his 'wife',[83] given passage to Europe at the request of Governor King.

Meanwhile Baudin continued to alienate his remaining friends with his manner of command and his failure to support and promote such dedicated officers as François Ronsard. These tensions were also noticed by his British hosts: Governor King, for example, thought it diplomatic not to invite Lieutenant Pierre Milius (who before the arrival of the *Géographe* had been a frequent visitor) to Government House while Baudin was in Port Jackson. 'Strengthened by my own innocence', wrote a wounded Milius to King, 'I do not try in any way to escape the blows he aims at me; I confine myself to my sorrows and to pitying him.'[84] Despite the deaths in the expedition's ranks, Péron and Lesueur were not entirely deprived of scientific company, for the mineralogist Bailly, the hydrographer Faure and the botanist Leschenault were now transferred from the *Naturaliste* to the *Géographe*. With Louis de Freycinet placed in command of the newly acquired *Casuarina*, the expedition's three vessels set sail together from Port Jackson on 18 November 1802.

— 13 —

King Island

Many a green isle needs must be
In the deep wide sea of Misery,
Or the mariner, worn and wan,
Never thus could voyage on
Day and night, and night and day

PERCY BYSSHE SHELLEY, *Lines Written*
among the Euganean Hills

THE *Naturaliste*, although destined to return to France early, kept company with the *Géographe* and *Casuarina* as they sailed south along the New South Wales coast. Baudin's intention was to continue survey work in Bass Strait, particularly King Island, and then return to Kangaroo Island off the South Australian coast. The passage to the strait was rough with frequent electrical storms. Three days out from Port Jackson, the French encountered the English sealing schooner *Endeavour* bearing Nathaniel Cogswell,[1] the American supercargo from Alexandre Lecorre's vessel, the *Entreprise*. From him, Péron and his colleagues learned that Lecorre's sealing and trading expedition from the Ile de France had been shipwrecked off the Two Sisters islands in Bass Strait and that Lecorre and five of his crew had been drowned.[2] It was a sombre warning of the treacherous waters they were about to re-enter. But Péron was also outraged by the dangerous stipulations that had been imposed on Lecorre by Governor King, based, in his belief, on the arrogant breadth of Britain's territorial claims in the region.[3] After quoting from Governor Phillip's instructions, Péron observed:

... one can see that half of New Holland, all the Bass Strait islands and Van Diemen's Land are included in the English instrument of possession and, in fact, that New Zealand and most of the archipelagos of the great [Pacific] ocean are also part of this new empire ... In arrogating to herself the possession of this vast expanse of earth and sea, it seems that England has had her principal aim the contriving of a plausible pretext for keeping other nations away from her very important fishing areas and thereby appropriating to herself the immense profits which the commerce and products of these distant climates might offer. Faithful to this system of exclusion and monopoly, the governors of Port Jackson overlook none of the means at their disposal for assuring the interests and alleged rights of their country.[4]

On 3 December 1802 the *Naturaliste* and *Géographe* rounded Wilson's Promontory and three days later anchored in Sea Elephant Bay on the east coast of King Island. Not long after, the *Casuarina*, which had been separated for some days, was reunited with her consorts. At King Island, final preparations were made for the departure of the *Naturaliste*. Baudin went aboard her with young Antoine Guichenot, the surviving gardener, to check on the condition of the plant seedlings and the live animals and birds. All were fine, except for the last remaining kangaroo, which had died of an abscess on the thigh. Baudin took the opportunity to send a pig, two sheep and a dozen chickens (apparently from his personal store) for the nourishment of the ailing mineralogist Louis Depuch. However, he had little sympathy for Hamelin's officers who, having squandered their victualling money, had only a dozen salted pigs between them for the voyage back. Almost to a man, they snubbed Baudin, and he recorded in his journal that he was 'very happy to have no farewells to make to them'.[5] In his *Voyage*, Péron declared that when the *Naturaliste* finally weighed anchor on the evening of 8 December,

All eyes followed her for a long time, and when she finally disappeared over the horizon there was a look of sadness on each man's face. So far from home and in an unhappy situation such as ours, one feels more keenly the need to see one's country again; and when this sweet prospect seemed to vanish before us, was it possible not to envy the lot of our friends and companions, who were already indulging in the hope of being soon reunited with their families and their gentlest and dearest affections?

François Péron, stipple engraving by Conrad Westermayer from a portrait by Jean-Henri Cless. This portrait was probably completed by Cless shortly after Péron returned to France in 1804. Although its veracity has been questioned, anatomical assessment has established a strong match with the facial proportions of Lesueur's 1810 portrait. The artist appears to have acknowledged Péron's blind right eye.
(National Library of Australia pic-an9814355)

'Cérilly où Péron est né et mort', sketch (c. 1810) by Charles-Alexandre Lesueur. Péron was born and died in Cérilly; Lesueur's sketch shows the steeple of the eleventh-century church of Saint-Martin.
(Muséum d'histoire naturelle du Havre, Collection Lesueur, 35004)

Cérilly, Place du Marché, postcard, unknown photographer *c.* 1905. Péron's lover Anne-Sophie Petitjean lived in the house with the second arched entrance on the left. Directly opposite, on the extreme right, is the small doorway that led to the stables where Péron died in December 1810. The clock tower is that of the Hôtel de Ville where Péron was employed for almost two years. (ALAIN PETINIOT)

'Napoléon Bonaparte, Premier Consul de la République française', hand-coloured mezzotint *c.* 1803 by William Dickinson after a portrait by Antoine-Jean Gros. The Baudin expedition was dispatched on the orders of First Consul Bonaparte.

Nicolas Baudin, mezzotint by François Bonneville from a portrait by Louis François Jauffret. Baudin's command style made him many enemies. His extraordinary navigational achievements were long overlooked largely because of the injustice done to him by Péron in the official account of his expedition.
(National Library of Australia pic-an9288315)

'Charles-Alexandre Lesueur', ink sketch by Valerian Gribayedoff, after a portrait (1818) by Charles Willson Peale now in the Academy of Natural Sciences, Philadelphia. Lesueur, Péron's closest friend, made an outstanding contribution to the natural history and artistic record of Nicolas Baudin's expedition. After the fall of Napoleon he spent many years in the USA.
(Christine Gribayedoff Rios)

'Nouvelle-Hollande, Ile Bernier, kangarou à bandes', hand-coloured stipple engraving by Choubard from an original sketch by Charles-Alexandre Lesueur, plate 27 from the *Atlas* for Péron's *Voyage de découvertes aux Terres australes* (1807). On Bernier Island in Shark Bay, Péron collected the banded hare-wallaby (*Lagostrophus fasciatus*), which is now extinct on the mainland. (National Library of Australia pic-an7573688)

'Timor, vue de la rade, de la ville et du fort de Coupang', engraving by Victor Pillement completed by François-Denis Née from an original sketch by Charles-Alexandre Lesueur, plate 39 from the *Atlas* for Péron's *Voyage*. This sketch of Kupang harbour shows the expedition vessels, *Géographe* and *Naturaliste*, at anchor.

(NATIONAL LIBRARY OF AUSTRALIA PIC-AN7568625)

OPPOSITE: 'Terre de Diemen, Arra-Maïda', stipple engraving by Barthélemy Roger from a portrait by Nicolas Petit, plate 12 from the *Atlas* for Péron's *Voyage*. Péron met Arra-Maïda on Bruny Island in late January 1802.

(NATIONAL LIBRARY OF AUSTRALIA PIC-AN7573644)

'Terre de Diemen, Ile Maria, tombeaux des naturels', engraving by Victor Pillement completed by Marie-Alexandre Duparc from an original sketch by Charles-Alexandre Lesueur, plate 16 from the *Atlas* for Péron's *Voyage*. Péron excavated an Aboriginal cremation site at Cape des Tombeaux, Maria Island, but it seems unlikely that he took any remains. This image also appears in copper bas-relief on Péron's tomb.

'Terre de Diemen, navigation, vue de la côte orientale de l'Ile Schouten', hand-coloured engraving by Claude-François Fortier from a sketch by Charles-Alexandre Lesueur, plate 14 from the *Atlas* for Péron's *Voyage*.

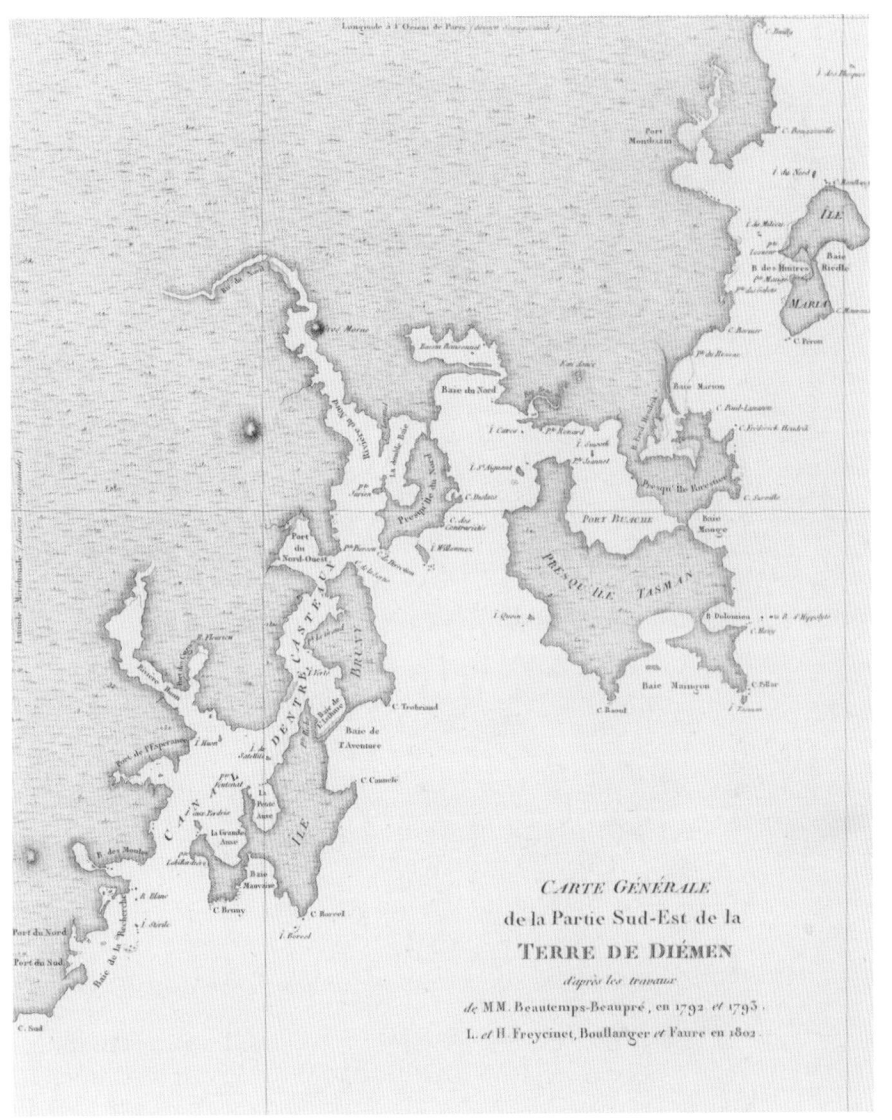

'Carte générale de la partie sud-est de la Terre de Diemen', by Louis de Freycinet
from the *Atlas* to Péron's *Voyage*, plate 3. A chart of the east coast of
Tasmania surveyed by the Baudin expedition.

(National Library of Australia map-raa1-s7)

'Nouvelle-Hollande, Nouvelle Galles du Sud, vue de la partie méridionale de la ville de Sydney, capitale des colonies anglaises aux Terres Australes et de l'embouchure de la rivière de Parramatta 1803', engraving by Victor Pillement completed by Marie-Alexandre Duparc from an original sketch by Charles-Alexandre Lesueur, plate 38 from the *Atlas* for Péron's *Voyage*. The Baudin expedition spent five months at Port Jackson, and Péron became intimately familiar with the nascent settlement.
(National Library of Australia pic-an7568621)

opposite: 'Nouvelle-Hollande, Cour-rou-bari-gal', hand-coloured stipple engraving by Barthélemy Roger from a portrait by Nicolas Petit, plate 18 from the *Atlas* for Péron's *Voyage*. (National Library of Australia pic-an7573661)

'Nouvelle-Hollande, Ile King, l'éléphant-marin ou phoque à trompe (*Phoca proboscidea*), vue de la Baie des Eléphants', engraving by Victor Pillement completed by Marie-Alexandre Duparc from an original sketch by Charles-Alexandre Lesueur, plate 62 from the *Atlas* for Péron's *Voyage* (2nd edn, 1824). Péron would devote an entire chapter to elephant seals (*Mirounga leonina*), which have long disappeared from King Island.
(NATIONAL LIBRARY OF AUSTRALIA PIC-AN7570306)

'Nouvelle-Hollande, Ile Decrès, casoar de la Nouvelle-Hollande', hand-coloured engraving by Lambert, *aîné* after a sketch by Charles-Alexandre Lesueur, plate 36 from the *Atlas* for Péron's *Voyage*. Kangaroo Island was once home to a distinctive species of emu (*Dromaius baudinianus*), much smaller and darker than those of the mainland and driven to extinction by the mid-1820s. Dogs were used to capture two live specimens, and Lesueur's sketches formed the basis of this engraving.
(NATIONAL LIBRARY OF AUSTRALIA PIC-AN7568611)

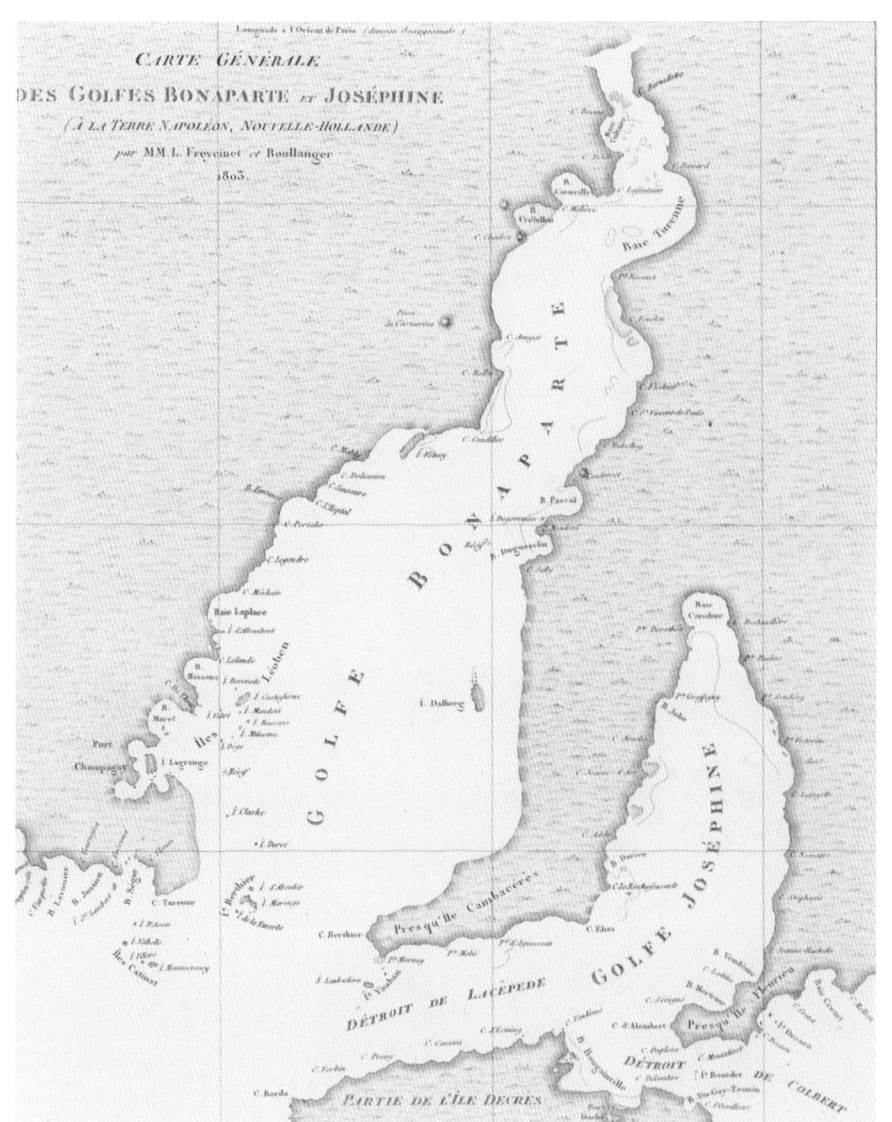

'Carte générale des Golfes Bonaparte et Joséphine (à la Terre Napoléon, Nouvelle-Hollande)', by Louis de Freycinet from the *Atlas* (part 2, 1811) to *Voyage*, plate 7. This chart of the South Australian coast bears imperial toponyms either as a result of Péron's calculated sycophancy or the suffocating narcissism of the Napoleonic despotism—or both. (NATIONAL LIBRARY OF AUSTRALIA MAP-RAA1-S11)

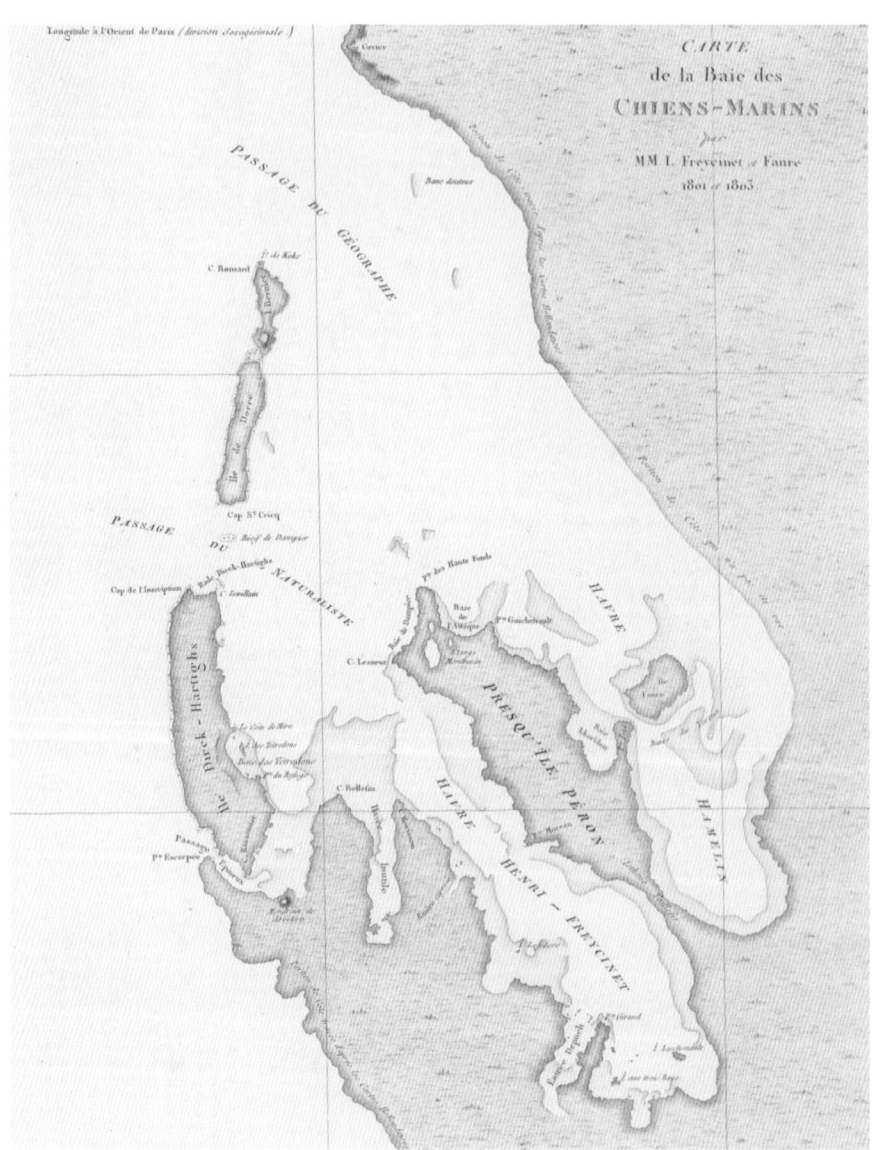

'Carte de la Baie des Chiens-Marins', by Louis de Freycinet from the *Atlas*
(part 2, 1811) to *Voyage*, plate 13. This chart of Shark Bay shows the peninsula
where Péron nearly lost his life and which still bears his name.

Flying foxes, Timor, hand-coloured engraving by Choubard from a watercolour by
Charles-Alexandre Lesueur, plate 35 from the *Atlas* for Péron's *Voyage*.
(National Library of Australia pic–an7568607)

'Habitation de Mme Querivel, Ile-de-France', engraving by Jacques Gérard Milbert,
plate 35 of Milbert's *Voyage pittoresque à l'Ile-de-France, au Cap de Bonne-Espérance, et à l'ile
de Ténériffe*, A Nepveu, Paris, 1812. This engraving shows the house in Port Nord-Ouest
(Port Louis) in which Nicolas Baudin died in September 1803.
(National Library of Australia s6826)

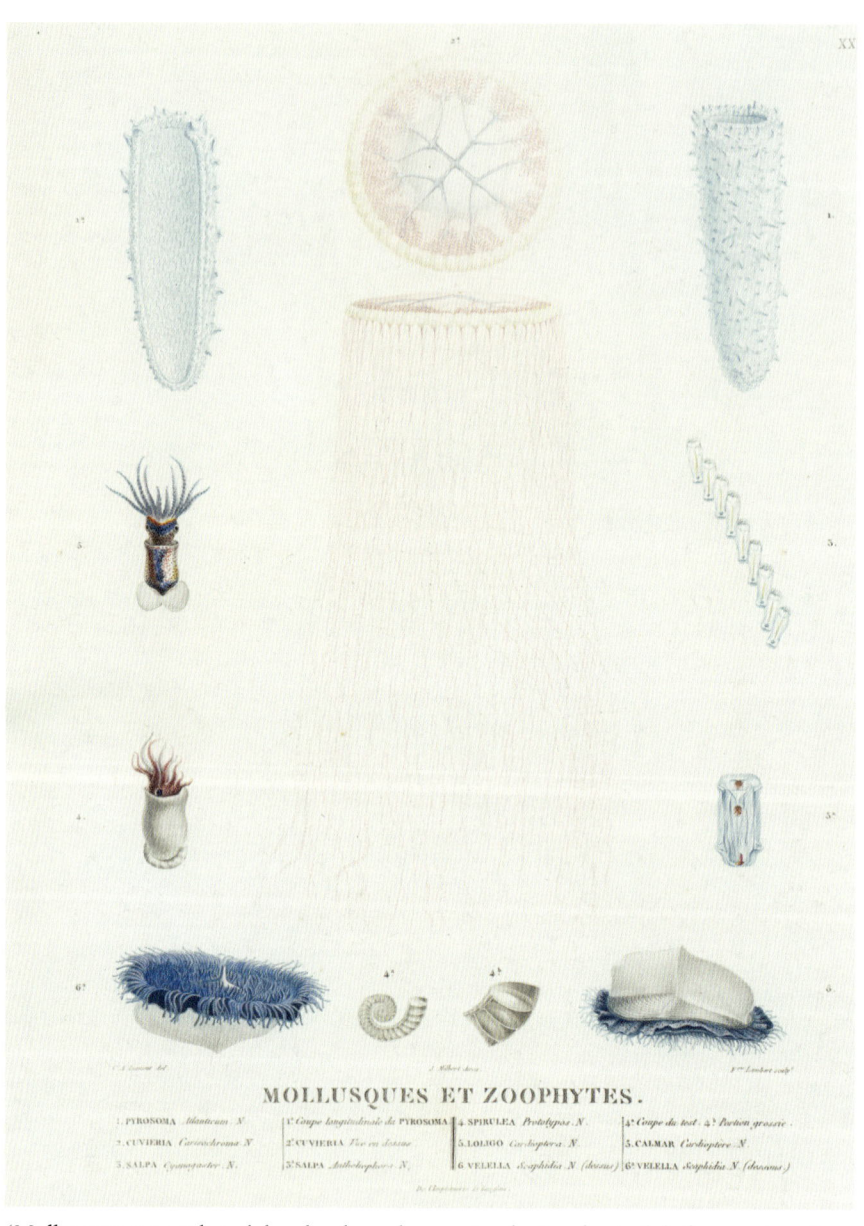

MOLLUSQUES ET ZOOPHYTES.

'Mollusques et zoophytes', hand-coloured engraving by Lambert, *aîné* after a watercolour by Charles-Alexandre Lesueur, plate 30 from the *Atlas* for Péron's *Voyage*. Péron's studies of 'mollusca' would ultimately include pioneering anatomical and physiological observations, as well as the collection of many previously undescribed species.

Lizars sc.

PERON.

Engraved for the Naturalist's Library.

François Péron, engraving by William Home Lizars for Sir William Jardine's *Naturalist's Library*, 1836, from an original portrait by Charles-Alexandre Lesueur now in William Henry Smith Memorial Library, Indiana Historical Society, Indianapolis. This is one of several engravings based on Lesueur's sketch completed a few days before Péron died. (EDWARD DUYKER)

'Cérilly étable où est mort mon estimable ami Péron, 14 décembre 1810'. The stables
where Péron died in December 1810; sketch by Charles-Alexandre Lesueur. At the time
it was thought that the air of cow stables was beneficial to tuberculosis cases.
(Muséum d'histoire naturelle du Havre, Collection Lesueur, 35006-1)

'Cérilly—Monument François Péron', postcard published by Moreau-Mériguet,
c. 1915. This north-westerly view of the Péron monument shows the naturalist's
family home in the background (centre left). (Alain Petiniot)

Péron must also have had a degree of disappointment at being parted from the collections he had made to date. It is little wonder that, before he even returned to France, many of the natural treasures he collected would be unpacked, studied and (in some instances) published, by leading scientists at the Muséum national d'histoire naturelle in Paris.

The day after the *Naturaliste* set sail, Baudin put ashore eight stowaways from Port Jackson with some bread and clothing, but refused their request for knives. In his journal, Baudin tells us that the English sealers already established on the island 'were not at all pleased by their arrival, fearing bad behaviour from them'.[6] Ironically, five would stowaway again with the aid of the sealers, before the expedition departed King Island.

One stowaway he did not put ashore was an escaped convict named Mary Beckwith. Baudin asserted that she was from a good family, that rather than entering a convent she had journeyed to Port Jackson to accompany her mother who had been convicted of taking a length of muslin and that he intended to 'set her down somewhere in the Moluccas' where she might find a happy fate.[7] Although Governor King might have decided to look the other way, it has been suggested by historian Anthony Brown that Baudin's substantial donation of fifty pounds to the infant colony's Female Orphanage might have been proferred as advance compensation for taking Mary Beckwith as a clandestine passenger. Baudin admitted making representations to King on Beckwith's behalf and must have known that she was a convicted felon; he certainly acknowledged that she had no 'authentic permission' to leave the colony. Péron does not mention Beckwith, but Henry de Freycinet wrote scathingly that Baudin had 'embarked with him a public girl for his personal use', and Lesueur recorded in his journal that Beckwith had relationships with other members of the crew.[8]

Once part of the land bridge between mainland Australia and Tasmania, King Island had been surrounded by the invading waters of Bass Strait since the end of the last Ice Age. It had no indigenous inhabitants when discovered by Captain William Reid in command of the schooner *Martha* in 1799.[9] Although visited by a number of sealers, the island had never been circumnavigated or properly charted. This was the task Baudin gave the geographer Pierre Faure when he set off in a longboat commanded by Midshipman Charles Baudin.

No sooner had Faure departed than the schooner *Cumberland* from Port Jackson arrived with Acting Lieutenant Robbins in command and Surveyor General Charles Grimes aboard. Their mission, as outlined in a letter quoted by Péron, was to reassert British territorial claims to Van Diemen's Land and south-western New South Wales (on the basis of Governor Phillip's Act of Possession of 1788) and to shadow the French until they were certain that their activities had 'nothing to do with any kind of invasion of British territory in these regions'.[10] Furthermore, according to Péron, Baudin was warned in a letter that any attempt at French settlement would be construed as a breach of the 'bonds of friendship' recently re-established with Britain and would be forcibly opposed. The letter Péron quoted has not survived in the original. Although its thrust differs little from King's surviving copy published in the *Historical Records of New South Wales* and loosely translated in Baudin's own journal, it is a different letter.

There are several reasons why Péron might not have wanted to include King's actual letter to Baudin in his account. First, he might not have wanted to give any printed legitimacy to King's use of the name 'Storm Bay Passage', rather than 'D'Entrecasteaux Channel', in deference to Bruny d'Entrecasteaux's discovery of the channel in 1792. Second, he might not have wished to acknowledge British territorial claims by repeating Governor King's declared 'intention of sending a vessel to the southward to fix on a place of settlement'.[11] And finally, he might have been reluctant to risk being identified as the source of the embarrassing reports of French colonial ambitions in Van Diemen's Land, which spurred the British pantomime of flag-raisings and musket volleys over French heads on King Island; this was because Governor King's letter to Baudin referred to the purported location for a French settlement given to Colonel Paterson 'by a gentleman of your ship'.[12] It is noteworthy that King's letter refers to a 'gentleman' rather than an 'officer' from the *Géographe*. Although there appear to have been naval officers who mouthed similar sentiments, Péron was by his own admission on intimate terms with Colonel Paterson, and Engineer Ronsard's journal confirms that it was indeed Péron who informed Colonel Paterson that the expedition 'had the plan to make a settlement on d'Entrecasteaux's Channel'.[13]

Péron might have thought his statements a legitimate assertion of French rights in the region, yet he made them in a charged atmosphere. Just two years before, while war still raged between Britain and France, Labillardière's *Relation* (1800) had suggested that the D'Entrecasteaux Channel 'might present great advantages to a commercial nation'.[14] The arrival of Baudin's expedition at Port Jackson, after resurveying the same channel, was bound to cause suspicion.

The arrogant British response made several patriots aboard the French vessels seethe with anger.[15] Baudin, nevertheless, chose to make a dignified response to King. First, in an official reply, he made it clear that if he had orders to linger in Van Diemen's Land for political reasons (and he didn't), he would have 'remained there without keeping it a secret';[16] but then in a frank private letter he showed himself to be particularly enlightened with regard to the rights of the indigenous inhabitants (although not the long-suffering Celts of Scotland and Brittany):

> To my way of thinking, I have never been able to conceive that there was justice or even fairness on the part of Europeans in seizing, in the name of their governments, a land seen for the first time, when it is inhabited by men who have not always deserved the title of savages or cannibals that has been freely given them; whereas they were still only children of nature and just as little civilised as your Scotch Highlanders or our Breton peasants, etc. who, if they do not eat their fellow-men, are nevertheless just as objectionable. From this it appears to me that it would be infinitely more glorious of your nation, as for mine, to mould for society the inhabitants of its own country over whom it has rights, rather than wishing to occupy itself with the improvement of those who are very far removed from it by beginning with seizing the soil which belongs to them and which saw their birth.[17]

And, in marked contrast to Péron's praise for Britain's convict transportation policy, Baudin added:

> … had this principle been reasonably adopted you would not have been obliged to form a colony by means of men branded by the law and made criminals by the fault of a government which has neglected them and abandoned them to themselves. It follows therefore that not only have you to reproach yourself with an injustice in having seized their land, but also in having transported on to a soil where the crimes and diseases of Europeans were unknown all that could retard the progress of civilisation, which has served as a pretext to your Government.[18]

Péron first landed on King Island on 10 December, in company with the botanist Jean-Baptiste Leschenault, the mineralogist Joseph Bailly, the artist Charles-Alexandre Lesueur and the surviving gardener Antoine

Guichenot. They appear to have come ashore near the Blowhole between the present town of Naracoopa and Cowper Point. The 'very hard and very compact shell-grit', which Péron refers to, must have been the cream-coloured Middle Miocene marly limestone—rich in Bryozoan and Ostracodan shells—which is readily visible as a platform on the beach.[19] Since this limestone also forms the bed of the Blowhole Creek[20] and Péron noted its presence 'from the seashore right into the interior of a neighbouring valley', we can assume he followed the creek some way inland.

Not surprisingly, it was the coastal flora and fauna that captured Péron's attention. 'All the shores', he tells us, 'were covered with a great quantity of *Fucus*, which for the most part formed new species.' In using the Linnean generic name *Fucus,* he was speaking of seaweeds in very general terms, but clearly when he referred to 'sturdy fragments of *F. gigantinus*', he meant the bull kelp. Today harvested kelp from the island is one of the world's most important sources of alginates for use in foods, cosmetics, pharmaceuticals and a wide range of industrial products.

As the name of the bay suggests, the sandy shore was covered with a 'prodigious number' of what are now known as elephant seals (*Mirounga leonina*). They have long disappeared from the island as a result of the depredations of early nineteenth-century sealers. Péron would devote an entire chapter of his *Voyage* to these creatures in which he lovingly described their habits. But he was also shocked by the environmental crime unfolding before his eyes and offered an impassioned warning of extinction, which is yet another landmark in Australian ecological writing:

> Until now, the animals of which we are speaking, guided by some wise instinct, have known how to conceal themselves from the wrath of the human race. Far from the regions in which it dwells, secluded on wild and lonely islands, these great seals were able, without enemies or fears, to outdo each other in multiplying and growing. Henceforth everything is changed for them; and if it was formerly possible for them to find protection from the voracity of the inhabitants of these climes, they will not now escape the mercantile greed which appears to have sworn the annihilation of their race. Indeed, the English have invaded these retreats, which for so long protected them; they have organised massacres everywhere, which cannot fail shortly to cause a noticeable and irreparable reduction in the population of these animals.[21]

Péron continued with great empathy:

> No sooner do they see themselves being attacked than they try to get away. If their retreat is cut off, they shake violently; an expression of despair comes into their eyes and they dissolve into tears. I, myself, saw one of these young females shedding copious tears while one of our sailors (a cruel, wicked man) amused himself, every time she opened her mouth, by smashing her teeth with the broad end of one of the oars from our long-boat. This poor animal filled one with pity; her whole mouth was bleeding, and tears streamed from her eyes.[22]

In fact, such weeping is an anthropomorphic misapprehension, for the lacrimal glands in seals produce a steady stream of tears to protect the eyes—with the aid of a nictitating membrane—from saltwater, wind and abrasive sand.

Although Péron was shocked by the brutality of the sealing industry, he soon made close friends with a number of the sealers on the island, in particular Daniel Cooper.[23] Cooper was an old Bass Strait hand. As early as 1799 he had sailed with Charles Bishop on the *Nautilus* and been part of a sealing party deposited on Cape Barren.[24] On King Island, he appears to have been part of a group of ten sealers, at least two of whom were Irish political deportees, but he also lived with a Hawaiian woman from Maui. Cooper and his men had killed and skinned many seals over the previous months and had long filled all their casks with seal oil (highly sought-after because it burns without odour or smoke). For this reason they were impatient for their ship to return in order to take their spoils to China for sale.

Péron and his companions soon discovered what all visitors to King Island soon discover: exposed to the wild expanse of the Southern Ocean and Bass Strait, the island is very wet and very windy. On 13 December 1802, not long after the savants had entertained their British watchdogs —Grimes and Robbins—with a frugal meal, Péron's tent was upturned and shredded by the wind, leaving him and his companions completely exposed to the torrential rain. Matters were made worse by a lack of food or arms to go hunting. An angry Péron blamed Baudin for not providing them with provisions before the storm forced the *Géographe* to stand out to sea. In her hasty withdrawal, her longboat was sunk when the tow rope ripped out the thwart it was secured to. Any prospect of collecting shellfish for food was thwarted by the storm, which turned the beach into a maelstrom of boiling surf. Curiously, Péron suggests that their hunger was made worse by high levels of ferrous oxide (actually tannin) in the water they drank from the creek. Faced with hunger and exposure, Péron tells us they owed salvation to the sealers, who generously accommodated them at their camp 'six miles' to the north—presumably on the estuary of the Sea Elephant River near Cowper Point.

The sealers' camp consisted of four huts 'made of bits of wood driven into the ground and joined on the angle at the top' with 'rough pieces of bark' covering the gaps between the timbers. Cooper occupied one hut with his Hawaiian wife, and the rest of the party occupied the other three. A great fire, fed with large tree trunks, burned day and night to keep the men warm and enable them to cook emus (Péron called them 'cassowaries'), wombats and kangaroos in a large cauldron. On a trestle in Cooper's 'smoky manor', the French were served a meal of native game: beasts and birds cooked unceremoniously together in the same pot. Yet Péron remarked: 'These masses of different meats, essentially delicate and well cooked in their own juices, provided a savoury meal, even though we had to eat them without bread or biscuit or any other similar substance.' He added that the 'sealers all enjoyed the most vigorous good health'.[25]

Despite the generous hospitality Péron received, the young zoologist was clearly troubled by the broader human impact on the island, and he wrote prophetically:

> In order to sustain the enormous quantity of meat that they consume, the sealers use a method as simple as it is cheap. On the deserted islands of which we are speaking, the different species of animals placed there by Nature have been able, over the centuries, to increase undisturbed. And so there are numerous herds of each species there, the most important on King Island being the kangaroo and the cassowary— equally swift in movement—and the wombat, with no notion of flight or of self-defence. Any method of hunting is sufficient for this last. As for the cassowaries and kangaroos: in order to catch them, the sealers have trained dogs which beat the woods by themselves and seldom fail to strangle several of these animals each day ... a small number of such dogs, if left on the island, would have been sufficient to destroy the whole stock of these innocent animals.[26]

The small endemic subspecies of emu (*Dromaius ater*) and the wombat are now extinct on King Island.

Péron seized the opportunity offered by his close company with the sealers to ask detailed questions about the life and habits of the emu. In an age in which zoology was still dominated by the collection and cataloguing of dead specimens, rather than the study of the habits of living creatures, Péron's thirty-three-point questionnaire represents an important exercise in gathering information (albeit second-hand) on the behaviour of a particular animal. He sought detailed responses—very probably from Daniel Cooper—on flocking, mating and egg-laying habits, plumage changes, size, natural enemies, diet, speed and whether the emu could swim. But he also asked questions relating to domestication and even on the uses of emu grease. The original document still survives in Le Havre[27] and was published in 1899.[28]

Péron spent almost a fortnight on King Island because the *Géographe*, which had been blown eastward beyond Wilson's Promontory, did not return until 23 December. Anxious after the disappearance of the expedition's mother ship and dependent on the generous hospitality of the sealers during the harsh weather conditions, Péron complained bitterly of Baudin's 'miserable obstinacy in refusing arms and supplies to the men he dispatched to settle on the shore'.[29] When the storm finally passed, he resumed his zoological observations and, with the aid of Lesueur, collected several fish[30] and numerous invertebrates, which were later described by Lamarck. These included at least six new sponges,[31] four species of calcareous tube worm,[32] four new species of mollusc[33] and the acorn barnacle *Acasta glans*.[34] Among the crustaceans he collected was the type specimen of a scyllarid lobster, which in 1815 was named *Ibacus peronii* in his honour by the English zoologist William Elford Leach.[35] Péron also tells us that the 'reptile family' provided him with 'two types of lizards and two snakes'. Although it has not been possible to locate these museum specimens in Paris, it seems likely that the snakes—which he tells us 'were both armed with venomous fangs'[36]—were the tiger snake (*Notechis ater*) and the lowland copperhead (*Austrelaps superbus*).

Baudin finally sent a landing party to retrieve his savants on 24 December, and appears to have been annoyed that Péron 'seeing nothing but molluscs at every step, had amused himself by missing the first boat'.[37] Péron, however, seems to have assumed, correctly, that he could return with the second boat bearing Ronsard and the ship's carpenter, who were seeking timber for the construction of the new longboat. Although the scientists and Pierre Faure's survey party were safely back aboard the *Géographe* by Christmas Eve, their departure was delayed until the arrival of the slow and leaky *Casuarina* on 27 December.[38] Reunited, the expedition pulled away from the scrub and heath-crowned dunes of Sea Elephant Bay, only to be separated again, soon after, in the vast anonymity of the Southern Ocean.

— 14 —

Kangaroo Island

All that is told of the sea has a fabulous sound to an inhabitant of the land, and all its products have a certain fabulous quality, as if they belonged to another planet, from seaweed to a sailor's yarn, or a fish story. In this element the animal and vegetable kingdoms meet and are strangely mingled.

HENRY DAVID THOREAU, *Cape Cod*

BEFORE leaving King Island, Baudin had informed Louis de Freycinet, aboard the *Casuarina*, that he was heading for Flinders' Kangaroo Island and that he intended to anchor on the east coast. Although the two vessels soon lost sight of each other, Baudin felt reasonably confident that they would be reunited at his next anchorage. The men of the *Géographe* gained their first view of the island—in particular its rugged eastern end—at dawn on 2 January 1803. Although Flinders named Cape Willoughby on this same eastern extremity, he did not name the peninsula from which it juts. On Freycinet's chart of New Holland (1808), the previously unnamed peninsula bore the name 'Presqu'île de La Galisonnière'. For all the criticisms heaped on Péron for appending French names to Flinders' prior discoveries, it is worth noting that since August 1874 this same peninsula, which was first surveyed in its entirety and first named by the French, has honoured a Christian name of an American lawyer, David Dudley Field, father-in-law of South Australia's Governor Anthony Musgrave.[1] It would seem that for Anglo-Saxon sensibilities, 'Dudley' was preferable to the name of one of France's greatest naval heroes, who was responsible, as Péron gleefully pointed out, for the defeat of the unfortunate Admiral Byng at Minorca![2]

Having lost his longboat in the storm off King Island, Baudin conducted his circumnavigation of Kangaroo Island with the *Géographe*. In his journal he refers to the island as 'Ile Borda' in honour of Jean-Charles de Borda, the French naval officer, mathematician and astronomer who developed a number of nautical and geodesic instruments and helped pioneer the introduction of the metric system; he is credited with having coined the word 'metre'. However, by the time Freycinet's *Atlas* went to press, the island would bear the name of the Minister of Marine, Denis Decrès.

Early on 4 January Baudin proudly completed his circuit of the coast —charting the west and south of the island (unseen by Flinders) for the first time. Two days later, he anchored in Western Cove. On arrival, Baudin decided to use his dinghies to survey Nepean Bay, search for fresh water and find suitable timber to complete construction of the replacement longboat. There was even more work to be done when, on 7 January, the *Casuarina* was reunited with the *Géographe*. Caulkers were put to work in an attempt to remedy the little schooner's leaking hull, and the smiths were busied repairing one of her anchors and forging new hoops for her topmasts.[3]

On 9 January, Péron made his first landing on Kangaroo Island in the company of Baudin, Leschenault, Guichenot and two of the English stowaways. He found 'not the slightest trace of man's presence'.[4] Furthermore, the lack of human predators had encouraged the growth of a substantial kangaroo population, and the expedition used a sealer's dog (brought from King Island) to hunt them. The hunters were spectacularly successful, taking twenty-seven live kangaroos—soon reduced to seven penned in two dismantled cabins near the gangway of the *Géographe*—and many others killed for immediate consumption. Perhaps with the dodo of Mauritius in mind, Péron worried that 'the innocent and gentle race of kangaroos would surely be destroyed in several years by a few dogs'.[5] His fears would have been better placed with regard to the island's distinctive emus (*Dromaius baudinianus*), which were much smaller and darker than those of the mainland and were driven to extinction by the mid-1820s.[6]

The dogs were used to capture two live specimens the day before the expedition departed the island,[7] and Lesueur made a number of sketches[8] that would form the basis for plate xxxvi engraved by Lambert *aîné* for Péron's *Voyage*. These dwarf emus joined three others from King Island already aboard the *Géographe* (in addition to two previously dispatched on the *Naturaliste*). Only two would survive the voyage—apparently the pair from Kangaroo Island rather than King Island—and shortly after their arrival they were presented to Mme Bonaparte. She, however, only kept them until February 1805, when they were handed over to the Ménagerie at the Jardin des plantes, where they joined the surviving emu transported on the *Naturaliste*. The latter bird died some time before 1809, while the emus from Kangaroo Island both died in 1822.[9] Their bones were thought to be the only surviving remnants of their species until additional emu skeletons were found in the Kelly Hill Caves, in the current Cape Bouguer Wilderness Protection Area, in 1924.[10]

It was on Kangaroo Island that Péron encountered the Australian sea lion. Although he established the original generic name *Otaria* (from Greek *otarion* = small ear), and provided the basis for the family name 'Otariidae' coined by Joshua Brookes in 1828,[11] he was not the first to note the distinction between seals with discernible ear lobes and the true seals or Phocidae.[12] As Françoise Debard has pointed out, this honour must be accorded to Buffon. Significantly, in one of his manuscripts, Péron made reference to page 304 of volume vi of the supplements to Buffon's *Histoire naturelle* in which this division of the seals is mentioned.[13] Péron christened the Australian sea lions *Otaria cinerea*, but in 1934 Tom Iredale and E. L. Troughton transferred them to the genus *Neophoca*.[14] Nevertheless, the generic name *Otaria* survives because of the South American sea lion *Otaria byronia* (Blainville, 1820).

Despite his previous concerns about the ruthless and brutal nature of the sealing industry in Bass Strait and the threat of extinction that it posed (not just to seals), Péron dispassionately remarked that such an industry on Kangaroo Island 'would offer valuable profits' and even suggested that the 'Bay of Springs' (present-day Hog Bay)[15] 'would provide the sealers with enough water for their consumption, while the kangaroos and cassowaries [emus] would supply them with a wholesome and inexhaustible source of food'.[16] This contradictory position perhaps came from Péron the imperialist, rather than Péron the ecologist. Since the Baudin expedition had been the first to circumnavigate the uninhabited island, Péron might have believed France had a right to take possession and exploit it. This never happened, but it remains to be said that thanks to the rapacity of the sealers who established themselves on the island in 1806, the Australian sea lion—which has a non-annual breeding cycle—is now a very rare species with a total population of between 10 000 and 11 000 individuals on the

Western Australian and South Australian coasts, including a mere 400 to 500 individuals on Kangaroo Island.[17]

If Péron actually returned to France with a specimen of the sea lion, its whereabouts is unknown. According to his own reckoning, he collected specimens from 336 animal species, but gave a very incomplete breakdown. However, he did assert that the island furnished him with fifty-four species of insects, in what he believed to be thirty-three different genera, and a surprising twenty-six species of sponge.[18] Although the island did not present him with many opportunities to collect freshwater amphibia, he did sight or collect a significant number of reptiles with Lesueur's assistance. These included the type specimens for the tawny dragon *Amphibolurus decresii* (Duméril and Bibron), closely related to the bearded dragon whose type specimen he had collected at Port Jackson, and those of the skinks *Egernia whitii* (Lacépède), *Lampropholis guichenoti* (Duméril and Bibron), *Hemiergis decresiensis* (Fitzinger) and *Hemiergis peronii* (Fitzinger).[19] At least five of the molluscs he collected on Kangaroo Island—almost certainly including the type specimen of the pipi *Paphies cuneata*—would find their way into Lamarck's *Histoire naturelle des animaux sans vertèbres*. However, by that time they were almost all species for which Lamarck lacked publishing priority.[20]

Péron tells us that Kangaroo Island, 'like all the other uninhabited islands of New Holland … was a meeting-place for great flocks of land birds and sea-birds'.[21] Although his notebook (with its unpublished manuscript names) does not have enduring taxonomic ornithological significance, as an eco-historical snapshot, it contains details of an impressive number of species he observed on the island.[22]

In contrast to the ornithological richness of the island, there appears to have been considerable disappointment at the very small number of fish that were caught when, on 12 January, Péron and Leschenault joined a fishing party made up of two boats with a draw net.[23] According to Péron: 'All our usual methods of fishing and all our searching produced scarcely a dozen species of fish—new ones, admittedly, but five or six of them are not normally eaten.'[24] The latter appear to have included a porcupine fish, probably a poisonous *Diodon nichthemerus*, sketched by Lesueur and described by Péron in his notebook.[25] Others appear to have been seaweed-eating parrot fish and wrasse (Labridae), known for their soft tasteless flesh. The 'triggerfish' to which Péron refers appear to have included the blue-finned *Balistoides viridescenes* and perhaps one of almost a dozen species of leatherjacket belonging to the Monacanthidae family caught locally.[26] However, 'of all the fish on the island', Péron wrote, 'the most astonishing is a species of shark, which grows to a length of 15 to 20 feet and is very common in Bougainville [now Nepean] Bay'.[27] This was probably a great white shark, *Carcharodon carcharias*. Péron speculated that it fed on seals, given the seemingly small number of fish in the bay. Péron's attention was also drawn to the diversity of species living in the shallow coastal waters. In his opinion the shores of the island presented an immense field for the naturalist's research.[28] They remain so as they contain a rich variety of intertidal invertebrates. Like Péron, the modern visitor can readily find 'brilliant sea-anemones', such as *Actina tenebrosa*, dark red with iridescent blue and sometimes white and pink spots on its tentacles, and *Anthothoe albocincta*, white with green and orange longitudinal stripes on its column, or be drawn to 'beautiful starfish', like *Patiriella gunnii*, shimmering in shades of red, pink, blue or even purple below the surface of the water.

Baudin, for his part, seems to have still viewed Péron's collecting with amusement rather than admiration. When the naturalists returned with the fishing party of 12 January, he wrote that Leschenault 'had had no luck on his excursion and arrived with only two or three plants that he did not know; but Citizen Péron was full of joy at having collected three or four molluscs, two small lizards and half a dozen ear-shell'. And to leave no doubt of how trifling these gatherings were in his eyes, he added that the ear-shells were 'like the ones that the sailors have filled their chests with'.[29]

Baudin, however, had more pressing matters on his mind. Once the *Casuarina* was repaired, Louis de Freycinet was ordered to sail with the hydrographer Boulanger to survey what we now know as the Gulf of St Vincent and Spencer's Gulf (including Port Lincoln) to the north. Baudin's written orders to Freycinet (in addition to his journal references to him) remained severe in tone and reflect his unceasing coolness and resentment towards his subordinate despite his obvious diligence and talent. With 'very fine weather and a fresh southerly breeze'[30] the *Casuarina* set sail late on the evening of 10 January with thirty days' supply of water. After completing his survey work, Freycinet was ordered to return to Kangaroo Island. If the *Géographe* was no longer there, he was to proceed to the islands of St Peter and St Francis (Nuyts Archipelago), the next rendezvous point.

Meanwhile, efforts to complete the new longboat were frustrated by the lack of suitable timber. Baudin tells us in his journal that sixty eucalypts were chopped down, but all were found to be rotten in the centre. After

Casuarinas were selected as an alternative, Baudin was injured when one fell unexpectedly and a branch knocked him off his feet. Sufficient timber was finally gathered, and Baudin even took a turn sawing the needed planks. Nevertheless, he complained that, with the exception of Ronsard, his other officers 'were careful not to show up' and had 'not gone near the longboat' since it had been on the stocks.[31] Péron, however, wrote:

> Everybody was eager to contribute to the success of his enterprise; those who were not sufficiently skilful to turn carpenter became pit-sawyers; and we had a fine, big boat even before we had reached King George Sound ... Thus, the devotion of a small number of men triumphed over every obstacle, made good of all the needs, multiplied all the resources and prepared the way for the fine results that we were to make of our expedition one of the most glorious undertakings of its kind.[32]

After another day lost waiting for the return of the *Casuarina*, but made happier by the capture of two emus, the *Géographe* weighed anchor on 1 February and sailed west along the broadening expanse of Investigator Strait in the hope of meeting the expedition's schooner. When he came to write his *Voyage*, Péron would take yet another swipe at Baudin for 'abandoning our consort whose pressing needs were known to us and whose assistance was indispensable for the remainder of our operations'.[33] There are some grounds, however, to believe that Baudin harboured a degree of indifference towards Freycinet's fate. In his journal he wrote that he was 'leaving the *Casuarina* to her good fortune, as she has chosen to leave us to ours'.[34] At 2.00 p.m. the *Casuarina* was indeed sighted in the distance sailing in an easterly direction but, to Baudin's surprise, she failed to change direction. The hydrographer Boulanger, however, would later write to Baudin expressing his surprise that the *Géographe* had not heaved to.[35] Shortening sail overnight (denied by Péron), Baudin was again disappointed when there was still no sign of the schooner at daybreak. Whether indifferent or confident of an eventual rendezvous off Nuyts Archipelago, Baudin made for the deep embrace of the Great Australian Bight.

— 15 —

Nuyts Archipelago

*I have not had the felicity, like the primitive navigators, who discovered
uninhabited islands, to contemplate the face of the ground as it came from
the hand of the Creator.*

JACQUES-HENRI BERNARDIN DE SAINT-PIERRE, *Etudes de la Nature*

THE *Géographe* sailed west for much of 3 February 1803 before heading
north-north-west during the afternoon in a heavy south-westerly swell.
Although it was still summer, the gusting winds brought icy rain. So much
so that, on the following morning, two kangaroos were found dead,
apparently from exposure: 'soaked with rain and the continuous mist',[1]
despite a heavy tarpaulin over their pen. The five surviving marsupials
were then transferred to two cabins begrudgingly vacated by Leschenault
and Ransonnet. Aside from altering cabins to accommodate live zoological specimens, the carpenters continued to work busily on the longboat.

By 5.00 p.m. on the afternoon of 6 February, the *Géographe* was abeam
of the island of St Peter (32° 17′ S 13° 35′ E), which had been discovered
by the Dutch explorers Pieter Nuyts and François Thyssen during the
voyage of the *Gulden Zeepard* in 1627. The day before, the *Casuarina* had
been a degree west of the nearby island of St Francis because of an error,
Freycinet asserted, in the longitude he had been given.[2] Thwarted in his
efforts to sight the *Géographe*, with his rudder brace broken and with only
four days' supply of water left, Freycinet felt he had little option but to sail
directly to the expedition's next rendezvous point—King George Sound—
where he knew he would be able to obtain fresh water. It was a desperate

dash, with the water ration halved yet again and with biscuits reduced by a further three ounces. Fortunately the gamble paid off. Blown west by the unrelenting winds, Freycinet deliberately drove the damaged *Casuarina*, with only 'a few bottles of water left on board', aground in the Sound.[3]

Meanwhile, on the *Géographe* there was great anticipation that a survey of the mainland coast immediately north of the archipelago might reveal a vast strait effectively separating New Holland from New South Wales. As Péron put it: 'Everything gave us hope of solving at last the great problem of the wholeness of New Holland. Filled with this hope, we crowded on sail towards the numerous islands lying on the horizon.'[4] Theories about a strait dividing the continent had emerged a century before with William Dampier—whose voyage accounts were in the *Géographe*'s library—who speculated that the tidal range in the southern part of De Wit's Land suggested a 'passage or strait going through eastward to the great South Sea'.[5] Others thought it might connect with the Gulf of Carpentaria and, as Matthew Flinders put it, 'thence to the unknown part of the South Coast, beyond the Isles of St Francis and St Peter'.[6] But, as Flinders also mused, 'whether this opening were the entrance to a strait, separating Terra Australis into two or more islands, or led into a mediterranean sea, as some thought; or whether it were the entrance of a large river, there was, in either case, a great geographical question to be settled ...'[7] Baudin would certainly help resolve the issue but without a glorious new discovery. Indeed, after the *Géographe*'s meticulous survey of Denial Bay, Péron was forced to concede that 'far from discovering there the entrance to that immense strait that we were searching for, we could not find so much as the merest trace of a stream or even a freshwater spring'.[8]

Péron, nevertheless, was excited by the opportunity to collect on the island of St Peter (which was renamed Eugène Island in his *Voyage* and in Freycinet's *Atlas* in fawning honour of Bonaparte's stepson Eugène de Beauharnais). Having decided to 'stay another day for the natural history of the region', Baudin organised a hunting party for the following day, and the naturalists were eager to join in. With the exception of Péron, who had accompanied Bonnefoy and the astronomer Bernier to the head of the bay in the longboat the day before, the savants had, in Baudin's words, 'remained peacefully on the ship through fear of not being comfortable in a boat that might spend one or two nights ashore'.[9] Péron's earlier landfall, however, sparked tension after the expedition's commander recorded that it had been very brief and his labours 'not very fruitful'.[10] When Péron read these comments in Baudin's journal he was angry enough to insert the following note: 'I went in spite of you. The objects that I collected on the excursion in question were very interesting and numerous. Read my zoological comments.'[11]

Péron set off in a boat for St Peter Island with Leschenault and Lesueur on 10 February 1803. Roughly fourteen kilometres long and four kilometres wide, St Peter is the largest island in Nuyts Archipelago and rises to a mere forty-four metres at its highest point (Mount Younghusband). It remains an uninhabited island to this day.[12] This fact would in itself have thrilled Péron's readers in an age when many dreamt of distant islands either untouched by the corrupting hand of man (as encountered by Defoe's Robinson Crusoe) or as the setting for communal perfection as in More's *Utopia* (1516) or idyllic innocence and simplicity as in Bernardin de Saint-Pierre's *Paul et Virginie* (1787) or Bougainville's account of Tahiti. Yet one wonders whether Péron ever realised the irony of the satirist Jonathan Swift's location of the asymmetrical insular dystopias, Lilliput and Blefescu, in the vicinity of Nuyts Archipelago: 'north west of Van Diemen's Land … in the latitude of 30° 2′ south'![13]

While Leschenault botanised, Péron tells us he 'surveyed the seashore'. In particular he was drawn to a spit of sand that stretched from the northeastern tip of the island almost to the mainland. Commencing his collecting when the tide was out, Péron was soon so utterly engrossed in the rich marine life of the bank that he failed to notice the rapidly incoming waters when the tide changed. Alerted by a sailor named Lefebvre,[14] he made good his retreat, but soon faced renewed danger when the shallow inlet he had crossed earlier in the day became a surging tide race. Up to his chest in water, exhausted and a 'stranger to the art of swimming', Péron had no doubt that he was saved by the 'zeal of the good Lefebvre' and wrote:

> He alone guided me in the midst of the rising waves; in the deepest places his arm supported me. In a word, this brave man did everything to prevent my drowning. But, despite all his care, it would certainly have occurred had he not managed, by dint of groping and testing, to discover a sand bank over which there was not much water and which led us close to the shore that we were trying to reach.[15]

Given Péron's record of absent-minded, near-exhausted, late returns, one wonders whether Lefebvre was his minder—perhaps on Baudin's orders. No one else appears to have been present when he came close to drowning. But the *Voyage* also offers a romantic hint of Man Friday (in the form of a rough but honest sailor) coming to the aid of Robinson Péron, cast-away for a day and a night on his desert isle.

In his *Voyage*, Péron tells us that he found the island rich in 'molluscs, worms, echinoderms and soft zoophytes' and that he 'alone gathered more than two hundred species belonging to these different groups'. Among the shellfish, he tells us, there were a 'great number of new species of rare beauty'.[16] There can be no doubt of the significance of the invertebrate collections made on the island, particularly when viewed from the per-spective of those new species that were ultimately published by Lamarck, including what Péron described as 'venus-shells, tellens and dazzling trochus-shells'.[17] Among those with a direct attribution to Péron and his gatherings in Nuyts Archipelago are the type specimens of *Venerupis distans* (= *Irus distans*), *Tellina albinella* (= *Tellinella albinella*), *Tellina capsoides* (= *Serratina capsoides*) and *Perna nucleus* (= *Isognomon nucleus*).[18] One trochus shell collected by Péron was published by Lamarck: this was *T. calyptrae-formis*;[19] but the type specimen is believed to have come from Maria Island off the Tasmanian coast rather than St Peter Island.

In addition to an acorn barnacle, *Balanus roseus*,[20] it would appear that Péron collected the holotype of Lamarck's *Spongia syphonoides* (= *Dactylia syphonoides*).[21] As the modern (Greek derived) generic name suggests, these are 'finger sponges', and Péron made reference to the 'thick, flabby, elastic covering' that is characteristic of their very flexible fibre skeletons. Lamarck wrote that this sponge inhabited 'the seas of New Holland at the islands of Saint Peter and Saint Francis'[22] and made direct reference to Péron. Most (if not all) of the surviving Australian sponge specimens from the Baudin expedition preserved in Paris appear to have been found among beach backwash, rather than removed directly from the seabed.[23] Given Péron's poor swimming abilities, this should not be a surprise, but he does make reference to 'a large bank of alcyonium in Decrès Bay', which is suggestive of a closer scrutiny of the seabed, perhaps made while traversing by boat. (In the past *Alcyonium* had a broader meaning, which included sponges.)

Péron's notebook for this period of the voyage also indicates that he took a particular interest in crustaceans in the waters surrounding the island. These included several unidentified pistol shrimps (Alpheidae), so named for the startling defensive cracking sound they generate with the dactyl and notch of their large claw; a *Caphyra* crab (Portunidae) and, most particularly—since he wrote descriptions of twenty-two and eighteen lines in length—two specimens of the crab *Schizophrys aspera*, commonly called 'sea toads' by Australians because of their stout shape and mottled, horned carapace. Péron clearly believed his two specimens belonged to two different species and gave them the manuscript names *Inachus insolita* and *I. variolosus*.[24] However, his descriptions were never published, and it was not until 1834 that Henry Milne-Edwards[25] published the name *Mithrax aspera* (later included in the genus *Schizophrys*).[26] Although the type locality is unknown, Péron's specimens from Nuyts Archipelago might have syntype status along with another specimen he collected at King George Sound.

Péron was unable to discover any trace of fresh water on St Peter. Nevertheless, this low, sparsely vegetated island, largely covered with an 'arid, deep and mobile' layer of sand, was home to a significant population of what we now call tammar wallabies. Four were killed by Lesueur and, because none were seen on the mainland, Péron referred to them as the 'Eugène Island Kangaroo'. He added: 'Each of these quadrupeds weighs from eight to ten pounds; their fur is thick, with very fine hair, and is a beautiful russet colour, verging on brown.'[27] Péron never published a detailed zoological description but, seven years after his death, Anselme-Gaëtan Desmarest did so under the name *Kangarus eugenii*[28] (= *Macropus eugenii*). Sadly, these beautiful wallabies are now extinct on St Peter Island (the source of the original type specimen) and on the South Australian mainland. Tiny populations of a kindred Western Australian subspecies— the first Australian marsupials ever to be described by Europeans—still survive in their original habitats, while in New Zealand descendants of introduced pairs of the now-extinct South Australian subspecies[29] have ironically become a pest.

While on the island Péron also observed what he thought was a new species of sea lion. In fact, his *Otaria albicollis* was a male of the species that he had already named *O. cinerea* (= *Neophoca cinerea*) on Kangaroo Island, but there he had seen only females and juveniles. Once again Péron specu- lated on the possibilities for a local sealing industry, albeit one sustained with fresh water supplied from King George Sound.[30] He also searched for birds, but found that the 'extreme barrenness' of the island had apparently 'repelled the winged species'.[31] Nevertheless, he did observe a 'kind of flycatcher' with low trailing wings and a raised outspread tail, which reminded him of a miniature farmyard turkeycock.[32] This was very prob- ably a willie wagtail (*Rhipidura leucophrys*) or a grey fantail (*R. fuliginosa*), familiar to most Australians. Furthermore, Péron's *Voyage* contains mention of a 'small, blue penguin',[33] a cormorant with a 'black back and a blue breast' (*Phalacrocorax* sp.?) and pelicans, sighted in Tourville Bay and at the head of the inlet on St Peter Island, which avoided capture. His notebook for the period also records five different species of gull.[34] 'As for reptiles', wrote Péron, 'we collected only one new species of lizard, belonging to the skink family.'[35] This was almost certainly his alcohol-preserved type specimen[36] of the south-western crevice skink *Egernia napoleonis* described by J. E. Gray in 1838. (Gray's specific epithet '*napoleonis*' even made direct reference to Péron's declared collection point, 'Terre Napoléon'.)[37]

Péron's reflections on the small number of insects and hence land birds on the island are evocative of modern ecological notions of equilibrium:

> … while the herbivorous and granivorous species are kept away from these infertile lands by the almost total lack of food, the insectivorous birds—so numerous and varied in all other parts of the continent—are forced to go elsewhere for the same reason. Thus everything is linked in Nature's great scheme of things; thus, the life story of the weakest beings is related to that of the most powerful. These marvellous links often escape our notice; but when we do manage to perceive them, we are astonished equally by the importance of their consequences and by their simplicity.[38]

Ecological interdependence and balance are strong themes in the work of Jacques-Henri Bernardin de Saint-Pierre, who is referred to in Péron's notebooks, and it seems likely that, aside from *Voyage à L'île de France* (1773), Péron had read *Etudes de la Nature* (1784)[39] in which Saint-Pierre declared that the habits of birds are 'equally contrasted' and that 'everything in Nature is in strict alliance'.[40]

Péron also recognised that the 'abundance of shellfish and marine worms' explained the presence of large numbers of seabirds and coastal waders on the island. Yet although he realised that some species on the island, such as the wagtails, were adapted to eating ants, lack of permanent water might better explain the absence of many seed-eating species, such as finches and doves,[41] and even humans, whose absence Péron attributed solely to 'complete ignorance of navigation'.[42] There clearly was sufficient (seed-bearing) vegetation to sustain a significant marsupial population —let alone migratory birds during more favourable periods of the year—

but Péron was unaware that tammar wallabies drink less than other wallabies, can even maintain their fluid levels by drinking seawater and have a larger renal capacity and colon size—and hence greater alimentary water conservation—than other wallabies.[43]

Seemingly well pleased with his collections and observations, Péron spent the night with his companions at their landing place, before leaving the island for the *Géographe* at six o'clock the next morning.

— 16 —

King George Sound

Often 'tis in such gentl temper found,
That scarcely will the very smallest shell
Be moved for days from where it sometime fell,
When last the winds of heaven were unbound.

JOHN KEATS, *On the Sea*

ON the morning of 11 February 1803, the *Géographe* left her anchorage in Murat Bay.[1] Later that day, after surveying a number of other islets and reefs, she reached the point where, because of lack of water, d'Entrecasteaux had broken off his eastward survey of the southern coast of New Holland on 3 January 1793.[2] Baudin felt some satisfaction that he had completed a significant cartographic task and that his chart, combined with Beautemps-Beaupré's from the earlier French expedition, would 'supply exact knowledge of the whole of this area, so long unknown to Europeans'.[3]

As the *Géographe* sailed west, the sight of storm petrels announced nothing more intimidating than a heavy swell, an ample display of light-ning and the distant drum-roll of thunder. By 17 February the favourable winds enabled Baudin to anchor near Seal Island, within the embrace of King George Sound. The next morning he lowered his boats to recon-noitre one of the finest natural harbours of Western Australia's south coast. Péron was no mariner, but he soon appraised the strategic significance of the sound, which covered more than ninety square kilometres and com-prised three 'principal basins', including Princess Royal Harbour—where the port of Albany is now located—which offered 'a good depth everywhere and could hold the biggest warships'.[4] Discovered by George Vancouver in September 1791, King George Sound not only offered shelter, it could also provide fresh water all year round.

While the expedition replenished its water casks and the sailors washed their linen and hammocks, Baudin dispatched one of his boats under the command of Midshipman Jacques-Joseph Ranssonet, with ten days' supplies, to survey the coast 'lying between Vancouver's Mount Gardner and d'Entrecasteaux's Bald Island'. And he ordered another boat under the command of Midshipman Charles Baudin, with the geographer Pierre Faure aboard and six days' supplies, to 'make a complete tour of the bay and of the two ports … [and] to survey them'.[5]

Baudin was already aware of the advance arrival of the *Casuarina*, from a flag placed on the summit of Seal Island and the presence of ten of her casks at the watering place, but he did not send a boat to find her. However, the following morning Louis de Freycinet reported to Baudin and received a frosty reception. The record of recriminations—including the geographer Charles Boulanger's polite but frank letter to Baudin, detailing the need for more precise instructions and agreed signals, in addition to adequate water and victuals for the *Casuarina*[6]—leave little doubt that poor communication and misunderstanding were the roots of the problem. Unfortunately, relations between Baudin and Freycinet only worsened. On 21 February, Baudin visited the *Casuarina*, beached at the head of Princess Royal Harbour, and recorded that she was 'in complete disorder and singularly dirty'. Freycinet attempted to explain that this was 'an inevitable consequence of the situation she was in'. Baudin, however, was in no mood for excuses and ordered Freycinet to move the *Casuarina* to the *Géographe*'s anchorage, within two days, and to replenish with fresh water and firewood.[7]

While all these activities were underway, Péron began to investigate the Sound. His account of its steep and rocky shores in his *Voyage* betrays a continued adherence to elements of Wernerian 'Neptunist' orthodoxy. For Péron, the exposed local 'granite' (actually Archaean granitic gneiss) was essentially 'primitive';[8] that is to say, among the first precipitates of the primordial ocean that Abraham Gottlob Werner naïvely imagined once covered the earth. Nevertheless, Péron does appear to have believed in 'uplift' and might have seen the areas of overlying quaternary dune limestones as offering a clue to when this occurred, judging by at least one of Baudin's sarcastic comments about his geological ideas.[9] Be that as it may, he correctly recognised an ancient weathered landscape very much lacking nutrients, yet supporting 'one of the areas richest in plant life that it is possible to find'.[10] Indeed he tells us that Leschenault collected 'more than two hundred species of plant, many of them new', and added, 'such a profusion of plants seems to contradict all that I have related to do with the general sterility of the soil'.[11] And in the exposition of his ideas, Péron made reference to notions that came remarkably close to some Darwinian concepts:

> ... for much of the year, the whole countryside is lacking in fresh water. Everywhere else but in New Holland, the vegetation of such an area would be miserable; and yet, in this respect, there is nothing richer, more elegant, more magnificent, even than these very places. Innumerable bushes, intermingled with larger trees, *fight everywhere for this dry, burning ground* [my italics]. They form (so to speak) a succession of enchanting groves ... plants unknown in Europe; there, shine the most brilliant and most agreeably perfumed flowers; and throughout the countryside their evergreen foliage creates an air of freshness that lends a charm to these regions and pleasantly enlivens the view. What happy illusion, what amiable artifice Nature seems to employ to disguise the sterility of that she has imposed on these shores![12]

However, this was not yet a truly evolutionary understanding, for these were plants, in Péron's words, '*created* [my italics] for this wild continent'. He had no notions of natural selection, yet he tells his readers that these species 'appear to delight in the heat and dryness'. In New Holland, 'Nature's inexhaustible variety shines forth, however, undeveloped these creatures may be, *they have each been given a distinct area* [my italics]. They are established in certain regions, and it is there that they are most numerous, largest and most beautiful. They degenerate in proportion to the distance that they are from that point, and the species finishes by dying out.'[13]

This was not a prescient recognition of evolutionary adaptation, in which certain characteristics of an organism could favour its prospects of survival in a particular environment and thus help establish a population of favourably adapted organisms. Nevertheless, it was recognition of physiological adaptation, in which change in an organism (such as failure to mature in size or perhaps even survive) takes place in response to specific geographically bound environmental conditions, such as sunlight intensity, temperature, nutrition levels or predation. These are all important components of modern evolutionary thought—as are the notions of ecological equilibrium that Péron expressed in his account of his visit to St Peter Island in Nuyts Archipelago. Endemism is also a fundamental biological concept, and Péron, who recognised the distinctiveness of Australian species, can perhaps be seen as a precursor of Alfred Russell Wallace, whose zoogeographical demarcation of the Asian from the Australasian (marsupial) faunal region[14] is still remembered with the term 'Wallace Line' and with 'Wallacea' for the zone of mixing. But rather than take credit for novel biogeographical ideas, Péron—perhaps more mindful of the benefits of sycophancy than humility—tells his readers that the beginnings of this new science were 'gloriously marked' by the 'beautiful geographico-zoological divisions' of Lacépède and the 'hydrographico-zoological work' of Fleurieu.[15]

Ironically, while King George Sound engendered much animated ecological thought on Péron's part, when Charles Darwin (who, along with Alfred Russell Wallace, would solve the riddle of species diversity by proposing the mechanism of natural selection and evolutionary adaptation) visited the same harbour in March 1836, he would write that during his voyage he had not passed 'a more dull and disinteresting time'.[16] Neither Australia's offshore southern islands nor King George Sound would be Péron's Galapagos, and the scientific world would have to wait another half century for the illumination of the Darwinian Revolution.

In his *Voyage*, Péron wrote: 'Of all the places where we have sojourned in New Holland, King George Sound is (after Shark Bay) the one that has provided us with the greatest abundance of fish.'[17] Here he found mackerel (*Scomber australisicus*) in numbers that 'would have sufficed for the needs of a considerable fleet', pike (*Dinolestes lewini*), wrasse (*Pseudolabrus parilus*), shark (*Heterodontus portusjacksoni*, *Furgaleus ventralis*, *Emissola antarctica*), mullet (*Mugil cephalus*), Sampson fish (*Seriola hippos*) and sweep (*Scorpis aequipinnis*), weedy sea dragons, rays and 'morays' (more likely conger eels, *Gnathophis habenata*).[18]

Readily visible at the head of the harbour were 'whale remains', which 'plainly indicated that an enormous cetacean had but lately perished in that place'.[19] Humpback and southern right whales can still be seen breaching and rolling in the local waters; and Frenchman Bay, in King George Sound, the site of a whaling station until 1978, now houses a whaling museum. Péron also saw a number of seals in the water, but he and his companions 'were unable to catch a single one to determine the species'.[20] Ashore, he appears to have been more successful collecting a specimen of the slender tree-frog. One of only three endemic tree-frogs in south-west Western

Australia, it is notable for its high-pitched screeching call. Péron thought it belonged to the genus *Hyla* (later his compatriots Lesson, Duméril and Bribon did, too), but today it is included in the genus *Litoria* and bears the specific name *adelaidensis*, given to it by J. E. Gray, who published the first description of a specimen collected by John Gould.[21]

In his *Voyage*, Péron tells his readers that land and sea birds in the region of the Sound were 'rare' and very wary, which he thought was a result of being 'habitually hunted by the natives'.[22] Their scarcity is apparently confirmed by Péron's notebook, which contains no mention of birds during his landfall.[23] More fruitful was the sandy intertidal zone of the shore. This was Péron's now familiar hunting ground. Here he found 'fleshy zoophytes' constituting 'rich and numerous species', including the type specimens of another two sponges described by Lamarck—*Spongia turgida* (= *Fasciospongia turgida*) and *Alcyonium putridosum* (= *Oceanapia putridosa*)[24]—and among the 'magnificence and variety'[25] of the shellfish, the type specimens of Lamarck's molluscs: *Mactra australis*, *Solemya australis* and *Tellina margaritina*.[26] In sharp contrast to the Tasmanian Aborigines, the indigenous Minang dialect–speaking people of the Nyungar language group steadfastly avoided eating shellfish[27] and thereby contributed to the rich variety on the shores. Collecting 'one hundred and sixty species', according to his own reckoning, Péron was surrounded by 'so many riches' that it became impossible to indicate 'the most precious'.[28]

The expedition's landfall had still more surprises to offer. During his survey of the coast near Cape Vancouver, Ransonnet was amazed to encounter a ship at anchor in a 'pretty bay' below Mount Gardner. This was the ninety-nine-ton snow *Union*, from New York, under the command of Captain Isaac Pendleton.[29] He had hopes of obtaining a cargo of 20 000 seal-skins for sale in China, but was disappointed at the scarcity of these sea mammals in the Sound. Baudin would direct him to Kangaroo Island. There he spent four months killing hapless seals and constructing a thirty-five-ton vessel, the *Independence*, on the north-east of the island at a place that has been known as American River ever since. In his *Voyage*, Péron alluded to the fate of Alexandre Le Corre in Bass Strait, before exclaiming: '... how fortunate Captain Pendleton will have been, if he has been able to escape the ruin that the English prepare in these remote regions for the ship-owners of all nations.'[30] Pendleton did escape ruin in Bass Strait, but the lure of lucre is a fateful master: on 1 October 1804, after a visit to Port Jackson and Norfolk Island, he, his supercargo John Boston and six crew members were massacred while in search of sandalwood on Tongatabu.[31] And some months later, the *Union*, under the command of Pendleton's first mate, Daniel Wright, was completely wrecked near Sandalwood Bay in Fiji.[32]

It was from other members of the expedition, particularly Baudin, Faure and Ransonnet, that Péron gained information on the indigenous inhabitants of the Sound. Faure and Baudin did not meet any of the Aborigines; nevertheless, they observed two circular clearings, '3 to 4 feet in circumference', on opposite banks of the estuary of a large stream (the King or the Kalgan River) flowing into Oyster Harbour, each ringed with eleven spears coated with red resin and stuck in the ground. Péron speculated that they might have marked 'the territorial borders of two neighbouring tribes' or the graves of 'two warriors or two chiefs of enemy tribes, struck down in the same general or individual battle'. Although his vivid imagination inclined him towards the latter hypothesis, he did recognise that without further investigation (perhaps even excavation) he was reduced to 'the uncertainty of conjectures'.[33]

A mile further on, Faure reported ingeniously located dry stone dykes designed to trap fish at low tide. (The Nyungar people are known to have used spears to take these trapped fish; surprisingly, they did not use hooks or nets.)[34] Ransonnet and his boat crew did actually encounter a group of eight indigenous inhabitants during their coastal survey. This was after seeking shelter in a small bay near Bald Island. The group comprised at least five men, accompanied by three women (who soon slipped away) and several handsome dogs. Ransonnet repeatedly tried to exchange all that he had at his disposal—including coat buttons, handkerchiefs and old jackets—for one of the dogs (presumably dingos), but failed. This seems to have been because the dogs were a crucial aid to hunting kangaroos. However, Ransonnet did receive an axe with a stone head fastened with 'mastic', which Péron and his colleagues considered 'valuable' because of the remarkably hard manner in which it had set. This axe was almost certainly a *kodja*—a distinctive Nyungar tool with a head fashioned from two stones (one sharpened, the other flat) bonded with *Xanthorrhoea* resin around a wooden handle.[35]

While Baudin was well pleased by the young gardener, Antoine Guichenot, collecting 'more than one hundred and fifty different species' and growing sixty-eight specimens in pots—efforts that he considered 'work and not wit'—he had contrasting expectations for Péron's and Leschenault's forthcoming reports, which he believed would be the product of 'all wit and no work'. In the same journal entry (25 February), he ignored Péron's zoological responsibilities and referred to him, with what seems to have been sarcasm, as 'our observer of mankind'.[36] His criticism of Péron's efforts appear unfair. There is no dispute about the paucity of his anthropological observations at King George Sound, but (like Baudin himself) Péron lacked any personal encounter with the indigenous inhabitants there. Baudin's resentment might actually have stemmed from Péron's attendance of a grand reunion dinner organised by Freycinet, aboard the *Casuarina*, on the evening of 25 February. Baudin, who might not even have been invited, fumed at what he considered to be Freycinet's misdirected priorities and relaxed discipline. For the expedition's commander, the men of the *Casuarina* should not have been off fishing, hunting in the hills or relaxing at the dinner table when there was still firewood to be cut. Wanting to shame his officers, he supervised the woodcutting and watering parties himself. In his journal, Baudin left little doubt of his anger towards Freycinet: 'I was in a mood to give him a thorough dressing-down in order to teach him his duty and also that he should not waste his time in pleasure when there is urgent work to be done.'[37] The next day Freycinet did indeed receive a severe reprimand— one Baudin hoped he would never forget 'as much for the good of the Service as for himself'.[38] But by this time Freycinet, with stoic resolve, knew he could never please the expedition's commander. As for Péron, Baudin refused to acknowledge anything significant in his efforts at King George Sound. And just before their departure, he wrote contemptuously: 'Citizen Péron ... will be able to write a volume on worms and molluscs. He has one or two cases of broken shells, for in several places along the shore one can shovel them up. These, he claims, should help him to establish the period at which New Holland must have risen from the floor of the sea.'[39]

— 17 —

Back to Shark Bay

To those who live in a state of rude familiarity with the sea it becomes natural to regard the wind as an individuality, and the rocks as sentient beings.

VICTOR HUGO, *The Toilers of the Sea*

THE expedition set sail from King George Sound at about 4.30 a.m. on 1 March 1803.[1] Instead of giving Freycinet the opportunity for clarification while both vessels were still at anchor, Baudin chose to give him his instructions in the form of written orders that were to be opened only at sea. His plan was to finish the survey of Geographe Bay, fix the position of St Allouarn Island, then, after a brief call at Rottnest Island, search for sea turtles in Shark Bay before visiting North West Cape. In his instructions, Baudin left it up to Freycinet to decide whether or not to accompany the *Géographe*, but intimated that in the event of another separation his subordinate would be held 'personally answerable to the authorities in France for the expenses incurred'.[2] Despite this, Freycinet was given four to five months of supplies—enough to sail directly to the Ile de France if necessary. Through his instructions to Freycinet and generous victualling of the *Casuarina*, Baudin must have sought to absolve himself of responsibility for his consort in the event of another separation.

It was not long before the two vessels were separated again. Progress towards Cape Leeuwin had been slow because of the contrary winds, so on 5 March Baudin decided to order Freycinet to make a closer investigation of the coast for 'some ports which could be of use to navigators'.[3] Baudin expected Freycinet to make a prompt return and report on his findings, but after two days of tacking and waiting, he persuaded himself (incorrectly) that the skipper of the *Casuarina* had simply been 'looking for a separation in order to head for Ile-de-France'.[4] Freycinet would not be vindicated until the vessels were reunited at Rottnest Island. There he explained that because of the winds, he had not been able to approach the coast (between Wilson Head and Point Hillier) until the following morning. When he did, he gained a view of what today is known as William Bay. Sailing west, he passed another three bays, hazardous reefs, Point Irwin (which he named 'Cape Lacroix' in honour of one of France's 'most learned geometricians') and rounded Rocky Head and Point Nuyts, before attempting to rejoin the *Géographe*. No sooner had the *Casuarina* stood out to sea than she was swallowed up by heavy fog. Lanterns were raised on the mast heads and flares were fired, but to no avail. Freycinet therefore decided to press on alone and hope for a rendezvous off Rottnest Island. En route, he completed the survey of Geographe Bay—dodging numerous dead whales floating eerily on the waves—and plotting the cape that would be named after Péron, near present-day Rockingham, south of Fremantle.

On the day the *Casuarina* reached the *Naturaliste*'s old anchorage off Rottnest Island, the *Géographe* anchored off Wonnerup Inlet on Geographe Bay where Timothée Vasse had disappeared among the waves on 8 June 1801 and where Péron had almost come to grief the day before. Clearly seeking to discredit Baudin further, Péron wrote:

> All eyes were then fixed on the nearby beach; we could see some very big fires quite close to the shore. It was there, precisely opposite our anchorage, that poor Vasse had been left for dead in the middle of the dark night ... The horror of such an abandonment had never ceased to inspire in us grief and bitterness; and, although it had been dictated by the most disastrous circumstances, no one aboard the *Géographe* had been able to get over it. Furthermore, those great fires—the like of which we had not seen during our first visit—filled every heart with an involuntary agitation, an anxiety both painful and tender. The weather was superb, the sea perfectly calm; the very winds, blowing gently from the west, seemed to invite us to undertake a search—fruitless, perhaps, but at least easy, as well as sacred ... Oh! how deep and general was the sadness when, on the following morning, our Commander gave the order to leave and sail away from those fires still burning on the shore![5]

As Frank Horner has pointed out, the other journals of the expedition do not corroborate Péron's assertions about the emotions aboard the *Géographe* at the time.[6] Furthermore, Freycinet did not search for Vasse either, but in an age sensitive to the plight of the castaway (be it in the form of Selkirk, Crusoe, La Pérouse or Bligh), Vasse might have been a potent instrument of Péron's vengeance against Baudin. It should also be noted that Vasse was not just a humble assistant helmsman aboard the *Naturaliste*. He came from an influential family—his father had been a member of the Council of Five Hundred during the Directory—and they had sought news of him as early as the summer of 1800 when he suddenly quit his post in the war ministry and disappeared.[7] Demonstrable (even genuine) concern for such an individual might yet bring other rewards for an ambitious young man like Péron. Ironically, he would later discount rumours which circulated in Paris, between 1804 and 1807, that Vasse had survived.

On 13 March, the *Géographe* was reunited with the *Casuarina* off Rottnest Island. After their most recent separation, Baudin had resolved to remove Freycinet from the command of the schooner. However, when his subordinate explained that the mist on the coast had thwarted their reunion before rounding Cape Leeuwin, Baudin found his excuse reasonable and changed his mind. The expedition did not linger. Although the *Casuarina* had difficulty keeping up with the *Géographe*, both vessels passed the Houtman Abrolhos without incident (other than the deaths of yet another wallaby and emu injured aboard in rough seas) and rounded Dirk Hartog Island on 16 March. The following day the vessels anchored off the tip of the Peron Peninsula, and Baudin dispatched two boats, under the command of Ransonnet, to search for turtles.[8] Péron was surprised to see their crews return soon after in a state of 'panic-stricken terror', having encountered a group of a hundred formidable indigenous inhabitants intent on resisting their landing.[9] Ransonnet's party, however, might have unwittingly interrupted a ceremony or other communal gathering of the local Malkana people; but it should be remembered that turtles were a prized Aboriginal food source[10] and that the *Endeavour* expedition faced a violent local reaction when Cook's sailors took eight or nine female turtles during their sojourn on the north Queensland coast in July 1770.[11] Ransonnet gathered only a dozen turtles because it was not the egg-laying season. This was in marked contrast to his earlier visit aboard the *Naturaliste* when the ship's boats were filled with turtles within minutes.

When Péron landed, he was disappointed to find no trace of the Aborigines other than their huts. Mindful of his ineffective anthropological efforts and tantalised by William Dampier's descriptions of the magnificent shellfish of the area, in his *Voyage* he gave a laborious justification for renewed zoological endeavours (in the company of an armed sailor), on the grounds that Stanislas Levillain's collections—during the *Naturaliste's* earlier landfall at the same anchorage—had been dispersed after his death and had allegedly even found their way into British hands as a result of 'incautious prodigality' at Port Jackson. So strident was his rationalised scientific nationalism that he declared: 'In every instance it must be considered a sort of crime in the eyes of a man of honour to hand over the fruit of these labours to foreigners—even enemies of one's country.'[12]

In search of replacement specimens, Péron decided to traverse the northern end of the peninsula, now named in his honour, to reach the promising shallows at Herald Bluff. It was a tiring walk over brilliant white sand that reflected sunlight painfully into his eyes. Unfortunately, the waters proved surprisingly barren. Climbing the neighbouring dunes he asserted he could see the east coast of the peninsula and convinced himself that the specimens gathered during the *Naturaliste's* landfall must have come from there. Returning to the *Géographe* he allegedly reported his fruitless efforts to Baudin and requested the use of a boat to take him 'as far as the sand-banks' or alternatively 'an escort of armed men, in order to get there by land'. According to Péron, Baudin refused both requests. Undeterred, on the morning of 19 March, Péron went ashore in the longboat along with a party ordered to boil seawater to replace the expedition's scanty supply of salt. This time he explored the western end of the tip of the peninsula and found three caverns near Cape Lesueur, which, judging by the ashes of fires and the presence of numerous footprints, he believed were used as dwellings. For Péron the lives of the inhabitants were indeed harsh, and for the European visitor no other country was to be feared more because of its extremes and sudden changes of temperature and humidity than this part of New Holland—responsible, he believed, for 'infirmities, illnesses and death'.[13]

The following day, Baudin dispatched the artist Nicolas Petit—two years Péron's junior and a former student of Jacques-Louis David—to sketch 'the native village and the shape of the huts', together with the gardener Guichenot to collect plants. 'Of the naturalists', Baudin wrote, 'Citizen Péron was the only one to go ashore, the others considering that the land did not merit any more careful an examination than they had already made along the small stretch that they had been able to see or visit.'[14] A half-mile from their landfall a rock pool encrusted with an abundance of crystalline salt was discovered; it was soon reported to one of the officers. Six hundred pounds of salt was collected, which more than replaced that which was used in salting the plentiful fish caught locally. (The waters of Shark Bay are high in salt because of the low precipitation and the high evaporation rates; in Hamelin Pool, which adjoins the peninsula, the waters contain almost twice the salt levels of normal seawater.)

Péron was still determined to visit the east coast of the peninsula and persuaded Guichenot and Petit to accompany him. According to Baudin, Péron—'the most thoughtless and most wanting in foresight of everyone aboard'—had assured the gardener and the artist that he had consulted a chart of the peninsula, that it was only a league in width and that they had 'much more time than they needed for the excursion he was proposing'. Guichenot was apparently promised 'a good collection of new plants' and Petit 'a great variety of entertainment'.[15] After walking for four hours without reaching their objective, Guichenot (according to Baudin) then raised concerns about returning to the longboat in time for the agreed departure time. Péron reportedly excused their delay on a failure to bear sufficiently to the left. According to his *Voyage*, they reached their objective at about 10.00 a.m. Péron was delighted:

> All my presumptions became a certainty: we found those sand-banks, those gentle waters and those beautiful shellfish that we had come to seek on that shore. By means of the flats, one could wade a long way out, the water scarcely reaching one's knees; and it was sufficient (as it were) to plunge one's hand into the sand in order to pull out the most beautiful shells. At the same time various shoals of fish swam fearlessly around us.[16]

However, among these shoals of fish were 'several large sharks', and when one came suddenly towards Petit, he fired his musket at it. The danger was certainly real; the sailor Lefèvre, Péron's worthy companion on St Peter Island, was attacked by a shark in the nearby Hamelin Pool and narrowly escaped with his life, thanks to three other sailors who came to his rescue. Péron and Guichenot soon quit the water, not, according to Péron, for fear of the sharks but because they feared the discharge of the musket might draw the attention of the Aborigines, whom they believed had only recently been present on the beach. While Péron and Guichenot hurriedly dressed, they repeatedly urged Petit to come with them and hide in the bush. Instead, he mocked them from the shallows.

Nicolas Petit's bravado soon turned to terror when loud cries were heard and a 'troop of natives'—Péron would eventually count fourteen men armed with clubs and spears—poured down from the dunes near Guichenault Point. Fleeing the water, Petit grabbed his clothes and ran half-naked towards his comrades. As he approached, Péron and Guichenot loaded their weapons—Baudin, however, asserted that the musket was borrowed from the steward and was 'found to work no longer'—and promised each other they would fire only as a last resort. But rather than run and further embolden the shrieking band about to fall upon them, Péron and his companions began to walk calmly in their direction.[17] This resolute action, by three men who must have seemed strangely costumed and ghostly pale, disconcerted their Malkana pursuers. Péron writes that 'after a few moments of uncertainty and deliberation', the Aborigines retreated 'slowly and without sign of fear or disorder'.[18]

Although clearly relieved, Péron had no regrets about any lost opportunities for cultural exploration. Having returned to the vantage point of the dunes, the Aborigines, according to Péron, 'seemed to be insisting that one of us go to them on his own'. The three young men made no move. 'After replying to them for a time with similar cries and gestures', wrote Péron, 'we bade them some sort of farewell and peacefully continued on our way back along the shore.'[19] Baudin seems to have been entirely justified in his harsh judgment that they had 'missed the finest opportunity that had arisen to communicate with the natives'.[20] He was equally disappointed that Petit had not sketched any of them.

Péron asserted that, soon after losing sight of their former pursuers, he and his companions began to head back across the neck of the peninsula in order to rejoin the landing party. According to Baudin's investigations, they continued looking for shells, several of which had already been found by the men of the *Naturaliste* in great numbers. He was scathing in his assessment of Péron:

> The leader of the party—the citizen who, until now, has caused us nothing but trouble and anxiety when he has been ashore with no-one to watch over and guide him—preferred to waste the remaining time roaming along the shore, rather than return. Thus they only

started back when it was certain that they would not reach the boat before the time fixed for departure, even supposing that they had taken the most direct route.[21]

There is no doubt that Péron and his companions lacked food and water. The Peron Peninsula is largely composed of a red Pleistocene Aeolian sandstone and is covered with dunes of red sand. In some of the interdunal depressions there are ephemeral playa lakes, which are called *birridas* by the local Aboriginal people.[22] Péron does not appear to have seen any of these precious seasonal water sources, which must have sustained the people he had just seen. Although the sun was no longer overhead, it reflected fiercely off the dunes in the breezeless air. Heavily laden with specimens, they sucked small pebbles in the vain hope of a 'few drops of saliva'. According to Baudin's journal, when night fell the three became lost, but this throws the time sequence out completely. They appear, in fact, to have become lost during the afternoon, and when they finally found the coast again (realising what little progress they had made), the certain route it offered seemed a safer option than attempting a shortcut across the peninsula.

By this stage, all three were severely dehydrated and suffering from heat stress. According to Péron, Guichenot, who was carrying a heavy load of shells on behalf of his colleague,[23] collapsed, 'pale and disfigured, his eyes growing dull'. Something had to be done quickly. Fortunately, the coast offered an opportunity to plunge in the sea. The effects were miraculous, as Péron recorded: 'A sweet freshness seemed to penetrate every pore; the burning in our mouths diminished; the painful gnawing at our stomachs ceased as if by magic; we felt some strength returning ... In a word, this salutary bath probably saved us from death.'[24] Abandoning their shoes and some of their clothes, they trudged on in the shallows. After sunset they were heartened by a breeze and decided to leave the water once more to cut across the tip of the peninsula. Despite their state of extreme fatigue, their spirits soared at the sight of a large bonfire in the distance. Péron tells his readers that just two hundred paces from the landing place, 'we fell as though senseless on the sand; our good friends hurried to our side; they lifted us up and supported us and, lighting several fires around us managed to rekindle the flame of life that was at the point of exhaustion'.[25]

It was now 10.30 p.m. Aboard the *Géographe*, Baudin had already come to the conclusion that the landing party had not returned because of the 'absence of some people, Citizen Péron being unquestionably one of them'.[26] Nevertheless, he had repeatedly ordered the return of the boat by firing a canon. When the first discharge brought no response, he ordered another, again in vain, and then decided to fine Bonnefoy de Montbazin thirty francs for his disobedience—the cost of the powder expended. Ashore, Bonnefoy had felt morally bound to remain until Péron, Guichenot and Petit were found.

When they finally reached the shore party, their ordeal was still not over. Péron tells us that 'no food or drink of any kind remained in the longboat'. Furthermore, he and his companions had to spend the night in their wet clothes, and in the morning they found that their return to the *Géographe* was delayed by their lack of a compass and the presence of a heavy morning mist, which made navigation impossible. By the time they reached the *Géographe*, Péron and Guichenot were almost on the point of complete collapse. Unable to give a report to Baudin, he was nevertheless shocked to learn that Bonnefoy had been fined for refusing the order that would have seen him and his companions abandoned in mortal peril ashore. His reaction was bitter: 'Wretched man! In order to save his life in Timor, I had shared with his doctor the small supply of quiquin [quinine] that I was saving for myself.'[27] In an appendix to the chapter recounting these events, he criticised Baudin for the bare rations he issued for excursions, which did not take unforeseen circumstances into account. With considerable justification, he also took issue with the meagre allowance of one pint of water per man as 'absolutely inadequate to the needs of sailors, who, under a burning sun had sometimes to row for an entire day. It was the same for the naturalists, who, through the nature of their work, were obliged to make long excursions over scorching sands.'[28] Unfortunately, Baudin had to manage water as his most precious resource. Severe water restrictions were not unusual during such voyaging, two centuries ago, and were very probably the cause of the chronic nephritis and cystitis that ultimately killed Matthew Flinders at the age of forty.[29]

Péron considered his most significant anthropological finding of the visit to have been the dismissal of the notion (going back to de Vlamingh's 1697 report of gigantic human footprints) that the local inhabitants were a race of giants. These people were of 'ordinary height—even small', he wrote, and were characterised by 'spindliness of limb and ... slenderness of form'.[30] Similarly, in his view, his most significant zoological finding was the dismissal of reports that hippopotami inhabited Shark Bay. This had first been propagated by William Dampier, who recorded that he had found a hippopotamus's head in the stomach of a shark in the bay. Baudin, who claimed to have killed several hippopotami on the African coast, thought he recognised a 'perfect resemblance to the hippopotamus' in the description and the actual teeth brought back by his men from Faure Island in Hamelin Pool. But what Dampier had seen was 'half-decomposed by digestion', and what the men of the *Géographe* had seen was 'half-decomposed' in the sand. When Péron examined the teeth he found they 'differed fundamentally' from a hippopotamus and correctly judged that they were 'from a dugong'.

Despite his harrowing ordeal ashore, Péron left Shark Bay, on 23 March, full of satisfaction at his efforts resolving 'two problems of equal importance to the zoology and physical history of New Holland'.[31] Baudin, however, made no mention of either of these conclusions; he had had enough of Péron: 'This is the third escapade of this nature that our learned naturalist has been on, but it will also be the last, for he shall not go ashore again unless I myself am in the same boat. And the limits that I shall set to his excursions will not be broad enough to allow him to delay the boat's departure or to stray too far.'[32]

Final surveys

My terminus near,
The clouds already closing in upon me,
The voyage balk'd, the course disputed, lost,
I yield my ships to Thee.

WALT WHITMAN, *Prayer of Columbus*

BAUDIN'S next objective was to verify the position of North West Cape and to investigate the so-called 'Willem's River' of Dutch charts.[1] Unfortunately, by the middle of 24 March he had not made land. Seeking the astronomer Pierre-François Bernier's assistance, he realised that the longitude he had sought to confirm incorporated a chronometer's error from his first visit, which he had not allowed for. In his journal Baudin wrote, 'I had nothing to say in reply to this and recognised my error.'[2] And as Frank Horner put it, 'For once he did not blame his subordinate.'[3]

Baudin did not explore Exmouth Gulf or attempt to determine whether a strait separated Exmouth Peninsula from the mainland. He continued his resurveying of the Western Australian coast and on 28 March charted the reef-ringed Monte Bello Islands, only one of which had been sighted during their previous coasting. On 29 March the expedition reached Dampier Archipelago, and the following day the *Géographe* anchored off Depuch Island (20° 37′ S 117° 44′ E), known as Womalantha to the local Ngarluma people. Although it now honours the expedition's mineralogist, Baudin referred to the island as Ile des Amiraux, and Lamarck mistakenly read this name as 'Ile des animaux' when he published the habitat location for his *Donax epiderma*—one of the molluscs that Péron presumably collected with a dredge on the offshore shoal where they were anchored.[4] For several days after leaving this anchorage, the vessels were too far from land to chart it, because of banks and reefs, but Péron gained renewed opportunities to collect 'a host of species of marine life hitherto unknown'. These included a 'prodigious number of sea-snakes' in 'every colour and various sizes', some the 'thickness of an arm and no less than 5 to 6 feet long'.[5] One specimen,[6] that of a highly toxic horned sea-snake, *Acalyptophis peronii*, was preserved in alcohol and fifty years later served as the holotype for André Duméril's description.[7]

What particularly attracted Péron's attention in these waters was a greyish microscopic organism, which covered the sea for 'more than 20 leagues from east to west'. He believed this was the 'sea-sawdust' reported by Banks and Solander during the *Endeavour* voyage.[8] This was very likely a species of *Trichodesmium*, an algal-like cyanobacteria that produces chlorophyll in its outer cytoplasm and thereby photosynthesises oxygen. This planktonic genus is also related to the colonies of cyanobacteria, attached to the seabed, which produce the world-famous stromatolites of Hamelin Pool in Shark Bay, one of the most ancient of all life forms.[9] According to Louis de Freycinet, Péron intended to 'return, some day, in a separate work, to this remarkable phenomenon of the ocean'. Although he found no trace of this manuscript among Péron's papers, Freycinet wrote: 'He hoped to be able to prove then that all these wonders of yellow sea, sea of milk and especially sea of blood, spoken of by so many celebrated writers of Antiquity, are not as absurd as people nowadays have been pleased to say that they are.'[10] Indeed, Péron was on the right track, for the Red Sea and the Yellow Sea are now generally believed to owe their names to blooms of *Trichodesmium*. Significantly, Charles Darwin also noted Péron's observations in this area.[11]

On 2 and 3 April there were anxious hours while the *Géographe* negotiated the vast shoals of the Amphinomes Bank, with the *Casuarina* sounding warily ahead. By 8 April, free of calms, contrary currents and perilous shoals, the expedition once more began to sail close to the coast, which Péron found 'less-dreary' than before and with greenery that had a 'soft freshness about it'.[12] This was the coast between Dampier's landfall at Roebuck Bay (where the 'Port of Pearls' Broome is now located) and the expansive reach of King Sound. The expedition charted Capes Boileau and Bertholet, but mistook Gantheaume Point and Emeriau Point for islands, before clearing Cape Leveque in stormy weather. On 15 April, in

the wake of still more tempests, another island was sighted that was ultimately named in honour of General Louis de Caffarelli, mortally wounded
during Bonaparte's siege of Acre in Palestine in 1799. In the week that
followed, other islands—Fontanes, Tournefort, Augereau and Championet
—were added to the chart of the Bonaparte Archipelago first sighted in
August 1801. Cape Chateaurenaud (on Bigge Island) was sighted on
21 April but mistaken for part of the mainland, mainly because of smoke
from what appeared to be Aboriginal fires. That night the expedition
anchored north-west of the Montalivet Islands.

Progress was slow in the next few days off the northern Kimberley
coast, and on 24 April, Baudin took advantage of a calm to dispatch a boat
to reconnoitre Cassini Island, named for the dynasty of French astronomers of Italian descent. Louis Barbe (a young sailor from Dunkirk) and
Guichenot were ordered to accompany it and respectively to collect any
birds and plants ashore. Péron was undoubtedly disappointed not to have
accompanied them and, with implicit criticism of Baudin, wrote: 'It would
have been desirable for this interesting section of the coast—which until
that day, had not been examined by any European—to have been explored
with regard to geography and natural history; one must regret, therefore, that
the command of this craft should have been entrusted to a simple sailor.'[13]

At dawn the following day, Péron and his companions sighted the boat
returning to the *Géographe*, but were surprised to see it suddenly change
course and enter what appeared to be a strait or bay. It did not reappear
until midday and no explanation for its diversion was available until it
returned to the mother ship at 2.00 p.m. Then it was learned that the boat
crew had spotted four Malay praus and, while pursuing them, had sighted
another two at anchor. Although the Malays had set sail and fled, one boat
was overtaken 'by the show that the men made of firing on them if it continued to row'.[14] The frightened men aboard were dressed and armed in
a manner very similar to those the expedition had met in Timor. When
the French made their peaceful intentions clear, a wary cordiality prevailed.
The French boat crew was offered water by the Malays, and Guichenot
was given some finely chopped tobacco. Although the Malays invited the
Géographe's boat to follow them, its poorly armed boat crew thought it
more prudent to report back to Baudin instead.

On learning of the presence of the Malays, Baudin decided to find out
why they were there and 'whether they were permanently established'. He
placed the master helmsman Ignace Fortin in charge of the ship's boat to

reconnoitre. Freycinet was ordered to follow in the *Casuarina* and maintain a watchful presence, but the currents separated him from Fortin's craft, and he found himself leeward of the island. Fortin would discover that the Malays were from Macassar and part of a fleet of two dozen praus collecting *trepang*—holothurians, also known as sea slugs or bêches-de-mer. Their elderly commander was the only one who possessed a compass, and it was a mere 'two inches in diameter and extremely poorly made'. He also learned that this was an annual voyage made by 'several flotillas'.

On this part of the Australian coast the Macassans appeared to have very poor relations with the indigenous inhabitants; Péron recorded that their watering parties rarely returned 'without the spilling of blood on one side or the other' and that one of the Macassans had only just been killed and several others wounded. Péron believed that the Macassans had 'discovered New Holland many centuries before Europeans, themselves knew of the existence of the great Asian archipelago'.[15] Modern historical research, however, has revealed that these voyages probably began sometime after the Dutch restricted other Macassan trading enterprises in 1667. No mention of the trade appears in Dutch sources before 1754 despite the probability that Macassan skippers had access to Dutch cartographic information long before. The trading voyages of the trepangers continued until the first decade of the twentieth century. Significantly, many of the Macassan boats were owned by Dutch merchants.[16]

When he wrote his account of these events, Péron was well aware that the trepangs were sold to an eager Chinese market. Indeed, they are still used in soups and cooked with vegetables in China. Péron, however, seized on their reputation as an aphrodisiac—based mainly on their phallic shape—to launch a moral tirade against the Chinese: '... no people in the world', he wrote, 'carry further the refinement of corruption and debauchery.'[17] Yet despite his moral condemnations and warnings of dangerous physiological consequences associated with the use of aphrodisiacs, he had no ethical qualms when he hinted that the little-exploited holothurians of the shores of Ile de France—barely any smaller than those of New Holland—might sell for a very high price in China.[18]

Unable to land on Cassini Island, Péron seems to have consoled himself with the fact that the shells collected by Guichenot and Barbe belonged, with a few exceptions, to the same species as had already been collected in Timor. Nevertheless, he seems to have been tantalised by reports that an 'entire section' of the island was composed of coral and calcareous material, as had fascinated him in Timor, and surprised by Baudin's decision to depart immediately after the boat had returned to the *Géographe*. The presence of the trepang occasioned the naming of the vast banks they traversed as the Holothurian Reefs, but the frequent calms ultimately thwarted Baudin's plans to continue his survey of De Witt's Land, and he decided to make for Timor again in order to replenish.[19]

Timor's highest peaks were sighted at sunset on 3 May, and the expedition anchored in Kupang Bay late on the evening of 6 May. In the morning, Péron accompanied the officers and remaining savants in their courtesy call on the Governor. After so many deaths during their first visit in 1801, there was still more unsettling news that their previous host, Governor Lofstett, had died of fever and that a number of the Timorese notables they had befriended had also passed away. Lofstett's replacement, Johannes Giesler, was himself seriously ill. Although destined to die from his malady, he attended to the expedition's victualling needs and arranged for Baudin to reside in Governor Lofstett's former residence and for the naturalists and astronomers to take up lodgings in Fort Concordia. It was from Geisler that they also learned of the departure of Matthew Flinders (bound for Port Jackson via Cape Leeuwin) on the *Investigator* a month before.[20]

Old friendships and nicknames were revealed. Lesueur, for example, was remembered as *orang mati bourou* (bird-killer man), and the mineralogist Bailly was recalled as *orang bato* (pebble man).[21] Perhaps Péron was known as *orang kerang* (shell man)! Between 16 and 20 May Péron and his fellow naturalists accompanied excursions by the officers to purchase provisions. These forays gave them an opportunity to add to their collections.[22] The expedition suffered less from illness during its second sojourn in Timor, a third as long as its previous visit, yet its members witnessed the ravages of endemic dysentery and fever among others, such as the crew of the American vessel *Hunter*, which had to be sold when she had insufficient healthy hands to sail her.

During the final stages of the reprovisioning of the *Géographe* and *Casuarina*, Péron and Lesueur decided to travel to the swamps of Babau, at the head of Kupang Bay, to hunt crocodile. They set off early on the morning of 26 May, riding bareback, apparently because of a superstition prohibiting the use of saddles. As we shall see, Péron was deeply impressed by the local Timor ponies, which stand only eleven to twelve hands high but are agile, strong and sure-footed. With a Timorese entourage of nine— five on horseback and four on foot—they headed east through coastal forest to the hamlet of Oba where wealthy Madame van Esten—whom they had come to know during their first visit—resided on land expropriated by her late husband, a former governor, from the unfortunate Rajah of Néâs.[23] Then they made for the shore and walked the length of Passir-Pandjang[24] to Kelapa Lima[25] before reaching the charming village of Oesapa-Ketjil,[26] where a hospitable elderly man entertained them with a meal of rice and coconut. Nearby was the Oesapa River. The road, which swung inland, along the course of the river, offered a pleasant view of two, low-lying, mangrove-fringed islands in the estuary. Here, the two naturalists noted large numbers of aquatic birds roosting in the branches and awaiting the exposure of familiar feeding grounds at low tide. To the west the road was fringed with towering coconut palms, and the enveloping silence was broken only by the solicitous cooing of doves. Péron appears to have relished the walk in the midst of these 'most agreeable' woods to reach the village of Oesapa-Besar,[27] inhabited by 300 to 400 people. Here, he and Lesueur were able to cross the Oesapa River and then reach Nonsouis, along 'narrow, rocky tracks that were frequently intersected by deep ravines'.[28] Beyond this village, Péron was thrilled by the sight of a round-up of horses and wrote vividly:

> The freedom enjoyed by these animals ... makes them impatient, quick in their movements and impetuous in their running. Should they get away from the herd, their guardians, gripping the shoulders of their mounts with their knees, follow them immediately. The men move through the trees like lightning and manoeuvre these rapid steeds so skilfully, that they avoid the trees in their path and run (or fly, rather) as though in open country. It is in this way that they catch up with the straying horse—with a lightness and flexibility of which nothing in Europe can give any idea. These horsemen, like the fabulous cen-taurs, appear to form one body with the horses they ride.[29]

Making their way back down to the coast, Péron, Lesueur and their Timorese companions meandered through several more villages (includ-ing present-day Tarus) and crossed the Penfoei River to reach the pros-perous hamlet of Nobaki, which was surrounded by fields of maize, sugar cane and rice. Plunging once more into dense forest and passing through another two villages, they finally reached Babau, eight leagues from Kupang. High on a hill, surrounded by groves of coconut and tamarind trees, they were received at the home of the local Rajah, a small, thin, lively man with a jovial countenance. From the Rajah's redoubt they could see the wide neighbouring plain intersected by rivers and marshes and flanked by the imposing Anmfoa Mountains. Their goal, on the morrow, was to reach the wetlands to the north, but when they explained their dangerous quest, they were met with horror and were only able to find two guides willing to show them where they could hunt crocodiles. And these guides were reluctant conscripts, enlisted by the Rajah with 'menaces on the one hand and promises and entreaties on the other'.[30]

Péron and Lesueur made their way warily: fording deep rivers on bridges comprised of single coconut palm-trunks, and negotiating the length of narrow embankments amid the knee-deep mud of paddy fields. As they searched for crocodiles they were threatened with abandonment by their nervous guides. Finally, on the sharp bend of a river, one of the massive reptiles (an Indo-Pacific 'saltwater' crocodile *Crocodylus porosus*) was sighted twenty-five paces away, partly submerged and apparently asleep. Lesueur recounted what happened next:

> I aimed at it immediately in order to hit it below the axilla; and, since the animal was side on to me, I fired in such a way as to break its back-bone and succeeded. As soon as the monster felt itself wounded, it tried to hurl itself into the water. This it could not manage, and so we watched as it tossed and thrashed with fury. It bled freely and, after a few minutes, seemed to us to be close to death. Being quite certain then that it could not escape, we decided to put off until the next day the task of skinning it.[31]

This was not quite the stuff of François Boucher's famous romantic painting *La Chasse au Crocodile* (1739), in which one fearless hunter wedges a baton between the jaws of the ferocious reptile and turbaned lancers attack each flank.[32] But Péron and Lesueur were determined to bring their quarry home to France with as little risk and damage as possible. Returning to Babau, with their now relieved and even boastful guides, they recruited a dozen men to help recover the crocodile's body. It was now 28 May. Back at the river's edge and waist deep in mud, Péron and Lesueur dissected the animal before slinging its remains beneath two bamboo poles. None of the porters would touch the dead animal and, when they returned to the Rajah's house, Péron recorded that they were made to 'put down the sacrilegious burden' and were required to undergo a purification ceremony before their host would approach them. According to Péron:

All the Malays—men, women and children—formed a circle around us; and, despite the rules of European propriety, we had to undress completely. Since the trough could only hold one person at a time, M. Lesueur and I got into it, one after the other. Two slaves brought large vessels full of water and emptied them over our heads; in this manner, we each received about twenty ablutions ... While all this was happening, a Malay used a long bamboo pole to lift our clothes up and, without otherwise touching them, put them in the pool of a nearby spring. When we were thus sufficiently purified, the rajah had us given large native sarongs, in which we dressed ourselves. From that moment on, all the people came up to us without fear ...[33]

Traditionally, the Timorese claimed totemic descent from the crocodile. And among some of the nearby peoples of the Philippines and Borneo there were certainly taboos associated with killing them, based on a belief in their important spiritual (even god-like) status.[34] A detailed scientific description of the Nile crocodile had been published by Joseph Nicolas Laurenti in 1768,[35] but when Baudin's expedition left France, Johann Gottlob Schneider had not yet published his pioneering description of an Indo-Pacific crocodile, believed to have been collected in Sri Lanka.[36] Therefore Péron and Lesueur's obsessive efforts in Timor should be seen in the context of their perceptions of a gap in the zoological literature of the time and the dearth of crocodile specimens in European museums.

On their last night in Babau, Péron and Lesueur enjoyed a festive evening of music, song, dance and pantomime—beside a great fire lit beneath the spreading canopy of a number of large tamarind trees. Very early on the morning of 29 May they bade farewell to the people of Babau and were accompanied as far as the Meniki River by the Rajah's daughter. The remains of the crocodile were tied to a horse led by a slave using a rope '50 to 60 feet long' in order to avoid contamination. Passers-by, warned by the escorts, fled into the woods to skirt the procession from the greatest possible distance.

It would seem that only the Dutch Governor's recommendations to a subservient and obliging Rajah could have enabled the naturalists to collect such a specimen amid such intense fear and revulsion. The excursion and all the portage costs, however, were borne entirely by the naturalists themselves. Unfortunately for Péron and Lesueur, despite their best efforts, by the time they reached Kupang the crocodile skin had begun to putrify and had to be tossed in the sea. Only the skeleton could be saved, and to this day it is preserved in the Muséum national d'histoire naturelle in Paris. Ultimately their specimen was utilised by Cuvier for his osteological study of living (as opposed to fossil) crocodiles published in 1808.[37]

Perhaps the most significant outcome of the excursion to Babau was the affirmation of Péron and Lesueur's friendship and scientific partnership. Although they had occasionally worked together during previous landfalls, both men had been more inclined towards solitary endeavours. The difficult journey to the crocodile-infested marshes signalled the firm establishment of a close professional relationship that would endure until Péron's death and find its fullest expression in their joint publications.

By the end of May Baudin was ready to sail from Timor, but then six of his sailors deserted from the *Géographe*. With the assistance of the Dutch authorities a search was mounted. On 1 June, two of the missing men thought better of their actions and returned voluntarily. Two more were captured on Buru Island off the northern shore of Kupang Bay, but the remaining two evaded the search parties altogether. They were joined by four of seven pigs who jumped from *Casuarina*—perhaps with a presentiment of their fate—and could not be recovered. The astronomer Pierre-François Bernier, suffering from a fever and convinced that the expedition would yet be the death of him, also sought to remain in Timor until his health recovered, but then reconsidered when the importance of his work was impressed upon him. And the engineer Ronsard sought to leave the expedition in Timor after a vote by the crew overwhelmingly chose Henry de Freycinet, over his candidacy, as their commander if the consumptive Baudin (who was now spitting blood) died before the completion of the expedition. Baudin repeatedly refused Ronsard permission to leave at Kupang, but soothed his ruffled feathers by inviting him to share his table, command his boat and be 'independent of all on board and under his [Baudin's] orders alone'.[38]

One member of the expedition, however, was permitted to remain in Timor because of illness: Leschenault. In the 1824 edition of the *Voyage* we are told that the botanist had an unfortunate experience with a toxic root called *mahé*. This might have been the root of *Phyllanthus acidus*, known as *salmélé* or *tjermélé* in Timor, a member of the Euphorbiaceae family.[39] Although its acidic fruit is eaten, its root—sometimes used medicinally in very diluted infusions—is known to be a highly toxic purgative. Whatever the species Leschenault examined (or experimented with), the painful effects were recorded with some precision:

His lips had barely touched the treacherous root before his face almost immediately became horribly puffed up. For several days he could not speak or swallow anything apart from liquids, and all the skin inside his mouth sloughed off. The symptoms that he experienced in this instance were so violent, that there seems no doubt that had he had the misfortune to swallow the merest morsel of the root, death would soon have followed.[40]

Ironically, there was one person aboard the *Géographe* whom Baudin wanted to rid himself of in Timor but failed: the young convict girl, Mary Beckwith, whom he had taken aboard at Port Jackson. According to Lesueur's journal, she threatened to commit suicide in Kupang when Baudin tried to disembark her. Drunk and deeply distraught, she was eventually allowed to return to the captain's cabin.

Baudin departed Timor on 3 June, determined to resume his survey of the Western Australian coast, which he had broken off at the eastern end of Bonaparte Archipelago. Two days out of Kupang the condition of the astronomer Bernier suddenly worsened. He was probably fortunate to have lapsed into unconsciousness before he was treated with cantharides. Sometimes called Spanish fly, this was a preparation made from the body of the blister beetle, *Cantharis vesicatoria*.[41] What Leschenault suffered in his mouth, Bernier would suffer on his back. Containing an intense inflammatory irritant, cantharides was used as a vesicant to form large blisters and thereby draw serum from the blood, an alternative to blood-letting mistakenly used to treat fevers since ancient times. For all the scientific advances of the previous decade, such 'remedies'—based on Galenic notions of humoral disequilibrium—were still part of the contemporary pharmacopoeia, and Péron very probably assisted Surgeon Lharidon in his misguided ministering to poor Bernier in his final hours. He died at 4.30 on the morning of 6 June, aged only twenty-three, and was buried at sea.

On the evening of 10 June the expedition skirted the Holothurian Banks and two days later anchored close to Cape Rulhiere and Lesueur Island. In the days that followed, the prevailing contrary winds forced the vessels to make continual short tacks in order to follow the coast. On the evening of 17 June they anchored off Cape Dusséjour and the following day sailed close to Lacosse Island, in the stretch of water that separates Joseph Bonaparte Gulf from Cambridge Gulf—on the western arm of which lies the modern port of Wyndham—before making for the open sea once again. Ahead lay 'a very long bank running parallel to the shore'. Here Péron, with Lesueur's assistance, would make significant zoological discoveries and occasion the naming of the Medusa Banks. Among the new species they collected were their beautiful purple jellyfish *Aequorea purpurea* (= *Zygocanna purpurea*), *Eudora undulosa* and *Berenix thalassina* (= *Toxorchis thalassina*).[42] These were followed, soon after, on the coast of Arnhem Land, by *Aequorea pleuronata* (= *Zygocanna pleuronata*), which Péron described as of a 'hyalino-crystaline' colour.[43]

After traversing Joseph Bonaparte Gulf, the expedition's next view of land was Cape Dombey, named in honour of yet another French naturalist. Continuing their northerly coasting, on 23 June they sighted what they thought was an island (in fact two islands later named in Péron's honour) off the northern tip of Anson Bay.[44] And at midday on 26 June, they came abeam of the sheer cliffs of the south-western tip of Bathurst Island, which was ultimately named Cape Fourcroy in honour of Péron's former teacher at the Paris Medical School. Baudin spent most of that night on deck because of the shallow waters.[45] After rounding the northern coast of Melville Island, the *Géographe* and the *Casuarina* entered the Arafura Sea. Despite Baudin's stubborn determination to reach the Gulf of Carpentaria, the prevailing easterlies—sometimes stirred into heavy drenching squalls— forced him to continue tacking and drove him as much north as east. By the end of the first week of July 1803, the expedition was in the middle of the Arafura Sea, two hundred nautical miles west of Cape Vals on the southern coast of New Guinea.

Even if Baudin strictly rationed his water, the expedition would have had only three weeks to spare before starting to sap the forty days' supply it needed to reach the Ile de France. Furthermore it had only one month's supply of biscuits, and twenty crewmen were sick with either dysentery or venereal disease. When told on 7 July that several of the animals aboard were also very ill and that the emus were refusing to eat (and had to be force-fed mashed rice), Baudin, who was himself spitting blood, took the decision to head for home.[46] 'This decision', wrote Freycinet, 'for which each one of us had been yearning and had awaited as the signal for our deliverance, produced a joy that was as keen as it was natural.'[47]

— 19 —

The voyage home

When late I fear'd a wandering course to keep,
Or scarce return, escaping from the deep,
With shrouds and tackle torn—But now, behold
The approaching bay its welcome arms unfold!

LODOVICO ARIOSTO, *Orlando furioso*

WHEN Baudin made the decision to set a homeward course, numerous
members of the expedition spent the whole night on deck (despite poor
weather) and frequently checked the compass 'for fear that they had not
heard aright'.[1] The *Géographe* reached the Ile de France on 7 August 1803.
There can be no doubt of the elation aboard after the privations, illnesses
and dangers the men had experienced. Letters from family and friends
awaited them. As Louis de Freycinet put it: 'He who has a good mother,
a tender father or a beloved wife can appreciate the sweet emotions which
then filled the hearts of those of us fortunate enough to receive glad
tidings of their families.'[2] A surviving letter from Lesueur indicates that he
had four letters from his father waiting for him.[3] And although they were
not yet home, they were among compatriots. Friendships established
during their previous visit were soon reaffirmed. Péron, for example, made
contact with a number of his colleagues who had quit the expedition
during its first sojourn, including the botanist Jacques Delisse and the
artists Pierre Le Brun and Jacques Milbert.[4] He also learned that André
Michaux had died of fever in Madagascar, the previous October, and he

sought to establish the location of the botanist's papers. There was sadness, too, when members of the expedition learned that their colleague, the mineralogist Depuch, had died of dysentery shortly after the *Naturaliste* had called at the island on her way back to France.[5]

The majority of the *Géographe*'s crew was hospitalised on arrival, and several deaths followed, including that of Baudin himself. His lungs eaten away by what was almost certainly tuberculosis, the expedition's commander passed away on 16 September 1803, in the Port Louis home of Alexandrine Kerivel,[6] the widow of a prominent local Jacobin.[7] In his final days Baudin had shown visitors pieces of his lungs coughed up and preserved in a jar of alcohol—observing with black humour: 'Are the lungs indispensable to life? … You see I no longer have any, yet I still exist.'[8]

From Freycinet's account it would appear that Péron, along with all the officers and scientists, attended Baudin's funeral, conducted with full naval honours. Midshipman Charles Baudin acknowledged his 'great strength of spirit in his last days', but wrote: 'His funeral was nothing less than dismal: he was universally detested.'[9] Even his last resting place is uncertain.[10] Whether Baudin and Madame Kerivel were lovers is also uncertain; he ended his days with her, but she was not mentioned in his will; nor was his convict shipboard mistress, Mary Beckwith. The latter certainly reached the Ile de France, where she sought assistance from Baudin's younger brother Augustin, then in command of a neutral Danish merchant vessel from Tranquebar on the southern Indian coast.[11]

Péron also met a number of neutral foreign visitors, including American mariners from vessels largely engaged in the lucrative trade in booty taken by local privateers. They included a Mr Noble, owner of the *Fanny*, and her skipper Captain Smith. Like Baudin's brother, they arrived from the Danish colony of Tranquebar.[12] Another foreigner he met was Walter Robertson,[13] who was a prisoner of war rather than a neutral. He had travelled to the Ile de France for his health during the Peace of Amiens and found himself a prisoner when the peace crumbled. Fortunately for him, he was allowed to leave the island aboard the neutral American ship *Bellisarius*, the year after Péron met him. By this time Matthew Flinders was also a prisoner of war on the island, but destined to face a much longer detention; and it was Robertson who was entrusted with his papers, letters and his historic chart, which bore for the first time the name 'Australia'.[14] Péron and Freycinet, however, never saw this map or even a copy of it before the publication of the official account of their voyage, despite nineteenth-century British accusations of plagiarism.[15]

Although we do not have a published narrative by Péron for his second visit to the Ile de France, we do have his manuscripts in the form of brief notes, which he declared his intention to 'one day write up with more care'.[16] In addition we have Louis de Freycinet's account, and he tells us: 'MM. Péron and Lesueur—the only zoologists then remaining to us— busied themselves with a most careful and persevering study of the fish to be found on these shores.'[17] Indeed, Péron's 'Diarium Zoographicum'[18] for this period contains descriptions of more than seventy local fish, many of which were sketched by Lesueur.[19] Péron also collected numerous crustacea,[20] including, it would seem, the type specimen of the lobster *Scyllarus squammosus* described by Henry Milne-Edwards in 1837.[21] Furthermore, Michel Jangoux has suggested that the type specimen of the echinoderm *Mithrodia clavigera* (Lamarck, 1816), was collected by Péron and Lesueur at the Ile de France.[22]

It is also clear that Péron, along with Guichenot, revisited Jean-Nicolas Céré, director of the botanical gardens at Pamplemousses. His correspondence with Céré reveals a very warm friendship and professional association.[23] In the quarter surrounding the botanical gardens and in the environs of the powder magazine (now St James' Anglican Church) in Port Louis, close to where Baudin died, Péron made notes on bladder ailments that affected the locals. Aside from renewing his friendship with Jacques Delisse (who was now working as a pharmacist), and with local doctors Nils Bergsten and Johann Stadtmann, Péron met two other significant medical figures on the island: Arnaud Lapeyre—chief medical officer to the military garrison, who had reported favourably to the Colonial Assembly on the advantages of practising vaccination in the colony[24]—and Jean-François Guillemeau, whom Péron probably already knew from his student days in Paris. Like Péron, Guillemeau had served in the military with distinction before undertaking medical studies. He had sustained himself as an assistant in the laboratory of Antoine-François de Fourcroy and had then taken part in public vaccinations at the Salpêtrière. Péron appears to have taken a strong interest in Guillemeau's local vaccination campaign, which had begun on his arrival in the colony (as a ship's medical officer the previous June)[25] in the midst of a smallpox epidemic. Both men probably had another bond. Guillemeau was a staunch Bonapartist.[26] If Péron had not already become a Bonapartist, he was soon to ally himself closely with the administration of the First Consul, who was about to squander the fragile peace with Britain by thwarting diplomatic efforts to resolve outstanding differences between the two great powers.

Major political changes began to take place at the Ile de France shortly after Péron's arrival at the colony. General Charles Decaen, with a French naval squadron and 800 troops aboard two transports, arrived on 17 August after failing to reassert French authority over Pondicherry as stipulated under the terms of the Peace of Amiens. Fearing that British prevarication over these terms was simply a prelude to an imminent renewal of hostilities, he had withdrawn to reinforce French forces at the Ile de France. Nine days after Baudin's death, the corvette *Berceau* arrived with news that a state of war had indeed existed between Britain and France since May and that Decaen had been named Captain General with command over all French forces in the Indian Ocean. The next day, 26 September, Governor Magallon submitted to his authority.[27] Although the colony came under Decaen's direct military rule, as an extension of Bonaparte's dictatorship, the Captain General gained the support of the colonists by making no moves to abolish slavery and doing his best to reform the colony's parlous finances.

There is evidence that, with the altered military situation, Decaen sought to augment Vice Admiral Linois's naval squadron with the able-bodied crew members of the *Géographe*. According to Lesueur,[28] Péron led the fight to keep the expedition intact, drafting a long letter first to the island's civilian administration on 14 October and twenty-four hours later to Decaen himself:

> We, the undersigned officers and naturalists of the staff of the corvette *Géographe*, consider that the commandeering of a great number of sailors of our crew and their transfer aboard a ship of war of the Republic, has obviously compromised our expedition, in a seemingly contrary manner to the most precise instructions of the government, to the orders of the First Consul himself, which cannot but be regarded by the enemies of France as an act of violation of the neutrality consented to for us by all the nations and guaranteed by the French people themselves ...[29]

There is a lack of evidence regarding what happened next and whether Péron's tenacious advocacy took the form of a personal confrontation with Decaen, as Alphonse Fleurieu believed.[30] Pierre Milius and Louis de Freycinet make only limited mention of the changes brought about by renewed war and the eventual departure of Linois's squadron on cruise. Decaen's own papers are incomplete.[31] We do, however, have Péron's own list of those he came to know at the Ile de France, and this does confirm that he actually met Decaen (in addition to his predecessor Governor Magallon), Vice Admiral Linois and several of the captains in the naval squadron.[32] On 10 December 1803, two months after drafting the letter signed by himself and the other officers and naturalists, Péron wrote personally to Decaen and asserted that Baudin's expedition had secret orders to gather intelligence on British settlements in New Holland under the guise of scientific endeavours. 'We needed to appear estranged from politics', wrote Péron, 'occupying ourselves only in collections of natural history.'[33]

Could these surprising claims—which have no documentary foundation other than those in Péron's own hand[34]—have been yet another means employed by Péron to persuade Decaen to allow the *Géographe* to return to France? We might never know. But it is worth remembering that during his first visit to the Ile de France Baudin had suspected his ships were being deliberately delayed at the island so that their crews could be conscripted in the event of a British attack.[35] Unable to secure adequate supplies, he also intimated secret instructions: 'that the Government has not undertaken in today's circumstances an expedition like mine without having an objective of a utility more solid and useful than the simple collection of objects of curiosity or passing fancy'.[36] Péron took a similar tack: 'this expedition criticised in its rationale by the very narrow-minded administrators of this colony, was, in its origin and its objective, one of the most brilliant and important conceptions to have distinguished our government.'[37]

Péron's report on the British colonisation of New Holland deals in great part with Port Jackson and was drafted, according to Péron, at the behest of Decaen. It pointedly examined how military action might be taken against the young British colony and advocated a French conquest with the aid of Irish political prisoners. 'The Irish in chains are silent now', wrote Péron, 'but if ever our country's government, alarmed by the rapid increase of this colony, planned to seize or destroy it in the name of France, all the Irish arms would rise.'[38] For the authorship of this memoir, Péron has been called a spy who dishonourably abused local hospitality. Others, such as Sir Ernest Scott, have dismissed such assertions: 'The imputation is unjust to Peron, who had not "spied" in Port Jackson, because the English there had manifested no disposition to conceal. Nothing that he reported was what the Government had wished him not to see; they had helped him to see all that he desired; and his preposterous political inferences, though devoid of foundation, hardly amounted to a positive breach of hospitality.'[39]

Yet there are ample corollaries when it comes to British ambitions and intelligence gathering in the French colony that Decaen now defended. Twenty years before, Colonel Charles Cathcart had visited the Ile de France on a British diplomatic mission and almost certainly made a secret report on the French naval build-up there, which, according to Alan Frost, helped to precipitate the decision to establish a convict colony at Botany Bay.[40] Before the ultimately successful British invasion of the Ile de France in 1810, the Swedish doctor Nils Bergsten (whom it will be remembered Péron met and befriended during his first visit) also supplied secret information and an actual plan of attack.[41] And Matthew Flinders, after being exchanged as a prisoner of war on parole, prepared charts of Port Louis (by then Port Napoléon) and suitable landing places for a British invasion force, together with four quarto pages of intelligence, at the behest of Vice Admiral Bertie.[42] Perhaps not surprisingly, the French historian Henri Prentout suggested a certain symmetry between Flinders and Péron.[43]

The former soldier Péron was obviously an ardent patriot, but circumstances suggest that his memoir on the British establishments was not simply grounded in a determination to impress Bonaparte's hand-picked commander in the Indian Ocean. Whatever the truth, Decaen allowed the *Géographe* to depart the island and seized the opportunity to use her to send dispatches to his superiors—in breach of the conditions of her passport —by replacing the geographer Pierre Faure with his personal envoy, his aide-de-camp, Laurent Bichon de Barois. Faure would spend the rest of his life on the island as a mathematics teacher and died there in 1855.[44] In the wake of Baudin's death, Pierre Milius assumed command of the *Géographe* on the orders of Vice Admiral Linois.[45] He had arrived at the Ile de France on the *Naturaliste*, recovered his health and was now the most senior surviving officer of the expedition, rather than Henry de Freycinet. With her reprovisioning completed and her crew largely restored to good health, the *Géographe* departed the Ile de France on 16 December 1803. She was not accompanied by the *Casuarina*, because the little schooner had been decommissioned in late August.

There was profound gratitude on the part of the officers and men for the hospitality, kindness and gifts extended to them by the colonists. A few days before departing the colony, Péron took delivery of a hundred juvenile gouramies (*Osphronemus goramy*)—in twelve inadequate containers less than three litres in size—which he sought to transport to France as breeding stock. Unfortunately for Péron, these freshwater fish, which were considered good eating in China and the Ile de France, all died before the *Géographe* reached the Mozambique Channel. The expedition was also given breadfruit tree seedlings, originally transported to the Ile de France by d'Entrecasteaux's gardener, Félix Delahaye, from Tonga, in the hope that they might be 'acclimatised' in 'some parts of Italy, France and Spain'.[46]

After entering the Mozambique Channel, the *Géographe* was struck by two days of violent squalls, but was left undamaged. The coast of Natal was sighted on 30 December and, with the aid of the southerly currents, the Cape of Good Hope was soon rounded. On the afternoon of 3 January 1804, the *Géographe* dropped anchor in Table Bay. The next day Milius dispatched an officer to present his compliments to Governor Jan Willem Janssens, and on the evening of 5 January the Governor invited the officers and savants to dine with him.

Earlier in his military career, Governor Janssens had fought against the invading French, but had then been made 'First Commissioner' to the French troops in the French-created 'Batavian Republic'. He had also made a number of official visits to France and presumably spoke French, which might be one reason why he was able to strike up such a warm and friendly relationship with the officers and savants of the visiting French expedition. Janssen's appointment as governor of the Cape had taken place only in the wake of the signing of the Peace of Amiens. Nevertheless, he had quickly made a point of familiarising himself with a great deal of the Cape—between Cape Town and Plettenberg Bay—and regaled his visitors with first-hand ethnographic observations, including information on the so-called Boschisman (Bushman) or Khoisan people. It would seem that Péron's curiosity was immediately tweaked because of the famous size of the buttocks of Khoisan women and their reputed genital 'apron'— sometimes uncharitably referred to as a 'penis' or 'tail'. If he did not already have some grounding in published references to this subject before his visit—through his own wide reading or through his discussions with other travellers in South Africa (such as Colonel Paterson at Port Jackson)—he now gained it with the aid of his hosts. In his own memoir on the subject, for which Lesueur provided graphic illustrations, Péron wrote: 'One of my first concerns on arriving at the Cape was to find out, for myself, exact information on the famous *apron*.' The unusual nature of this particular anatomical characteristic 'was too spicy', he wrote, 'not to excite the curiosity of the majority of the individuals attached to the staff of our vessel'.[47] And he added, 'My friend L'Haridon, physician of our corvette, made very particular personal observations on the kind of orgasm to which this part is said to be susceptible.'[48]

Péron did not make such intimate admissions himself, but according to the memoir he eventually wrote on the subject, he accompanied the director of medical services at the Cape Colony, Reinier de Klerk Dibbetz, to the hospital where he first examined seven or eight 'Hottentot' women who did not have the 'apron' and then examined a number of 'Boschisman' women who, without exception, had a large elongation of what Péron quickly realised was actually the *labia minora*—not some strange additional organ.

Péron got on particularly well with Dr Dibbetz, who was also a poet and an avowed revolutionary. As a result of his political beliefs, he had spent many years in exile in France, before returning to the Netherlands and pioneering the introduction of Edward Jenner's vaccination methods. After accepting the most senior medical post at the Cape, he had been put in charge of the medical commission that directed efforts to introduce smallpox vaccination in the Dutch colony. Péron, who had also studied the pioneering vaccination campaigns of Nils Bergsten, Johann Stadtmann, Jean-François Guillemeau, Léonard Laborde and Arnaud Lapeyre at the Ile de France, would in due course write a report on Dibbetz's work, which was apparently submitted to the Comité centrale de vaccine in Paris.[49]

The *Géographe* remained three weeks at the Cape of Good Hope and departed on 24 January 1804 bearing still more live animals, thanks to Governor Janssens: two young lions, three leopards, two ostriches, a female zebra, a male gnu, two porcupines, two chacma baboons, a dwarf mongoose, a civet and a pair of Cape rails.[50] To avoid the fate of the *Naturaliste*—which reached Le Havre on 7 June 1803, but not before being stopped by an English frigate and escorted to Portsmouth for the examination of her passport[51]—Milius made for the port of Lorient in Brittany. Aside from some illness aboard and more than a week becalmed, it was a relatively uneventful voyage back to Europe. Péron appears to have busied himself revising and expanding his secret memoir on British establishments in New Holland. After an absence of more than forty-one months, the *Géographe* reached the Breton coast on 25 March. Louis de Freycinet calculated that in all her courses she had sailed a sum total of 51 000 nautical miles.

— 20 —

Back in France

Long have they voyaged o'er the distant seas,
And what a heart-delight they feel at last,
So many toils, so many dangers past,
To view the port desired …

ROBERT SOUTHEY, *She Comes Majestic*
with Her Swelling Sails

PÉRON arrived back in France in the last months of the Consulate: a repressive police state with no free press and few remaining republican virtues—a state at war and subordinate to the needs of the military. It was the same month in which the hapless young Duke d'Enghien was kidnapped and summarily executed in the fosse of the Château de Vincennes on the orders of the First Consul for Life. Yet despite this thuggish repression, many *émigré* nobles had voluntarily returned during the seeming stability of the Peace of Amiens. Like them, Péron must have gawked at the strange new fashions that had blossomed during his absence. Men had begun to sport long sideburns and wear high-collared jackets and beaver hats with extravagantly curled brims. Women's dresses had begun to lose their neo-classical purity and now had fitted bodices, pleats and standing ruffs. It was an age of brash speculation and altered patterns of patronage, in which merit, power and corruption formed new and inventive alliances. And these were stormy new seas that Péron would now have to navigate.

Hopeful of a continued scientific association with the treasures of the expedition, Péron wrote to Denis Decrès, Minister of Marine, on 27 March and declared his leading role in the gathering of the collections. In the process he cast more mud on Baudin's reputation.[1] He also reported the deaths of his scientific colleagues and boldly requested formal permission to supervise the disembarkation and transportation to Paris of fifty-four cases—which he described as 'containing my collections and all packed by me with much care'—in addition to responsibility for 'all that which could affect their wellbeing and their conservation'. Perhaps in the hope of a still more reflective role, although he did not formally raise the issue of writing the official narrative of the expedition, he added: 'I have not told you anything of my other labours; it will suffice for me to assure you that in no case have I neglected to gather all that appeared to me to be interesting for our government with regard to political and commercial relations. The English establishments on the east coast of New Holland have most particularly drawn my research and meditations.'[2] Concluding his letter, Péron requested the earliest possible reply from the minister because his health, he asserted, was 'very frail', and it was only the fear of losing in an instant the 'fruit of suffering and fatigues' (the collections) that could make him sacrifice much-needed rest.[3]

Two days later, the Naval Prefect of Lorient, Antoine Thévenard—himself a former minister of marine and well disposed to the sciences—wrote to his superior in support of Péron's request. In his opinion, it was an 'absolute necessity' to inspect the contents of the chests and 'conveniently arrange their diverse parts' before transporting them. Thévenard, after whom Cape Thevenard on Kangaroo Island is named, also informed the minister that Péron was about to leave for Paris to receive his 'particular instructions' and added that the expedition's only surviving naturalist had 'knowledge' that appeared to him to be 'equal to his zeal'.[4] Péron appears to have departed on 31 March,[5] leaving Lesueur to surpervise the collections. Ultimately it was not Péron but Geoffroy Saint-Hilaire who was dispatched by the Muséum to supervise the unloading and transportation of the collections across Brittany and central France. By this time, the First Consul's extravagant spouse, Joséphine, was also taking a keen interest in the live exotic animals that the expedition had brought back, and Thévenard received two letters from her within a fortnight. No animals had died aboard the *Géographe* during the final leg of the voyage, and Geoffroy was assisted in their disembarkation by Mme Bonaparte's bird keeper, Lefèvre; the amazing menagerie was transported to Paris in a convoy of carriages.[6] En route, a jackal belonging to Milbert escaped and created havoc until recaptured by Lesueur.[7] The seedlings and other living plants were transported under Guichenot's care to the Jardin des Plantes in suspended tubs.[8]

On 10 April, from his lodgings in the Hôtel de Strasbourg on the rue Montmartre, Péron again wrote to the Minister of Marine and informed him that he had been in Paris some days. Intimating that he wished to visit his family, residing eighty leagues from the capital, he declared that the minister could do him a 'great service' with an 'appointment' conferring the sum of 600 francs to satisfy his 'most urgent requirements'.[9]

Péron soon had strong support for a more generous appointment. On 27 June, the professors of the Muséum national d'histoire naturelle recommended to the minister that he should receive the salary of 'premier zoologist' backdated to when Bory de Saint-Vincent retired from the expedition at the Ile de France. This meant a salary of 4200 francs per annum. The professors also requested backdated promotions for Lesueur,[10] Bailly, Guichenot and Petit, who had also assumed more senior roles in the wake of desertions and deaths.[11]

The report of the Muséum committee was fulsome in its praise: 'Our job is to make known the services they have rendered to science, but our task will not be perfectly completed until we have obtained for them, from a generous and just government, the compensation due for their labours.' And since the results of the voyage were 'among the richest and the most useful for the progress of natural history', the minister was invited 'to furnish to the authors the means to publish the materials they have collected'.[12] Péron followed up with yet another letter—not only requesting the Minister of Marine backdate his pay but also grant him a further six-year appointment in order to publish the results of the expedition and 4000 francs to cover his victualling and other debts incurred while gathering collections for the government. Unfortunately, Denis Decrès did not respond sympathetically: in the same month he dismissed both back-dated promotions and continued salaries for the publication of scientific results.[13] As we shall see, he would eventually change his mind. But by this time, Péron had gained the attention of Madame Bonaparte and the 'director' of her gardens at Malmaison, François Brisseau de Mirbel,[14] after whom the Australian plant genus *Mirbelia* is named. For all her frivolity, Joséphine was genuinely appreciative of the natural splendours brought back to France by hardworking zoologists, botanists and gardeners. Indeed, Malmaison would become a focus for several important natural history publications and splendid artistic endeavours. Only the year before, Etienne Ventenat had published his *Jardin de La Malmaison* and with it descriptions of a number of Australian plants were published for the first time.

Joséphine's apparently warm letters to Péron have not survived, but a copy of his reply to her, on 12 May 1804, is preserved among the Lesueur Collection in Le Havre. In it he informed Madame Bonaparte that he was putting the insect collection in order and that he would not fail to make a choice of species for her on the basis of 'uniqueness of form or the elegance of colour'. Nevertheless, this would still conform with her intention 'to take no unique individual, or even any that are rare or few in number'. He also informed Madame Bonaparte that he was sending her 'one or two small cases of seeds and fruit' and a 'great quantity of apparel, weapons and utensils of the savage peoples of Van Diemen's Land, Maria Island, New Holland and of many archipelagos of the South Seas, very suitable objects to figure in the important collection of this kind you are preparing and lacking, so to speak, in Europe'.[15] (This thoroughly catalogued gift of the expedition's ethnographic collection was presented on 29 May 1804 with the approval of the Muséum, since the Société des Observateurs de l'Homme—for whom the collection was originally gathered—was now defunct. It included a rich collection from Oceania given by Surgeon George Bass. Part of the collection was pillaged in 1815; the rest was sold to an unknown purchaser or purchasers after the death of Joséphine's son Eugène de Beauharnais in 1829.)[16] Furthermore, Péron advised his prospective patron that he was writing on her behalf to the 'Cape of Good Hope, the Ile de France and even Madagascar' in order to obtain the collections she desired from 'these countries'. And finally, in response to the good wishes that Madame Bonaparte had offered him in her previous letter, Péron pleaded for her intercession, so that he could publish the results of his work carried out under the 'auspices of her glorious spouse'.[17]

About the same time, or soon after, Péron drafted a letter to Bonaparte himself and requested permission to publish the 'Zoography of New Holland' at government expense. He would never publish such a work, and his drafts of further pleading letters became ever more sycophantic after the First Consul for Life abjured his republican commitments, declared himself Emperor and reinvented his Corsican family and gang of generals as a new aristocracy.

When Péron wrote again to the Minister of Marine he made much of Madame Bonaparte's favour and her imminent preparedness to make a submission to her husband on his and Lesueur's behalf. Nevertheless, yet another of his draft letters to the Empress, this time written with Lesueur, suggests that the two men remained extremely anxious about their financial predicament and their scientific prospects. Declaring that Her Imperial Majesty 'was never more indispensable' to the fulfilment of their hopes, they advised her that their 'salaries were almost completely owing'; they had been 'refused the smallest sums'; they had 'pressing needs' and 'obligations of honour to fulfil'; and their labours were 'suspended'.[18] There is ample evidence that Joséphine was kindly and considerate in her efforts on behalf of those she thought worthy of promotion and patronage. But gaining the attention of the Emperor was problematic even for the Empress; he was often absent from Paris and distracted by his vain ambition to leap the Channel—as if it were a mere ditch—and mete out a Marengo to the English on the fields of Sussex or Kent.

Péron, nevertheless, pressed on with his work with the apparent blessing of the professors of the Muséum and perhaps even with financial assistance from his home *département*. He had certainly not forgotten his native Allier and, with the approval of the Muséum,[19] made a substantial donation to the new Lycée de Moulins of 'rare and precious' natural history specimens—including 124 mounted birds, 111 shells and corals and 10 cases of butterflies and beetles[20]—which he had collected 'on the distant beaches of the extremity of the southern world'. He arranged this gift with a covering letter to the Prefect of Allier, on 23 May 1804, and made only one stipulation: that the specimens carry the label 'Given by M. Péron of Cérilly'.[21] But just in case the prefect was inclined to hesitate in accepting the offer, Péron prodded him with news of the imminent arrival of commissioners from Milan and a professor from Montpellier authorised to make large collections for their respective museums.[22] Today, Péron's specimens are largely dispersed or destroyed, but at least one large shell in the present-day Lycée Banville, in Moulins, still bears a leather label inscribed with the words 'Nouvelle Hollande'.[23] Perhaps the generous gift was also a call to attention: the son of the poor tailor's widow from Cérilly had returned to France a savant and traveller of note, a 'somebody'. Rare and exotic natural history specimens were valuable, and Péron might have sought to gain favour with the authorities in Moulins, should he need to quit Paris and find sponsorship or employment in his home *département*. According to Louis Audiat, Empress Joséphine even sought a local chair in 'physic and natural history' for him.[24]

During his first ten months back in France, Péron published five major papers in several prestigious scientific journals. These dealt with zoological subjects, such as the new genus *Pyrosoma* (a salp or swimming sea squirt) he had discovered[25] and the animals he observed between Timor and Van Diemen's Land.[26] They included palaeontolgical observations and geo-logical ideas;[27] oceanographic observations on the temperature of the sea at different depths;[28] and speculations on dysentery and the prophylactic benefits of the chewing of betel in the tropics.[29] But these articles also ranged far beyond their purported titles and promoted the achievements of the expedition. In his account of the genus *Pyrosoma*, for example, he proudly declared:

> Twice we have traversed the Atlantic Ocean in its entire length; twice we have rounded the Cape of Good Hope; as many times again we have circled Van Diemen's Land and rounded the most southerly cape in that part of the world; on five or six occasions we have crossed Bass Strait; during two different periods we have sailed along the coast of New Holland, and the south-west coast, more interesting again; twice we have visited the archipelago of St Peter and St Francis, coasted on two occasions the sea that bathes Nuytsland; thrice we have rounded Cape Leeuwin, explored as many times the Edels, Witt and Eendracht coasts, sailed along our course to the Aru Islands, and did not return to Europe until we had traversed the Indian Ocean four or five times in several directions, and crossed the Tropic of Capricorn seven times at different longitudes, sailing thus north to south a line of more than 60° [in latitude] (1800 leagues) and west to east describing a route of more than 190° [in longitude] (3800 leagues).[30]

Then, speaking specifically of himself and Lesueur, without mentioning his now-dead colleagues, he wrote: 'Not only have we doubled or even tripled the number of known species in almost all the genera, but we have also observed several which were not included in any of those previously established, and which consequently will form new divisions in the numerous classes of the molluscs and in those of the zoophytes.'[31]

Péron's paper 'Mémoire sur quelques faits zoologiques applicables à la théorie du globe', read to members of the Institut in October 1804 and published shortly after, generated significant debate because it recorded numerous locations in Van Diemen's Land, New Holland and Timor where marine fossils could be observed up to 1500 feet above sea level. For Péron, 'one of the most beautiful results of modern geological research, one of the most incontestable also, was the certainty of the sojourn of the sea at great elevations above its present level'. Although he made no mention of Werner and his Neptunist theory, Péron did refer to the 'great catastrophes of nature and their terrible effects'—geological notions that Cuvier would soon refine. The article, however, provoked a 25-page response by Lamarck in the *Annales du Muséum*. In this paper he wisely asked whether 'it is the level of the seas which have lowered, or if it is the lands which are raised to so place the coral soils and the debris of marine bodies above the actual level of the seas'. Rejecting catastrophist notions, Lamarck argued that the many fossilised tropical invertebrate species observed by Péron, and others, in temperate latitudes, not only provided evidence of gradual climatic change and shifts in the locations of the poles but also gradual change in the centre of gravity and displacement of the seas on a spheroidal globe.[32] Ultimately modern tectonic plate theories of continental drift, collision (and resultant uplift) would explain the palaeontological and geological evidence both Lamarck and Péron had tentatively begun to assess in their own respective ways. However, on a more personal level, this geological debate illustrates that Péron—who just a few years before had left France a mere student—now drew the attention of some of the great scientific intellects of his era.

Another example is Péron's gynaecological paper, 'Observations sur le tablier des femmes Hottentotes', which he read to members of the Institut in January 1805. Although it was officially approved by Labillardière and Cuvier in March, it was not published in his lifetime and appeared in print only after being rediscovered nearly eighty years later. Nevertheless, the substance of Péron's paper was reported in the *Magasin encyclopédique*,[33] where it was in turn criticised by Charles Dumont, who—distrusting observations made exclusively in a hospital and questioning Péron's ethnic terminology—argued that there was 'perhaps still a right to doubt whether the bizarre excrescence in question [the enlargement of the *labia minora*] pertains to all individual females of a particular race of Africans'.[34] Péron defended himself in an article published in the *Journal de Physique, de chimie et d'histoire naturelle* in the same year largely with quotations from other (sometimes racist) authors,[35] but this debate—and European male fascination with the genitalia of these women—would ultimately have a broader significance as part of the conceptualisation of the intersecting categories of race and sex in the nineteenth century and help explain the tragic fate of Saartje Baartman, the so-called 'Hottentot Venus', who was exhibited like a circus freak in Britain and France in the five years after Péron's death.[36]

On 30 September 1804 the Minister of Marine made the very welcome decision to pay Péron and Lesueur a salary of 4400 francs from the date they had respectively assumed their function as 'naturalist and draftsman'.[37] There were rumours, however, that the 'very apathetic' secretary of the Minister of Marine had been charged with the task. Péron's correspondence with the Freycinet brothers, who were then in Antwerp, indicates that by early 1805 he had seized the initiative, resolved to publish an historical account of the voyage himself and begun writing. Meanwhile, Lesueur was hard at work on the illustrations.[38] The work of Nicolas Petit, the other surviving artist of the expedition, would only figure posthumously in these plans; tragically, in December 1804 two weeks before his planned marriage, he died of gangrene after his leg was injured in a fall attempting to avoid a carriage in a Paris street.[39]

Péron's star continued to rise in Paris. He was already a corresponding member of the Société médicale d'Emulation when he departed with Baudin's expedition. Although he never completed his medical studies, on 2 February 1805 he became an adjunct member of the Société de Médecine de Paris. Less than three weeks later the Société de l'Ecole de Médecine elected him an 'associate adjunct' member, with the approval of the Minister of the Interior. And in March he became a resident member of the Société philomatique. He seems also to have been elected a member of the Société d'Instruction médicale. But by far the most prestigious accolade of all was his election as a corresponding member of the Classe des Sciences physiques et mathématiques of the Institut impérial, France's peak scientific body, on 14 October 1805.[40] It was probably about this time that the Strasbourg-born artist Jean-Henri Cless, who was then working in Paris, completed a portrait of Péron that was later engraved by Conrad Westermayer.[41]

Although Péron would utimately gain the permission of the Minister of Marine to write the official account of the voyage, he did not gain an undertaking to pay for its publication.[42] If the government were to foot the bill, the funds would have to come from the Minister of the Interior. The two friends appear to have worked through 1805 and the first half of 1806, making renewed representations to the Institut impérial for support during this period and presumably living on their back pay. The report the Institut handed to the government on their efforts, drafted by Georges Cuvier and dated 9 June 1806,[43] echoed many of the themes in Jussieu's Muséum report of 1804: how responsibility for the scientific work of the expedition had devolved to Péron and Lesueur; how they had gathered collections of more than 'one hundred thousand specimens of animals, large and small' and 'discovered more new animals than all the naturalist voyagers of our times'. The report indicates that all the zoological and anthropological descriptions had been 'revised and were ready for the press'. The review of the subjects covered would suggest that the first volume of Péron's *Voyage* already existed in draft form. It noted the scientific articles Péron had already published—and which would be reprinted in the *Voyage*—and remarked that, in addition to manuscripts, he possessed materials 'for numerous other publications on the most important subjects'. Indeed the report goes on to state that Péron's labours 'appear to be of the utmost consequence both to the statesman and philosopher. Perhaps a work more curious or interesting has never been presented to one or to the other.'[44]

Cuvier's report indicates that, by June 1806, the government had already resolved to publish Péron's *Voyage*. Nevertheless, the official imperial decree actually dates from 4 August 1806. In it, the government undertook to publish only the first three volumes—historical, anthropological, physical and meteorological—at government expense, with natural history to be published by subscription.[45] At the time, there was no Minister of the Interior. The chemist Jean Chaptal had resigned because of his disapproval of the transition from consulate to empire. His successor, Jean-Baptiste de Nompère de Champagny, who took office on 8 August, was a loyal Bonapartist with a strong naval background. Champagny appears to have taken a keen personal interest in Péron's project and read draft chapters forwarded to him through the ministry's secretary general, Péron's friend Jean-Marie Degérando, who it will be remembered was a leading member of the Société des Observateurs de l'Homme and had drafted anthropological advice before the expedition's departure.[46] Frank Horner has argued that the imperial toponyms for the *Voyage* were adopted by Péron and Freycinet while the former was still employed by the Minister of Marine in the 'hope of reviving the flagging interest of the Emperor', rather than through coercion as Matthew Flinders and Conrad Malte-Brun believed.[47] The truth might be somewhere in the grey shadows of the middle ground; Péron's correspondence with Degérando clearly indicates that his draft chapters were not only subject to the personal scrutiny of the minister but also were susceptible to change.

There is little doubt of Péron's calculated sycophancy, yet this should still be considered in the context of the suffocating hubris and narcissism of the Napoleonic despotism and the culture of subservience, exaggerated court etiquette and flattery on which the self-styled heir to the Roman emperors and Charlemagne now insisted. The insertion of 'Terre Napoléon' on the chart of southern Australia was only one arrogant example that characterised the period. In Brittany the town of Pontivy became 'Napoléonville'; in the ravaged Vendée, La Roche-sur-Yon was reconstructed as 'Napoléon-sur-Yon' and the neighbouring towns of Le Poiré, Le Bourg and Beaulieu, all had 'sous-Napoléon' appended to their names. Major fortifications in Ostende (Belgium) and Almaraz (Spain) were also 'baptised' in the Emperor's name. Even in the distant outpost of the Ile de France, Captain General Decaen changed the name of Port Nord-Ouest (formerly Port Louis) to Port Napoléon and Mahébourg to Port Impérial in 1804.[48] And in August 1806, the island of Réunion (formerly Bourbon) was renamed 'Ile Bonaparte'.[49] Flinders, who was a prisoner of war at the Ile de France at the time, would have been well aware of these surrounding toponymic changes and of the political culture that demanded the propitiation of the demigod Bonaparte.[50]

It should also be remembered that if Péron's *Voyage* had been privately published, it would still have required the imprimatur of the imperial censor. It seems very unlikely that Péron, Freycinet and Lesueur could have issued such a politically sensitive atlas and accompanying narrative with names that were entirely of their own choice or that recognised the names of the Englishman Flinders—even if such names were known to them— or the prior geographical and territorial claims of France's enemy. Conrad Malte-Brun, who knew Péron personally, certainly believed that he was troubled by the lack of acknowledgement to Flinders in the *Voyage* and declared: 'M. Péron, the French scientist, conversing on the subject of the discoveries of the English navigator, always appeared to us agitated by a secret sorrow, and gave us to understand that he regretted not having the freedom to say all he knew about them.'[51]

During the Restoration and six years after Péron's death, Louis de Freycinet would conveniently absolve himself of responsibility for the imperial toponymy of the official account when he wrote the preface to volume ii of the *Voyage*. Although he shifted the blame on to his late friend, he did so with subtle acknowledgement of the norms and difficulties of the period. 'Péron had conceived the project of all the names of all the places we had visited', wrote Freycinet, and he added, 'this project had been adopted by the authorities; it thus had to bear the imprint of the epoch during which our expedition had been undertaken and the circumstances in which Péron had written the account.'[52] For his part, Péron referred only to what 'our geographers have named'[53] when he mentioned Cape Peron on Maria Island, christened in his honour.

In times of despotism or foreign occupation, there are those who actively collaborate and make Faustian contracts out of conviction or self-interest and still more who passively collaborate because they have little choice. Napoleonic France was in many respects the precursor of the totalitarian dictatorships of the twentieth century. As in those dictatorships, Bonaparte crushed all free expression of opinion with ruthless censorship and sought to control the very minds of his subjects; he also co-opted a generation for the prosecution of aggressive war, conquest and the fulfilment of a megalomaniacal sense of destiny.[54] Péron was only one of many obedient subjects—but also careerists and hero-worshippers—who helped to legitimise Bonaparte's rule; in his (and Freycinet's) case with the Emperor's name written large across the expedition's *Atlas*. But we must not forget that science was then very much subordinate to the Emperor's will. The Ecole polytechnique, for example, had already been militarised and, in the year the first volume of Péron's *Voyage* appeared (1807), Bonaparte made it abundantly clear that he believed the Institut impérial existed to fulfil his wishes and that its members had no right to object to tasks he assigned.[55]

In such an environment, is it really possible that Baudin would have been any less compliant than Péron, had he lived to write the official account of the expedition? It seems unlikely. He too was an obedient servant of the then First Consul and diligently fulfilled his orders—even to the extent of ripping out cabins to satisfy Mme Bonaparte's whim for living Australian animals. His recompense might have been the honour of a Baudin Peninsula or a Cape Baudin, where today the map bears the names of Péron and Freycinet. And perhaps some of his sarcastic manu-script names, such as Cap des Mécontents and Anse des Maladroits, might have survived, instead of Cape Naturaliste and Vasse River (Wonnerup Inlet) on Geographe Bay, to commemorate the unfavourable opinion he held of some of his men.

Yet for all his pioneering navigational achievements and his efforts facilitating the transport of live specimens, Baudin was ignored by Jussieu and Cuvier in their respective reports. This was strangely evocative of James Cook's initial treatment. It seems hard to believe now, but when the *Endeavour* returned to Britain in 1771, the press made sparse mention of her commander's extraordinary seamanship. An ignorant modern reader perusing the London press of the time could be forgiven for thinking Cook a mere chauffeur for the naturalists Banks and Solander.[56] So, too, Jussieu and Cuvier seem to have been more interested in the work of Péron and Lesueur than in those parts of the Australian coast charted for the first time by Baudin, Hamelin, Freycinet and the hydrographers Faure and Boulanger.

— 21 —

Final years

And men go abroad to admire the heights of mountains, the mighty
billows of the sea, the broad tides of rivers, the compass of the ocean, and
the circuits of the stars, and pass themselves by.

AUGUSTINE, Confessions

PÉRON moved lodgings frequently during his final years. It was some
time before May 1804 that he left the Hôtel de Strasbourg on the rue
Montmartre and moved to 284 Grande Rue, Belleville,[1] then just a village
of a thousand souls on a steep slope on the eastern edge of Paris, now a
crowded suburb. Although it enjoyed broad views of the capital and the
surrounding countryside, he did not stay there long. Belleville was far from
his collections and from his professional colleagues. By June 1804, perhaps
after an intervening visit to his family in Cérilly, Péron is known to have
moved into lodgings at 499 rue Copeau (now rue Lacépède),[2] on the
corner of rue de la Clef, close to the Jardin des plantes and the Muséum.
Late nineteenth-century buildings now occupy the corner where the
Voyage de découvertes aux Terres Australes was prepared for publication. It is
often stated that Lesueur resided with Péron, and Jacqueline Bonnemains
has drawn attention to their formal deed of association, dated 15 prairial
an XII (8 June 1804).[3] Although they might have shared lodgings during
their work on the text and illustrations for the *Voyage* and *Atlas*, Lesueur
is also known to have resided at 15 rue Copeau, and it is by no means
certain that Péron lived there too. It is to be expected that professional
correspondence to both should have gone to one address for the sake of

convenience. Given the lack of a journal or first-person reminiscences during this relatively obscure period of Péron's life, these fragmentary surviving letters and the addresses they bear offer the only real clues to his movements.

Although Paris was now Péron's home—and it is hard to imagine that he could have been happy long separated from the city's bookshops, libraries, learned institutions and fertile intellects—his family, and perhaps his heart, remained in Cérilly. On 3 August 1806, his mother died; she was just seven weeks short of her sixtieth birthday. It was a difficult period for Péron's sister Rosalie, who was not yet thirty and had only recently been widowed with three children.[4] The contents of her home had been carefully itemised on 18 July 1806, and 188 items of furniture and personal effects were auctioned on 7 August (four days after Madame Péron's death) to pay her husband's debts.[5] Péron's mother probably lived with Rosalie, but whether her remaining effects were also included in this sale is unclear. There is no surviving inventory of her separate possessions. Inheritance can often be a source of dispute and bitterness in a family, but the Péron family had little to squabble over, if they squabbled at all. Rosalie remained close to her brother—who is said to have lived modestly in order to assist her and her surviving sister Cécile.[6] Ultimately one of Rosalie's sons, apparently with Lesueur's encouragement, became a priest, and she ended her days with him in his parish of Vorly near Bourges[7] in 1844.[8]

Péron was deeply affected by his mother's death, and his grieving appears to have coincided with a marked deterioration in his own precarious health.[9] It would seem that he returned to France already infected with the tuberculosis that would kill him.[10] One can speculate that it might have been a legacy of the crowded confines of the *Géographe* and that he might even have contracted it from Baudin himself, long before reaching the Ile de France. Maurice Girard asserted that the decline in Péron's health began at the Cape of Good Hope.[11] The poor diet of the voyage could not have helped his condition. Those who knew him recorded that his chest condition worsened rapidly in France. Joseph Deleuze wrote: 'he suffered very much; the fever and the cough did not leave him; the remedies produced no effect.'[12] Fever and headaches robbed him of sleep and sapped his body of strength; yet still he pressed on with his work.[13]

The first volume of Péron's *Voyage* was published by the Imprimerie impériale in 1807. Péron is reported to have personally presented a copy to the Emperor after Mass on the morning of Sunday 10 January.[14] Two German editions, one published in Tübingen, the other in Weimar, appeared in 1808. The following year Richard Phillips, of Bridge Street, Blackfriars, published an English translation that contained numerous errors and had much of its scientific content abridged.[15] The original work, despite the injustices done to Baudin, remains an important work of early nineteenth-century French travel literature. Throughout the text, Baudin is referred to simply as 'the commandant' or 'our leader' and is not named personally. 'Commandant' might have been the usual form of address for Baudin during the expedition, but in the *Voyage* there seems little doubt that this formality was not deference but vindictive exclusion of Baudin from the narrative. In contrast, Baudin's subordinates are mentioned by name—as are the explorers Tasman, Cook, Marion Dufresne, d'Entrecasteaux, Bass and Flinders. Péron, as the official chronicler of the expedition, had to concern himself with the achievements of exploration and cartography, in addition to natural history. Although Jussieu and Cuvier can perhaps be forgiven for the natural history focus of their official scientific reports and their failure to mention Baudin, Péron cannot. Baudin, for all his faults and abrasiveness, should have been appropriately acknowledged and more fairly treated. But Péron was in no mood to be magnanimous to the man who would have left him for dead on the parched shores of Shark Bay, in March 1803, and who fined the officer whose disobedience saved his life. His vengeance was to expunge Baudin's name from the record and magnify his every failing.

Yet Péron's actions seem out of character. He appears to have been deeply sensitive to the feelings of others even if he was argumentative and strong-willed. On 14 October 1796, for example, he wrote to Henri Dufour after mocking him in verse while they were rivals for the hand of Sophie Petitjean: 'Accept my very sincere and ardent excuses,' he implored. 'My heart is not wicked ... it is delicate ... it is generous ... it is sensitive. But I have committed a blunder ... and nothing else.'[16] Péron was certainly aware of his own shortcomings, as his frank self-assessment of November 1800 reveals:

> Inconsistent, thoughtless, quarrelsome, indiscreet, too full of opinions, unable to yield for reasons of convenience, I am able to make enemies and alienate myself from my best friends. These faults are the result of my education and the state of independence in which I have lived. I know that they tarnish the qualities I might possess, but such is the force of habit that my efforts to correct myself have been useless so far. However, if I am reproaching myself, I do not blush about them. I feel

that my heart is unconnected to any harm that I might have caused, and the regret that I experience leaves me with a clear conscience. These imperfections of the spirit are redeemed by the qualities of the heart. Kind, sensitive, generous, I have never purposely caused any harm to anyone. My friends have often had to experience my vivacity; often they had to complain about my indiscretions; often they had to complain about my thoughtlessness, my stubbornness; they have always praised my gentleness, my affection, my kindness … This last quality has always singled me out. At college, in the army, it brought me the esteem and the friendship of all those I have been in contact with. It made me loved by these unfortunate men, who, as victims to the fury of their princes, became prey to the French armies … Young, enthusiastic, misfortune has always had a sacred grip on me. In spite of the accusations against my compatriots [in Germany], I was always loved and esteemed … Unconcerned by the ways and customs of society, possessing an impetuous imagination that never bent to authority, of a dangerous and sometimes dishonest and imprudent frankness, too sure of my opinions that I maintain without reserve, full of heedlessness and inconsistency, I have often alienated my friends; but no sooner had passion given way to reason, I have blushed at my outburst. I find those I have offended, showing regrets and apologies so real, that they pardon me. Thus all the friendships that I have made either at college or in the army, or in Paris have survived. Few of them have ever had to complain about me, but all of them are still as attached to me as I am to them …[17]

It is not unusual to reflect on one's role in past events, but 'reconstruction' can sometimes lead to self-deception. Despite his considerable personal talents and achievements, Péron's later record of ambition and vindictiveness inevitably leads us to doubt his declaration: 'I have never purposely caused any harm to anyone.' However, there is no doubt that Péron made many enduring friendships during his voyage with Baudin. Although he grieved the loss of many of his colleagues and was prepared to honour their names in the text of his *Voyage*, he was also prepared to enhance, subtly, his own scientific reputation at their posthumous expense. In Baudin's case, however, he was prepared to destroy a posthumous reputation. Yet by now he himself was dying, and his own posthumous reputation was at stake.

As his health worsened, Péron's friends rallied to him. The botanist Aimé Bonpland (1773–1858), a former military surgeon who had accompanied Alexander von Humboldt during his South American travels and was now superintendent of Empress Joséphine's gardens, took great pains to organise a visit by him to Malmaison. In the gathering winter weather of November 1808, Bonpland organised a carriage to collect Péron. Explaining his arrangements, he informed his friend: 'Do not worry about the return; we will arrange all for the better.'[18] Péron was also treated by his former teacher Jean-Nicholas Corvisart—Napoleon's personal physician[19] and one of the pioneers of modern cardiology and percussive diagnosis.[20] Furthermore, he received medical advice from his friend Pierre-François Keraudren.[21] 'All his friends', wrote Lesueur, 'counselled him to go to the south of France and, after their good advice and lively solicitations, he decided to go.' Lesueur, ever loyal to his ailing friend, decided to accompany Péron to Nice where he could avoid the rigours of winter. The artist's sketchbook offers a precious historical window to their route.[22]

After farewells to a number of their former shipmates, the two friends departed Paris 'amidst ice and frost' on 21 January 1809. They reached Lyon six days later, travelling via Chalon and Mâcon. Here they embarked on a boat and 'abandoned themselves to the rapid current of the Rhône'.[23] On their first day afloat, Lesueur finished five sketches by the time they reached the shaded banks of Vienne. Over the next few days, they sailed past the hills and vineyards of Tain, through the precipitous gorge of Tournon, past the ruined castle of Châteaubourg—overlooking the Rhône's confluence with the Isère—and skirted Valence with the Vivarais to the west and the vast natural fortress of the Vercors to the east. It would seem that they then disembarked at Montélimar and made their way to the village of Saulces, a few kilometres south of Loriol. André Maury suggests that this was because Péron was 'exhausted by the fatigues of the journey and very glad to take a couple of days' rest'.[24] This is plausible, since their visit to the parents of Henry and Louis de Freycinet, who resided there, was unannounced.

Lesueur was quickly struck by the beautiful Australian species growing locally and was immediately reminded of the tragic efforts of the gardener Riedlé and other scientists on Baudin's expedition. Today, the Freycinet family home still backs on to groves of beautiful trees—perhaps descendants of those planted on the alluvial plain by the seafaring brothers after their visits to many a distant shore. And far from the sea, Louis de Freycinet, who would return to Australian waters in command of an expedition of his own,[25] now lies buried in the silt and gravel of the local cemetery.[26]

Péron and Lesueur made a very favourable impression in Saulces during their three-day visit. Freycinet senior, writing to his son Henry, in Le Havre, declared it was an 'agreeable surprise to be visited by friends as precious to the heart as distinguished by merit', and added, 'with what consternation have I hugged Péron and Lesueur in my arms!' Although Freycinet *père* thought that the distractions of travel and research would be good for Péron's body and soul, he felt that, for a prompt recovery, Péron would need 'less action and vehemence in conversation'. This, in itself, tells us a great deal about Péron's passionate and engaging manner. Monsieur de Freycinet certainly recognised it as the mark of 'an exquisite sensibility and of an ardent imagination'. Péron, he judged, was 'very amiable'.[27] Elisabeth de Freycinet concurred; writing to Henry herself some days later, she declared: 'How this young savant is amiable. He has an energy and warmth in the commerce of amity which is rendered very precious to his friends.'[28]

In neighbouring Loriol, Péron and Lesueur took the opportunity to visit the geologist Barthélemy Faujas de Saint-Fond, famous for his travels in Europe and the British Isles—where he met Sir Joseph Banks and Adam Smith—and for his books on Alpine natural history, volcanism and volcanic mineralogy. According to Elisabeth de Freycinet, they were so warmly received by Faujas that they 'almost did not depart'.[29] Faujas was a vigorous opponent of Werner's ideas, and his work on the extinct volcanoes of the Vivarais and the volcanic origins of basalt made a significant contribution to the undermining of Neptunism. Nevertheless, Faujas also held some quaint ideas. The year Péron and Lesueur visited him, he asserted (in volume iii of his *Essai de Géologie*) that metal ores grew plant-like underground![30]

On 1 February, after three days in the area of Saulces, the travellers took their leave of the Freycinet home—Lesueur made a parting gift of two of his sketches of the house—and were escorted by Monsieur de Freycinet to Montélimar. They then continued their journey overland to Fontaine de Vaucluse, which they found devoid of beauty and located beneath a barren calcareous rock bearing the ruins of the château where the poet Petrarch had resided 450 years before. (A column in his honour was inaugurated in 1804.) Lesueur, however, found sufficient inspiration in the wild decrepitude of the scene for a sketch. The eponymous fountain of the village impressed him by the quantity of water that gushed forth and fed a stream that supplied the inhabitants (and it would seem the visitors) with 'excellent eels and delicious trout'. Over the next couple of days the two friends visited the former papal town of Avignon, then crossed the Durance on the 46-arch timber Pont de Bonpas and followed the river upstream to Orgon.

The Provençal village of Orgon is notable for its Lower Cretacious fossils, and it is tempting to speculate that Faujas de Saint-Fond suggested they visit, since he must have known that Péron was keenly interested in marine fossils above modern sea level. Here, on the extreme north-east of the chain of the Alpilles, one can find striking specimens of *Requienia ammonia* and *Toucasia carinata*—extinct sessile species of mollusc with large spiral valves thirteen centimetres high—which lived cemented to rock platforms beneath the sea 135 million years ago. Lesueur dated his sketch of the Château d'Orgon 6 February 1809 but made no other remarks on the sleepy village. Five years later, Bonaparte would not find it so tranquil: he received a violent reception on his way to exile on Elba and had to don the uniform of one of his foreign military escorts in order to escape peril.[31]

After passing through verdant Lambesc, Péron and Lesueur traversed the ancient weathered landscape of the Var and then the mountains of the Esterel to reach Nice, via Fréjus, Cannes and Cagnes. This was shortly after 9 February, and they found lodgings in a house on one of the limestone hills with expansive views of the Mediterranean and the neighbouring coast. This was recently occupied territory, which, like Avignon, had been annexed by the French revolutionary armies in 1792. In 1805, just four years before Péron and Lesueur's visit, Bonaparte's administration had reminded the curates in neighbouring Villefranche that they were forbidden to preach in Italian.[32] Nevertheless, the locals still refer to the harbour by its Genovese name 'la darse'.

In their next six months on the Mediterranean, Péron and Lesueur threw themselves into a renewed régime of writing and scientific research and experimentation—the latter with the aid of a boat loaned to them by Commissaire Godet, the senior naval officer of the port. Despite the relative shallowness of the Mediterranean, the sheltered waters off Nice and particularly Villefranche plunge rapidly offshore. Even today Villefranche is the location of important marine research and is home to the Observatoire océanologique, which incorporates the Russian zoological laboratory established in 1888 under Alexis de Kortoneff.[33]

Quite a number of species collected by Péron and Lesueur off Nice had never before been scientifically described. In early March 1809, for example, they netted a medusa of two to three centimetres in diameter with nine tentacles. Although they would jointly publish the name *Foveolia bunogaster*, the laconic description given by the ailing Péron was not accompanied by Lesueur's extraordinarily detailed illustration and, sixty years later, the Russian zoologist Ilja Metschnikov did not realise their priority when he published his name *Cunina probosciedea* for the same species. This was also the fate of their *Foveolia lineolata* (= *Solmissus albescens*, Gegenbaur, 1856). Hence today, Péron's original names for these jellyfish are regarded as *nomina oblita*. However, his denomination for a tiny (seven to eight millimetre) hyaline-coloured medusa with distinctive yellow internal organs, which was netted on the morning of 24 March, has survived: *Aglaura hemistoma*. And another medusa caught off Nice— although it has undergone generic revision—has retained the specific epithet bestowed when Péron and Lesueur published their brief pioneering description: *Melicerta fasciculata* (= *Koellikerina fasciculata*).[34]

These Mediterranean species were included in a descriptive table of 120 medusae—all those then known—which Péron had resolved to co-author with Lesueur. In addition to species already described by other naturalists, they included species the pair had collected on Baudin's expedition and in Le Havre. The plan was for Péron's descriptions to be accompanied by Lesueur's magnificent illustrations. Although their published *tableau* carried detailed reference numbers for plates and figures, an explanatory footnote admitted that these were not yet engraved. Nevertheless, the authors hoped 'to do something useful to science and agreeable to naturalists' by publishing the prepared catalogue.[35] Less than two months after the Battle of Waterloo, the newly resurrected Académie des Sciences did publish fourteen of Lesueur's plates, and in 1879 the German zoologist Ernst Haeckel made use of them, together with Péron and Lesueur's catalogue, for the taxonomic determinations of his *Das System der Medusen*. Yet it was not until 1995 that Péron's more detailed manuscript 'Histoire générale des méduses' was published with reproductions of Lesueur's exquisite watercolours.[36] This 'histoire générale' incorporates a number of individual *mémoires*, and two of these, dealing with the genus *Aequorea*, were read to members of the Institut by Péron (at meetings on 21 November and 5 December 1808) and later published.

The manuscript of the final memoir also reveals that Péron's admiration for Bonaparte might have dampened shortly before his departure for

Nice. When Bonaparte was still First Consul, Péron had intended to name a medusa he had collected in Tasmanian waters in his honour, but by 5 December 1808 he had crossed out Bonaparte's name and substituted the specific name *eurodina*.[37] Was this excision a private statement of disillusionment or simply a reconsideration on the grounds that a jellyfish might not flatter a man who chose the eagle and the bee for his insignia? We might never know, but it is a telling fact that Péron's zoological names are largely descriptive or honour other scientists. Indeed they are surprisingly free of references to the Bonapartes. In the wake of the atrocities in Spain, unceasing global war and the squandering of one generation of conscripts after another, the charisma of the Machiavellian Bonaparte might have started to wear thin for Péron. Perhaps more importantly, the ambitions and perspective of a dying man are different from those of a young careerist seeking to flatter those in power. Péron had now taken charge of his own destiny.

In the journal he kept in Nice, Lesueur wrote that, for Péron, the gathering and study of delicate marine creatures was 'of all pleasures, the sweetest and the most agreeable'.[38] But he did not confine himself to the study of medusae. With Lesueur he collected other coelenterates (such as siphonophores and velellids) and urochordates (such as sea squirts and salps), just as he had on Baudin's expedition. However, the Mediterranean was more familiar to European scientists, and many of the species to which he triumphantly gave new manuscript names, between mid–March and early April 1809, had already been described by some of the great traveller-naturalists of the previous generation, such as Peter Pallas and Pehr Forsskål.[39] This is not to suggest that Péron was unaware of his predecessors. His bibliographic notes—surveying references by more than thirty scientific authors between 1559 and 1808[40]—and several unfinished manuscripts[41] suggest that he planned a major work on velellids perhaps similar to that which he envisaged for the medusae. Thus he sought to consolidate the work of his predecessors with his own collecting in northern and southern waters. Even in Nice he corresponded with his colleagues, receiving, for example, a letter from Pierre Marcel de Serres in Montpellier, answering questions on known velellids in the Mediterranean.[42]

Péron lived long enough to publish only a fraction of his work in Nice (essentially on the medusae); nevetherless three years after his death, Lesueur published an account of the species that he and his friend had collected there.[43] It was even translated and published in the German journal *Isis* in 1817. Similarly, although Péron did not live to see the publication of the second volume of his *Voyage*, he continued to work on it in Nice. We know this because on 29 July 1809 he dispatched the manuscript of a chapter to the Minister of the Interior.[44] (At the time of his death he had written thirty chapters and notes for the remainder—all of which were handed over to Louis de Freycinet in March 1815 for completion, and published in 1816.)

Inevitably, Péron must have felt anger, frustration and depression at the implications of his illness—in particular the thwarting of his scientific career, but perhaps also the prospect of marriage and fatherhood, although no one like Sophie Petitjean appears to have entered his life. Moreover, the sheer pain and exhaustion of his symptoms must have been both physically and psychologically debilitating. There is no more powerful antidote for vanity and egotism. Despite this, he seems to have laid the foundations for a consciously heroic death. In a letter to Louis de Freycinet, which appears to have been written while he was still in Nice, Péron revealed both a serene resignation and a determination to make the most of the time he had left:

> Never, I swear to you, my dear Freycinet, have I worked more than at the moment; it is the same for Lesueur: we leave our beds only to work; we only stop work, with regret, to take our meals; and without the atrocious pain which consumes me, I would never have been more happy, more fortunate: this is the truth which I attest to you: on [my] honour this is living! I do not know a sweeter pleasure than that which occupies one in things useful and honourable … Seeing your friend, so close to the grave, working so constantly, you would feel animated by the most noble courage.[45]

Work certainly diverted Péron's attention from his impending fate. In Nice, besides collecting marine specimens and working on the second volume of his *Voyage*, he resumed oceanographic experiments begun during the Baudin expedition. It will be remembered that he had observed the temperature of seawater to fall with depth in the Atlantic. Nevertheless, he remained aware of seemingly anomalous observations by Luigi Marsigli and Horace-Bénédict de Saussure, in the Mediterranean, and Donati in the Adriatic. Saussure, the famous Swiss polymath and Alpine explorer, had conducted experiments in Nice and also expected temperatures to fall with depth, as he had observed in Alpine lakes. In October

1780 he had used an alcohol thermometer submerged in a wooden container for twelve hours—with the bulb of the instrument encapsulated in a coating of wax, resin and oil—to record temperatures at 147 and 300 fathoms.[46] He too was surprised to find that even at 300 fathoms the temperature in the Mediterranean was 10.6°.[47] Given these observations, Péron had decided to conduct his own observations in the same waters. On 24 June, he and Lesueur were summoned by their boat crew very early in the morning. At 4.00 a.m. they measured the outside air temperature and recorded 16° (one degree lower than the surface temperature of the sea) before enclosing their thermometer in a container similar to that which they had used on Baudin's expedition. Péron, burdened with pain and failing strength, decided not to embark in the boat, and so Lesueur proceeded a considerable distance offshore, without him, before plunging the instrument 300 feet below the surface. An hour later, he hauled it up and established that at that depth the water temperature was 11°—six degrees lower than at the surface.[48]

Over the next month they conducted further experiments in the deeper waters between Nice and Villefranche. Lesueur's journal indicates that on 14 July (the twentieth anniversary of the fall of the Bastille) they plummeted their instrument 2125 feet and measured 10° water temperature when it was recovered. They were never able to sound deeper, but their temperature readings remained largely consistent with those of their predecessors. Temperatures fell, but nothing like the way they did in the Atlantic, where Péron had measured a fall of 19° below surface temperature at 2144 feet.

In 1804, Péron had unconvincingly speculated that, since 'all the observations of Marsigli and of Donati were made in places encumbered with sponges, corals, alcyons etc.', perhaps zoophytes accumulating at the bottom of the sea somehow influenced sea temperatures. There is, of course, an ecological association between many of these creatures and warmer waters, but it is not *they* that heat the waters, rather it is the injection of warmer currents or the effects of insolation and the atmosphere on a relatively shallow body of water that can produce more homogeneous readings. Péron might already have realised this, but by late July 1809 he was increasingly unable to venture out by boat to test his ideas. And from his prospect ashore, he could only watch Lesueur ply his course through the waters busy with sardine fishermen.[49] The last of their temperature experiments—which contributed to a broader understanding of isothermal zones—was completed on 3 August. Soon others would take up the subject.[50]

When Péron left the Mediterranean coast for Paris, via his native Cérilly,[51] in August 1809, he would never see the sea again. He did not return to rue Copeau (at least not at first), for the artist Jacques Milbert —now the director of publication for the *Voyage*—wrote to him on 30 September at a new address, a certain 'maison de l'Enelore'—apparently on the eastern end of the rue de Longchamp, which runs between the Bois de Boulogne and the place d'Iéna. This was then on the outer edge of Paris, near the Porte Dauphine. Close by were remnants of the ancient forest that once covered the entire valley of the Seine and that, five years later, occupying British and Prussian troops would almost completely reduce to firewood. Here, it would seem, Péron continued the writing of the second volume of the *Voyage* and completed (or oversaw the publication of) another wide-ranging series of scientific articles co-authored with Lesueur. In addition to their joint work on the medusae, they published articles on the conservation of zoological specimens in alcohol;[52] pteropods (a group of planktonic snails sometimes called sea butterflies because of their wing-like fins);[53] *Firola* (a macroplanktonic genus of gastropod);[54] and the habitat of seals and other marine animals.[55]

Time is the fire in which we all burn and, although Péron burned brightly for a time in Nice, he had no prospect of recuperation or cure. Joseph Deleuze tells us that soon after Péron's return to Paris he 'relapsed into a worse state than he was in before his departure'. Deleuze recorded that he saw Péron frequently and sought to give him hope, but that he 'spoke of his end with a surprising tranquillity'.[56] Determined to finish his days in his birthplace, close to his two beloved sisters, Péron made a final farewell to his friends in Paris and set off for Cérilly. Once again, Lesueur was his devoted travelling companion.

Tuberculosis, in its pulmonary form, is a disease caused by respiratory infection with *Mycobacterium tuberculosis*, first identified by Robert Koch in 1882. The pathological lesions in the lungs are called tubercles, and these had been described by Giovanni-Battista Morgagni in his *De Sedibus et Causis Morborum* as early as 1761.[57] However, it was one of Péron's fellow students under Corvisart, Gaspard Laurent Bayle, who first employed the term 'tuberculosis' and described the relation between pulmonary tuber- culosis and the disease in other organs.[58] Despite significant advances in the pathology of the disease, its treatment in the early nineteenth century was still deeply influenced by classical medical authorities. Hippocrates, for example, had advised those afflicted with consumption to 'buy a cow, drive the cow to the mountains, and live off the cow'.[59] His later Arab disciples, Avicenna and Rhazes, also espoused the virtues of fresh milk and dry air.[60] But it was not just milk that was regarded as beneficial in the treatment of tuberculosis; the very air of stables was regarded as salutary.[61] In 1804, Etienne Sainte-Marie declared that there was 'no air more advantageous' than 'lacteal air' that one 'breathes in a cow stable'.[62] Treatment by *instabulation* required the patient to be lodged with two to six young cows, which were fed aromatic herbs and had their dung removed every three hours.[63]

We know Péron showed great interest in the immunological protection offered by cowpox vaccination against smallpox. Could he have seen milk and stable remedies as another credible medical benefit associated with cows? It would appear so. On arrival in Cérilly on 19 October 1810,[64] he was accommodated in stables belonging to his old classmate, Jean-Gilbert Bonnet, later mayor of the town during the Bourbon Restoration. Bonnet's residence comprised three buildings that embraced two court-yards between the then Grande Rue and the rue du Foirail.[65] Lesueur sketched the scene inside the stables and either he or one of Péron's sisters milked a cow whenever Péron felt a desire for sustenance. Lesueur also sketched Péron, three days before his death, seated by the fire, reading. The severe weight loss that usually characterises consumptive patients is evident in Péron's drawn cheekbones and generally emaciated appearance. He was soon unable to write and little able to read. Instead Lesueur read con-stantly to him, ceasing only when Péron drifted into sleep.

Tuberculosis can spread into other organs, but in the lungs the large cavitating lesions cause the patient to cough up blood (haemoptysis) and severely reduce the amount of tissue available for respiration. Péron had long displayed the symptoms of exhaustion and feverish sweats. In Cérilly, the general toxemia and breathlessness of his condition reached the stage of complete respiratory failure. Joseph Deleuze, perhaps on the basis of Lesueur's testimony, suggests that Péron 'plunged into a kind of medita-tion, it seemed, to lie in wait for death, to observe it'. It is hard to believe that he did not think of Baudin and the irony of their shared fate during his final days. Perhaps, also, he was reminded of the deaths of his parents. Did he grapple, anew, with losing his father so young? Did he struggle, once more, to remember his face, his voice, his touch ...? Or perhaps it was the lingering bitter-sweet memory of Sophie Petitjean, who had predeceased him by six years,[66] that engaged him in the blurred kaleidoscope of his final reveries. The bare documentary record we have indicates that in the early hours of 14 December 1810, Lesueur answered Péron's request for a little milk. Péron squeezed his friend's hand, turned towards him one last time, then slipped from consciousness. By 3.00 a.m. he was dead, aged only thirty-five.[67] The next day he was buried in the local cemetery with a simple black cross bearing only his name.

— 22 —

Epilogue

There came to his grave-side,
In decent mourning, from the county's ends,
Those scattered friends
Who had liv'd the boon companions of his prime ...
RUPERT BROOKE, *The Funeral of Youth: Threnody*

SHORTLY after Péron's death, the director of the Muséum ordered seals
to be placed on the doors of his Paris lodgings until natural history objects
he had borrowed for study were returned. The Muséum also requested the
Minister of the Interior 'not to yield to any of the applications made in
favour of the sisters of M. Péron, or seeking to obtain sums intended to
facilitate the publication of the results of the voyage, until the Muséum has
regained possession of everything that has been removed from the collection brought together by the naturalist'.[1] Poor Lesueur, attempting to
complete his drawings of fish, reptiles and sponges, was even threatened
with litigation if he caused any obstruction to this reclamation. Mindful of
the vulnerability of Péron's impoverished sisters (now that they had lost
their principal benefactor), Lesueur arranged in April 1811 for his portrait
of their brother to be engraved[2] and sold for their benefit.[3] Fortunately,
by the following month, Lesueur's difficulties with the Muséum were
resolved, and he was even offered compensation for the costs incurred by
the seals 'in consideration of the services of the late M. Péron'.[4]

In 1811 Lesueur sought support to honour Péron with a splendid
tomb bearing the allegorical image of a demasted and shrouded *Géographe*.

Péron's friend, Pierre-François Keraudren, even composed an elegant com-
memorative inscription: '… he is withered like a tree charged with the
most beautiful fruit which succumbs to the excess of its fecundity.'[5]
Unfortunately, no funds could be found to realise this ambition,[6] and
Lesueur could honour his late friend only by reprinting 300 copies of
Alard's and Deleuze's respective elegies.[7]

Lesueur remained in Paris until 1815, continuing his scientific work,
but bitter that he was not entrusted with the task of completing the second
volume of Péron's *Voyage*. Expecting the loss of his imperial pension after
Napoleon's final abdication, he signed a contract to accompany William
Maclure on a scientific expedition to the West Indies and the United
States. He and Maclure arrived in New York in May 1816 and then set up
base in Philadelphia for several geological tours. After his contract expired,
Lesueur remained in the United States continuing his scientific observations, but supplementing his income by giving drawing lessons. Among his
pupils were the daughters of Joseph Bonaparte. In 1825 he participated in
the foundation of Robert Owen's utopian settlement at New Harmony,
Indiana. Although Owen's social experiment failed, Lesueur continued his
zoological observations in Missouri, Illinois and Tennessee. He planned a
twelve-part work, *Fish of North America*, but only the first two parts were
published. Following further valuable ethnographic and geological studies,
he returned to France in 1837.[8]

News of Lesueur's return eventually reached Péron's family in Allier.
Rosalie wrote to him, on 2 February 1839, to welcome him home and to
advise him of renewed plans to honour her 'unfortunate brother' in
Cérilly.[9] These plans had been initiated by Péron's old friend, the artist
Henri Dufour, who, in 1836, sought subscriptions for a commemorative
edifice[10] to be located in the new 'Place Péron' created by the demolition
of Cérilly's ancient ramparts.[11] Members of the family of the notary Pierre
Petitjean (who had died in 1822) also wrote to Lesueur to invite him
to attend the inauguration as their guest of honour.[12] He accepted and,
on 8 June 1842, flanked by two rows of National Guards and holding the
arm of the prefect, Lesueur headed the procession that walked solemnly
towards the monument, bearing Péron's bronze bust, in addition to
inscriptions and bas-relief scenes from Baudin's expedition. It was also a
mausoleum for, on 23 February 1842, the naturalist's remains had been
exhumed from the local cemetery and reinterred within the embrace of
its grey Volvic basalt.[13]

Whether it was the tiresome length of the speeches, or the summer heat, it was all too much for Péron's godson, François Bonnet, in whose father's stable the naturalist died: he dropped dead of a stroke in the middle of the formalities. All thought of festivity disappeared, and the town was plunged into mourning, which carried over to the younger Bonnet's funeral the next day. Not surprisingly, Lesueur was moved to reflect on his last painful visit to Cérilly, thirty-two years before, which had also ended with a funeral.[14]

After Péron's death, Lesueur came into possession of his friend's manuscripts, which were part of their joint working papers. Technically, the government would have had a claim on all that was drafted while they were in its employ. But in the wake of Napoleon's final defeat at Waterloo, Lesueur seized the opportunity to lay claim to documents that were, in the words of Gustave Lennier, an early curator of the Muséum du Havre, 'abandoned by the government to their authors Péron and Lesueur after the proposal to publish the last two volumes of the voyage had been given up'.[15] Some were cared for by Lesueur's family; others went with him to the United States. After his death, on 12 December 1846, these papers (including Péron's manuscripts) remained with Lesueur's relatives. One crate of early documents and drawings is known to have still been in the possession of his niece in 1874. Between 1883 and 1918, most of Lesueur's collection was sold or donated to the museum in Le Havre, and an additional forty portfolios of manuscripts and drawings were given to the natural history museum in Paris.

In the Allied bombardment of 5 September 1944, the Le Havre museum was completely gutted; Péron's manuscripts, and Lesueur's papers and luminous watercolours, would have been lost forever had not the shrewd curator, André Maury, removed the priceless Lesueur Collection for safekeeping during the early days of the German occupation.[16] Today, they continue to bear witness to a splendid vision of the natural world and to one of the great friendships and scientific partnerships in the history of maritime exploration.

Glossary of scientific terms

Asteroideas *See Echinodermata*

Beroe (from Greek mythology = Berói, daughter of Oceanus) A genus of comb jelly (ctenophora) that feeds on other comb jellies. It is characterised by a sac-like body without tentacles, but with a large oral opening used to engulf prey whole. Beroes use eight comb rows for propulsion and employ macrocilia to break off pieces of their prey, which are encountered blindly. Parts of their bodies are also luminescent.

binomial (from Latin *binominis* = two names) Each species of plant or animal is designated by a two-part name, which reflects the genus to which it belongs, and its own species name, for example, *Eucalyptus* (genus) *globulus* (species).

Bryozoa (from Greek *bryon* = moss + *zoa* = animals) Small invertebrate aquatic creatures animals now classified in the phyla Entoprocta and Ectoprocta that colonise rocky surfaces, shells and even algae. Each animal has a distinct alimentary canal. In fossil form they are often an abundant component of limestones. Bryozoan colonies are often called 'sea mats' or 'lace corals'.

catastrophism (from Greek *katastrophi* = overturning) A theory that ascribed species extinctions, sharp breaks in the fossil succession and major geomor-phological changes (such as the advance and retreat of the sea) to periodic 'revolutions' or catastrophes. It is most closely associated with Georges Cuvier, one of the founders of vertebrate paleontology; however, in recent years neo-catastrophists have posited asteroid impact as a possible explanation for the dinosaur extinctions.

Cephalapoda (from Greek *kephale* = head + *poda* = feet) The cuttlefishes, squids and octopuses, invertebrate animals belonging to the mollusca that have well-developed nervous systems and relatively large brains.

Crustacea (from Latin *crusta* = crust or shell) Predominantly aquatic arthropods with segmented bodies, an exoskeleton and paired, jointed limbs—including the decapoda (lobsters, crabs, shrimps), stomatopoda (mantis shrimps), euphausiacea (krill) and the only sessile group, cirripedia (barnacles). Lamarck was the first to use the term in its modern zoological sense in 1801, but Cuvier had used it in a more general sense, in 1798, to include other arthropoda (jointed limbed animals), such as arachnids and insects.

Echinodermata (from Greek *ekhinos* = spiny + *derma*, skin) Radially symmetrical marine animals of which there are approximately 7000 described living species and about 13 000 fossil species (dating back to the Precambrian) without any freshwater or terrestrial forms. Most live on the sea bottom. They include the Echnoidea or sea urchins, the Holothuroidea or sea cucumbers (trepang, bêche de mer), and the Stelleroidea or sea stars, which are further divided into two subtypes: Asteroideas (true sea stars, which have arms connected to each other) and the Ophiuroideas (brittle stars and basket stars, which have a distinct boundary between arm and central disk).

endemic (from Greek *en* = in + *demos* = people) A term applied to plants and animals found only in a certain area.

genus (from Greek *genos* = race, stock) A taxonomic group of closely related species (plural: genera).

Holothurian (from Greek *olothoiryon*) Sea cucumbers, trepang, bêche de mer. The Holothuroidea are distinguished from other Echinodermata by being elongated, bilaterally symmetrical and lying on their sides. Holothurians have a thick and elastic body wall with a worm-like mouth–anus axis. The mouth is normally surrounded by between 8 and 30 feelers used to filter food. They have no arms, but do have three rows of leg-like ambulacras. There are 1100 described extant species around the world.

holotype (from Greek *olos* = whole, entire + *typos* = impression, figure) A single specimen (except in the case of a hapantotype representing different stages in the lifecycle of a species) designated the type specimen by the original botanical or zoological author when the description of a species was first published.

lectotype (from Greek *lectós* = chosen + *typos* = impression) The specimen (or image) selected as the type of a species when the original author of a name failed to designate one.

materia medica (Latin = healing materials) Pharmaceutical remedies used in medicine.

Medusa (from Greek, *Medusa* = one of the gorgons) In Greek mythology, after Medusa slept with Poseidon, an outraged Athena turned the only mortal gorgon's hair into living snakes. For Linnaeus, the snake-like appendages of Medusa's head were reminiscent of the stinging tentacles attached to the umbels of jellyfish and inspired his naming of a genus. Today Medusazoa is a collective term applied to several taxonomic classes that belong to the phylum Cnidaria—to which sea anemones and coral polyps also belong—within the infrakingdom Coelenterata.

megalop (from Greek, *megalo* = large + *op* = eye) Originally a name for a supposed genus of crustacean, now applied to a post-larval stage for crabs.

Mollusca (from Latin *mollis* = soft) One of the largest phyla of invertebrates, comprising more than 50 000 highly diverse living species and about 35 000 fossil species dating from the Cambrian. Molluscs have soft bodies and usually (but not always) have a prominent shell. They include the pelecypoda (bivalves), the gastropoda (snails and slugs), polyplacophora (chitons), scaphopoda (tusk shells) and the cephalapoda (octopuses, squids and cuttlefish).

Neptunists (from Latin, *Neptunus* = god of the sea) A term applied to those who believed that water was the fundamental agent of geological change. In the seventeenth century such notions were associated with John Woodward, who saw marine fossils as evidence of the Noachic flood. In the eighteenth century Neptunism was closely associated with the writings of Abraham Gottlob Werner, who maintained that the entire globe was originally covered by a turbid universal ocean, from which so-called primitive rocks, such as granite and other crystalline rocks, were precipitated. (For a survey of Abraham Gottlob Werner and his ideas, see Adams, *The Birth and Development of the Geological Sciences*, pp. 209–27.) These ideas were opposed by the Vulcanists, who advocated the primacy of heat and volcanic action, and later the Plutonists, associated with the brilliant Scottish geologist James Hutton, who drew attention to intrusive igneous formations.

nomen nudum (Latin = bare name, plural *nomina nuda*) A scientific name that has been published or mentioned without a complete description and is thus effectively ignored.

nomen oblitum (Latin = forgotten name, plural *nomina oblita*) Names that have remained unused for many years and are effectively senior synonyms.

Nudibranchia (from Latin *nudus* = naked + *branchia* = gill) Gastropod marine molluscs (*sea slugs*) without shells.

Ophiuroideas *See Echinodermata.*

Salps *See Thaliacea.*

Siphonophores (from Greek *siphon* = pipe, tube + *phóros* = bearer) Delicate pelagic hydrozoans with long filamentous tentacles belonging to the phylum cnidaria (along with the medusazoa). They are either floating colonies or free-swimming.

species (Latin = appearance, form, kind) A taxonomic classification for a group of organisms with common characteristics, capable of breeding and producing fertile progeny.

syntype (from Greek *syn* = alike + *typos* = impression) A specimen belonging to a type series from which neither a holotype nor a lectotype has been selected or designated. The syntypes constitute the name-bearing type collectively.

taxonomy (from Greek *taxis* = arrangement + *nomos* = law) Among the natural sciences, the description, naming and classification of living things. Scientists name and revise the names of plants and animals on the basis of their knowledge of a species and its relationship to other species. In the past, botanists studying plants in different parts of the world sometimes gave different names to the same species. Under the International Code of Botanical Nomenclature, a species can have only one name. Beginning with those published in Linnaeus's *Species Plantarum* (1753), the oldest name has priority. Similarly, under the International Code of Zoological Nomenclature the starting date is the tenth edition of Linnaeus's *Systema naturae* (1758). Taxonomic revision can take place not simply as a result of discovering an older name; it can take place as a result of a better understanding of the differences or similarities in a taxon (plural taxa), a general term for any taxonomic rank from subspecies to division. Thus a given species can be moved from one genus to another. Although its generic name can change, its specific epithet usually does not. Decisions are made by the International Commission on Zoological Nomenclature, which was founded on 18 September 1895.

Thaliacea (from Greek *thaleia* = blooming) The salps: small, free-swimming, barrel-shaped, zooplankton belonging to the subphylum urochordata (tunicates).

Tunicates *See Urochordata.*

type specimen (from Greek *typos* = impression, figure) The museum or herbarium specimen selected by a taxonomist to serve as a basis for naming and describing a new species. Where the original specimen has disappeared, an illustration can have 'type' status.

Urochordata (from Greek *oirá* = tail + *khord* = cord) Sea squirts, which have motile larvae displaying a tubular nerve chord normally lost in the adult form. They are also known as tunicates because of the gelatinous tunic of the adults; these have pharyngeal gill slits that trap food as water is drawn through with the aid of ciliated cells; *see also Thaliacea.*

Glossary of French terms

As they appear in the text; in some cases already translated into English.

abbé (from Greek *abbas* = father) A title given to abbots, priests without the charge of parishes and members of the secular clergy. Between February and August 1790 a number of laws were passed that abolished religious orders and monastic vows, and allowed for the election of bishops and priests in French dioceses; members of the clergy were also required to take an oath of allegiance to the civil constitution. The Abbé Pierre Marchand, Péron's clerical mentor in Cérilly, took this oath.

Académie des Sciences *See Institut.*

Ancien Régime (old regime) The social and political structure in France before the Revolution, based on absolute monarchy. It consisted of three orders: the clergy, the nobility and the Third Estate or commons (peasantry and bourgeoisie).

aîné (fem. ainée) eldest, elder.

brumaire (from French *brume* = fog) The second month of the French republican calendar; the equivalent of the northern hemisphere autumn period 22 October to 20 November. It is particularly remembered for Napoleon's *coup d'état* of 18 brumaire (9 November 1799).

capitaines de vaisseau (ship's captain) The most important rank among the French navy's *officiers particuliers*. Nicolas Baudin held this rank. The immediate superiors of the *capitaines de vaisseau*, after 1791, were the *contre-amiraux* or rear admirals. Hamelin held the more junior rank of *capitaine de frégate* as did Le Bas de Sainte-Croix.

chevalier (knight) A title by which the upper level of the French nobility separated itself from the rest of the nobility, who were merely *écuyers* (esquires). The title was used by high officers of the royal household, the chancellor and holders of *fiefs de dignité*, but was appropriated by lesser nobles towards the end of the Ancien Régime. Members of the order of Saint-Louis, created by Louis XIV in 1693 as a reward for outstanding military conduct, were also entitled to call themselves *chevalier*. Orders of chivalry were abolished by the Constituent Assembly in 1791, but the title 'chevalier' was reinstated with the creation of the *Légion d'honneur* in 1804.

commissaire de guerre (commissioner of war) A senior officer charged with the administration and supply of the army. Legislation in October 1791 fixed their number at twenty-three, which was increased to twenty-five in May 1792. They were later replaced by the *intendants militaires*. It was a *commissaire de guerre* who reviewed Péron and the 2nd Battalion of volunteers from Allier in February 1794.

comte (count) A title of landed nobility ranking next after a *marquis* and corresponding to the British earl.

Directory (French = *directoire*) The constitution of 22 August 1795 vested executive authority in five directors: Barras, Reubell, Letourneur, La Reveillière-Lépeaux and Sieyès. The latter promptly retired and was replaced by Carnot. They were assisted by the Council of Five Hundred and the Council of Ancients (made up of 250 members). The Directory was overthrown by Bonaparte's *coup d'état* of 9 November 1799, which initiated the dictatorship of the Consulate.

Ecole[s] de Santé (Schools of Health) On 4 December 1794, after five months of debate, the National Convention voted to create three new. medical schools: in Paris, Montpellier and Strasbourg. The intention was to meet a desperate need for doctors (exacerbated by continuing war and the previous abolition of all of France's medical faculties and surgical colleges) and completely overhaul medical training such that the previously separate disciplines of general medicine, surgery and materia medica were taught together in the same schools, along with a program of clinical instruction. These radical reforms effectively marked the birth of modern medical education.

Estates General (French = *Etats généraux*) An ancient assembly of the three estates (clergy, nobility and Third Estate or commons) first summoned by the King of France in 1301, but which before the Revolution had not met since 1614. Summoned by Louis XVI to resolve France's financial crisis, it met at Versailles on 5 May 1789. From the ranks of the Third Estate and a number of reformist members of the clergy and nobility emerged the self-declared National Assembly on 17 June.

floréal (from Latin *floris* = a flower) The eighth month of the French republican calendar; the equivalent of the spring period 20 April to 19 May.

franc French monetary unit. On 7 December 1793 the National Convention decreed that the principal monetary unit of the Ancien Régime, the *livre*, was to be decimalised and henceforth known as the *franc*. The following year the convention decreed that the new one-franc coin would weigh five grams. The old coins effectively coexisted with the new until Napoleon, who issued coins bearing his own image, ordered their removal from circulation.

frimaire (from Latin *frigus* = cold) The third month of the French republican calendar; the equivalent of the northern hemisphere autumn period 21 November to 20 December.

fructidor (from Latin *fructus* = fruit) The final month of the French republican calendar; the equivalent of the northern hemisphere summer period 18 August to 16 September.

germinal (from Latin *germino* = to sprout) The seventh month of the French republican calendar; the equivalent of the northern hemisphere spring period 21 March to 19 April.

Girondins (Girondists) A moderate middle-class group of republicans mainly composed of deputies to the Legislative Assembly and the National Convention who came from the Gironde region of south-western France. Led by Brissot, Roland and Pétion, they advocated the overthrow of the monarchy, anti-clerical measures and an aggressive foreign policy, but opposed the excesses of the Commune and the violent measures of the Jacobins. In the wake of French reverses on the battlefield and increasingly radical popular hostility and violence, they were overthrown on 2 June 1793 and twenty-one of their leaders guillotined on 31 October 1793.

Institut (Institute) In 1666, during the reign of Louis XIV, Jean-Baptiste Colbert founded the Académie [royale] des sciences to promote scientific endeavours in France. Although suppressed by the National Convention in 1793, it was effectively reconstituted as a principal part of the new Institut national in 1795 (and Institut impérial after Napoleon crowned himself emperor). In 1816 the name 'Académie des sciences' was resurrected, but to this day it remains part of the Institut. The Institut originally had three 'classes': physical sciences and mathematics, literature and fine arts, and moral and political sciences. In January 1803 Bonaparte reorganised the Institut into four classes: physical sciences and mathematics, literature and fine arts, French language and literature, history and ancient literature, and fine arts. In the process he rid himself of his ideological critics by abolishing the class of moral and political sciences.

intendant During the Ancien Régime, the senior administrator of a province, roughly equivalent to a governor and, before 1799, a senior administrator responsible for the fiscal supervision of a naval base or *arsenal*. The rank of *intendant* was briefly resurrected during the Restoration; *see also* prefect.

Jacobins The most radical of revolutionary associations, which took its name from its meeting place in the former Dominican convent in the rue Saint-Jacques. Its members included the 'Mountain' faction of Maximilien Robespierre, Jean-Paul Marat and Louis Florelle de Saint-Just. The Jacobins ruled France during the Terror and were overthrown on 9 thermidor (27 July 1794). Their principal leaders were guillotined.

Jardin des Plantes Originally the Jardin du Roi, the royal botanical garden, it was established on a six-hectare site by Louis XIII in 1635. Initially it functioned as a physic garden for medicinal and useful plants. Together with the *ménagerie*, where exotic animals were kept, it gradually became a centre for the study of all branches of the natural sciences. Renamed the Jardin des

Plantes in 1792, the following year it became home to the new Muséum national d'histoire naturelle. In this institution, several of Péron's friends and mentors, including Georges Cuvier, Faujas de Saint-Font and Bernard Lacépède, gained influential professorial chairs.

livre (from Latin *libra* = pound) The common monetary unit of France before the introduction of the franc. It was equivalent to the value of a *livre* or pound of silver and was divided into twenty *sols* (or *sou*) and each *sol* into twelve *deniers*. The famous gold coin, the *Louis d'or*, was valued at twenty-four livres. Before the Revolution, a modest meal or a seat at the Comédie française could be purchased for one livre. A bowl of *café au lait* at a street stall cost about two sols. A Paris labourer earned between 300 and 500 livres a year. A professorial stipend was about 1900 livres a year.

marquis A title of landed nobility ranking immediately below a *duc* (duke) and above a *comte* (count). It originally referred to the ruler of a *marche* or frontier territory.

messidor (from Latin *messis* = harvest) The tenth month of the French republican calendar; the equivalent of the northern hemisphere summer period 19 June to 18 July.

Muséum national d'histoire naturelle *See Jardin des Plantes.*

National Assembly (French = *Assemblée nationale constituante*) On 17 June 1789, the representatives of the Third Estate in the Estates General were joined by reform-minded representatives of the nobility and clergy, and declared themselves to be a National Assembly. After refusing Louis XVI's orders to disband and sit as separate estates, on 9 July the representatives proclaimed themselves to be a National Constituent Assembly. On 22 December 1789, the voting procedures drafted by the assembly gave suffrage to adult males older than twenty-five with tax and residential qualifications. The National Assembly was succeeded on 1 October 1791 by the National Legislative Assembly (*Assemblée nationale législative*), which in turn was succeeded on 21 September 1792 by the National Convention. The National Convention, which proclaimed the republic on 22 September, was succeeded by the Directory in 1795. It was overthrown by Napoleon Bonaparte in the *coup d'état* of 18 brumaire (9 November 1799), which initiated the Consulate and laid the foundations of the empire.

National Convention *See National Assembly.*

National Guard (French = *garde nationale*) Citizen militia established in Paris on 13 July 1789 to ensure law and order. The first commander was the marquis de Lafayette, hero of the American War of Independence.

National Legislative Assembly *See National Assembly.*

nivôse (from Latin *nivosus* = snowy) The fourth month of the French republican calendar; the equivalent of the northern hemisphere winter period 21 December to 19 January.

pluviôse (from Latin *pluvia* = rain) The fifth month of the French republican calendar; the equivalent of the northern hemisphere winter period 20 January to 18 February.

prairial (from French *prairie* = meadow) The ninth month of the French republican calendar; the equivalent of the northern hemisphere spring period 20 May to 18 June.

prefect (French *préfet* from Latin *praefectus* = an overseer) Bonaparte's Consulate (and later his empire) was a highly centralised authoritarian state. By means of the Law of 28 pluviôse an VIII (17 February 1800), the First Consul installed prefects as the representatives of his all-powerful state in each of France's regional *départements*. The previous year the term was also applied to the *intendants de la marine et des colonies*, who held a commission equivalent to a *lieutenant-général* and were responsible for the fiscal supervision of a naval base or *arsenal*—in such ports as Toulon, Marseilles, Rochefort, Brest and Le Havre or in such colonies as Martinique, Saint-Domingue and the Ile de France.

procureur (attorney, advocate) A legal representative in seigneurial courts and provincial *parlements* (courts); generally equivalent to English 'solicitors'. A *procureur du roi* acted as a public prosecutor in a royal court of law.

sans culottes (French *sans* = without + *culotte* = breeches) Radical republican manual workers who proudly wore trousers rather than the knee breeches associated with the aristocracy of the Ancien Régime and the bourgeoisie.

Terror (French = *La Terreur*) The intensely fearful period of denunciations, mass arrests and executions that began with the fall of the Girondins on 2 June 1793 and ended with the fall of Robespierre on 27 July 1794. Initially those accused of being enemies of the Revolution were tried—and almost invariably condemned—by the *Tribunal révolutionnaire*, but in the final six weeks of the Terror (after a law passed on 10 June 1794) those arrested were executed without trial.

thermidor (from Greek *thermos* = hot) The eleventh month of the French republican calendar; the equivalent of the northern hemisphere summer period 19 July to 17 August. It is particularly remembered for the fall of Robespierre on 9 thermidor an II (27 July 1794) and the end of the Terror; hence the term 'post-thermidor'.

vendémiaire (from Latin *vindemia* = grape harvest, vintage) The first month of the French republican calendar; the equivalent of the northern hemisphere autumn period 22 September to 21 October. It is particularly remembered for Bonaparte's dispersal of royalist insurgents in Paris on 13 vendémiaire (4 October 1795).

ventôse (from Latin *ventosus* = windy) The sixth month of the French republican calendar; the equivalent of the northern hemisphere winter period 19 February to 20 March.

Notes

Textual note

[1] See, for example, Cleland, 'Remarkable mistranslations in the English version (1809) of Peron's Voyage of Discovery'.

Introduction

[1] Quoted by Deleuze in 'Notice historique sur M. Péron', p. 272.

[2] See Duyker and d'Unienville, 'Faure, Pierre Ange François Xavier (1776–1855)'.

[3] See Chelin, 'Billard, Julien (c. 1781–1846)'.

[4] See Duyker, 'In search of Madame Kerivel and Baudin's last resting place'.

[5] Anonymous review, 'Emile Guillaumin, *François Péron*', *Bulletin de la Société d'Emulation du Bourbonnais*, tome 39, 1936, p. 112.

[6] Scott, *Terre Napoléon*, p. 76.

[7] ibid., pp. 251–2.

[8] See, for example, Marnie Bassett's comments in a footnote on page 65 of *The Governor's Lady*.

[9] Scott, *Terre Napoléon*, p. 238.

[10] ibid.

[11] The French historian Jean-Paul Faivre did much to rehabilitate Baudin in a number of scholarly articles published between 1938 and 1965. Then Christine Cornell's English translation of Baudin's journal (1974) made the expedition commander's account accessible to a new generation of scholars. In 1982, the Mauritian historian Madeleine Ly-Tio-Fane published important findings on Baudin's early career; see Ly-Tio-Fane, 'Contacts between Schönbrunn and the Jardin du Roi at Isle de France (Mauritius) in the 18th century: An episode in the career of Nicolas Thomas Baudin'. Five years later Frank Horner published *The French Reconnaissance* (1987). Although Horner's work remains the principal reference work on Baudin, the bicentenary of both the Baudin and Flinders expeditions stimulated renewed interest in this period of Australian coastal exploration. In 2000, Anthony Brown published *Ill-starred Captains:*

Flinders and Baudin (see my review in the *Journal of the Royal Australian Historical Society*, vol. 87, part 2, December 2001, pp. 290–2); in 2003, Ly-Tio-Fane published her study of Baudin's final visits to the Ile de France (*Le Géographe et le Naturaliste à L'Ile-de-France 1801, 1803: Ultime Escale du Capitaine Baudin*); and in 2004 Jean Fornasiero, Peter Monteath and John West-Sooby co-published *Encountering Terra Australis: The Australian Voyages of Nicolas Baudin and Matthew Flinders*.

12   In *The Navigators*, Klaus Toft does not stop with Péron's sins against Baudin; we are told that even his 'handling of the vast natural history collection entrusted into his care by Milius was lamentable' and that 'what Péron did not hand out to secure favours he kept for himself'. Furthermore, despite the fact that Professor Michel Jangoux (see his study 'Vers les Terres Australes') has done much valuable work identifying the many botanical specimens collected by Leschenault during the expedition, which are still preserved in the Muséum national d'histoire naturelle in Paris, Toft accuses Labillar-dière of claiming them as his 'private property' and asserts that they were then sold after his death; see pp. 301–2.

13   Marchant, *France Australe*, p. 115.

14   Horner, *The French Reconnaissance*, p. 76.

15   Jangoux, 'Les zoologistes et botanistes qui accompagnèrent le Capitaine Baudin aux Terres Australes'.

16   See, for example, the ideas of G. W. Stocking Jr. in his article 'French anthropology in 1800', taken up by Fornasiero, Monteath and West-Sooby, in *Encountering Terra Australis*. For my critical discussion of this position, see chapter 10 of this book.

17   Lamarck and Guyton, 'Rapport sur le mémoire de M. Péron sur les observations de la température de la mer'; Lamarck, 'Considérations sur quelques faits applicables à la théorie du globe, observés par M. Péron dans son voyage aux Terres Australes, et sur quelques questions géologiques qui naissent de la connaissance de ces faits'; Lamarck, 'Sur une nouvelle espèce de Trigonie, et sur une nouvelle huître, découvertes dans le voyage du capitaine Baudin'.

18   Péron, 'Mémoire sur quelques faits zoologiques applicables à la théorie du globe'.

19   Vallance, 'Origins of Australian geology', p. 26.

20   See, for example, Cuvier, *Discours sur les révolutions de la surface du globe et sur les change-ments qu'elles ont produits dans le règne animal*, p. 33.

21   For a survey of Abraham Gottlob Werner's ideas and Neptunism, see Adams, *The Birth and Development of the Geological Sciences*, pp. 209–27.

22   Péron, 'Ile de France ... nature de sol', MHNH, Coll. Lesueur, MS 15025; Péron, 'Port-Louis, île de France 25 ventôse an 9 [16 March 1801], MHNH, Coll. Lesueur, MS 15044; see also Bailly, 'Geognotische Bemerkungen über Isle de France'.

23   Lamarck, 'Sur une nouvelle espèce de Trigonie, et sur une nouvelle huître, découvertes dans le voyage du capitaine Baudin'.

24   Lamarck and Guyton, 'Rapport sur le mémoire de M. Péron sur les observations de la température de la mer'; see also Deacon, *Scientists and the Sea 1650–1900*, pp. 204–6.

25   Keraudren, 'Nécrologie [François Péron]'.

1. Cérilly

1   The novelist Charles-Louis Philippe (1874–1909) was a native of Cérilly.

2   Piboule and Bertrand, *Mémoire des communes Bourbonnaises*, pp. 62–3.

3   See BMS, 1768–78, Archives départementales de l'Allier, 2E/44/4.

4   Mitton, 'Généralités sur les églises de la région de Tronçais: Eglise Saint-Martin de Cérilly'.

5   The parish registers indicate that this was the average infant mortality rate for Cérilly at the time.

6   There might be an association between the house in question, the Gillet family and the 'trou Gillet', a small door that provided pedestrian and horse access through Cérilly's southern wall during the eighteenth century; see Bodard, *Cérilly et les environs, traditions, documents, légendes*: VI: *Les fêtes de la Révolution et le Citoyen Jean-François Bourgoing*, p. 8.

7   See Actes, notaire Pierre-Lazare Petitjean, 5 mars 1784, Archives départementales de l'Allier, 3E/11549.

8   Cérilly, BMS, 1779–87, Archives départementales de l'Allier, 2E/44/5.

9   Actes, notaire Pierre-Lazare Petitjean, 5 mars 1784, Archives départementales de l'Allier, 3E/11549.

10   See Actes, notaire Pierre-Lazare Petitjean, 5 mars 1784, op. cit.

11   See, for example, Hocquet, *Le Sel et le pouvoir*.

12   This might survive in the courtyard between the external cellar door and the entrance to the stables.

13   Whether it was a reflection of the financial insecurities of his childhood or the seeming normality of guests paying for their accommodation and food, Péron appears to have been continually surprised by the generous hospitality of his fellow man, be it peasants in Germany, Aborigines in Tasmania, British officers at Port Jackson, or rough sealers on King Island in Bass Strait, all of whom extended kindness without thought of money.

14   The Péron family possessed two large wine barrels.

15   The family owned three mills to grind tobacco and six stoneware pots to store its baneful leaves. Six pounds of rope tobacco (valued at nineteen livres, sixteen sols) was recorded in the house. A lockable counter, two pairs of scales and two weighing bags appear to have completed the tobacco merchant's ensemble; see Actes, notaire Pierre-Lazare Petitjean, 5 mars 1784, op. cit.

16   Five years before his death, François senior's name appeared in the parish registers as the declared guardian of a domestic servant named Marie Pegaud, who married in Cérilly on 29 April 1778; Cérilly, BMS, 1768–78, Archives départementales de l'Allier, 2E/44/4.

17   The valuers found the horse in reasonable health and estimated it to be worth ninety-three livres; Actes, notaire Pierre-Lazare Petitjean, 5 mars 1784, op. cit.

18   Péron to Jean-Baptiste Lesueur *c*. October 1804, MHNH, Coll. Lesueuer, MS 63026.

19   Actes, notaire Pierre-Lazare Petitjean, 10 juin 1785, Archives départementales de l'Allier, 3E/11549.

20   Cérilly, BMS, 1768–78, Archives départementales de l'Allier, 2E/44/4.

21   Alard, 'Eloge historique de François Péron'.

22   Audiat, *F. Péron*, p. 7.

23   Guillaumin, *François Péron*, p. 18.

24   Throughout François' childhood and youth, for example, the establishment of the widow Marie-Françoise Faure and Etienne Vidalin operated as a press and bookshop on the rue de Paris, in Moulins, near the Collège royal; see Fanaud, *Lettre de Noblesse de l'Imprimerie Moulinoise*, p. 14.

25   Moret, *Les Ecoles bourbonnaises avant 1789*, p. 80.

26   ibid., p. 78.

27 Bodard, op. cit., p. 4.
28 ibid., p. 6.
29 ibid., pp. 6–7.
30 ibid., pp. 78–9.
31 Deleuze, 'Notice historique sur M. Péron'.
32 See, for example, Olivier, 'Faune de l'Allier'; Berthoumieu and Bourgougnon, 'Matériaux pour la flore de l'Allier'; and Peyerimhoff, 'Matériaux pour la faune entomologique du Bourbonnais'.
33 Alard, op. cit.
34 Moret, op. cit., p. 81.
35 Deleuze, op. cit.
36 This was because the government of France's twenty-eight million people (see Dupaquier, *Histoire de la population française*, vol. iii., p. 63) was then grounded on unequal rights. The Church, as a separate and privileged estate in French society, numbered approximately 170 000 and had attracted the bourgeoisie to the priesthood in large numbers. The Church offered a means to further education, respect and security, for it controlled 6–10 per cent of the land (see Gibson, *A Social History of French Catholicism, 1789–1914*, p. 2) and was exempt from France's chief tax, the *taille*.

2. Revolution and war

1   Burley, in *Witness to Revolution*, p. 30; Doyle, *The Oxford History of the French Revolution*, pp. 86–7.
2   Péron, 'Ile de France: Végétation, mœurs des habitants', folio 16, verso, MHNH, Coll. Lesueur, MS 15028.
3   Cobban, *A History of Modern France*, vol. i, p. 237.
4   Peasant obligation to provide regular unpaid labour to the crown.
5   Bodard, 'Cahier de la ville et paroisse de Cérilly Pour les Etats-Généraux de 1789'.
6   Thompson, *The French Revolution*, pp. 1–5.
7   Léon, *Les anciennes forges de Tronçais*, pp. 3–4.
8   Hérault in 'Texte et documents: La Grande Peur en Bourbonnais'.
9   Tulard, Fayard and Fierro in *Histoire et dictionnaire de la Révolution française 1789–1799*, p. 317.
10 'Tableau des ecclésiastiques, fonctionnaires publics du Départment de l'Allier, qui ont prêté le serment ordonné par la loi du 26 décembre 1790', Archives nationales, D xiv 21, cited in Biernawski, *Un département sous la Révolution française, l'Allier de 1789 à l'an III*, p. 421. See also Joussain, 'Notes sur les curés de Cérilly d'après les recherches de l'abbé Louis Cabbane dans "Historique de la paroisse"'.
11 See 'Lettre au Ministère de l'Intérieur et à la députation du Bourbonnais, au sujet de la gendarmerie', Archives départementales de l'Allier, L 489, folo 191 recto.
12 See Cornillon, 'Comment le naturaliste François Péron de Cérilly fit la connaissance de Henri Dufour, artiste à Moulins et devint son ami'.
13 For an excellent historical study, see Blanning, *The Origins of the French Revolutionary Wars*.
14 On 24 January 1792, the French had demanded the renunciation of any treaties aimed at French sovereignty and assurances that Austria intended to keep the peace. If a satisfactory response was not received by 1 March, a state of war was deemed to have

existed between the two states. Austria, unable to comply without humiliation, soon gave France her pretext for hostilities.

15 Service historique de l'Armée de Terre, Vincennes, 16YC 23, 'Contrôle du 2e Bataillon des Gardes nationales volontaires du Département de l'Allier'.

16 Rousseau, 'Considérations sur le Gouvernement de Pologne et sur sa Réformation projetée' (section XII, 'Système militaire'), p. 1014.

17 Quoted by Bertaud in 'Du volontariat à la conscription 1789–1815'.

18 Dulac, *Les Levées départementales dans l'Allier sous la Révolution (1791–1796)*, tome i, pp. 116–20.

19 ibid., tome i, p. 120.

20 Guillaumin, *François Péron*, p. 18.

21 Rigondet, *François Péron*, chapter iii.

22 Dulac, op. cit., tome i, p. 116.

23 Flament, 'Note sur le 1er bataillon de volontaires de l'Allier (1791–1792)'.

24 Quoted by Verteuil, in 'Garnisons moulinoises et regiments bourbonnais'.

25 'Bureau du détail 1er Registre des déliberations des Administrateurs du Directoire du Département d l'Allier: 12 août 1791–24 août 1793', Archives départementales de l'Allier, L 60.

26 Guillaumin, op. cit, p. 18. Colin Wallace (*The Lost Australia of François Péron*, p. 6), however, would have us believe that François was so affected by the reaction of his family to his enlistment that he 'returned to the square, sought out the Recruitment Officer and asked for temporary leave to allow his family time to reconcile themselves to this abrupt change of circumstances. This was refused.' This seems to be a romanticised version of events based on a kernel of truth. François did request a deferment, but for reasons of health.

27 Péron's comrade Jean-Baptiste Brugière of the 2nd Company, quoted by Girard, *F. Péron*, p. 50; see also Brugière, 'Témoignage'.

28 Sérvice historique de l'Armée de Terre, Vincennes, 16YC 23, 'Contrôle du 2e Bataillon des Gardes nationales volontaires du Département de l'Allier'.

29 Jean-Baptiste Brugière quoted in Girard, op. cit., p. 17.

30 Dulac, op. cit., tome i, p. 124.

31 Delaunay, 'La Révolution française dans l'Allier (août 1792–septembre 1793)'.

32 ibid.

33 '57e séance du 27 septembre 1792 du Département de l'Allier', Archives départementales de l'Allier, L 54.

34 '53e séance du 21 septembre 1792 du Département de l'Allier', Archives départementales de l'Allier, L 54.

35 'Séance du 6 décembre 1792 du Département de l'Allier', Archives départementales de l'Allier, L 54.

36 Not only was the town critically dependent on imported grain, but also the grape harvest had failed, a parasitical infection had ravaged the local sheep, and there was virtually no oil or soap to be had; see Raillard, *Un coin du Morvan à travers l'histoire*, p. 294.

37 Sergeant Major Allard in Dulac, op. cit., tome i, p. 131.

38 ibid.

39 Perchet, *Histoire de Pesmes*, pp. 421–2.

40 Sergeant Major Allard in Dulac, op. cit., tome i, p. 133.

41 Germain, *La Marche et le Bassigny Barrois Mouvant*, pp. 142–3.

42 Péron, *Voyage de découvertes aux Terres australes*, tome i, p. 226 (Phillips trans., p. 177).

43 Sergeant Major Allard in Dulac, op. cit., tome i, p. 134.

44 Collet, *Charmes et ses environs*, p. 153.

45 Sergeant Major Allard in Dulac, op. cit., tome i, p. 136.

46 ibid., p. 138; see also Brugière, op. cit.

47 See Hess, *300 Jahre Festung Landau 1688/91–1988/91*.

48 ibid., tome i, p. 139.

49 Delageneste to his father, 1 avril 1793, in Dulac, op. cit., tome ii, pp. 212–13.

50 Delageneste to his parents, 5 avril 1793, in ibid., p. 214.

51 ibid.

52 Delageneste to his parents, 23 avril 1793, in ibid., p. 219.

53 Delageneste to his parents, 12 mai 1793, in ibid., p. 222.

54 Tullat to his mother, 7 mai 1793, in Picard (ed.), *Au service de la Nation: Lettres de volontaires (1792–1798)*, pp. 9–11.

55 Dulac, op. cit., tome i, pp. 139–40.

56 Eyer, *Wissembourg*, p. 53.

57 The 'Mountain' faction took its name from the fact that its members sat on the highest benches of the left side of the chamber. Its members were revolutionary radicals who espoused a highly centralised government for France.

58 See Watson, *Carnot*, pp. 73–4.

59 See Greer, *The Incidence of the Terror*, pp. 26, 37, 97, 106.

60 Forrest, *The Soldiers of the French Revolution*, p. 120.

61 Deputy to the Convention for 'Bas-Rhin'.

62 'Général Laubadère, Commandant en Chef-Landau—sa justification contre les accusations du representant du people Dentzel', Service historique de l'Armée de Terre, Château de Vincennes, GD/2s 43, pièce 52.

63 See Dossier Germain-Félix Tenet de Laubadère, Service historique de l'Armée de Terre, Château de Vincennes, GD/2s 63.

64 In 1793 Sergeant Major Allard believed there were 4000 civilians in Landau. This approximates the closest census (1796), which yielded a total civilian population of 4261. Laubadère calculated his rations on the basis of a total of 9190 mouths to feed.

65 'Mémoire de la vie politique et militaire du Général Laubadère défenseur de Landau' [*c.* 1803], Service historique de l'Armée de Terre, Château de Vincennes, GD/2S 43. pièce 6.

66 Laubadère, *Mémoire du Citoyen Laubadère,* p. 12.

67 'Notes et pièces justificatives' in Laubadère, *Mémoire*, p. 101.

68 'Biographie anonyme de Péron', Bibliothèque centrale du Muséum national d'histoire naturelle, MS 2528, folio 124.

69 Tullat to his mother, 7 mai 1793, in Picard (ed.), op. cit., p. 10.

70 Lettre de 23 prairial, an II, Vincennes, Xw 49 (Indre) cited by Forrest, op. cit., p. 162.

71 Dulac, op. cit., tome i, p. 140.

72 ibid.

73 Laubadère, *Mémoire*, p. 10.

74 For example: Audiat, op. cit., p. 11 (Audiat also stretches the siege of Landau to eight rather than five months); Dulac, op. cit., tome i, p. 141.

75 'Biographie anonyme de Péron', op. cit.

[76] Undated letter (*c.* 1796) from Péron to Henri Dufour, quoted by Cornillon, op. cit.

[77] According to M. J. L. Alard, this was after 'having given proof of a rare fearlessness and at the same time the greatest coolness in the face of danger'; see Alard, 'Eloge historique de François Péron'.

[78] Quoted in Cuneo d'Ornano, *Hoche, sa vie, sa correspondance*, p. 113.

[79] Bonnechose, *Lazare Hoche*, pp. 52–3, 64–5.

[80] See Jourquin (ed.), *Mémoires (1792–1815) du général d'artillerie baron Boulart*, p. 9.

[81] Dulac, op. cit., tome i, p. 156.

[82] ibid.

[83] ibid., pp. 157–60.

[84] Girault to Farjonnel, Dudenhofen, 21 germinal l'an II [10 April 1794], in Dulac, op. cit., tome ii, p. 229.

[85] Autobiographical note cited by Deleuze, op. cit.

[86] Péron frequently misspelt the names of acquaintances during his travels.

[87] 'Designatio deren Dudenhöfer Rauchhühner oder Herd-Gelder für 1789', appendix in Klotz, *Ortsgeschichte der gemeinde Dudenhofen/Pfalz*, pp. 254–6. The account of Péron's life by urologist Dr Georges Rigondet contains two invented sisters, 'Gretta' and 'Hilda', who tended the ailing Péron during his military service in the Rhineland in 1794. In a footnote Rigondet admits to having romanticised this episode, but tells us that his 'Kyner' family (farming a smallholding and tending a few cows, sheep and horses) is 'parfaitement authentique' (p. 62).

[88] Klotz, op. cit., pp. 150, 207, 235.

[89] His mill burned down in 1901 and was rebuilt by his descendants, who still live in the village; see Kinscherff, 'Die Mühle am Speyer-und-Woogbach'.

[90] Klotz, op. cit., pp. 107–8.

[91] See Blanning, *The French Revolution in Germany*, p. 246. Blanning points out that the more austere Protestant churches offered fewer iconoclastic opportunities.

[92] ibid., pp. 144–5.

[93] Cited by Deleuze in 'Notice historique sur M. Péron'.

[94] Acte de décès, Marie de Dudenhofen, Arrondissement Communal de Spire, 1808, Sterberegister, Stadtarchiv Speyer.

[95] For an account of the looting in Speyer (and a brilliant examination of the French occupation in general), see Blanning, op. cit., p. 117.

[96] Alard, op. cit.

[97] Jean-Baptiste Brugière quoted in Girard, *F. Péron*, p. 17.

[98] Péron's memoir, dated November 1800, quoted by Deleuze, op. cit.

[99] See Ambert, *Les Illustrations et célébrités du XIXe siècle, 7e série: biographie du général J.-J. Ambert, par le général Ambert son fils*.

[100] Stein, 'Revolutionäre Schulpolitik und schulische Stabilität im Arrondissement Kaiserslautern'.

[101] Péron added: 'Surprised by such marks of concern I asked myself what I had done to deserve it. What you have done, I remarked to myself: you have this unfortunate family, and you were moved to pity by their plight; you have sometimes shared with them your meagre ration of bread; you have inspired these sentiments in those who were subordinate to you, and the house in which you lived was peaceful. Today thankful people are showering you with blessings. This reflection on myself aroused in me a pleasant rejoicing. I told myself, if my kindness has made such an impression on angry men, I must always cultivate this quality, it must balance out the faults in my

character. I will always be kind, honest, generous even towards my enemies'; Péron's memoir, dated November 1800, quoted by Deleuze, op. cit.

[102] ibid.

[103] Girard, op. cit, p. 17, see also Brugière, op. cit.

[104] Dulac, op. cit., tome i, pp. 162–3; see also Service historique de l'Armée de Terre, Vincennes, 16YC 23, 'Contrôle du 2e Bataillon des Gardes nationales volontaires du Département de l'Allier'; see also Brugière, op. cit.

[105] Alard, op. cit., and Deleuze, op. cit.

[106] Girard, op. cit., p. 18; see also Brugière, op. cit.

[107] *Magdeburgische Zeitung* (articles on the arrival of prisoners-of-war), no. 94, 9 August 1794, p. 1; no. 99, 21 August 1794, p. 1; and no. 122, 14 October 1794, p. 1.

[108] Alard, op. cit., and Deleuze, op. cit.

[109] Anon., *Magdeburg als preussiche Festung um 1750: Ein Führer durch das Modell der Festung*, Magdeburger Schriftenreihe, n.d.

[110] Peters, 'Belagern und belagert werdern: Landeshaupstadt Magdeburg: Stadtplanung-samt Magdeburg', p. 50.

[111] Pilsudski, 'La psychologie du prisonnier'.

[112] Péron, *Voyage*, op. cit., tome i, p. 375 (Phillips trans., p. 277).

[113] In discussing the contents of prisons, Pilsudski offered a clue to the possible genesis of a naturalist: 'One finds insects and animals, which penetrate by any means. And it is the pure truth that one finds prisoners who take a liking to bugs, who make an object of their study [and] crystallise their need to live independently around such a repugnant insect'; Pilsudski, 'La psychologie du prisonnier'.

[114] ibid.

[115] Deleuze, op. cit.

[116] Wiehle, '1525–2000: Vierhundertfünfundsiebzig Jahre Stadtbibliothek Magdeburg'.

[117] An indication of the breadth of Péron's reading can be gleaned from his discussion of 'phosphorescence of the sea' in chapter v of his *Voyage de découvertes aux Terres Australes*. After citing Aristotle and Pliny, he declared: 'I have not borrowed from the observations of those not liable to either enthusiasm or exaggeration. It will suffice to mention Cook, La Pérouse, Labillardière, Vancouver, Banks, Sparman, Solander, Lamanon, d'Après de la Mannevillette, Le Gentil, Adanson, Fleurieu, Marchand, Stavorinus, Spallanzani, Bourzets, Linnaeus, Pison, Hunter, Byron, Beal, Adler, Rathgeb, Martens, De Gennes, Hierne, Daglet, Dicquemarre, Bacon, Lescarbot, Locflingtus, Shaw, Sloane, Tachart, Dombey, Ozanam, Barter, Tarnström, Marsigli, Kalm, Nassau, Pontoppidan, Morogue, Phipps, Poutrincourt, Heittmanne, Kirchmayer, Anson, Frezier, Lemaire, Vanneck, Rhumpe, Rogers, Drake etc.' See: Péron, *Voyage*, op. cit., tome i, p. 38 (Phillips trans., pp. 35–6); see also Brugière, op. cit.

[118] Deleuze, op. cit., p. 255; Brugière, op. cit.

[119] Thionville had been encircled for fifty-five days by 19 600 Austrians, 7000 Prussians and 13 000 émigré French troops. But under the spirited command of General Georges Félix de Wimpfen the defenders had hung on until the blockade was broken; Lentz, 'La Révolution à Thionville (1789–1799)'.

[120] See Chimello, *Avec le Club des Jacobins, la Révolution au quotidien*, pp. 25–6.

[121] Cuneo d'Ornano, op. cit., p. 131.

[122] Roth (ed.), *Histoire de Thionvillle*, p. 157.

[123] Bodard, *Cérilly et les Environs … VI*, pp. 74–5; Brugière, op. cit.

[124] Alard, op. cit., p. vii.

3. Medical student

[1] Quoted in a footnote by Bodard in *Cérilly et les Environs, traditions, documents, légendes*: VI, p. 75.

[2] Maurice Girard believed that Péron's work 'in the dry badly kept archives' was particularly valuable for a future naturalist, for it helped him 'to understand the advantages of a methodical classification and perfected in him the spirit of order'; see Girard, *F. Péron*, p. 18.

[3] Bodard, op. cit., pp. 68–71.

[4] ibid., p. 74.

[5] Cornillon, 'Comment le naturaliste François Péron de Cérilly fit la connaissance de Henri Dufour, artiste à Moulins et devint son ami'.

[6] Archives départementales de l'Allier, 'Séance publique du 9 Vendemiaire an 4e', L 480, folio 46 verso.

[7] Weiner, 'French doctors face war, 1792–1815'.

[8] Ramsey, *Professional and Popular Medicine in France, 1770–1830*, p. 75.

[9] Gallot, *Vues générales sur la restauration de l'art de guérir*, p. 9. Gallot ministered to my grandmother's ancestors, who hailed from the same village in the Vendée.

[10] Boerhaave's students also established clinical schools in Edinburgh and Vienna. Clinical medicine was also taught in Padua and Pavia.

[11] Ackerknecht, 'Paris hospitals around 1800—A new era in medicine'.

[12] Quoted by Weiner, in 'French doctors face war, 1792–1815'.

[13] Ramsey, op. cit., p. 51.

[14] Bodard, 'Cahier de la ville et paroisse de Cérilly pour les Etats-Généraux de 1789'.

[15] Bodard, 'Cérilly sous l'Ancien Régime: Chirurgiens-apothicaires'.

[16] 'Liste d'inscription des élèves qui suivent les cours de l'Ecole de Médecine à Paris, à commencer du 1er nivôse an VI', Archives nationales, AJ[16] 6412A★.

[17] Montaiglon, 'Description d'un salon peint par François Boucher'.

[18] Marvillet, Le Caer et al., *Nomenclature officielle des voies publiques et privées*, p. 576.

[19] Bibliothèque nationale, estampes Va 260a.

[20] See Dupont, *Dictionnaire historique des médecins*, pp. 127, 219, 249, 298, 305, 450, 466, 562.

[21] See Swords, *The Green Cockade*, pp. 90, 216, 238.

[22] For an excellent biography, see Smeaton, *Fourcroy: Chemist and Revolutionary 1755–1809*.

[23] Huguet, *Les professeurs de la faculté de médecine de Paris*, pp. 102–4.

[24] ibid., pp. 273–4.

[25] Péron, *Voyage de découvertes aux Terres Australes*, tome ii, p. 102 (Cornell trans., p. 83).

[26] Brockliss, 'L'enseignement médical et la Révolution: Essai de réévaluation'.

[27] Thirteen naturalists, 21 mathematicians, 3 astronomers, 17 civil engineers, 4 architects, 8 draughtsmen, 10 artists, 15 interpreters and 22 printers; see Tulard, Fayard and Fierro in *Histoire et dictionnaire de la Révolution française 1789–1799*, p. 246.

[28] See Warner, *The Battle of the Nile*.

[29] 'Registre journalier des élèves inscrits pour suivre les cours des deux semestres de l'an VII; feuillets décadaires des signatures des élèves pour l'an VI et l'an VII', Archives nationales, AJ[16] 6413. Jean-Noël Halle could have been an important influence on Péron's anthropological ideas since he was also a member of the Société des Observateurs de l'Homme. Marie-Joseph Alard tells us admiringly that, despite the demands

of his medical studies, Péron continued to read poetry and study history, geography, jurisprudence, mathematics, astronomy, physics and chemistry; that 'Latin flowed from his pen with the same ease as French', and that he also studied Greek, Italian, English and Spanish; see Alard, 'Eloge historique de François Péron'.

4. Savant

[1] Anonymous summary of François Péron's life, Bibliothèque centrale du Muséum national d'histoire naturelle, Paris, MS 2528.

[2] Now no. 14 place Marx-Dormoy in Cérilly.

[3] Cornillon, 'Comment le naturaliste François Péron de Cérilly fit la connaissance de Henri Dufour, artiste à Moulins et devint son ami'.

[4] Péron, 'Ile Maria—Observations anthropologiques—ventôse an X [February–March 1802]', MHNH, Coll. Lesueur, MS 18040.

[5] Acte de baptême de Sophie-Anaïs Coupery, 20 octobre 1799, Archives départementales de l'Allier, 2E/44/7.

[6] Debard, *François Péron (1775–1810)* ..., pp. 25–6.

[7] Bodard, *Cérilly et les Environs, traditions, documents, légendes*: VI, p. 107.

[8] With witty understatement, Sir Ernest Scott commented: 'Mademoiselle was unkind —because the lover was poor, his biographer says; but we must not forget that he was also one-eyed. Many ladies prefer a man with two'; Scott, *Terre Napoléon*, pp. 156–7. As has already been stated, Péron appears to have been blind in, rather than missing, one eye.

[9] Draft letter, Péron to a friend, MHNH, Coll. Lesueur, MS 14047.

[10] Acte de mariage d'Anne-Sophie Petitjean avec Pierre Raby de la Lande, 16 février 1803, Archives départementales de l'Allier, 2E/44/8.

[11] Acte de décès d'Anne-Sophie née Petitjean, 30 août 1804, Archives départementales de l'Allier, 2E/44/13.

[12] Linné, *Système sexuel des végétaux: Suivant les classes, les ordres, les genres et les espèces, avec les caractères et les différences: Première édition française calquée sur celles de Murray et de Persoon, augmentée et enrichie de notions élémentaires, de notes diverses, d'une concordance avec la Méthode de Tournefort et les Familles naturelles de Jussieu, etc., etc par N. Jolyclerc, Chez Ronvaux*, Paris an VI [1798]. I am grateful to M. Daniel Gulon, a former mayor of Cérilly, for drawing my attention to Péron's personal copy bearing the following inscription: 'François Péron du Dépt de l'Allier, Etudt. de médecine à Paris le 1er therm. an VI [signed] Péron'.

[13] 'Registre d'inscription des élèves qui suivent les cours de l'Ecole de Médecine (an VIII) ...', Archives nationales, AJ[16] 6415.

[14] Cuvier, *Eloge historique de M. Richard*, p. 15.

[15] Kunth, 'Richard, Louis Claude Marie'.

[16] Cuvier, op cit., p. 15.

[17] Kunth, op. cit.

[18] Richard, 'Instructions partielles pour les voyageurs naturalistes; instructions sur la minéralogie ...', Bibliothèque centrale du Muséum national d'histoire naturelle, MS 46.

[19] 'Registre d'inscription des élèves qui suivent les cours de l'Ecole de Médecine (an VIII) avec liste alphabétique des élèves qui ont signé les feuillets décadaires pour l'an VIII', Archives nationales, AJ[16] 6415.

20 Marvillet, Le Caer et al., op. cit., p. 571.

21 Richard lived at no. 531 rue Copeau. He was made a Chevalier de la Légion d'honneur on 25 August 1819; see Archives nationales, LH 2322/37.

22 Péron, *Voyage*, tome i, p. 42 (Phillips trans., p. 38).

23 ibid., tome ii, p. 59 (Cornell trans., p. 46).

24 In the sixteenth century, Leonhart Fuchs, Conrad Gesner, Caspar Bauhin and Guillaume Rondelet were all medical men; so too were Engelbrecht Kaempfer, Joseph Pitton de Tournefort and Sebastien Vaillant in the seventeenth century. Similarly, in the eighteenth century, the founder of modern plant and animal taxonomy, Carl Linnaeus; such great traveller–naturalists as Daniel Solander, Johann George Forster and Jacques-Julien Houtou de Labillardière; and such scientific luminaries as Albrecht von Haller, Louis Daubenton, Bernard de Jussieu and Antoine Laurent de Jussieu, were also doctors by training.

25 Horner, *The French Reconnaissance*, pp. 24–5.

26 Ly-Tio-Fane, 'Contacts between Schönbrunn and the Jardin du Roi at Isle de France (Mauritius) in the 18th Century: An episode in the career of Nicolas Thomas Baudin'; see also Horner, op. cit., pp. 25–8.

27 Horner, op. cit., pp. 29–34.

28 For the account of this semi-official expedition, see Ledru, *Voyage aux îles Ténériffe, la Trinité, Saint-Thomas, Sainte-Croix et Porto Ricco …*

29 Jean-François de Galaup de La Pérouse (1741–c. 1788) was ordered to follow up on James Cook's surveys in the Pacific. He sailed from Brest in August 1785 and, after crossing the Atlantic and entering the Pacific, he visited Easter Island, the Hawaiian Group, Alaska, California, Macau, the Philippines, Siberia, Samoa and Norfolk Island before reaching Botany Bay on 26 January 1788. He and his men departed on 10 March 1788, never to be seen by Europeans again.

30 Antoine-Raymond-Joseph Bruny d'Entrecasteaux was born in Aix-en-Provence on 8 November 1737. He entered the navy as a *garde de la marine* in 1754 and rose rapidly through the ranks. In May 1791 he was given command of the expedition ordered to search for La Pérouse. The expedition visited Tenerife, Cape of Good Hope, Van Diemen's Land, New Ireland, Admiralty Islands, Ambon, Esperance Bay (Western Australia), Van Diemen's Land again, Tongatapu and Balade (New Caledonia). The expedition then passed Vanikoro Island (unaware that the relics of La Pérouse's expedition were strewn upon its reefs), confirmed the location of the principal islands of the Solomons, and discovered and surveyed the D'Entrecasteaux and Trobriand islands in the Louisiade Archipelago. Finally, just before his death on 20 July 1793, d'Entrecasteaux accomplished important survey work on the coasts of eastern New Guinea and northern New Britain.

31 Antoine-Laurent de Jussieu to the Minister of Marine, 12 thermidor an 6 [20 July 1798] Archives nationales, Paris, AJ[15] 569, folios 152–3.

32 'Le capitaine de vaisseau Nicolas Baudin, aux membres de l'Institut national à Paris, Séance des 16 et 17 ventôse de l'an VIII de la République française [7 et 8 mars 1800]', in Bonnemains, Argentin and Marin (ed.), *Mon voyage aux Terres Australes: Journal personnel du commandant Baudin*, p. 31.

33 This sequence of events is based on Baudin's account in the first chapter of his 'Journal personnel'; see Bonnemains, Argentin and Marin (eds), op. cit., p. 32.

34 'Mémoire pour servir d'instruction particulière au citoyen Baudin, capitaines des vaisseaux de la République, commandant les corvettes le Géographe et le Naturaliste dans

le voyage d'observations et de recherches relatives à la géographie et à l'histoire naturelle, dont la conduite et la direction lui sont confiées', in Bonnemains, Argentin and Marin (eds), op. cit., pp. 74–5.

35 For Baudin's exchange of correspondence with Pierre-Alexandre Forfait, Minister of Marine, see Bonnemains, Argentin and Marin (eds), op. cit., pp. 34–7.

36 Michaux (sometimes also spelt Michaud) was in debt and insisted that the government fulfil its promise of partial reimbursement of his previous travel expenses before he would join another expedition. He also demanded letters of introduction to the administrators of the Dutch East Indies and the Ile de France and the 'freedom to embark 50 reams of paper and six trunks containing my provisions'; see 'Michaud aux citoyens membres de la Commission nommée pour le voyage scientifique, Paris 24 Thermidor an 6 [11 August 1798]', Archives nationales, AJ[15] 569, folio 335 recto and verso.

37 'Registre d'inscription des élèves au cours de l'Ecole de Santé avec table alphabétique pour l'an IV et l'an V', Archives nationales, AJ[16] 6411.

38 See Ledru, op. cit.

39 See Duyker, 'Maugé, René (c. 1761–1802)'.

40 See Duyker, 'Levillain, Stanislas (1774–1801)'.

41 See Duyker, 'Riedlé, Anselm (1768[sic.]–1801)'.

42 Bory de Saint-Vincent went into exile in Belgium after the fall of Napoleon, returned to publish the seventeen-volume *Dictionnaire classique de l'Histoire naturelle*, and undertook further scientific travels in the Peloponnese (1828) and Algeria (1840–42). Of particular relevance to Péron's story is Bory's *Voyage dans les quartre principales îles des mers d'Afrique* ... (1804).

43 Pelte, 'Bory de St Vincent, Geneviève Jean Baptiste (1778–1846)'.

44 See Duyker, 'Bernier, Pierre-François Bernier (1779–1803)'.

45 Cape Faure on Schouten Island (off Tasmania) and Faure Island (off the Western Australian coast) were named in his honour; see Duyker and d'Unienville, 'Faure, Pierre Ange François Xavier (1776–1855)'.

46 See Duyker, 'Bailly, Joseph-Charles (1777–1844)'.

47 Toussaint, 'Milbert, Jacques Gérard (1766–1840)'; see also Milbert, *Voyage pittoresque à l'Ile de France* ...

48 Vinson, 'Garnier, Michel (1753–c. 1820)'.

49 Undated testimonial (c. 1800) on behalf of Pierre Louis Lebrun 'architecte dessinateur', signed by Pierre Joseph Redouté and other artists, Archives nationales, Paris, AJ[15] 569 pièce 343.

50 Péron, *Observations sur l'anthropologie* ...

51 Published by Jean de Laet in his *Historia naturalis Brasiliae* (Leyden, 1648).

52 *Tractatus topographicus et meteorologicus Brasiliae, cum observatione eclipsis solaris. II. Commentarius de Brasiliensium et Chiliensium indole ac lingua*, etc. (1658).

53 Péron, *Observations sur l'anthropologie* ...

54 Ducros and Ducros, 'Point d'histoire: Nouvelle anthropologie au temps de la Révolution'.

55 [De] Gérando, *Considérations sur les diverses methodes à suivre dans l'observation des peuples sauvages*.

56 Hervé, 'A la recherche d'un manuscrit: Les instructions anthropologiques de G. Cuvier pour le voyage du *Géographe* et du *Naturaliste* aux Terres Australes'.

57 Jussieu to the Minister of Marine, 19 thermidor an 8 [7 August 1800], Archives nationales, Marine BB[4] 997, dossier 1, folio 74 recto and verso; see also 'Physiciens et

naturalistes nommés pour accompagner le Capitaine Baudin', Archives nationales, AJ[15] 569, pièce 367. Later, in a report to Baudin, Péron would reveal his disappointment: 'I requested so earnestly in Paris that I should be permitted to occupy myself exclusively with this subject [anthropology], to which all my passions, all my sympathies, all my reading, all my thoughts had been turned exclusively from that time. My entreaties were unavailing; I did not obtain the title I craved, and that of Zoologist imposed upon me the obligation to devote myself without reserve to that aspect of natural history, and you have seen me from that time occupied ceaselessly with the duties and activities which scrupulousness and honour had equally put me under an obligation to carry out'; see Péron [addressed to 'Citoyen Commandant'], 'Ile Maria, Observations anthropologiques, ventôse an X [February–March 1802]', MHNH, Coll. Lesueur, MS 18041.

5. To the shoals of Capricorn

1 Péron, *Voyage*, tome i, p. 14.
2 Bory de Saint-Vincent, *Voyage dans les quatre principales îles des mers d'Afrique ...*, tome i, pp. 8–9.
3 Baudin, *The Journal of Post Captain Nicolas Baudin*, p. 20.
4 Péron, *Voyage*, tome i, p. 13 (Phillips trans., p. 17).
5 Bory de Saint-Vincent, op. cit., tome i, p. 21.
6 Bernier, 'Journal', Archives nationales, Marine, 5JJ 46.
7 Baudin, op. cit., p. 35.
8 ibid., p. 24.
9 Bory de Saint-Vincent, op. cit., tome i, pp. 78–9.
10 ibid., pp. 49–50.
11 See Caillé, *Un savant montpelliérain: Le Professeur Auguste Broussonet (1761–1807)*.
12 See Roux and Bonnemains, 'Les poissons du "Voyage de découvertes aux Terres Australes" (1800–1804) étudiés par F. Péron et C.-A. Lesueur: Collection iconographiques des dessins de C.-A. Lesueur du Muséum d'histoire naturelle du Havre', fascicule 2–3, p. 46.
13 Baudin, op. cit., p. 26.
14 Riedlé, journal, Bibliothèque centrale du Muséum national d'histoire naturelle, Paris, MS 1688.
15 Baudin, op. cit., pp. 26–8.
16 Péron, *Voyage*, tome i, p. 15 (Phillips trans., p. 18).
17 Péron wrote: 'The ancients, who knew but little of the Canaries, having made them the abode of the blessed, some enthusiastic authors fancy themselves obliged to repeat all the ideal and poetical descriptions of the pagan mythology, when writing on the subject of these islands. Hence we have recently seen the fertility of the Canaries celebrated in a manner which is totally repugnant both to reason and experence', Péron, *Voyage*, tome i, p. 17 (Phillips trans., p. 20).
18 Péron, *Voyage*, tome i, p. 15 (Phillips trans., p. 18).
19 Baudin, op. cit., p. 24.
20 For some interesting background, see Santana Perez and Monzón Perdomo, *Hospitales de La Laguna durante el Siglo XVIII*.
21 Guimera Peraza, 'Bernardo Cólogan y Fallon (1772–1814)'. The family name was originally Kilcolgan.

22 Hernandez Suárez, 'Breves biographifias actualizadas de personajes Canarios'.

23 The author visited these gardens (which were first laid out by the architect Nicolas Edouardo) in December 2002.

24 'Etat des plantes apportées du Jardin des plantes du Val-de-Grâce et de chez le citoyen Celse [sic] pour le Jardin botanique de Ténériffe établi à l'Oratava' in Bonnemains, Argentin and Marin (eds), *Mon voyage aux Terres Australes: Journal personnel du comman-dant Baudin*, pp. 127–8.

25 Bory de Saint-Vincent, op. cit., tome i, p. 24.

26 Péron, *Voyage*, tome i, p. 26 (Phillips trans., p. 26).

27 Horner, *The French Reconnaissance*, pp. 94–5.

28 Deacon, *Scientists and the Sea 1650–1900: A Study of Marine Science*, pp. 183–4.

29 For Wales's rejection of Forster's claim to have conducted the experiments, see *Remarks on Mr Forster's Account of Captain Cook's Last Voyage Round the World*, p. 21.

30 Forster, *Observations Made During a Voyage Round the World*, pp. 55–6.

31 See Deacon, op. cit., pp. 191–3.

32 Péron, 'Sur la température de la mer soit à sa surface, soit à diverses profondeurs'.

33 Deacon, op. cit., p. 204.

34 Péron, 'Notice sur quelques applications utiles des observations météorologiques à l'hygiène navale'.

35 Baudin, op. cit., p. 37.

36 Gicquel, Journal, Archives nationales, Marine 5JJ 55; see also Baudin, op. cit., p. 74.

37 ibid., p. 46.

38 But in calling them *orties de mer* (sea nettles) he confused them with sea anemones. Pierre Belon used the term *orties de mer* to describe sea anemones in his *De aquatilibus* in 1553.

39 For a summary of the early literature on medusae, see Goy, *Les Méduses de François Péron et de Charles-Alexandre Lesueur*, pp. 95–106.

40 During the *Endeavour* voyage, Banks and Solander repeatedly used their periods becalmed near the equator to great advantage: lowering a boat (which belonged to Banks) and collecting large numbers of 'sea blubbers' and other pelagic marine speci-mens in the waters surrounding the ship. Beaglehole (ed.), *The* Endeavour *Journal of Joseph Banks 1768–1771*, vol. i, pp. 168–74.

41 Péron wrote: '… the study of the animals of this family was especially recommended to me by Citizens Cuvier and Lamarck. I have not neglected to respond to their wish. I have collected everywhere that which is profitable to my researches and I have the satisfaction to present a collection in this genre equally interesting and numerous': see 'Tableau général d'une partie des espèces observées dans les diverses classes du règne animal … remise par le Citoyen Péron au Citoyen Commandant, Messidor an 10 de la République, MHNH, Coll. Lesueur, MS 21003–1.

42 Jangoux, '*L'expédition du Capitaine Baudin aux Terres Australes: Les observations zoologiques de François Péron pendant la première campagne (1801–1802)*'.

43 Stanislas Levillain, carnet, MHNH, Coll. Lesueur, MS 14040.

44 Bonnemains, Bustaret and Breton, 'Etude codicologique des manuscrits et dessins de méduses (1800–1810) de François Péron et Charles-Alexandre Lesueur'.

45 Goy and Breton, 'Les Méduses de François Péron et Charles-Alexandre Lesueur (1775–1810 et 1778–1846) Révélées par les vélins de Lesueur'; see also Kramp, 'Synopsis of the Medusae of the World', p. 273.

46 Péron, *Voyage*, tome i, p. 42 (Phillips trans., pp. 38–9).

47 One was *Nomeus albula*, Mesuschen 1781; the other was a species of Myctophidae, *Argyropelecus olfersi*, which would have to wait almost thirty years before being described by Georges Cuvier.
48 Péron, *Voyage*, tome i, pp. 44–5 (Phillips trans., p. 40).
49 ibid., p. 44 (Phillips trans., p. 40).
50 Bonnemains and Carré, 'Siphonophores et velelles observés par F. Péron et C.-A. Lesueur au début du 19e siècle', p. 41.
51 Péron, *Voyage*, tome i, pp. 46–7 (Phillips trans., p. 42).
52 ibid., p. 45 (Phillips trans., p. 41).
53 Quoted by Bonnemains and Branconnot, 'Les tunciers pélagiques: Salpes et pyrosomes étudiés par François Péron et Charles-Alexandre Lesueur au début du XIXe siècle', p. 46.
54 ibid.
55 Péron, 'Zoographia Hollandiae-novae marium alluentium illam—No VI—Baie des Chiens—Côtes du Nord-Ouest—Traversée de la N[ouv]elle Hol[lan]de à Timor'. MNHH, Coll. Lesueur, MS 65006.
56 Péron, *Voyage*, tome i, pp. 38–9 (Phillips trans., p. 36).
57 ibid., tome i, p. 41 (Phillips trans., p. 37).
58 Péron, 'Nuits des tropiques', MHNH, Coll. Lesueur, MS 07006 B recto.
59 Gicquel, Journal, Archives nationales, Marine 5JJ 55.
60 Baudin, op. cit., p. 44.
61 Lieutenant François Baudin was related neither to his superior Nicolas Baudin nor to Midshipman Charles Baudin.
62 Horner, op. cit., p. 68.
63 ibid., p. 110.
64 Baudin, op. cit., p. 104.
65 Horner, op. cit., p. 111.

6. Ile de France

1 Péron, 'Ile de France: Végétation, mœurs des habitants', MHNH, Coll. Lesueur, MS 15028.
2 In 1807, there were 6489 Europeans (mainly French), 65 367 slaves of African and Malagasy origin, and 5912 *noirs libres* (free blacks); Barnwell and Toussaint, *A Short History of Mauritius*, appendix 3, p. 255.
3 Péron, 'Ile de France: Végétation, mœurs des habitants', op. cit.
4 See d'Unienville, *Histoire politique de l'Isle de France* (3 vols).
5 Baudin, op. cit., p. 121.
6 Decrès, Minister of Marine, to Bonaparte, First Consul, 3 ventôse an X (22 February 1802), Archives nationales, Marine BB⁴ 995, item 2, folio 90.
7 Gicquel, Journal, Archives nationales, Marine, 5JJ 55.
8 Péron, *Voyage*, tome i, p. 61 (Phillips trans., p. 52).
9 'Etat nominatif des personnes [du Géographe] qui sont restées à l'île-de-France sous different prétextes', in Bonnemains, Argentin and Marin (eds), *Mon voyage aux Terres Australes: Journal personnel du commandant Baudin*, pp. 178–9.
10 Baudin to Jussieu, 24 avril 1801 in Bonnemains, Argentin and Marin (eds), op. cit., p. 173.
11 See Duyker, 'Gicquel Destouches, Pierre-Guillaume (1770–1824)'.

12 Deleuze, 'Notice historique sur André Michaux'.

13 Horner, *The French Reconnaissance*, p. 121.

14 Péron, 'Port-Louis, île de France 25 ventôse an 9', MHNH, Coll. Lesueur, MS 15044.

15 Bory de Saint-Vincent, *Voyage dans les quatre principales îles des mers d'Afrique*, tome i, p. 163.

16 ibid., p. 192.

17 Baudin, *The Journal of Post Captain Nicolas Baudin*, p. 122.

18 Péron, *Voyage*, I, pp. 49–52.

19 See Rouillard and Guého, *Le Jardin des Pamplemousses 1729–1979*.

20 Liste de Végétaux, folio 10 verso et 11 recto, MHNH, Coll. Lesueur, MS 15028 cont.

21 Péron, *Voyage*, tome i, pp. 57–8 (Phillips trans., p. 49).

22 See the anonymous portrait in Ly-Tio-Fane, *Mauritius and the Spice Trade*, opposite p. 100.

23 See Ly-Tio-Fane, 'Contacts between Schönbrunn and the Jardin du Roi at Isle de France (Mauritius) in the 18th century'.

24 See D'Emmerez de Charmoy, 'Céré, Jean-Nicolas de (1737–1810)'.

25 Péron, 'Personnes recommandables de l'île de France', MHNH, Coll. Lesueur, MS 15032 (no. 1392).

26 ibid.

27 Péron, two sheets incomplete, MHNH, Coll. Lesueur, MS 15030.

28 Péron, 'Ile de France: Végétation, mœurs des habitants', op. cit.

29 ibid.

30 ibid.

31 d'Unienville, 'Laborde, Léonard Clair (1752–1824)'.

32 Péron, 'Ile de France: Maladies (lèpre et maladie des voies urinaires) et nature de sol', MHNH, Coll. Lesueur, MS 15025.

33 Nagapen, 'Dr Nils Bergsten erudite mémorialiste et directeur de clinique recherché'; see also Toussaint, 'Bergsten, Nils (1769–1852)'.

34 Regnard, 'Stadtmann, Jean Frédéric (1762–1807)'.

35 Péron and Lesueur, 'Tableau des caractères génériques et spécifiques de toutes les espèces de Méduses connues jusqu'à ce jour', p. 356. Their *C. forsakell*, named in honour of the great Swedish naturalist Pehr Forsskål, is not taxonomically valid other than as a synonym. Lesueur's striking watercolour illustration (which the uninitiated might think an image sketched underneath and underwater, rather than from above) appears to be indistinguishable from the species Forrskål himself named *Medusa andromeda*, forty years earlier on the Red Sea and which was published posthumously in 1775. Hence, although Péron recognised that the species belonged to a distinctive new genus, Forsskål's prior specific epithet *andromeda* has priority. Péron, however, was clearly inspired by the fact that in Greek mythology the beautiful Cassiopeia, wife of King Cepheus, was the mother of the equally beautiful Andromeda!

36 Kramp, 'Synopsis of the Medusae of the world', p. 349; Goy, *Les Méduses de Péron et Lesueur*, pp. 326–8.

37 Péron, Carnet 'pense-bête': 'Souvenirs des diverses époques de ma vie', MHNH, Coll. Lesueur, MS 15031.

38 Péron, *Voyage*, tome i, p. 51 (Phillips trans., pp. 44–5).

39 Reforestation of denuded areas was also ordered, and a forest service was established in 1777. Furthermore, in 1791, the Colonial Assembly pioneered legislation to control

the pollution of water by sugar mills and indigo factories. Seven years later regulations came into force to protect diminishing fish stocks; see Grove, *Green Imperialism*, pp. 199–222.

[40] For the birds Péron noted, see his *carnet* (notebook), 'île de France', MHNH, Coll. Lesueur, MS 15032.

[41] Gicquel, Journal, Archives nationales, Marine, 5JJ 55; according to Bory de Saint-Vincent, these goods were sold at between 200 and 400 per cent profit in a local store; see Bory, *Voyage dans les quatre principales îles des mers d'Afrique*, tome i, pp. 186–7.

[42] Baudin, op. cit., pp. 135–6.

[43] ibid., p. 129.

[44] Quoted (my translation) from 'Méditations sur l'objet de notre voyage', MHNH, Coll. Lesueur, MS 15007 [*sic*], by Jangoux in 'Les zoologistes et botanistes qui accompagnèrent le Capitaine Baudin aux Terres Australes'.

7. A course for New Holland

[1] Baudin, *The Journal of Post Captain Nicolas Baudin*, p. 137.

[2] ibid. ('Plan of itinerary for Citizen Baudin'), p. 2.

[3] Péron, *Voyage*, tome i, p. 64 (Phillips trans., p. 55).

[4] ibid.

[5] ibid., p. 65 (Phillips trans., p. 55).

[6] Péron, *Voyage*, tome i, p. 26 (Phillips trans., p. 26).

[7] ibid., p. 63 (Phillips trans., p. 54).

[8] Horner, *The French Reconnaissance*, p. 142.

[9] Baudin, op. cit., p. 152.

[10] ibid., p. 158.

[11] ibid.

[12] Péron, *Voyage*, tome i, p. 66 (Phillips trans., p. 56).

[13] Lamarck, *Histoire naturelle des animaux sans vertèbres*, tome ii, p. 356.

[14] Walton, *Zoological Catalogue of Australia*, vol. 12, Porifera, p. 458; see also Topsent, 'Eponges de Lamarck conservées au Muséum de Paris'.

[15] Péron, *Voyage*, tome i, p. 68 (Phillips trans., p. 58).

[16] Baudin, op. cit., pp. 166–8.

[17] It was then completely unknown, and the name on Lesueur's illustration suggests that he and Péron considered it a wrasse, for it was provisionally named *Labrus giganteus*. This incorrect designation, however, was never published, and it was not until 1860 that the Dutch naturalist and physician Pieter Bleeker included this species in the genus *Lutjanus* as *L. nematophorus*; see Roux and Bonnemains, 'Les poissons du "Voyage de découvertes aux Terres Australes" (1800–1804) étudiés par F. Péron et C. A. Lesueur: Collection iconographiques des dessins de C.-A. Lesueur du Museum d'histoire naturelle du Havre', fascicule 1, p. 43.

[18] The Port Jackson shark had been described less than a decade before from a specimen collected by a member of the First Fleet in New South Wales, but Péron seems not to have realised this at the time. With its bull head and banded markings, Lesueur was inspired to sketch it four times. Péron noted that there was 'nothing like it in the Mediterranean', and it seems that they initially intended to name it in honour of one or both of the Freycinet brothers; see Péron, *carnet*, MHNH, Coll. Lesueur, MS 65011; see also Roux and Bonnemains, op. cit., fascicule 2, p. 42.

19 Péron, *Voyage*, tome i, p. 70 (Phillips trans., p. 59).

20 Horner, op. cit., p. 147.

21 Baudin, op. cit., p. 173.

22 Péron, *Voyage*, tome i, p. 71 (Phillips trans., pp. 59–60).

23 ibid., p. 73 (Phillips trans., p. 61).

24 *Salicornia australis* has now been superseded in Western Australia by *Sarcocornia quinque-flora* (beaded samphire); it is a decumbent perennial herb or shrub, which grows in sand, sandy loam, clay, moderately saline soils, swamps, estuaries and salt lakes. *Sarcocornia blackiana* is also a decumbent perennial herb that grows in sand, silt, swampy or periodically waterlogged saline areas and estuaries. Péron might also have seen a kindred species of *Atriplex*.

25 Labillardière, *Novae Hollandiae plantarum specimen*, tome ii, p. 30.

26 Péron, *Voyage*, tome i, p. 76 (Phillips trans., p 64).

27 ibid., p. 82 (Phillips trans., p. 68).

28 ibid., pp. 83–4 (Phillips trans., p. 69).

29 Baudin, op. cit., p. 178.

30 ibid., p. 181.

31 Péron, *Voyage*, tome i, p. 97 (Phillips trans., p. 79).

32 Baudin, op. cit., p. 184.

33 Péron, *Voyage*, tome i, p. 98 (Phillips trans., p. 80).

34 See Serieyx, *Wonnerup: The Sacred Dune* and Duyker, 'Vasse, Timothée (1774–c. 1801)'.

35 On 19 April 1838 George Fletcher Moore (an early Irish settler in the Swan River colony) visited Wonnerup and wrote a letter to the *Perth Gazette*, which was published on 5 May. In it he dismissed as 'improbable' reports that Vasse had remained 'two or three years' with the natives before being rescued by an American vessel, then being taken prisoner to England by a British cruiser. Nevertheless, Moore did not dismiss Aboriginal testimony that Vasse had survived and was cared for by the Aborigines but died some time later 'near Toby's Inlet at the south-eastern extremity of Geographe Bay'.

36 Baudin, op. cit., p. 184.

37 ibid., p. 185.

38 Péron, *Voyage*, tome i, pp. 102–3 (Phillips trans., p. 84).

8. Shark Bay

1 Péron, 'Observations sur la Baie du Géographe [June 1801]', MHNH, Coll. Lesueur, MS 08039; see also Péron, 'Topographie, aspect général de la baie du Géographe par le citoyen Péron' [June 1801], MHNH, Coll. Lesueur, MS 08040.

2 Although Péron's notebook for Terre de Leuwin (carnet 65006) contains reference to an abundance of bird calls that 'resemble that of the warbler', we must turn to a manuscript in Lesueur's hand for a more general survey thought to be actually by Péron: 'Oiseaux de la Baie du Géographe', MHNH, Coll. Lesueur, MS 79058.

3 Bory de Saint-Vincent, *Voyage dans les quatre principales îles des mers d'Afrique* …, tome i, p. 161.

4 Aside from the English botanist James Edward Smith's *Specimen of the Botany of New Holland* (1793, which described sixteen Australian species sent to Britain by Surgeon John White of the First Fleet), Péron had no possible access to a botanical reference work devoted specifically to New Holland. The first part of Labillardière's magnificent *Novae Hollandiae plantarum specimen* would not appear for another two and a half

years. Péron therefore relied on the Linnean canon and earlier works that described Pacific species, such as J. R. and J. G. A. Forster's *Characteres Generum Plantarum* (1776) and Joseph Gærtner's *De Fructibus et Seminibus Plantarum* (1788).

5   Ironically this was also the fate of the first French on Australian soil; see Duyker, 'The first French in Australia: The soldiers of the *Batavia*'.

6   Baudin, *The Journal of Post Captain Nicolas Baudin*, pp. 191–2.

7   Jangoux, 'Les Astérides (Echinodermes) des Terres Australes ramenés par l'expédition Baudin (1800–1804): Catalogue commenté des dessins inedits de Charles-Alexandre Lesueur conservés au Muséum d'histoire naturelle du Havre'.

8   Lamarck, *Histoire naturelle des animaux sans vertèbres*, tome vi, part i, p. 150.

9   As a record of their visit they left an inscribed pewter plate, nailed to an oak post. It remained there until February 1697, when members of Willem de Vlamingh's expedition took it to Batavia, but not before replacing it with another pewter plate inscribed with both the original text and a record of their own visit. The original plate is today preserved in the Rijksmuseum in Amsterdam. When Louis de Freycinet landed on Dirk Hartog Island in July 1801, he sought to take de Vlamingh's plate back to France, but was forbidden to do so by Hamelin. Indeed the captain of the *Naturaliste* set up the plate again on a new post. However, in 1817, when Freycinet returned in command of his own expedition, there was no one to thwart him, and he returned to France with the precious pewter memorial. It was finally returned to Australia by the French Government in 1947 and is today preserved in the Western Australian Maritime Museum in Perth.

10   Péron, *Voyage*, tome i, p. 104 (Phillips trans., pp. 84–5).

11   In the journals these islands are referred to as the Iles Stériles.

12   In the journals Shark Bay is referred to as the Baie des Chiens-Marins (a reference to the dugongs).

13   Péron, *Voyage*, tome i, p. 105 (Phillips trans., p. 85).

14   ibid., p. 108 (Phillips trans., p. 87).

15   ibid., pp. 109–10 (Phillips trans., pp. 88–9).

16   Dakin, *Whalemen Adventurers in Southern Waters*, pp. 59–60, 212.

17   Playford, 'Geology of the Shark Bay Area, Western Australia'.

18   Péron very likely saw the shells of terrestrial gastropods, *Bothriembryon* sp.

19   Péron, *Voyage*, tome i, p. 111 (Phillips trans., p. 89).

20   The area is famous for the Shark Bay pearl oyster, *Pinctada albina*, on which the local pearling industry centred on Denham was based.

21   Lamarck, op. cit., tome v, p. 594.

22   Bernard Métivier has advised me that in the collection of the Muséum national d'histoire naturelle is a left valve, Lamarck's holotype, of *Venus crassisulca*. Inside this valve is a label (in the handwriting of Louis Dufresne, who was Lamarck's assistant for invertebrates): '*Venus luteola* P [probably for Péron] Baye des Chiens Marins n° 96 14 3'. Péron's apparent manuscript name, *Venus luteola*, was obviously not retained by Lamarck, who decribed it under a new one, *crassisulca*. In 1971 E. Fischer-Piette and Bernard Métivier published 'Révision des Tapetinae (Mollusques Bivalves)' in the *Mémoires du Muséum national d'histoire naturelle*, n.s., sér. A, Zoologie, vol. lxxi, 106 pp., 16 pl.) mention and figure (p. 41, pl. IX, figs 11–12), placing Lamarck's holotype in the genus *Paphia* as *P. crassisulca* (Lamarck).

23   Lamarck, op. cit., tome vi, part i, p. 208.

24   ibid., tome vi, part i, p. 24. In other instances Lamarck was too late. For example, his *Sanguinolaria livida* (ibid., tome v, p. 511), based on a specimen collected by Péron, had

already been published in 1815 by the English malacologist William Wood as *Sotellina biradiata*. And his *Cypricardia angulata* (ibid., tome vi, part i, p. 28) from Shark Bay remains a synonym for Heinrich Christian Friedrich Schumacher's *Trapezium bicarinatum* published in 1817.

25 Bonnemains and Jones, 'Les crustaces de la collection C. A. Lesueur (dessins et manuscrits)'; Lesueur also sketched a number of species that were later designated as belonging to the genus *Portunus*, but only one has retained this generic diagnosis (*P. emarginatus*), and it was collected at the Ile de France, not Shark Bay.

26 Péron, *Voyage*, tome i, p. 120 (Phillips trans., pp. 96–7).

27 Another luminous species, *Amphipholis squamata* (Delle-Chiaje, 1828), is also found at Shark Bay, but it is quite small.

28 George, *William Dampier in New Holland*, p. 34.

29 Several species of *Acacia* are found on Bernier Island: *A. coriacea*, *A. ligulata*, *A. rostellifera* and *A. synchronicia*; see Claymore and Markey, *A Floristic Survey of the Shark Bay World Heritage Area*, pp. 21–2.

30 Claymore and Markey, op. cit., p. 23, did not record any *Melaleuca* on Bernier Island. *M. cardiophylla* might now be extinct on the island; alternatively Péron might have observed *Pileanthus limacis* or a *Thryptomene*.

31 In a recent survey, *Cyperus bulbosus* was found on Dorre Island but not neighbouring Bernier Island; see Claymore and Markey, op. cit., p. 18.

32 Riedlé, journal, Bibliothèque centrale du Muséum national d'histoire naturelle, Paris, MS 1688.

33 George, op. cit., p. 131.

34 See Bauchot and Bauchot, 'Dessins de poissons et de mammifères de la collection du Muséum d'histoire naturelle du Havre', pp. 68–9.

35 Péron, *Voyage*, tome i, p. 116 (Phillips trans., p. 93).

36 ibid., tome i, p. 117 (Phillips trans., pp. 94–5).

37 ibid., tome i, p. 118 (Phillips trans., p. 95).

38 Carnet, Péron, 'Baie des Chiens Marins et Timor', MNHN, Coll. Lesueur, MS 65006.

39 Péron, *Voyage*, tome i, p. 118 (Phillips trans., p. 95).

40 Roux-Estève, 'Liste des amphibiens et reptiles des collections du Muséum National d'histoire naturelle de Paris'.

41 See Roux-Estève, 'Reptiles' in Bonnemains, Forsyth and Smith, *Baudin in Australian Waters: The Artwork of the French Voyage of Discovery to the Southern Lands 1800–1804* …, pp. 285–94.

42 Baudin, op. cit., p. 207.

43 Péron, *Voyage*, tome i, p. 123 (Phillips trans., pp. 98–9).

44 Baudin, op. cit., pp. 208–9.

45 ibid., p. 220.

46 Péron, *Voyage*, tome i, pp. 123–4 (Phillips trans., p. 99).

47 Albert Günther originally included this shark in the genus *Mustelus* in 1870.

48 André Marie Constant Duméril, one of the best-known of Cuvier's disciples; see Roux and Bonnemains, 'Les poissons du "Voyage de découvertes aux Terres Australes" (1800–1804) étudiés par F. Péron et C.-A. Lesueur: Collection iconographique des dessins de C.-A. Lesueur du Museum d'histoire naturelle du Havre', fascicule 1, p. 44; fascicules 2, 3, p. 44.

49 Roux, 'Les requins des côtes australiennes observés par Péron et Lesueur', pp. 34, 36.

50 'Citizen Péron', he wrote, 'whose extreme enthusiasm leads him to undertake every-thing without thought for the dangers to which he is exposing himself, went on a visit to the western part of the island and, as usual, went alone'; see Baudin, op. cit., p. 215.

51 ibid.

52 Péron, *Voyage*, tome i, p. 125 (Phillips trans., p. 100).

53 ibid.

54 ibid.

55 Baudin, op. cit., p. 215.

56 ibid.

57 Péron, *Voyage*, tome i, p. 125 (Phillips trans., pp. 100–1).

58 ibid., p. 126 (Phillips trans., p. 101).

59 'Le commandant en chef de l'expédition de découvertes au ministre de la Marine et des Colonies, quatorze vendémiaire an X [6 October 1801]', in Bonnemains, Argentin and Marin (eds), *Mon voyage aux Terres Australes: Journal personnel du commandant Baudin*, p. 362.

9. Timor

1 Horner, *The French Reconnaissance*, p. 164.

2 Baudin, *The Journal of Post-Captain Nicolas Baudin*, p. 245.

3 Péron, *Voyage*, tome i, p. 137 (Phillips trans., p. 109).

4 Baudin, op. cit., p. 252.

5 ibid., pp. 254–5.

6 Péron, op. cit., tome i, p. 142 (Phillips trans., p. 113).

7 ibid., p. 146 (Phillips trans., p. 116).

8 Jangoux, 'Les Astérides (Echinodermes) des Terres Australes ramenés par l'Expédition Baudin (1800–1804) …', p. 34.

9 Bonnemains and Jones, 'Les crustacés de la collection C.-A. Lesueur (dessins et man-uscrits)', p. 35.

10 The other fish collected or observed in Timor included: *Dactyloptena orientalis, Alectis indicus, Glossogobius* sp., *Hemiramphus quoyi, Nomeus albula, Chaetodon lunula, Platax* sp., *Equula fasciata, Holocentrus* sp., *Kutaflammeo sammara* and others identifiable only by family; see Roux and Bonnemains, 'Les poissons du "Voyage de découvertes aux Terres Australes" (1800–1804) etudiés par F. Péron et C.-A. Lesueur …'.

11 Lamarck, *Histoire naturelle des animaux sans vertèbres* …, tome v, p. 560.

12 ibid., tome vi, part i, p. 208.

13 ibid., tome vi, part i, p. 41.

14 Péron, op. cit., tome i, p. 146 (Phillips trans., pp. 116–17).

15 ibid.

16 Audley-Charles, *The Geology of Portuguese Timor*, pp. 28–35.

17 Péron, *Voyage*, tome i, p. 145 (Phillips trans., p. 115).

18 ibid., p. 150 (Phillips trans., p. 119).

19 ibid., p. 151 (Phillips trans., p. 120).

20 Baudin, op. cit., p. 239.

21 ibid., pp. 256–61.

22 ibid., pp. 132–3.

23 ibid., p. 133.

24 Horner, op. cit., p. 187.

25 Péron, *Voyage*, tome i, pp. 166–7 (Phillips trans., p. 132).
26 ibid., p. 164 (Phillips trans., p. 130).
27 Anselm Riedlé to André Thouin, Timor, 6 vendémiaire an X [27 September 1801], Bibliothèque centrale du Muséum national d'histoire naturelle, Paris, MS 100060.
28 Baudin in Bonnemains, Argentin and Marin (eds), *Mon voyage aux Terres Australes: Journal personnel du commandant Baudin*, p. 376.
29 See Duyker, 'Riedlé, Anselm (1768–1801)'.
30 Péron, *Voyage*, tome i, p. 133.
31 Baudin in Bonnemains, Argentin and Marin (eds.), op. cit., p. 376.
32 Péron, *Voyage*, tome i, p. 168 (Phillips trans., p. 134).
33 Letouzey, *Le Jardin des Plantes à la croisée des chemins avec André Thouin 1747–1824*, p. 526.
34 Péron, *Voyage*, tome i, p. 171 (Phillips trans., p. 136).
35 Péron, 'Observations sur la dyssenterie des pays chauds et sur l'usage du bétel'.
36 Péron, 'Notice sur quelques applications utiles des observations météorologiques à l'hygiène navale'.
37 Péron, *Voyage*, tome i, p. 170 (Phillips trans., p. 135).
38 The masts for the longboat were finished at sea; see Baudin, op. cit., pp. 277–8.

10. Van Diemen's Land

1   Péron, *Voyage*, tome i, p. 207 (Phillips trans., p. 163).
2   Baudin, *The Journal of Post Captain Nicolas Baudin*, p. 267.
3   Péron, *Voyage*, tome i, p. 210 (Phillips trans., p. 165).
4   Carnet, Péron, 'Zoologie: Animaux observés pendant la traversée de l'île de Timor à la Terre de Diemen du 22 Brumaire au 23 Nivôse an X', MHNH, Coll. Lesueur, MS 65013.
5   Baudin, op. cit., p. 277.
6   Lacépède, *Histoire naturelle des cétacées*, p. 43.
7   Péron, *Voyage*, tome i, p. 218 (Phillips trans., p. 171).
8   See Duyker (ed.), *The Discovery of Tasmania*.
9   See Duyker, *An Officer of the Blue*.
10 See Duyker and Duyker (eds, trans) *Bruny d'Entrecasteaux: Voyage to Australia and the Pacific 1791–1793*.
11 Péron, *Voyage*, tome i, p. 220 (Phillips trans., p. 173).
12 ibid., tome i, p. 221 (Phillips trans., pp. 173–4).
13 ibid., tome i, p. 222 (Phillips trans., p. 174).
14 ibid., tome i, p. 223 (Phillips trans., pp. 174–5).
15 ibid., tome i, p. 81 (Phillips trans., p. 67).
16 Historians have questioned whether the indigenous Tasmanians could produce fire themselves. See Plomley, *The Tasmanian Aborigines*, p. 25; Ryan, *The Aboriginal Tasmanians*, p. 11.
17 Péron, *Voyage*, tome i, p. 224 (Phillips trans., pp. 175–6).
18 Honigman, *The Development of Anthropological Ideas*, p. 82.
19 Moore in his introduction to Degérando, *The Observation of Savage Peoples*, p. 21.
20 ibid., p. 33.
21 ibid., p. 34.
22 Péron, 'Mémoire sur quelques faits zoologiques applicables à la théorie du globe, lu à la Classe des Sciences physiques et mathématiques de l'Institut national (Séance du 30

vendémiaire an XIII)', p. 478. Péron's exact words are: 'De la différence absolue des deux races de la Nouvelle-Hollande et de la terre de Diémen, ainsi que de l'absence du chien sur cette dernière, j'ai cru pouvoir tirer la conséquence, que la séparation de ces deux régions doit remonter à une époque beaucoup plus ancienne qu'on ne pourroit le soupçonner d'abord.'

23 Stocking, 'French anthropology in 1800'.

24 Arbuthnot was the author of *An Essay Concerning the Effects of Air on Human Bodies*, 1731, which was translated into French by Boyer de Pebrandié (*Essai des effets de l'air sur le corps-humain*, Jacques Barois fils, Paris, 1742) and profoundly influenced Montesquieu (and Péron, if not directly, then indirectly); see Dedieu, *Montesquieu et la tradition politique anglaise en France*.

25 Initially we are told that Péron 'seemed to support the notion of racial difference', but even this cautious restraint soon gives way to unequivocal accusations of racism; see Fornasiero, Monteath and West-Sooby, *Encountering Terra Australis: The Australian Voyages of Nicolas Baudin and Matthew Flinders*, pp. 356, 370, 380.

26 Quatrefages, *Hommes fossiles et hommes sauvages: Etude d'anthropologie*, p. 296.

27 Jones, 'Images of natural man', pp. 39, 63–4.

28 Sankey, 'François-Auguste Péron: Le mythe de l'homme sauvage et l'écriture de la science'.

29 Dyer, *The French Explorers and the Aboriginal Australians 1772–1839*, pp. 46, 50.

30 'Physiciens et naturalistes nommés pour accompagner le Capitaine Baudin', Archives nationales, AJ[15] 569, pièce 367.

31 Carnet, Péron [addressed to 'Citoyen Commandant'], 'Ile Maria, Observations anthropologiques, Ventôse an X [February–March 1802]', MHNH, Coll. Lesueur, MS 18041.

32 Plomley, *The Baudin Expedition and the Tasmanian Aborigines 1802*, p. 15.

33 Some of Lamarck's habitat statements with references to Van Diemen's Land appear to be wrong. For example, *Arca semi-torta* (= *Trisidos semitorta*), *Histoire naturelle des animaux sans vertèbres*, tome vi, part i, p. 37, and *Conus pontificalis*, ibid., tome vii, p. 459, synonymous with Péron's still-valid *Conus dorreensis*, must have been collected in Western Australia.

34 Lamarck, op. cit., tome vi, part 1, p. 59.

35 Turner, 'The D'Entrecasteaux Channel, Terre de Diemen, 13th January–16th February 1802: A comparative marine survey of the voyage by Baudin, by Elizabeth Turner, Tasmanian Museum, Hobart, Tasmania, 20th March and 8th April 2002', unpublished typescript.

36 Lamarck, op. cit., tome vi, part 1, p. 5.

37 ibid., tome v, p. 495.

38 ibid., tome v, p. 483.

39 ibid., tome v, p. 599.

40 ibid., tome v, p. 451.

41 Péron, *Voyage*, tome i, pp. 225–6 (Phillips trans., p. 177).

42 ibid., tome i, pp. 227–8 (Phillips trans., p. 178).

43 ibid., tome i. p. 230 (Phillips trans., p. 180).

44 In his *Discours sur l'origine et les fondements de l'inégalité parmi les hommes* (Amsterdam, 1755), Jean-Jacques Rousseau sought to define *sauvage* or 'natural' man as uncorrupted by morality, the arts, sciences and private property and living in serenity without the stress and conflict of civilised society.

45 Péron, *Voyage*, tome i, p. 231 (Phillips trans., p. 181).

46 ibid., tome i, pp. 231–2 (Phillips trans., pp. 181–2).

47 For example, Carl Linnaeus's *Mimosa, Protea, Thesium* (1753), *Casuarina* (1763) and *Melaleuca*; J. R. and J. G. A. Forster's *Embothrium* and *Euodia* (1776); Carl Linnaeus the Younger's *Banksia* (1781); l'Heritier de Brutelle's *Eucalyptus* (1788); Gaertner's *Metrosideros* (1788); James Edward Smith's *Xanthorrhoea* (1789) and *Conchium* (1798); Henry Andrews' *Correa* (1798) and Labillardière's *Exocarpos* (1800). Although Péron's description of Van Diemen's Land appears to have been influenced by Labillardière's *Relation* (1800), when he came to write his official account, some years later, it is uncertain whether he made use of Labillardière's *Novae Hollandiae plantarum specimen* (1804–06) —given his retention of such names as *Protea* and *Metrosideros* in an Australian context. His knowledge of the *Correa* and its cultivation in France can be explained by his eventual familiarity with the Empress Joséphine's garden and with Etienne Ventenat's work *Jardin de La Malmaison* (Paris, 1803–05), which overturned Labillardière's synonym *Mazeutoxeron* (published in his *Relation*) in favour of Henry Andrews' prior publication.

48 Baudin, op cit., p. 308.

49 Geoffroy-Saint-Hilaire, 'Note sur un nouveau genre de mammifières de l'ordre des rongeurs sous le nom d'hydromys'.

50 Péron, *Voyage*, tome i, p. 240 (Phillips trans., p. 188).

51 Lamarck, 'Sur une nouvelle espèce de Trigonie …'

52 Péron, op. cit., tome i, p. 241 (Phillips trans., p. 188).

53 ibid., tome i, p. 242 (Phillips trans., pp. 189–90).

54 Baudin, op. cit., p. 316.

55 This was not the first scientific collection of lichen in Australia; that honour belongs to Labillardière, who collected *Cladia retipora* (Coral Lichen) in either 1792 or 1793.

56 Péron, *Voyage*, tome i, p. 248 (Phillips trans., p. 193).

57 Péron, 'Mémoire sur quelques faits zoologiques applicables à la théorie du globe …'

58 Péron, *Voyage*, tome i, p. 250 (Phillips trans., p. 195).

59 For more on Bellefin, see Guicheteau, 'La vie et la grande aventure du "chirurgien navigans" Jérôme Bellefin'; for a useful study of the expedition's medical officers, see Southwood and Simpson, 'Baudin's doctors: French medical scientists in Australian waters, 1801–1803'.

60 ibid., tome i, pp. 252–3 (Phillips trans., p. 197). Given this statement, Fornasiero, Monteath and West-Sooby appear excessive in their assertion that Péron dismissed all Tasmanian women 'as extremely repugnant' and considered the notion of sexual relations with them as 'below contempt'; op. cit., p. 370.

61 Péron, *Voyage*, tome i, p. 253 (Phillips trans., p. 197).

62 ibid.

63 ibid., tome i, p. 255 (Phillips trans., p. 199).

64 Nicolas Petit, watercolour, gouache and ink, MHNH, Coll. Lesueur, MS 20004-3. The name Arra-Maïda appears on the engraving published as plate XII in the *Atlas* of Péron's *Voyage* (1807).

65 Péron, *Voyage*, tome i, p. 256 (Phillips trans., p. 199).

66 ibid., tome i, p. 256 (Phillips trans., p. 200).

67 ibid.

68 For an account of the voyage see Mortimer's *Observations and Remarks made during a Voyage to the Islands of Tenerife, Amsterdam, Maria's Island near Van Diemen's Land …*

69 Péron, 'Histoire naturelle. Topographie générale de l'île Maria sur la côte orientale de la Terre de Diemen', MHNH, Coll. Lesueur, MS 18043.

[70] ibid., translated in Plomley, Cornell and Banks, 'François Péron's natural history of Maria Island, Tasmania'.

[71] See Werner, *Kurze Klassification und Beschreibung der Verschieden Gebirgsarten*, Walther, Dresden, 1787.

[72] Péron, 'Histoire naturelle. Topographie générale de l'île Maria sur la côte orientale de la Terre de Diemen', MHNH, Coll. Lesueur, MS 18043, translated in Plomley, Cornell and Banks, op. cit.

[73] Péron, 'Ile Maria—Observations de phisique et d'histoire naturelle—Ventôse an X', MHNH, Coll. Lesueur, MS 18041.

[74] Buch, 'Observations sur les volcans d'Auvergne'.

[75] Buch, 'Einige Bemerkung über die geognostiche constitution von Van Diemens Land'.

[76] See, for example, Péron's observations on the volcanic geology of the Canary Islands and Mauritius: 'Ile de France ... nature de sol', Coll. Lesueur, MHNH, MS 15025; and Péron, 'Port-Louis, île de France 25 ventôse an 9 [16 March 1801]', Coll. Lesueur, MHNH, MS 15044.

[77] Péron, 'Histoire naturelle ...', translated in Plomley, Cornell and Banks, op. cit.

[78] D'Aubuisson de Voisins, *Traité de Géonosie*, Strasbourg, 1819, vol. i, p. xiv, quoted by Adams, op. cit., p. 227.

[79] Geoffroy-Saint-Hilaire, 'Note sur les espèces du genre dassyure'.

[80] Wakefield and Waterhouse, 'Some revision in Antechinus (Marsupialia)'.

[81] Geoffroy-Saint-Hilaire, 'Note sur un nouveau genre de mammifières de l'ordre des rongeurs sous le nom d'hydromys'.

[82] Péron, 'Ile Maria—Observations de phisique et d'histoire naturelle—Ventôse an X', MHNH, Coll. Lesueur, MS 18041.

[83] Goy, *Les Méduses de Péron et Lesueur: Un autre regard sur l'expédition Baudin*, pp. 364–74.

[84] Péron, 'Histoire naturelle. Topographie générale de l'île Maria sur la côte orientale de la Terre de Diemen', MHNH, Coll. Lesueur, MS 18043.

[85] Péron, 'Ile Maria—Observations anthropologiques', MHNH, Coll. Lesueur, MS 18040.

[86] ibid.

[87] ibid.

[88] Péron, *Voyage*, tome i, p. 285 (Phillips trans., p. 221).

[89] Rousseau, *Discours sur l'origine et les fondements de l'inégalité parmi les hommes* (Amsterdam, 1755); for an English translation by G. D. H. Cole, see vol. 38 of *Great Books of the Western World*, p. 350.

[90] Régnier quoted by Jamin in 'Note sur le dynamomètre de Régnier'.

[91] Jones, op. cit., footnote p. 46.

[92] Péron, op. cit., tome i, p. 287 (Phillips trans., p. 223).

[93] Cuvier, 'Note instructive sur les recherches à faire relativement aux différences anatomiques des diverses races d'hommes', in Copans and Jamin (eds), *Aux origines de l'anthropologie française: Les Mémoires de la Société des Observateurs de l'Homme en l'an VIII*, pp. 171–6.

[94] Péron, *Voyage*, tome i, p. 266 (Phillips trans., p. 208).

[95] Lesueur, sketch, MHNH, Coll. Lesueur, MS 18017.

[96] Péron, *Voyage*, tome i, p. 268 (Phillips trans., p. 209).

[97] Péron, 'Ile Maria—Observations anthropologiques', op. cit.

[98] See Fornasiero, Monteath and West-Sooby, op. cit., p. 380.

[99] If we are to assess Péron in the context of notions of genocide and racist intellectual superiority, we should at least judge him by his own words. His comments on the

Dutch treatment of Bushmen in South Africa serve as an adequate demonstration of his humanity and his belief that the intellect is not immutably constrained by race: 'It frequently happens that the settlers (and even the other tribes who surround the bushmen) hunt or round up these unfortunate people and, without pity or remorse, kill all whom they find. The Dutch, however, sometimes keep the young children in order to bring them up to be shepherds for their flocks; but they claim never to be able, even when the children do grow up with them, to make them lose their first inclination to wander. It could be that this is also the result of the scant care that they take of them or, more precisely, the result of a total absence of education'; see Péron, tome ii, pp. 310–11 (Cornell trans., p. 262).

[100] Baudin, op. cit., p. 340.
[101] Péron, *Voyage*, tome i, p. 240 (Phillips trans., p. 188).
[102] In 1804 Péron appears to have read this memoir at a meeting of the Société Philomatique; see Péron, 'Notice d'un mémoire sur les animaux observés pendant la traversée de Timor au Cap Sud de la Terre de Van Diemen'.
[103] Jangoux, 'L'expédition du Capitaine Baudin aux Terres Australes: Les observations zoologiques de François Péron pendant la première campagne (1801–1802)', p. 5.
[104] Péron, *Voyage*, tome i, p. 307 (Phillips trans., p. 238).
[105] Baudin, op. cit., pp. 355–7.

11. Uncharted waters

[1] Péron, *Voyage*, tome i, p. 317 (Phillips trans., pp. 244–5).
[2] Horner, *The French Reconnaisance*, p. 211.
[3] James Grant's landfall, named in honour of his patron Captain John Schanck, Commissioner of the Transport Board.
[4] Péron, op. cit., tome i, p. 322 (Phillips trans., p. 248).
[5] For an impressive recent biography, see Estensen, *The Life of Matthew Flinders*.
[6] Giblin, 'Flinders, Brown and Baudin at Encounter Bay'.
[7] Péron, op. cit., tome i, p. 325 (Phillips trans., p. 251).
[8] Giblin, op. cit.
[9] Baudin, *The Journal of Post Captain Nicolas Baudin*, p. 380.
[10] Bougainville quoted by Horner, op. cit., p. 218.
[11] Baudin, op. cit., p. 380.
[12] ibid.
[13] ibid., p. 381.
[14] Flinders, *A Voyage to Terra Australis*, vol. i, p. 193.
[15] See, for example, Duyker, *Citizen Labillardière*, pp. 142, 144.
[16] Governor King to Baudin, 23 November 1802, in Bladen (ed.), *Historical Records of New South Wales*, vol. 4, p. 1007.
[17] Watson (ed.), *Historical Records of Australia*, series 1, vol. 3, 1801–1802, p. 698.
[18] Baudin, op cit., pp. 393–4.
[19] ibid., pp. 397–8.
[20] Péron, op. cit., tome i, p. 331 (Phillips trans., p. 255).
[21] ibid.
[22] Baudin, op cit., p. 401.
[23] Péron, op. cit., tome i, p. 333 (Phillips trans., p. 257).

24 Baudin to the Minister of Marine, 11 November 1802, Archives nationales, Marine BB⁴ 995.

25 Péron, op. cit., tome i, p. 334 (Phillips trans., p. 258).

26 On the east coast of Bruny Island, Adventure Bay was named by Tobias Furneaux in honour of his vessel, the *Adventure*, in 1773.

27 Péron, op. cit., tome i, p. 336 (Phillips trans., p. 260).

28 Baudin, op cit., p. 407.

29 Roux, 'Les requins des côtes australiennes observés par Péron et Lesueur', p. 34.

30 Freycinet, *Voyage de découvertes aux Terres Australes* …, tome iii, 1816, p. 12.

31 Péron, op. cit., tome i, pp. 338–9 (Phillips trans., p. 260).

32 'Expédition de découvertes: La corvette *Le Géographe*: Morts à bord ou dans les hôpitaux', Archives nationales, Marine BB⁴ 997, dossier 3, folio 124 recto.

33 Péron, op. cit., tome i, pp. 339–40 (Scott trans., *Terre Napoléon*, pp. 184–6).

34 Baudin to the Minister of Marine, 11 November 1802, Archives nationales, Marine BB⁴ 995.

35 Baudin, op. cit., p. 416.

12. Port Jackson

1 Péron, *Voyage*, tome i, p. 342 (Phillips trans., p. 262).

2 Flinders, *A Voyage to Terra Australis*, vol. i, p. 230.

3 Horner, *The French Reconnaissance*, pp. 238–9.

4 ibid., pp. 239–40; for the entries in Ronsard's journal see Archives nationales, Marine 5JJ 29, folios 365–7.

5 Bladen (ed.), *Historical Records of New South Wales*, vol. 4, pp. 949–50.

6 Péron, *Voyage*, tome i, p. 368 (Phillips trans., p. 271).

7 ibid., p. 369 (Phillips trans., p. 272). Well versed in the achievements of Arthur Phillip, Péron was impressed by the fact that one of the hospital buildings had come pre-fabricated with the First Fleet.

8 ibid.

9 ibid., p. 371 (Phillips trans., p. 273).

10 ibid., p. 370 (Phillips trans., p. 273).

11 Paterson, W., *A Narrative of Four Journeys into the Country of the Hottentots, and Caffraria In the Yeare One Thousand Seven Hundred and Seventy-Seven, Eight, and Nine*, J. Johnson, London, 1789. Péron might not have read the French edition of Paterson's book, published in 1790, but he must have read references to it when he read the account of Governor Phillip's voyage.

12 Macmillan, 'Paterson, William (1755–1810)'.

13 For the lengthy exchange of correspondence associated with this affair, see Bladen (ed.), *Historical Records of New South Wales*, vol. 4, pp. 977–1005.

14 ibid., pp. 962–6.

15 ibid., King to Baudin, 23 June 1802, p. 948.

16 ibid., Baudin to King, 22 June 1802, p. 948.

17 Péron, *Voyage*, tome i, p. 378 (Phillips trans., pp. 278–9).

18 Authorities in Sydney mistakenly registered the *Entreprise* as the *Surprise*.

19 Lecorre's father Josselin (1727–85) had participated in the expeditions of Bougainville and Marion Dufresne; see Duyker, 'Josselin and Alexandre Le Corre: Early French voyagers to Van Diemen's Land and New Holland'.

20 Cumpston, *First Visitors to Bass Strait*, pp. 15–17; see also Bateson, *Australian Shipwrecks*, vol. 1, pp. 33–4.

21 Baudin, op. cit., p. 427.

22 Péron, *Voyage*, tome i, pp. 375–6 (Phillips trans., p. 277).

23 Forster, *France and Botany Bay: The Lure of a Penal Colony*, p. 9.

24 Bassett, *The Governor's Lady*, note p. 65.

25 Péron to Charles-Mathieu-Isidore Decaen, Capitaine général, Isle de France, Port-Nord-Ouest, le 20 frimaire an 12 [12 December 1803], Archives du général Decaen, Bibliothèque municipale de Caen, vol. 92, folio 2, 14 pages recto-verso.

26 Péron, 'Mémoire sur les établissements anglais à la Nouvelle Hollande, à la Terre de Diémen et sur les Archipels du Grand Océan Pacifique au Citoyen Fourcroy, Membre du Conseil d'Etat'; 'Etat administratif et commercial des colonies anglaises aux Terre Australes'; 'Tableau général des colonies anglaises aux Terres Australes'; Tableau militaire des colonies anglaises aux Terres Australes'; 'Voyage de découverte aux Terres Australes: Tableau général des colonies anglaises aux Terres Australes'; MHNH, Coll. Lesueur, MSS 12001, 12002, 12005-1, 12006-1.

27 Péron's 'Tableau général des colonies anglaises aux Terres Australes' was published in tome ii of his *Voyage*, pp. 393–433 (original French edition).

28 Hamelin's journal, Archives nationales, Marine 5JJ 42, contains reflections on how the fortifications at Port Jackson could be overcome, and Péron, in his report to Decaen, later declared: 'M. Freycinet, the young officer, has specially researched the places around Port Jackson favourable to an invasion. He has, particularly, informed himself on the entrance to the port …'; see Péron to Charles-Mathieu-Isidore Decaen, Capitaine général, Isle de France, Port-Nord-Ouest, le 20 frimaire an 12, op. cit.

29 For Barrallier's account of his attempt (in French) see appendix A of Bladen (ed.), *Historical Records of New South Wales*, vol. 5.

30 Péron, *Voyage*, tome i (Phillips trans., p. 290).

31 ibid., p. 376 (Phillips trans., pp. 277–8).

32 ibid., p. 377 (Phillips trans., p. 278).

33 Lewinsohn, *A History of Sexual Customs*, pp. 245–6.

34 Péron, *Voyage*, tome i, p. 379 (Phillips trans., p. 280).

35 ibid., p. 380 (Phillips trans., p. 280).

36 Turbet, *The Aborigines of the Sydney District Before 1788*, p. 23.

37 Bellefin hailed from Crémieu (Isère) and was held in high regard by his colleague. See Duyker, 'Bellefin, Jérôme Claude (1764–1835)'.

38 Péron, *Voyage*, tome i, p. 380 (Phillips trans., p. 280).

39 Baker, *The Australian Language*, p. 301.

40 Péron, *Voyage*, tome i, p. 404 (Phillips trans., p. 295).

41 Donovan, *An Epitome of the Natural History of the Insects of New Holland, New Zealand, New Guinea, Otaheite* … [General Illustrations of Entomology, vol. 3], [pp. 1–2].

42 Cuvier, *Le Règne animal* …, Nouvelle édition [2nd edn], tome ii, p. 35.

43 Roux-Esteve, 'Liste des amphibiens et reptiles des collections du Muséum National d'histoire naturelle de Paris'.

44 Péron, *Voyage*, tome i, p. 407 (Phillips trans., p. 296).

45 See Walton (ed.), *Zoological Catalogue of Australia*, vol. 1, *Amphibia and Reptilia*, p. 41.

46 Duméril and Bibron, *Erpétologie générale ou Histoire naturelle complète des reptiles*, vol. 8, ii, p. 595.

47 White, *Journal of a Voyage to New South Wales*, p. 248.

[48] Roux-Estève, 'Liste des amphibiens et reptiles des collections du Muséum National d'histoire naturelle de Paris'. Its specific epithet is somewhat misleading and was probably occasioned by the bluish colour change the specimen (now lost) underwent after being preserved in rum.

[49] ibid.

[50] Lesson, 'Description de quelques reptiles nouveaux ou peu connus'.

[51] There are two syntypes (MHNP 4499 and MHNP 4500) in Paris, but the collection locality is not precise.

[52] Levi and Bergman, *Australian Genesis*, pp. 43–7.

[53] Péron, *Voyage*, tome i, p. 408 (Phillips trans., p. 296).

[54] ibid. (Phillips trans., p. 297); despite Péron's praise of Larra, one wonders whether his mention of the fact that his hospitality had to be paid for was a reflection of incipient anti-Semitism. The later unflattering comments on the Chinese in Timor and comparisons with the Jews in tome iv (pp. 86–7) of the *Voyage* (see chapter xxxii, p. 237 of the Cornell translation) might suggest some prejudice in this regard. However, this volume was completed by Louis de Freycinet; given the disappearance of the original manuscript, we cannot know for certain whether the published comments are actually Péron's. They do not appear in the chapters on Timor in tome ii of the 1816 edition, only in the 1824 edition.

[55] Levi and Bergman, op. cit., p. 46.

[56] Péron, 'Tableau militaire des colonies anglaises aux Terres Australes', MHNH, Coll. Lesueur, MS 12006-1.

[57] Péron, *Voyage*, tome i, p. 415 (Phillips trans., p. 302).

[58] This was Brush Farm; the original homestead is believed to have been located in the Dundas Valley to the west of present-day Marsden Road. Cox was also known to have been 'very closely associated' with the Irish nationalist Joseph Holt.

[59] Baudin, 'Lettre du capitaine Baudin à Mr Jussieu datée du Port Jackson le 20 brumaire an XI', Archives nationales, Marine BB⁴ 995.

[60] Péron, *Voyage*, tome i, pp. 417–18 (Phillips trans., p. 303).

[61] Baudin, 'Lettre du capitaine Baudin à Mr Jussieu datée du Port Jackson le 20 brumaire an XI', op. cit.

[62] Péron, *Voyage*, tome i, p. 420 (Phillips trans., p. 305).

[63] ibid., p. 429 (Phillips trans., p. 307).

[64] ibid.

[65] A memorial plaque commemorates the battlefield on Schofields Road, near the Vinegar Hill Wool Shed.

[66] Péron, *Voyage*, tome i, p. 431 (Phillips trans., p. 308).

[67] See Duyker, 'Lalouette de Vernicourt [dit de Clambe], Pierre (1754–1804)'.

[68] Péron, *Voyage*, tome i, p. 431 (Phillips trans., p. 308).

[69] See Chief Secretary Barry to the Government of New South Wales, 25 June 1811, enquiring about the existence of Mr de Vernicourt alias Baron Clambe with enclosed copy of a petition by Mrs de Vernicourt, National Archives, Mauritius, RB 8, folios 171–3.

[70] ibid., p. 432 (Phillips trans., p. 309).

[71] I am very grateful to Graham Wilson for sharing the fruits of his research relating to Lalouette de Vernicourt, especially among the Portland Papers (PI C 7/9) at the University of Nottingham and in the Colonial Secretary's Correspondence 4/3491, pp. 198–9, 202–3, State Records of New South Wales.

72 Many royalists, encouraged by Bonaparte's rapprochement with the Church, hoped that he might also reinstate the monarchy.

73 Pierre Lalouette was regent of the medical faculty in Paris from 1742 until his death on 14 August 1792. A lobe of the thyroid gland is named after him. For his 'boîte fumigatoire', with which he successfully treated 400 syphilis cases with mercury vapour, he was awarded an annuity for life. Delaunay, in *La vie médicale aux XVIe, XVIIe et XVIIIe siècles*, states that Lalouette was one of the rare doctors decorated with the Cordon noir de l'Ordre de Saint-Michel. He was ennobled in February 1773.

74 Adopting the name Lalouette de Vernicourt, Pierre appears to have joined the army as a *sous-lieutenant* in the Ile de France Regiment and departed Lorient on the *Flamand* on 9 February 1778. He was promoted to lieutenant in the same regiment on 10 October 1784 and again departed for the Ile de France on the *Breton* from Lorient on 19 December 1786. In Port Louis, on 6 August 1787, he married Légère Anne Apoline Grandemange d'Anderny, daughter of a lieutenant colonel in the infantry, and had three children. Lalouette de Vernicourt was promoted to the rank of captain on 2 June 1789. On 15 February 1803, Vernicourt's farm at Castle Hill, known as the Hermitage, was attacked by fifteen fugitives who had taken part in the failed Irish convict rebellion. The very first issue of the *Sydney Gazette* reported that his house was 'ransacked, and stripped of many articles of plate, wearing apparel, some fire and side-arms, provisions, spiritous and vinous liquors'. After his death, his estate was sold at auction by his administrator, Robert Campbell, on 3 August 1804. Vernicourt's widow did not learn of his death until 1811; see Duyker, 'Lalouette de Vernicourt [*dit* De Clambe], Pierre (1754–1804)'; Anon., *Sydney Gazette and New South Wales Advertiser*, vol. i, no. 1, Saturday, 5 March 1803, p. 3; vol. ii, no. 58, Sunday, 8 April, 1804, p. 3; no. 67, Sunday, 10 June 1804, p. 1; no. 73, Sunday, 22 July 1804, p. 2; see also Watson (ed.), *Historical Records of Australia*, series 1, vol. 3, pp. 109, 406.

75 Webb, *George Caley*, p. 1.

76 Péron to Charles-Mathieu-Isidore Decaen, Capitaine général, Isle de France, Port-Nord-Ouest, le 20 frimaire an 12, op. cit.

77 See Governor King to Lord Hobart, 1 March 1804, in Watson (ed.), *Historical Records of Australia*, series 1, vol. 3, p. 460.

78 Péron, *Voyage*, tome i, p. 386 (Phillips trans., p. 284).

79 Kass, *Parramatta: A Past Revealed*, pp. 62–3.

80 Péron, *Voyage*, tome i, p. 409 (Phillips trans., p. 297).

81 Meurant's conditional pardon was dated 18 October 1801 (State Records NSW item 4/4430 Reel 774). The *Sydney Gazette* reported his full pardon on 19 June 1803, p. 4. He married Rose (Rozetta) Martin on 27 May 1811 (NSW BDM vol. 3A/1224) and died on 4 November 1844.

82 Péron, *Voyage*, tome i, p. 417 (Phillips trans., p. 303); see also Bonnemains and Chappuis, 'Les oiseaux de la collection C.-A. Lesueur du Muséum d'histoire naturelle du Havre'.

83 James Thomson sailed to Sydney as surgeon on the *Atlantic* in 1791. According to Governor King's dispatch of 17 November 1802, Thomson had 'some time past laboured under an asthmatic complaint'. Dr Chris Cunneen, on the basis of a letter Thomson wrote as surgeon of the *Surprise*, has suggested that he did not arrive with a wife and, although he certainly left 'with his family', might have acquired a consort

and perhaps a child in Sydney. Although Thomson was 'on leave', by 22 February 1806 it was clear to Governor King that he had 'no intention of returning'; Cunneen, pers. comm., 30 March 2005; see also biographical details in McCormick, *First Views of Australia*, p. 329.

[84] Pierre Milius to Governor King, 9 July 1802, in Bladen (ed.), *Historical Records of New South Wales*, vol. 4, p. 951.

13. King Island

[1] Cogswell was the son of the American patriot Nathaniel Cogswell, of Rowley, Mass.; see Duyker, 'Cogswell, Nathaniel (1778–1832)'.

[2] Duyker, 'Josselin and Alexandre Le Corre: Early French voyagers to Van Diemen's Land and New Holland'.

[3] Frank Horner has argued that Governor King might have intended to separate sealing parties only to avoid potential conflict.

[4] Péron [and Freycinet], *Voyage*, tome ii, pp. 2–3 (Cornell trans., p. 4).

[5] Baudin, *The Journal of Post Captain Nicolas Baudin*, p. 441.

[6] ibid.

[7] Baudin, op. cit., p. 425.

[8] In 1800 Mary Beckwith was arrested and convicted with her mother (or stepmother) of stealing forty-six yards of printed calico. Although both were sentenced to hang, their sentences were commuted to transportation for life, and they arrived in New South Wales on the *Nile* on 14 December 1801. Mary's mother became the senior housekeeper of Richard Atkins, the newly appointed judge advocate, and is believed to have borne one or more of his illegitimate children. Atkins spoke French and is known to have entertained Baudin during his visit to Sydney, so it was perhaps through the judge advocate that the expedition commander met his future stowaway; see Brown, 'The captain and the convict maid: A chapter in the life of Nicolas Baudin' and Duyker, 'Beckwith, Mary (c. 1786–c. 1804)'.

[9] Cumpston, *First Visitors to Bass Strait*, p. 12.

[10] Péron [and Freycinet], *Voyage*, tome ii, p. 6 (Cornell trans., p. 6).

[11] Bladen (ed.), *Historical Records of New South Wales*, vol. 4, p. 1007.

[12] ibid.

[13] Ronsard, Journal, Archives nationales, Marine 5JJ 30, folio 42.

[14] Labillardière, *Relation du voyage à la recherche de La Pérouse ...*, tome i, p. 192 (Stockdale trans., p. 137).

[15] See Ronsard, op. cit., folio 42; Hamelin had already declared indignantly that the 'English are about to take from us the D'Entrecasteaux Channel, where it would however interest the French Republic very much to have a settlement', quoted by Horner in *The French Reconnaissance*, p. 264.

[16] Bladen (ed.), *Historical Records of New South Wales*, vol. 4, p. 1008.

[17] ibid., vol. 5, p. 826.

[18] ibid.

[19] Crespin, 'Middle Miocene limestones from King Island, Tasmania'.

[20] Jennings, 'The coastal geomorphology of King Island, Bass Strait, in relation to the relative level of land and sea', p. 4.

[21] Péron [and Freycinet], *Voyage*, tome ii, pp. 50–1 (Cornell trans., p. 40).

22 ibid., p. 52 (Cornell trans., p. 41).

23 Although Péron thought Cooper (whom he mistakenly called Cowper) had spent thirteen months on King Island, he appears to have arrived in June 1802 on the *Margaret*. It has been suggested that the French confused him with members of a sealing gang from the *Harrington* who christened the island the year before.

24 Cumpston, op. cit., p. 11.

25 Péron [and Freycinet], *Voyage*, tome ii, pp. 18–19 (Cornell trans., p. 15).

26 ibid., tome ii, p. 19 (Cornell trans., pp. 15–16).

27 'Cowper, chef des pêcheurs anglais de l'île King. Questionnaire très détaillé sur les Casoars [emus] et leur manière de vivre [in Péron's hand]', MHNH, Coll. Lesueur, MS 79054.

28 In Milne-Edwards and Oustalet, 'Note sur l'Emeu noir (*Dromaeus ater* V.) de l'île Decrès (Australie)'.

29 Péron [and Freycinet], *Voyage*, tome ii, p. 20 (Cornell trans., pp. 16–17).

30 *Hippocampus* sp., *Zeus faber* Linné, 1758; *Alabes rufus* (Macleay, 1881); and unidentified members of the Syngnathidae and Blenniidae families; see Bauchot and Daget, 'Poissons recoltés par C.-A. Lesueur et entrés dans les collections du Muséum national d'histoire naturelle de Paris' and 'Dessins de poissons et de mammifères de la collection du Muséum d'histoire naturelle du Havre'.

31 See *Spongia filamentosa, S. favosa, S. cellulosa, S. placenta, S. angulosa, S. vulpina*, in Lamarck, *Histoire naturelle des animaux sans vertèbres*, tome ii, pp. 355–6, 358, 376.

32 *Spiriorbis lamellosa* and *S. carinata, Serpula infundibulum* and *S. filaria*, ibid., tome v, pp. 359, 364–5.

33 Including *Crassatella kingicola* (= *Eucrassatella kingicola*), *Trigonia pectinata* (= *Neotrigonia margaritacea*), *Arca pistachia* (= *Barbatia pistachia*); see ibid., tome vi, part i, pp. 41, 63.

34 ibid., tome v, p. 398.

35 Holthuis, 'The scyllarid lobsters (Crustacea: Decapoda: Palinuridea) collected by F. Péron and C. A. Lesueur during the 1800–1804 expedition to Australia'.

36 Péron [and Freycinet], *Voyage*, tome ii, p. 13 (Cornell trans., p. 11).

37 Baudin, op. cit., p. 452.

38 There was some compensation for the delay when it was learned that Louis de Freycinet had accomplished valuable survey work in the Hunter Islands while his vessel was separated from the *Géographe*.

14. Kangaroo Island

1 The name 'Dudley' was first given to the eastern-most 'hundred' (administrative division) of the island and thereby to the peninsula; see Nunn, *This Southern Land: A Social History of Kangaroo Island 1800–1890*, p. 133.

2 Péron, *Voyage*, tome ii, p. 70 (Cornell trans., p. 58).

3 Baudin, *The Journal of Post Captain Nicolas Baudin*, pp. 454–63.

4 Péron, *Voyage*, tome ii, p. 76 (Cornell trans., p. 62).

5 ibid., p. 77 (Cornell trans., p. 63).

6 Milne-Edwards and Oustalet, 'Notice sur quelques espèces d'oiseaux actuellement éteintes qui se trouvent représentées dans les collections du Muséum d'histoire naturelle; l'Emeu ou Emou noir', and Milne-Edwards and Oustalet, 'Note sur l'Emeu noir (*Dromaeus ater* V.) de l'île Decrès (Australie)'.

7 Baudin, op. cit., pp. 471–3.

8 See MHNH, Coll. Lesueur, MS 79004.

9   See Jouanin, 'Les émeus de l'expédition Baudin'; see also Jouanin, 'La passion de la nature ou Joséphine amateur et mécène des sciences de la nature', in D'Arneville, Benoît, Chevalier, Chiappero, Jouanin and Ledoux-Lebard (eds), *L'Impératrice Joséphine et les sciences naturelles*, pp. 20–34.

10 Ruediger, *Border's Land: Kangaroo Island 1802–1836*, p. 14.

11 Scheffer in his *Seals, Sea Lions and Walruses: A Review of the Pinnipedia*, cites J. Brookes, *A Catalogue of the Anatomical and Zoological Museum of Joshua Brookes …*, London, 1828.

12 Debard, 'François Péron (1775–1810), zoologiste du voyage de découvertes aux Terres Australes: Remarques et observations sur les Pinnipèdes' (thesis), p. 257.

13 'Mémoire sur les phoques en général, sur ceux des Régions Australes en particulier et sur les avantages que les Anglais retirent de l'huile et des fourrures de ces derniers. 1ère section: Observations générales sur le genre Phoques', MHNH, Coll. Lesueur, MS 80 508.

14 Iredale and Troughton, 'Order Pinnipedia', p. 89.

15 Baudin was partly responsible for the modern name because he released pigs in the area in the hope that they would multiply and assist future mariners.

16 Péron, *Voyage*, tome ii, p. 78 (Cornell trans., p. 63).

17 Higgins, 'The unusual sea-lions of Kangaroo Island'.

18 Péron, *Voyage*, tome ii, pp. 81–2 (Cornell trans., p. 65–6).

19 Roux-Estève, 'Liste des amphibiens et reptiles des collections du Muséum national d'histoire naturelle de Paris, récoltés par Lesueur (1778–1846)'.

20 See Lamarck, *Histoire naturelle des animaux sans vertèbres*, tome v, pp. 481–3, 502, 547, tome vii, p. 120.

21 Péron, *Voyage*, tome ii, p. 78 (Cornell trans., p. 63).

22 These include gulls, petrels, terns, oystercatchers, flycatchers, finches, the Australian pelican (*Pelecanus conspicillatus*) and almost certainly the white-bellied sea-eagle (*Haliastur leucogaster*), the yellow-tailed black-cockatoo (*Calyptorhynchus funereus*), the Australian raven (*Corvus coronoides*), the bronzewing pigeon (*Phaps chalcoptera*), the superb fairy wren (*Malurus cyaneus*) and possibly the southern boobook (*Ninox novae-seelandiae*), if not another species of owl; see Péron, 'Zoographiae Hollandiae-novae mariumque alluentium illam—Descriptions zoologiques No. 3—île King—île aux Kanguroos—îles St Pierre et St François—Port du Roi Georges', MHNH, Coll. Lesueur, MS 65010.

23 Baudin, op. cit., p. 467.

24 Péron, *Voyage*, tome ii, p. 79 (Cornell trans., p. 64).

25 Péron, 'Zoographiae Hollandiae-novae mariumque alluentium illam—Descriptions zoologiques No. 3 …', op. cit.

26 Péron's description of scads and mackerel-like fish would also suggest that the fishermen of the expedition caught members of the Carangidae family, including perhaps the yellowtail kingfish, *Seriola lalandi*, later described by his compatriot Achille Valenciennes. For further information on the fish of Kangaroo Island, see Glover, 'Fishes' and 'Checklist of the inshore and inland fishes of Kangaroo Island', in Davies, Twidale and Tyler (eds), *Natural History of Kangaroo Island*, pp. 142–53.

27 Péron, *Voyage*, tome ii, pp. 79–80 (Cornell trans., p. 64).

28 ibid., tome ii, p. 83 (Cornell trans., pp. 66–7).

29 Baudin, op. cit., p. 467.

30 ibid., p. 466.

31 ibid., p. 470.

32 Péron, *Voyage*, tome ii, pp. 202–3 (trans. Cornell, p. 134).

33 ibid., p. 84 (Cornell trans., p. 67).

34 Baudin, op. cit., p. 472.

35 Charles-Pierre Boulanger to Baudin, 1 ventôse an 11 [20 February 1803], Archives nationales, Marine 5JJ 53.

15. Nuyts Archipelago

1 Baudin, *The Journal of Post Captain Nicolas Baudin*, p. 473.

2 ibid., p. 483.

3 Freycinet's account quoted at length in Péron [and Freycinet], *Voyage*, tome ii (Cornell trans., p. 104); see also Baudin's account of his interrogation of Freycinet after they were reunited at King George Sound; Baudin, op. cit., p. 483.

4 Péron [and Freycinet], *Voyage*, tome ii, p. 108 (Cornell trans., p. 84).

5 Dampier, 'An account of New Holland and the adjacent islands, 1699–1700' [extract from *Voyage to New Holland in the year 1699* (1703–09)] in Pinkerton, *Early Australian Voyages* ..., pp. 105–92 (see, in particular, p. 132).

6 Flinders, *A Voyage to Terra Australis*, vol. i, introduction.

7 ibid.

8 Péron [and Freycinet], *Voyage*, tome ii, p. 108 (Cornell trans., p. 88).

9 Baudin, op. cit., p. 478.

10 ibid.

11 ibid., note inserted by Péron.

12 Péron did not personally encounter any of the indigenous inhabitants on the South Australian coast and could only reiterate the reports of his companions who caught sight of two fleeing individuals at Tourville Bay. Yet, despite his lack of first-hand knowledge, he was prepared to write dismissively that they were 'undoubtedly reduced—like the wild natives of Leeuwin Land—to the use of brackish water', that for food they had 'only the uncertain products of hunting and fishing' and that they revived '(in possibly darker tones still) those dismal pictures of misery, hunger and barbarity'; see Péron [and Freycinet], *Voyage*, tome ii, p. 123 (Cornell trans., p. 98).

13 See Jonathan Swift, *Travels into Several Remote Nations of the World by Lemuel Gulliver* (1726), part i: *A Voyage to Lilliput*, chapter 1.

14 'Lefebvre' was probably Joseph Lefèvre, from Flanders, who joined the expedition at Tenerife as a stowaway. Identifying the man who rescued Péron on St Peter Island is made difficult by the fact that Péron later spelt his name 'Lefèvre'. There were sailors with both these names on the *Naturaliste*.

15 Péron [and Freycinet], *Voyage*, tome ii, p. 111 (Cornell trans., p. 90).

16 ibid., tome ii, p. 121 (Cornell trans., p. 97).

17 ibid.

18 Lamarck, *Histoire naturelle des animaux sans vertèbres*, tome v, pp. 507–8, 524–5, 531–2 and tome vi, part i, p. 142.

19 ibid., tome vii, p; 558. Lamarck commented on the similarity of this Trochus to Hampshire fossils described by Daniel Solander in Gustaf Brander's *Fossilia Hantoniensia* (1766) and to fossils from Gignon in his personal collection.

20 ibid., tome v, p. 392.

21 ibid., tome ii, p. 368.

22   ibid.

23   See appendix 3 of Fromont's 2002 survey of (mainly) Western Australian sponge specimens in Paris, in 'A Quest for Our Natural Heritage', Winston Churchill Memorial Trust of Australia, Churchill Fellowship Report, Canberra, 2002. Fromont also noted that all those from the Baudin expedition were dry specimens that did not 'retain external surface features' and lacked 'important morphological characters'.

24   Carnet, Péron, 'Zoographiae Hollandiae-novae marium que alluentium illam—Descriptions zoologiques No. 4—îles St Pierre et St François—Port du Roi Georges', MHNH, Coll. Lesueur, MS 65011. See also Bonnemains and Jones, 'Les crustacés de la collection C.-A. Lesueur (dessins et manuscrits)'.

25   Henry Milne-Edwards was born in Bruges of an English father, and studied and worked in Paris as a disciple of Georges Cuvier. His son, Alphonse Milne-Edwards, himself a specialist in decapod crustacea, became director of the Muséum national d'histoire naturelle and published Péron's questionnaire relating to the emus of King Island.

26   Davie, 'Crustacea: Malacostraca: Phyllocarida, Hoplocarida, Eucarida (part 1)', in Walton (ed.), *Zoological Catalogue of Australia*, vol. 19.3A, p. 311.

27   Péron [and Freycinet], *Voyage*, tome ii, p. 117 (Cornell trans., p. 94).

28   Desmarest, *Nouveau dictionnaire d'histoire naturelle* ..., tome 17, p. 38.

29   The tammar wallaby was first described by Europeans in François Pelsaert's account of the wreck of the *Batavia* in 1629. The South Australian origin of the tammar wallaby in New Zealand has been determined on the basis of skull morphological studies; see Poole, Wood and Simms, 'Distribution of the Tammar, *Macropus eugenii*, and the relationships of populations as determined by cranial morphometrics'.

30   Péron [and Freycinet], *Voyage*, tome ii, p. 119 (Cornell trans., p. 95).

31   ibid.

32   ibid.

33   Very obviously the familiar *Eudyptula minor novaehollandiae* of southern Australian coastal waters.

34   Carnet, Péron, 'Zoographiae Hollandiae-novae marium que alluentium illam—Descriptions zoologiques No. 4—îles St Pierre et St François—Port du Roi Georges', MHNH, Coll. Lesueur, MS 65011.

35   Péron [and Freycinet], *Voyage*, tome ii, pp. 119–20 (Cornell trans., p. 96).

36   Muséum national d'histoire naturelle, Paris, holotype 1242.

37   Gray, 'Catalogue of the slender-tongued saurians, with descriptions of many new genera and species (contd.)', p. 290.

38   Péron [and Freycinet], *Voyage*, tome ii, pp. 120–1 (Cornell trans., pp. 96–7).

39   According to Fornasiero and West-Sooby in 'Baudin's Books', Baudin did not have works by Bernardin de Saint-Pierre in his shipboard library.

40   Saint-Pierre, *Etudes de la Nature* (1784), vol. i (Hunter trans., 1796, p. 280).

41   Birds have no sweat glands and cool themselves by panting, but this involves evaporation of water, which must be replaced. Insect eaters and raptors regain fluid from their prey.

42   Péron [and Freycinet], *Voyage*, tome ii, p. 122 (Cornell trans., p. 98).

43   Lentle et al., 'Differences in renal and alimentary water conservation account for differences in the distribution of tammar and parma wallabies on Kawau Island, New Zealand'.

16. King George Sound

[1] Named in honour of the brave but brainless Marshal Joachim Murat (1767–1815), the twelfth child of an innkeeper, who married Bonaparte's youngest sister and was made King of Naples. Baudin, however, refers to Murat Bay as 'Baie des Saints'.

[2] Duyker and Duyker (eds, trans.), *Bruny d'Entrecasteaux: Voyage to Australia and the Pacific 1791–1793*, p. 134.

[3] Baudin, op. cit., p. 479.

[4] Péron [and Freycinet], *Voyage*, tome ii, p. 131 (Cornell trans., p. 105).

[5] Baudin, *The Journal of Post Captain Nicolas Baudin*, p. 484.

[6] Charles Pierre Boulanger to Baudin, 20 February 1803, Archives nationales, Marine 5JJ 53.

[7] Baudin, op. cit., p. 485.

[8] Péron [and Freycinet], *Voyage*, tome ii, p. 133 (Cornell trans., p. 108).

[9] Baudin, op. cit., p. 494; see his comment regarding Péron establishing 'the period at which New Holland must have risen from the floor of the sea'.

[10] Péron [and Freycinet], *Voyage*, tome ii, p. 139 (Cornell trans., p. 111).

[11] ibid.

[12] ibid., tome ii, p. 140 (Cornell trans., pp. 111–12).

[13] ibid., tome ii, p. 145 (Cornell trans., p. 115).

[14] See Wallace's *Malay Archipelago*, p. 11.

[15] Péron [and Freycinet], *Voyage*, tome ii, p. 147 (Cornell trans., p. 117).

[16] Darwin, *The Voyage of the Beagle*, chapter xix, p. 449.

[17] Péron [and Freycinet], *Voyage*, tome ii, p. 141 (Cornell trans., pp. 112–13).

[18] ibid., tome ii, p. 142 (Cornell trans., p. 113); see also Roux and Bonnemains, 'Les poissons du "Voyage de découvertes aux Terres Australes" (1800–1804) étudiés par F. Péron et C.-A. Lesueur: Collection iconographiques des dessins de C.-A. Lesueur du Muséum d'histoire naturelle du Havre'.

[19] Péron [and Freycinet], *Voyage*, tome ii, p 141 (Cornell trans., p. 112).

[20] ibid.

[21] Roux-Estève, R., 'Liste des amphibiens et reptiles des collections du Muséum national d'histoire naturelle de Paris, récoltés par Lesueur (1778–1846)'; see also Gray, 'Description of some new species and four new genera of reptiles from Western Australia, discovered by John Gould, Esq.'.

[22] Péron [and Freycinet], *Voyage*, tome ii, p. 141 (Cornell trans., p. 112).

[23] Péron, 'Zoographiae Hollandiae-novae marium que alluentium illam—Descriptions zoologiques No. 4—îles St Pierre et St François—Port du Roi Georges', MHNH, Coll. Lesueur, MS 65011.

[24] Muséum national d'histoire naturelle, Paris, holotype LBIM DT548 v. B Type DT3399 type v. A and holotype LBIM DT650, see appendix 3 of Fromont's 2002 survey of (mainly) West Australian sponge specimens in Paris, in 'A Quest for Our Natural Heritage', p. 24; see also Lamarck, *Histoire naturelle des animaux sans vertèbres*, tome ii, pp. 358–9, 402.

[25] Péron [and Freycinet], *Voyage*, tome ii, p. 142 (Cornell trans., p. 113).

[26] See Lamarck, op. cit., tome v, pp. 475, 489, 525.

[27] See Ferguson, 'Mokaré's domain'.

[28] Péron [and Freycinet], *Voyage*, tome ii, p. 143 (Cornell trans., pp. 113–14). For more information, see Wells et al. (eds), *The Marine Flora and Fauna of Albany, Western Australia*.

29   Wace and Lovett in *Yankee Maritime Activities and the Early History of Australia*, p. 86, give Pendleton's first name as Isaac. Péron says it was James, but he might have misheard 'Isaac' as 'Jacques' and mistranslated it. Bateson in *Australian Shipwrecks*, vol. 1, p. 38, says Pendleton's Christian name was John. According to Everet Hall Pendleton (born 1878), Captain Isaac Pendleton was the son of Captain Amos Pendleton (1728–1821) and Anna Foster, born on 22 November 1777 in Westerly, King's Co., Rhode Island; see *Brian Pendleton and his Descendants 1599–1910*.

30   Péron [and Freycinet], *Voyage*, tome ii, p. 157 (Cornell trans., p. 124).

31   The article about the massacre in the *Sydney Gazette*, 'Depositions respecting the ship *Union*, of America', of 28 October 1804, pp. 3–4, makes fascinating reading— especially because the massacre led to the rescue of a woman named Elizabeth Morey, the sole survivor of the previous massacre of the crew of the 400-ton American whaler, the *Duke of Portland*, wrecked on Tongatabu in June 1802. Pendleton's supercargo, John Boston, was the owner of the *Portland*.

32   Bateson, op. cit., vol. i, pp. 33, 38.

33   Péron [and Freycinet], *Voyage*, tome ii, p. 151 (Cornell trans., p. 119). Individual Minang family groups did have defined estates, and the later French voyage of Dumont d'Durville would meet Mokaré, the customary owner of the area around Princess Royal Harbour. He must have been an infant at the time of the Baudin expedition.

34   See Ferguson, op. cit., p. 124.

35   See ibid., p. 125.

36   Baudin, op. cit., p. 490.

37   ibid.

38   ibid., p. 491.

39   ibid., p. 495.

17. Back to Shark Bay

1   Baudin, *The Journal of Post Captain Nicolas Baudin*, p. 495.

2   Quoted by Horner, in *The French Reconnaissance*, p. 292.

3   Baudin, op. cit., p. 497. By the time Baudin reached Cape Leeuwin, he came to the conclusion that the expedition's previous survey of the coast was inaccurate—unfairly blaming his geographers (who had not had the benefit of a close approach). He therefore resolved to begin 'work on this whole coast afresh'.

4   ibid., p. 498.

5   Péron [and Freycinet], *Voyage*, tome ii, p. 197 (Cornell trans., p. 130).

6   Horner, op. cit., footnote, p. 294.

7   See Serieyx, *Wonnerup: The Sacred Dune*.

8   Baudin, op. cit., pp. 502–5.

9   Péron [and Freycinet], op. cit., tome ii, pp. 201–2 (Cornell trans., p. 134).

10   Turtle remains are well represented in archaeological sites on the peninsula; see Bowdler, 'Archaeological research in the Shark Bay Region, Western Australia: An introductory account'.

11   Duyker, *Nature's Argonaut*, pp. 201–2.

12   Péron [and Freycinet], op. cit., tome ii, p. 204 (Cornell trans., p. 135).

13   ibid., p. 209 (Cornell trans., p. 139).

14   Baudin, op. cit., p. 508.

15   ibid., p. 509.

16 Péron [and Freycinet], op. cit., tome ii, p. 216 (Cornell trans., p. 144).
17 Baudin's interrogations after the event would appear to corroborate this cool decision.
18 Péron [and Freycinet], op. cit., tome ii, p. 218 (Cornell trans., p. 145).
19 ibid.
20 Baudin, op. cit., p. 510.
21 ibid., p. 509.
22 Playford, 'Geology of the Shark Bay area, Western Australia'.
23 Péron acknowledges this; Baudin recorded that Guichenot was laden with twenty-five to thirty pounds.
24 Péron [and Freycinet], tome ii, p. 221 (Cornell trans., p. 147).
25 ibid., p. 222 (Cornell trans., p. 148).
26 Baudin, op. cit., p. 508.
27 Péron [and Freycinet], tome ii, pp. 123–4 (Cornell trans., p. 149).
28 ibid., 2nd edn, 1824, tome iii, p. 318 (Cornell trans., appendix F, p. 154).
29 Estensen, The Life of Matthew Flinders, p. 472.
30 Péron [and Freycinet], op. cit., tome ii, p. 219 (Cornell trans., p. 146).
31 ibid., p. 230 (Cornell trans., p. 153).
32 Baudin, op. cit., p. 510.

18. Final surveys

1 According to Horner, this was to determine whether the Exmouth Peninsula was separated from the mainland by a strait.
2 Baudin, The Journal of Post Captain Nicolas Baudin, p. 495.
3 Quoted by Horner, The French Reconnaissance, p. 292.
4 Lamarck, Histoire naturelle des animaux sans vertèbres, tome v, p. 548.
5 Péron [and Freycinet], Voyage, tome ii, p. 238 (Cornell trans., p. 161).
6 Holotype, Muséum national d'histoire naturelle, Paris, MNHP 7711.
7 Duméril, 'Prodrome général de la classification des serpents', p. 522.
8 Péron [and Freycinet], Voyage, tome ii, p. 239 (Cornell trans., p. 161).
9 Edgar, Australian Marine Life, p. 19.
10 See Freycinet's note in Péron [and Freycinet], Voyage, 1824 edition, tome iii, p. 348 (Cornell trans., appendix G, p. 173).
11 Charles Darwin wrote, 'Peron, the distinguished naturalist in the Voyage aux Terres Australes, gives no less than twelve references to discoloured waters of the sea'; see The Voyage of the 'Beagle', chapter 1, footnote p. 16.
12 Péron [and Freycinet], Voyage, tome ii, p. 241 (Cornell trans., p. 162).
13 ibid., p. 245 (Cornell trans., p. 165).
14 Baudin, op. cit., p. 539.
15 Péron [and Freycinet], Voyage, tome ii, p. 248 (Cornell translation, p. 167).
16 See Macknight, The Voyage to Marege.
17 Péron [and Freycinet], Voyage, tome ii, p. 248 (Cornell trans., p. 168).
18 ibid.
19 At this stage of the voyage Baudin interrupted his journal and did not resume it until his departure from Timor.
20 Péron [and Freycinet], Voyage, tome ii, p. 256 (Cornell trans., p. 176).
21 ibid., p. 257 (Cornell trans., p. 177).
22 ibid., p. 260 (Cornell trans., p. 178).

23 Lombard-Jourdan, 'François Péron et Charles Lesueur à Timor: Une chasse au crocodile en 1803'.

24 Passir-Pandjang = long beach.

25 Kelapa Lima = five coconut palms.

26 Oesapa-Ketjil = Little Oesapa.

27 Oesapa-Besar = Great Oesapa.

28 Péron [and Freycinet], *Voyage*, tome ii, p. 269 (Cornell trans., p. 181).

29 ibid.

30 ibid., p. 270 (Cornell trans., p. 182).

31 ibid., p. 271 (Cornell trans., p. 183).

32 Set on the banks of the Nile, Boucher's painting was originally commissioned by
Louis XV and is now in the Musée de Picardie in Amiens.

33 Péron [and Freycinet], *Voyage*, tome ii, p. 275 (Cornell trans., p. 185).

34 Trompf, 'Crocodillians and humans: Mythology, religion, art and literature'; see also
Lombard-Jourdan, op. cit.

35 J. N. Laurenti, *Specimen medicum, exhibens synopsin Reptilium emendatam cum experimentis
circa venena et antidota Reptilium Austriacorum*, Viennæ, 1768; only recently had Europeans
come to realise that the crocodile had a prominent place in ancient Egyptian religion
and mythology. Images of the crocodile-headed god Sobek (such as at the temple at
Isna) were drawn by Dominique Vivant Denon during Bonaparte's Egyptian expedition and would soon be published in the first volume of the *Description de l'Egypte*
(1809; plate 82).

36 In the second volume of his *Historiae Amphibiorum naturalis et literariae* (Jena, 1801).

37 Cuvier, 'Observations sur l'ostéologie des crocodiles vivans'.

38 Ronsard, Journal, Archives nationales, Paris, Marine 5JJ 30.

39 Santos, *Apontamentos para o estudo da flora de Macau e de Timor*, p. 43.

40 Péron [and Freycinet], *Voyage*, 1824 edition, tome iii, p. 418 (Cornell trans., p. 194).

41 Diluted solutions of cantharides were also taken as a diuretic and to treat impotence.
The irritation of the intestinal and genito-urinary tracts sometimes resulted in kidney
failure and other fatal consequences.

42 Péron and Lesueur, 'Des caractères génériques et spécifiques de toutes les espèces
de Méduses connues jusqu'à ce jour'; see also Kramp, 'Synopsis of the Medusae of the
world'.

43 Goy, *Les Méduses de Péron et Lesueur: Un autre regard sur l'expédition Baudin*, pp. 186–9.

44 Baudin, op. cit., p. 552.

45 ibid., p. 554.

46 ibid., p. 560.

47 Péron [and Freycinet], *Voyage*, tome ii, p. 290 (Cornell trans., p. 247).

19. The voyage home

1 Baudin, *The Journal of Post Captain Nicolas Baudin*, p. 560.

2 Freycinet in Péron [and Freycinet], *Voyage*, tome ii, p. 292 (Cornell trans., p. 250).

3 C.-A. Lesueur to his father, Jean-Baptiste Lesueur, 24 thermidor an XI de la
République [12 August 1803], MHNH, Coll. Lesueur, MS 63020.

4 The latter two, however, would return to France on the *Géographe*; see Milius, *Récit
du voyage aux Terres Australes par Pierre Bernard Milius, second sur le 'Naturaliste' dans
l'expédition Baudin (1800–1804)*, transcribed and edited by Bonnemains and Hauguel,
p. 53.

[5] See Jean-Baptiste Chanvalon (Ordonnateur-général, Ile de France) to the Minister of Marine, 21 fructior an 11 [8 September 1803], Archives nationales, Paris, Marine BB[4] 996, dossier 3, folio 59 recto & verso; see also Duyker, 'Depuch Monbuton, Louis (c. 1774–1803)'.

[6] The Kerivel home was near the powder magazine (the present St James Cathedral) in Port Louis. Jacques Gérard Milbert (1766–1840) published two sketches of the house and environs of Madame 'Querivel' (sic) as plates 33 and 34 of the magnificent atlas of his Voyage pittoresque à l'Ile de France, au Cap de Bonne Espérance et à l'Ile de Ténériffe (Paris, 1812). He wrote: 'It is in this house that our commander, M. Baudin, ended his career shortly after his return from the South Lands.'

[7] Duyker, 'In search of Madame Kerivel and Baudin's last resting place'.

[8] Charles Baudin quoted by Horner, The French Reconnaissance, p. 317.

[9] ibid.

[10] The Mauritian historian Auguste Toussaint believed Baudin was interred in the Kerivel family vault in Port Louis's Cimitière de l'Ouest, but perhaps the Genève family vault is a better bet, since Alexandrine (née Genève de St Jean) had two influential brothers on the island.

[11] In his private journal Matthew Flinders, who soon after was a prisoner of war at the Ile de France, records being visited in confinement by the younger Baudin and being asked his advice on the 'propriety of taking a young woman to India whom his brother had brought hither from Port Jackson'. Flinders neither recorded his advice nor the fate of the unfortunate younger Beckwith, who was by then eighteen years old. Thereafter she disappears from the historical record; see Brown, 'The captain and the convict maid: A chapter in the life of Nicolas Baudin', and Duyker, 'Beckwith, Mary (c. 1786—c. 1804)'.

[12] Toussaint, Early American Trade with Mauritius, p. 78.

[13] Péron mistakenly described Robertson as an English captain when he was in fact a surgeon who had worked for the British East India Company in Bengal. Flinders described him as 'a well-informed good man'.

[14] See Estensen, The Life of Matthew Flinders, pp. 341, 356.

[15] For a convincing dismissal of these accusations, we can do no better than turn to Ernest Scott who, in 1910, wrote: 'A critical examination of Freycinet's charts is alone sufficient to shatter the opinion that he utilised the drawings of the English navigator. Had he even seen them, his own work would have been more accurate than it was, and his large chart of New Holland would have been more complete … Freycinet's charts reveal not the faintest trace of the fresh discoveries which Flinders had achieved around east and north-east Australia, nor do they in any particular indicate that their manifold serious imperfections had been corrected by reference to Flinders' superb charts'; see Scott, Terre Napoléon, pp. 100–1.

[16] Péron, 'Souvenirs des diverses époques de ma vie', MHNH, Coll. Lesueur, MS 15031.

[17] Péron [and Freycinet], Voyage, tome ii, p. 296 (Cornell trans., p. 252).

[18] 'Diarium Zoographicum, no. XIII—Insula Franciae à 28 thermidoris an XIe ad usque 24 Frimarii an XIIe [15 August 1803–15 December 1803]', MHNH, Coll. Lesueur, MS 15022.

[19] Roux and Bonnemains, 'Les poissons du "Voyage de découvertes aux Terres Australes" (1800–1804) étudiés par F. Péron et C.-A. Lesueur: Collections iconographiques des dessins de C.-A. Lesueur du Museum d'histoire naturelle du Havre'.

[20] Bonnemains and Jones, 'Les crustacés de la collection C. A. Lesueur (dessins et manuscrits)'.

21 Holthuis, 'The scyllarid lobsters (Crustacea: Decapoda: Palinuridea) collected by F. Péron and C.-A. Lesueur during the 1800–1804 expedition to Australia'.

22 Jangoux, 'Les Astérides (Echinodermes) des Terres Australes ramenés par l'expédition Baudin (1800–1804): Catalogue commenté des dessins inedits de Charles-Alexandre Lesueur conservés au Muséum d'histoire naturelle du Havre'.

23 See, for example, Céré to Péron, 11 frimaire an 12 [3 December 1803], MHNH, Coll. Lesueur, MS 2632.

24 Rey, *Répertoire bibliographique des travaux des médecins et des pharmaciens de la marine française, 1698-1873*, and d'Unienville, *Histoire politique de l'Isle de France (1795–1803)*, p. 114.

25 Recensements, 24 September 1803, Mauritius Archives, KK2.

26 Guillemeau is later said to have attempted to visit his imprisoned idol during a stop at St Helena, on his way back to the Ile de France from France, in early 1816; see Foucart, *Le dernier des Guillemeau, esquisse biographique*, p. 12; see also Duyker and d'Unienville, 'Guillemeau, Jean-François (1772–1860)'.

27 d'Unienville, *Histoire Politique de l'Isle de France (1795–1803)*, p. 143.

28 Lesueur, 'Ile de France—escale du retour', MNHN, Coll. Lesueur, MS 15034.

29 'Expédition française de découvertes' [document in Lesueur's hand addressed to the administrators of the Ile de France and drafted by François Péron, see MNHN, Coll. Lesueur MS 15034] signed by Faure, Ransonnet, Boulanger, Freycinet, Bonnefoy, Lesueur, Péron, L'Haridon and Petit; MNHN, Coll. Lesueur, MS 15039.

30 Fleurieu, A., 'Recherches faites au Havre dans les papiers de Lesueur du 29 au 31 décembre 1910', MS A 567, Mitchell Library, Sydney.

31 Although Decaen's papers, preserved in Caen, are quite extensive, he never finished his memoirs, and thirty-eight years after his death many of his other personal papers were lost when his house in Montmorency was ransacked during the Franco-Prussian War; see Estensen, op. cit., p. 418.

32 Péron, 'Personnes recommandables de l'île de France', MNHN, Coll. Lesueur, MS 15032 (no. 1392).

33 Péron, report to General Charles-Mathieu-Isidore Decaen on the colonisation of New Holland, Port-Nord-Ouest, Ile de France, dated 20 frimaire 12 [12 December 1803], Archives du général Decaen, Bibliothèque municipale, Caen, vol. 92, folio 2, 14 pages recto-verso.

34 Reeth, *Nicolas Baudin et le Voyage aux Terres Australes (1800–1804)*, part iv, chapter iii.

35 Horner, op. cit. p. 116.

36 Quoted by Horner, op. cit., p. 136.

37 Péron, report to General Charles-Mathieu-Isidore Decaen, op. cit.

38 ibid.

39 Scott, op. cit., pp. 115–16.

40 Frost, *Convicts and Empire*, pp. 112–16.

41 Toussaint, 'Bergsten, Nils (1769–1852)'.

42 Estensen, op. cit., pp. 420–1.

43 Prentout, *L'Ile de France sous Decaen, 1803–1810*, p. 382.

44 Duyker and d'Unienville, 'Faure, Pierre Ange François Xavier (1776–1855)'.

45 Linois's order, dated 6 vendémiaire an 12 [29 September 1803] is included in Milius' journal; see Milius, op. cit. (Bonnemains and Hauguel ed.), p. 51.

46 Péron [and Freycinet], *Voyage*, tome ii, pp. 296–7 (Cornell trans., p. 253).

47 Péron and Lesueur, 'Observations sur le Tablier des Femmes Hottentotes, avec une note sur l'expédition française aux Terres Australes, et une étude critique sur la

Stéatopygie et le Tablier des femmes Boschimanes, par le Dr. Raphaël Blanchard', p. 16.

48 ibid., p. 19.

49 Péron, 'Vaccine: Son introduction au Cap Bonne-Espérance—Mémoire par Péron', MHNH, Coll. Lesueur, MS 19001. Although the manuscript has survived and is annotated 'Bulletin—Comité de vaccine', it is not known whether it was published, because reports and opinions on vaccination appeared in a wide rage of publications. They not only appeared in the principal medical journals (the *Recueil périodique de la Société de médicine* and the *Journal de médecine, chirirgie, pharmacie*), they also appeared in the two daily newspapers, the *Moniteur universel* and the *Journal de Paris*, and other published journals such as the *Magasin encyclopédique, Journal de Galvanisme, La Décade philosophique, Mercure de France, La Clef du Cabinet des Souverains* and *Mémoires de l'Institut national des sciences et arts*.

50 These were a gift for Mme Bonaparte's menagerie; see Milius, op. cit. (Bonnemains and Hauguel ed.), pp. 57–8; see also Geoffroy Saint-Hilaire, 'Note sur les animaux vivans venus à bord du *Géographe*'.

51 Péron [and Freycinet], *Voyage*, tome ii, pp. 293–4 (Cornell trans., p. 251).

20. Back in France

1 Intimating that Baudin had threatened the integrity of the natural history collections and perhaps even intended to sell part of it when he unloaded it at the Ile de France.

2 Péron to the Minister of Marine, 4 germinal an 12 [25 March 1804], Archives nationales, Marine BB⁴ 996, dossier 2, folios 37–38 recto and verso.

3 ibid.

4 Antoine Thévenard to the Minister of Marine, 6 germinal an 12 [27 March 1804], Archives nationales, Marine BB⁴ 996, dossier 3.

5 Péron's letter to the minister of 4 germinal an 12 [25 March 1804] is annotated with the date of his departure as reported by Thévenard.

6 Antoine Thévenard to the Minister of Marine, 16, 18 and 20 germinal an 12, Archives nationales, Marine BB⁴ 996, dossier 3; see also Geoffroy Saint-Hilaire, 'Note sur les animaux vivans venus à bord du *Géographe*'.

7 Milbert, *Voyage pittoresque à l'Ile-de-France, au Cap de Bonne-Espérance, et à l'ile de Ténériffe*, vol. ii, p. 36.

8 Antoine Thévenard to the Minister of Marine, 4 Germinal an 12 [25 March 1804], Archives nationales, Marine BB⁴ 996.

9 Péron to the Minister of Marine, 18 germinal an 12 [8 April 1804], Archives nationales, Marine BB⁴ 997 dossier 1, folio 44 recto.

10 Péron had urged this in a draft letter to the professors of the Muséum, MHNH, Coll. Lesueur, MS 22052.

11 Comité du Muséum, Séance du 15 messidor an douze [4 July 1804]; general report drafted by Jussieu, signed by Fourcroy, Vauquelin, Haüy, Desfontaines, Lamarck, Geoffroy Saint-Hilaire, Lacépède, van Spaendonck, Jussieu, Cuvier and Thouin; Archives nationales, Paris, AJ¹⁵ 106.

12 ibid.

13 See Decrès' marginal notes on the report, Archives nationales, Marine BB⁴ 995, dossier 2, folio 103.

14 Mirbel is mentioned in a number of Péron's letters, including one to the Freycinet brothers, in which he describes him as 'my friend'; see copy of a letter from Péron to

one of the Freycinet brothers, *c.* 1804, without postal address, original in the possession of Baron de Freycinet, Aubanais, Charente; MHNH, Coll. Lesueur, MS 22072.

[15] [Draft] Letter from Péron to Mme Bonaparte, 25? floréal an 12, MHNH, Coll. Lesueur, MS 22054.

[16] Péron, 'Inventaire général de tous les objets relatifs à l'histoire de l'homme recueillis pendant le cours de l'expédition ou remis à M. Péron, naturaliste zoologiste du Gouvernement dans cette expédition, et présentés par M. Geoffroy et lui à Sa Majesté l'Impératrice Joséphine le 9 prairial an XII'; see also Hamy, 'Les collections anthro-pologiques et ethnologiques du voyage de découvertes aux Terres Australes (1801–1804)'.

[17] [Draft] Letter from Péron to Mme Bonaparte, 25? floréal an 12, op. cit.

[18] [Draft] Letter from Péron and Lesueur to the Empress Joséphine, no date, MHNH, Coll. Lesueur, MS 22066.

[19] Letter from André Thouin, Secretary of the Administrative Assembly of the Professors of the Muséum national d'histoire naturelle, to Péron, 25 Thermidor an 12, MHNH, Coll. Lesueur, MS 21130.

[20] Girard, *F. Péron*, p. 263.

[21] This stipulation is surprising, since Péron had already declared that he had submitted all his collections, including private collections, to the Muséum.

[22] Complete text quoted by C. H. Dufour, in *Opuscule sur la statistique proprement dite et l'histoire de l'Art dans le département de l'Allier à partir de 1790*, pp. 8–9; also quoted by Audiat in *F. Péron (de Cérilly)*, pp. 101–3.

[23] The author visited the Lycée de Moulins in the company of Dr Françoise Debard on 15 November 2002 and surveyed the presumed remnants of Péron's collection.

[24] Audiat, *F. Péron*, p. 98.

[25] Péron, 'Mémoire sur le nouveau genre *Pyrosoma*'.

[26] Péron, 'Notice d'un mémoire sur les animaux observés pendant la traversée de Timor au Cap Sud de la Terre de Van Diemen'.

[27] Péron, 'Mémoire sur quelques faits zoologiques applicables à la théorie du globe, lu à la Classe des Sciences physiques et mathématiques de l'Institut national (Séance du 30 vendémiaire an XIII)'.

[28] Péron, 'Sur la température de la mer soit à sa surface, soit à diverses profondeurs'.

[29] Péron, 'Observations sur la dyssenterie des pays chauds et sur l'usage du bétel'.

[30] Péron, 'Mémoire sur le nouveau genre *Pyrosoma*', p. 439.

[31] ibid., p. 440.

[32] Lamarck, 'Considérations sur quelques faits applicables à la théorie du globe, observés par M. Péron dans son voyage aux Terres Australes, et sur quelques questions géologiques qui naissent de la connaissance de ces faits'.

[33] *Magasin encyclopédique*, tome iii, 1805, p. 195.

[34] Dumont, 'Lettre à M. Millin, sur le Tablier des Femmes hottentotes', p. 84.

[35] Péron, 'Reponse de M. Péron, naturaliste de l'expédition de découvertes aux Terres Australes aux observations critique de M. Dumont sur le tablier des femmes Hottentotes'.

[36] Saartjie Baartman was a Khoisan woman who arrived in London from South Africa in 1810 at the age of twenty as virtually a slave. She died five years later in France (probably of syphilis and tuberculosis) after being exhibited like a circus animal and studied as a curious representative of black African womanhood. Her genitalia and brain were displayed at the Musée de l'Homme in Paris until as recently as 1985, but were returned to South Africa in 2002; see McGeal, 'Homeward bound'; see also Le

Garrec, 'Rapport fait au nom de la Commission des Affaires Culturelles, Familiales et Sociales sur la Proposition de loi, adoptée par le Senat, relative à la restitution par la France de la dépouille mortelle de Saartje Baartman à l'Afrique de Sud'.

[37] Péron wrote an excited letter, copying and including the text of the minister's letter, to Lesueur's father, Jean-Baptiste Lesueur [c. October 1804], MHNH, Coll. Lesueur, MS 63026.

[38] Copy of a letter from Péron to Messrs Freycinet frères, Commandant les corvettes Le Phaëton et Le Voltigeur ..., Anvers [Antwerp], annotated 'Paris, Nivose an 13, 15 janvier [1805]', original in the possession of Baron de Freycinet, Aubanais, Charente; MHNH, Coll. Lesueur, MS 22071.

[39] Duyker, 'Petit, Nicolas Martin (1777–1804)'.

[40] For a detailed survey of Péron's membership of scientific societies, see Debard, op. cit., pp. 135–42.

[41] Although the veracity of this portrait has been questioned, this was mainly because of the misreading of the stylised typography of Cless's name and the belief that Péron lost an eye, rather than the sight in an eye, during his military service. Nevertheless, the general facial proportions are very similar to the portrait Lesueur would complete shortly before his friend's death. This, too, shows a consistent nose, zygomatic bones and cheek creases, so much so that two anatomists consulted by this author, Dr Carl Stephan and Professor Maciej Henneberg of the University of Adelaide, asserted that there was an 80 per cent probability that they were of the same man, despite being the work of two different artists and despite the emaciation depicted in Lesueur's 1810 portrait; pers. comm., 25 June 2004.

[42] This is implied by Péron's letter to the Minister of Marine in June? 1806; see BB⁴ 996, dossier 1, folio 87.

[43] Furthermore, the report was approved by Laplace, Bougainville, Fleurieu and Lacépède.

[44] Cuvier, 'Rapport fait au gouvernement par l'Institut impérial, sur le voyage de découvertes aux Terres Australes: Extrait du Procès-verbal de la Classes des Sciences physiques et mathématiques, séance du lundi 9 juin 1806', in Péron's Voyage, tome i, pp. i–xv (Phillips trans., pp. iii–viii).

[45] Extrait du décret Impérial, rendu au Palais de Saint Cloud le 4 Août 1806, MHNH, Coll. Lesueur, MS 22069-1.

[46] Jean-Marie Degérando to François Péron, 18 Xbre 1806, MHNH, Coll. Lesueur, MS 23010.

[47] Horner, The French Reconnaissance, p. 333.

[48] Toussaint, Port Louis: A Tropical City, pp. 59–60.

[49] Toussaint, Histoire des iles Mascareignes, p. 136.

[50] Even an anonymous British reviewer of volume 1 of the Voyage (thought to have been John Barrow, Secretary to the Admiralty) believed Péron was not independently responsible for the political claims of his book: '... he must have been betrayed by superior influence. Of M. Péron, as a man of general science, we are disposed to think highly; but we repeat, that in the publication of the work before us, we do not and cannot consider him as a free agent. It is brought forward, in the first place, under the immediate sanction of Buonaparte, in consequence of a report of the Imperial Institute'; see Quarterly Review, vol. iv, August 1810, p. 44.

[51] Malte-Brun, C., 'Mémoire sur la découverte de la côte sud-ouest de la Nouvelle-Hollande, ou de la Terre Flinders, de la Terre Napoléon, et de la Terre Grant', p. 289.

52 Freycinet's preface, in Péron [and Freycinet], *Voyage*, tome ii, p. viii.

53 Péron, op. cit., tome i, p. 263 (Phillips trans., p. 205).

54 I must admit to the profound influence of Pieter Geyl on this point. In the preface to the first Dutch edition of his masterly *Napoleon: For and Against*, drafted seven months before the Netherlands was liberated from Nazi tyranny, Geyl wrote: 'He [Napoleon] was a dictator who attempted to break with new legislation what resistance was left in the old society; who intensified his power in the State by means of a centralised administration; who suppressed not only all organised influence or control and expression of opinion, but free thought itself; who hated the intellect, and who entered upon a struggle with the Church which he had first attempted to enslave; and who thought that with censorship, police and propaganda he would be able to fashion the mind to his wish. He was a conqueror with whom it was impossible to live; who could not help turning an ally into a vassal, or at least interpreting the relationship to his own exclusive advantage; who decorated his lust of conquest with the fine-sounding phrases of progress and civilisation; and who at last, in the name of the whole of Europe, which was to look to him for order and peace, presumed to brand England as the universal disturber and enemy.' See Geyl, *Napoleon: For and Against*, pp. 8–9.

55 Hahn, *The Anatomy of a Scientific Institution*, p. 311.

56 See my review of this press coverage in Duyker, *Nature's Argonaut*, pp. 220–1.

21. Final years

1 Jacques-Joseph Ransonnet to Péron, Paris, 1 May [1804?], MHNH, Coll. Lesueur, MS 09029.

2 Marvillet, Le Caer et al., *Nomenclature officielle des voies publiques et privées*, p. 578.

3 Bonnemains, 'The history of the Lesueur Collection of the Muséum d'Histoire Naturelle du Havre'; see in particular p. 66 and footnote 21; Bonnemains cites MHNH, Coll. Lesueur, MS 64004.

4 Her late husband, Joseph Coupery, whom she married on 31 October 1798, was a saddler; Archives départementales de l'Allier, Yzeure, 2E 44/8.

5 Actes, notaire François Thibault de Beauregard: no. 266, 'Inventaire des effets de la communauté Coupery du 18 juillet 1806'; no. 278, 'Ventes des effets de la succession des effets de Joseph Coupery, des 7, 8, 10 août 1806'; no. 285, 'Liquidation … succession Coupery du 14 août 1806'; Archives départementales de l'Allier, Yzeure, 3E 11570.

6 Deleuze, 'Notice Historique sur M. Péron', p. 277.

7 Rosalie Péron femme Coupery to C.-A. Lesueur, rue St Etienne du Mont no. 16—Paris, 2 February 1839, MHNH, Coll. Lesueur, MS 63106.

8 'Fratrie de François Péron', appendix 2 of Françoise Debard's thesis, 'François Péron (1775–1810), zoologiste du voyage de découvertes aux Terres Australes …', p. 328.

9 Deleuze, op. cit., p. 277.

10 Biographie anonyme de Péron, Bibliothèque centrale du Muséum national d'histoire naturelle, Paris, MS 2528, folio 124.

11 Girard, F. *Péron, naturaliste, voyageur aux Terres Australes*, p. 51.

12 Deleuze, op. cit., p. 277.

13 Alard, 'Eloge historique de François Péron, Rédacteur du voyage de découvertes aux Terres Australes', pp. lxxij, lxxviij.

14 Anon., 'Intérieur', *Le Moniteur universel*, no. 13, mercredi, 13 Janvier 1808, p. 1.

[15] See Cleland, 'Remarkable mistranslations in the English version (1809) of Peron's Voyage of Discovery'.

[16] Quoted by Cornillon, in 'Comment le naturaliste François Péron de Cérilly fit la connaissance de Henri Dufour, artiste à Moulins et devint son ami', p. 17.

[17] Quoted by Deleuze, op. cit., p. 272.

[18] Aimé Bonpland to François Péron, Thursday, 17 November [1808], MS Cayrol, no. 617, folio 2, Bibliothèque de La Rochelle, published in Hamy, Aimé Bonpland, p. 20.

[19] Napoleon is reputed to have said, 'I do not believe in medicine, but I do believe in Corvisart.'

[20] The Austrian Leopold von Auenbrugg (1722–1809) first proposed chest percussion as a diagnostic aid in 1761. His method and his book, Inventum Novum, were both championed by Corvisart in France.

[21] A Cape Keraudren and Keraudren Island in Western Australia and Cape Keraudren on Hunter Island in Bass Strait are named after him.

[22] See Bonnemains, 'Charles-Alexandre Lesueur dans le Var en 1809'.

[23] Lesueur, 'Journal-Historique des expériences faites à Nice sur la température de la mer, par Péron et Lesueur, en 1809', MHNH, Coll. Lesueur, MS 10040, folio 1.

[24] Maury, 'Les œuvres mineurs de C.-A. Lesueur, voyageur et peintre naturaliste havrais (1778–1846): du Havre à Nice par la Vallée du Rhône', p. 9.

[25] Freycinet was accompanied by his wife Rose; for an English translation of her account, see Rivière (ed., trans.), A Woman of Courage.

[26] Louis de Freycinet's grave is the third from the gate on the right.

[27] Freycinet senior to Henry de Freycinet, 5 February 1809 [transcription by M. Jangoux, 1999, from the Archives Freycinet, carton 5; série 239], MHNH, Coll. Lesueur, MS 63046P.

[28] Elisabeth de Freycinet to Henry de Freycinet, 17 February 1809 [transcription by M. Jangoux, 1999, from the Archives Freycinet, carton 5; série 239], MHNH, Coll. Lesueur, MS 63047P.

[29] ibid.

[30] This concept was also accepted by Buffon and Fourcroy; see Adams, The Birth and Development of the Geological Sciences, pp. 245, 296.

[31] Tertian, Orgon, p. 172.

[32] Cane, Histoire de Villefranche-sur-Mer …, p. 76.

[33] See Tracou and Richard, Villefranche-sur-Mer: La Rade Etincelante.

[34] Goy, Les Méduses de Péron et Lesueur: Un autre regard sur l'expédition Baudin, pp. 288, 297, 355; Goy and Breton, 'Les Méduses de François Péron et Charles-Alexandre Lesueur (1775–1810 et 1778–1846) révélees par les vélins de Lesueur', p. 75; Kramp, 'Synopsis of the medusae of the world', pp. 85, 191, 251. Similarly their Oceania viridula, found in the English Channel, and their Oceania gibbosa, found at Nice, are considered to be the same species and have been included in the genus Eirene with their specific designation viridula; see Bonnemains, Bustaret and Breton, 'Etude codicologique des manuscrits et dessins de méduses (1800–1810) de François Péron et Charles-Alexandre Lesueur', p. 20.

[35] Péron and Lesueur, 'Tableau des caractères génériques et spécifiques de toutes les espèces de Méduses connues jusqu'à ce jour'. This appeared in vol. 14 of the Annales du Muséum national d'histoire naturelle with the imprint date 1809, but Jacqueline Goy has established that the actual publication date was in 1810.

36 See Goy, *Les Méduses de Péron et Lesueur*. Nevertheless, this was not without contro-
    versy; see also Bonnemains and Breton, 'A propos de l'ouvrage: "Les méduses de Péron
    et Lesueur, un autre regard sur l'expédition Baudin" par Jacqueline Goy'.
37 Goy, op. cit., p. 201.
38 Lesueur, 'Journal-Historique des expériences faites à Nice sur la température de la
    mer, par Péron et Lesueur, en 1809', op. cit.
39 For a discussion of Lesueur's sketches 75026, 65030, 65032 and 65087 in Le Havre,
    see Bonnemains and Branconnot, 'Les tunciers pélagiques: Salpes et pyrosomes étudiés
    par François Péron et Charles-Alexandre Lesueur au début du XIXe siècle'; for a dis-
    cussion of a pencil sketch entitled 'Protomedia uniformis', dated Nice, 24 March
    (MS 1734, no. 908, Muséum national d'histoire naturelle, Paris), which has been iden-
    tified as *Hippopodius hippopus*, originally described by Forsskål in 1776, see Bonnemains
    and Carré, 'Siphonophores et vélelles observés par F. Péron et C.-A. Lesueur au début
    du 19e siècle', p. 61.
40 For an index of these authors and the manuscripts in which they are cited, see Bonne-
    mains and Carré, 'Siphonophores et vélelles observés par F. Péron et C.-A. Lesueur au
    début du 19e siècle', p. 41.
41 See for example, Péron, 'Histoire du genre Vélelle et des 10 espèces de méduses que
    nous rapportons à ce genre', MHNH, Coll. Lesueur, MS 68261; Péron, 'Histoire du
    genre Vélelle—Historique', MHNH, Coll. Lesueur, MS 68309, and an untitled frag-
    ment of a draft (MHNH, Coll. Lesueur, MS 68310) dealing with five Mediterranean
    species of velellids, several others from the Atlantic and one from Tasmanian waters.
42 [Pierre] Marcel de Serres to Péron, Montpellier, 7 March 1809, MHNH, Coll.
    Lesueur, MS 68308.
43 Lesueur, C.-A., 'Mémoire sur quelques nouvelles espèces d'animaux Mollusques et
    Radiaires, recueillis dans la Méditerranée, près de Nice'.
44 Jacqueline Bonnemains in her article 'Charles-Alexandre Lesueur dans le Var en 1809'
    draws attention to the covering note for the manuscript chapter sent to the minister,
    MNHH, Coll. Lesueur, MS 23132.
45 The text of Péron's undated letter to Louis de Freycinet appears as a footnote in
    Alard's 'Eloge historique de François Péron', p. lxxiv.
46 Deacon, *Oceans*, p. 178.
47 Deacon, *Scientists and the Sea 1650–1900*, p. 205.
48 Lesueur, 'Journal-Historique des expériences faites à Nice sur la température de la
    mer, par Péron et Lesueur, en 1809', op. cit.; according to Bonnemains, for the results
    of this particular experiment, see MNHH, Coll. Lesueur, MS 10042.
49 Lesueur, 'Journal-Historique des expériences faites à Nice sur la température de la
    mer, par Péron et Lesueur, en 1809', op. cit.
50 The whaling captain William Scoresby the younger, a correspondent of Sir Joseph
    Banks, conducted measuring experiments in the Arctic between 1813 and 1817 on
    his vessel, the *Esk*. The measurement of seawater temperatures was also an important
    element of the global *Challenger* expedition (1872–76) and Fridtjof Nansen's *Fram*
    polar expedition (1893–96); see Deacon, *Scientists and the Sea 1650–1900*.
51 A sketch by Lesueur, dated Cérilly, 22 August 1809, indicates that they visited Péron's
    hometown on their way back to Paris.
52 Péron and Lesueur, 'La conservation des diverses espèces d'animation dans l'alcool'.
53 Péron and Lesueur, 'Histoire de la famille des Molluques Ptéropodes'.
54 Péron and Lesueur, 'Histoire du genre Firole: Firola'.

55   Péron and Lesueur, 'Notice sur l'habitation des animaux marins' and Péron and Lesueur, 'Notice sur l'habitation des phoques'.

56   Deleuze, op. cit., p. 278.

57   Meachen, *History of Tuberculosis*, p. 7.

58   Piery and Roshem, *Histoire de la tuberculose*, p. 250, and Meachen, op. cit., p. 9.

59   Quoted by Meachen, op. cit., p. 15.

60   ibid., p. 4; there is a certain irony that tuberculosis in its bovine form, which generally affects the bones and joints of humans, is contracted through infected milk.

61   See Read, *Essai sur les effets salutaires du séjour des étables dans la phtisie*.

62   Sainte-Marie, *Thèse sur le traitement de la phtisie*, Montpellier, 1804, quoted by Grellet and Kruse, *Histoire de la tuberculose: Les fièvres de l'âme 1800–1940*, p. 43.

63   Grellet and Kruse, op. cit., p. 43.

64   Audiat, *F. Péron*, p. 89.

65   Respectively the present place Marx-Dormoy and rue Joseph Dupechot; see Perchat, 'Où était l'étable de Jean-Gilbert Bonnet?'

66   Acte de décès d'Anne-Sophie née Petitjean, 30 août 1804, Archives départementales de l'Allier 2E/44/13.

67   Alard, op. cit., p. 279; see also Acte de décès de François Péron, Archives municipales, Cérilly.

22. Epilogue

1   Quoted by Bonnemains in 'The History of the Lesueur Collection of the Muséum d'Histoire naturelle du Havre', p. 66.

2   Receipt for 200 francs signed by Lambert (engraver), addressed to Lesueur, for the engraving of the portrait of Péron, 13 April 1811, MHNH, Coll. Lesueur, MS 06111; see also Lambert to Lesueur, 12 June 1811, demanding another 100 francs, MHNH, Coll. Lesueur, MS 06113.

3   Deleuze, op. cit., footnote, p. lxxix.

4   Quoted by Bonnemains, op. cit., p. 67.

5   Deleuze, 'Notice historique sur M. Péron', footnote, p. lxxx.

6   Debard, *François Péron (1775–1810), Zoologiste du Voyage de découvertes aux Terre Australes …*, pp. 175–6.

7   Receipt for 260 francs signed by Dubray (printer), addressed to Lesueur, for the printing of 300 elegies for Péron, 26 July 1811, MHNH, Coll. Lesueur, MS 06112, and invoice (132 francs), Imprimerie Delance et Belin, addressed to Lesueur, dated 10 September 1811, for the printing of 300 copies of the 'Notice historique de F. Péron', by Deleuze, MHNH, Coll. Lesueur, MS 24002.

8   See Bonnemains, 'Biography of Charles-Alexandre Lesueur'.

9   Rosalie Péron femme Coupery to C.-A. Lesueur, 2 February 1839, MHNH, Coll. Lesueur, MS 63106.

10   'Liste générale des souscripteurs au projet d'élever un monument funéraire à la mémoire de François Péron, naturaliste, voyageur, né à Cérilly, département de l'Allier', copy of an original in the Archives départementales de l'Allier, MHNH, Coll. Lesueur, MS 06125P.

11   Debard, op. cit., pp. 175–6.

12   Paul Petitjean, juge de paix du canton de Cérilly, to C.-A. Lesueur, 29 April 1842, MHNH, Coll. Lesueur, MS 63116; see also Emile de Rochefort to C.-A. Lesueur,

1 January 1839 and 12 January 1839, MHNH, Coll. Lesueur, MS 63104 and MS 63105.

13 Debard, op. cit., p. 176; a century after it was erected, the collaborationist regime in Vichy despoiled Péron's monument of its bronze bust for the fascist war effort. In 1955, when the monument and Péron's remains were moved some metres to the west to accommodate a new parking area, a concrete replica of the bust was reinstated. It was eventually replaced with a bronze casting.

14 See C.-A. Lesueur to Madame Laffon, 11 June 1842, MHNH, Coll. Lesueur, MS 63202.

15 Quoted by Bonnemains in 'The History of the Lesueur Collection of the Muséum d'Histoire naturelle du Havre', p. 67, from Lennier, *L'Expédition française aux Terres Australes*, Imprimérie de la Société Zoologique de France, Meulan, 1883, p. 7.

16 Bonnemains, op. cit.

Bibliography

Unpublished sources

AUSTRALIA

Hobart

Tasmanian Museum

Turner, E., 'The D'Entrecasteaux Channel, Terre de Diemen, 13th January–16th February 1802: A comparative marine survey of the voyage by Baudin, by Elizabeth Turner, Tasmanian Museum, Hobart, Tasmania, 20th March and 8th April 2002', typescript.

Sydney

Mitchell Library, State Library of New South Wales

MS A 567, Fleurieu, A., 'Recherches faites au Havre dans les papiers de Lesueur du 29 au 31 décembre 1910'.

FRANCE

Caen

Bibliothèque municipale, Archives du général Decaen

Volume 92, pièce 1, folio 2, 14 pages recto–verso, report from François Péron to General Charles-Mathieu-Isidore Decaen on the colonisation of New Holland, Port-Nord-Ouest, Ile de France, dated 20 frimaire 12 [12 December 1803]; National Library of Australia, Canberra, microfilm Mfm G/2190.

Cérilly

Archives municipales

Acte de décès de François Péron, 14 décembre 1810.

Eglise de Saint-Martin

Joussain, M., 'Notes sur les Curés de Cérilly d'après les recherches de l'abbé Louis Cabbane dans "Historique de la paroisse"', pp. 21, sq., undated typescript.

Le Havre

Muséum d'histoire naturelle du Havre (MHNH), Collection Lesueur

2632, Jean-Nicolas Céré to François Péron, 11 frimaire an 12 [3 December 1803].

06111, receipt for 200 F. signed by Lambert [engraver], addressed to C.-A. Lesueur, for the engraving of the portrait of Péron, 13 April 1811.

06112, receipt for 260 F. signed by Dubray (printer), addressed to C.-A. Lesueur, for the printing of 300 elegies for Péron, 26 July 1811.

06113, Lambert [engraver] to C.-A. Lesueur, 12 June 1811.

06125P, 'Liste générale des souscripteurs au projet d'élever un monument funéraire à la mémoire de François Péron, naturaliste, voyageur, né à Cérilly, département de l'Allier', copy of an original in the Archives départementales de l'Allier.

07006 (A–B), Péron, 'Nuits des tropiques'.

08032, Péron, 'Topographie générale de la petite île de Dorre'.

08034, Riedlé, 'Observations générales sur l'île Stérile faites par le citoyen Riedlé' [in Péron's hand].

08039, Péron, 'Observations sur la Baie du Géographe' [June 1801].

08040, Péron, 'Topographie, aspect général de la baie du Géographe par le citoyen Péron' [June 1801].

09006–08, Péron, observations on the south coast of New Holland [31 March – 1 April 1802].

09014–25, Péron, observations on the south coast of New Holland [7–18 April 1802].

09026, Péron, observations on the south coast of New Holland [21–30 April 1802].

09027, 'Animaux observés–Détroit de Bass'.

09029, Jacques-Joseph Ransonnet to Péron, Paris, 1 May [1804?].

09030, Jacques-Joseph Ransonnet, 7 ventôse [26 February 1803] (notes on a landing at King George Sound).

09032, draft letter by Péron presumably to the professors of the Muséum with observations on New Holland.

10002–1, sketch of the thermometer and container used by Péron to study the temperature of the sea at different depths.

10004, Guyton and Delambre's report on Péron's 'Mémoire sur la température de la mer soit à sa surface, soit à diverses profondeurs'.

10005, Péron and Depuch to Baudin, 8 prairial an IX [28 May 1801]: 'Expérience sur la température du fond de la mer'.

10106, François Etienne L'Haridon-Créménec to Péron [on reading Mémoire sur la phosphorescence].

10040, C.-A. Lesueur, 'Journal-Historique des expériences faites à Nice sur la température de la mer, par Péron et Lesueur, en 1809'.

10100–1, 'Observations sur la phosphorescence des eaux de la mer'.

12001, Péron, 'Mémoire sur les établissements anglais à la Nouvelle Hollande, à la Terre de Diémen et sur les Archipels du Grand Océan Pacifique au Citoyen Fourcroy, Membre du Conseil d'Etat'.

12002, Péron, 'Etat administratif et commercial des colonies anglaises aux Terres Australes'.

12005–1, Péron, 'Tableau général des colonies anglaises aux Terres Australes'.

12006–1, Péron, 'Tableau militaire des colonies anglaises aux Terres Australes'.

12007–1, Péron, 'Voyage de découverte aux Terres Australes: Tableau général des colonies anglaises aux Terres Australes'.

14040, carnet manuscrit de Stanislas Levillain, zoologiste de l'expédition Baudin.

14042, Notes sur les Canaries et particulièrement sur Ténériffe.

14046, François Péron to Jean-Marie Degérando, Secrétaire général du Ministre de l'Intérieur; date unknown.

14047, draft letter by François Péron to a friend [probably Anne-Sophie Petitjean].

15022, 'Diarium Zoographicum, no. XIII—Insula Franciae à 28 thermidoris an XIe ad usque 24 frimarii an XIIe [16 August 1803 to 16 December 1803]. Numerous Latin descriptions and several letters at the end of the notebook, together with 'Noms de personnes que j'ai connues à l'Ile de France'.

15024, 'Chapitre quatrième—séjour à l'île de France', in Péron's hand with text cross by Péron.

15025, notes in Péron's hand: 'Ile de France: maladies (lèpre et maladie des voies urinaires) et nature du sol'.

15026, notes in Péron's hand: 'Ile de France: maladies, nature du sol, végétation'.

15028, notes in Péron's hand: 'Ile de France: végétation, mœurs des habitants' [numbered 10–17 by him, with the previous pages missing]; 'Liste de Végétaux' [with modern botanical nomenclature completed by Dr Guy Rouillard, Curepipe, Mauritius], folios 10 verso and 11 recto.

15030, manuscript François Péron, 2 folios.

15031, carnet, Péron, 'Souvenirs des diverses époques de ma vie'.

15032, carnet, Péron, 'Ile de France', including (Nos 1388–93), 'Personnes recommandables de l'île de France'.

15034, C.-A. Lesueur, 'Ile de France—escale du retour'.

15039, 'Expédition française de découvertes' [document in Lesueur's hand addressed to the administrators of the Ile de France and drafted by François Péron], signed by Faure, Ransonnet, Boulanger, Freycinet, Bonnefoy, Lesueur, Péron, L'Haridon and Petit.

15044, manuscript in François Péron's hand, Port-Louis, Ile de France, 25 ventôse an 9 [16 March 1801].

18040, carnet, Péron, 'Ile Maria—Observations anthropologiques—Ventôse an X [February–March 1802]'.

18041, Carnet, Péron [addressed to 'Citoyen Commandant'] 'Ile Maria, Observations anthropologiques, Ventôse an X [February–March 1802]'; Carnet, Péron, 'Ile Maria—Observations de phisique et d'histoire naturelle—Ventôse an X' [February–March 1802].

18042, Carnet, Péron, 'Ile Maria: suite des observations de phisique et d'histore naturelle.

18043, 'Histoire naturelle. Topographie générale de l'île Maria sur la côte orientale de la Terre de Diemen'.

18044, Carnet, Péron, 'Terre de Diemen—1re vue le 23 nivôse an X [13 January 1802]'.

18045, Péron, 'Notice sur les végétaux de la Nouvelle-Hollande' [actually Van Diemen's Land].

18047, Péron, 'Hommes' [incomplete].

19001, Péron, 'Vaccine: Son introduction au Cap Bonne-Espérance'.

19005, 'Diarium Zoographicum, no. XIV—Caput Bonae Spei è 12 â die Nivosi adusque 3 am Pluviosi an 12 [3 January 1804–24 January 1804]'.

19070, 'Relâche au Cap de Bonne Espérance'.

21002–1, 'Descriptions zoologiques—Tableau général de tous les objets décrit dans les 10 numéros de mon journal zoographique remis au Commandant Baudin en exécution des ordres du ministre de la Marine et des Colonies'; signed Péron.

21003–1, Tableau général d'une partie des espèces observées dans les diverses classes du règne animal par le Citoyen François Péron élève zoologiste attaché à l'expédition française de découvertes commandée par le Citoyen Nicolas Baudin. Cette collection contenant 205 descriptions et 90 dessins qui les accompagnent en conformité des instructions du Ministre de la Marine a été remise par le Citoyen Péron au Citoyen Commandant [blanc] Messidor an 10 de la République; signed: Péron.

20004–3, Nicolas Petit, watercolour, gouache and ink [bust of Arra-Maïda, Van Diemen's Land].

21121, Voyage de Découvertes aux Terres Australes, Exécuté par ordre du Gouvernement sur les Corvettes le Géographe et le Naturaliste, pendant les années 1800, 1801, 1802, 1803 et 1804: Extraits du Décret du Gouvernement, et du Rapport qui lui a été fait, le 9 juin 1806, par la Commission de l'Institut, qui se trouvent également consignés dans la lettre de MM. les Professeurs du Muséum, du 14 juin 1806, sur les richesses en Histoire naturelle déposées au Muséum, à la suite des travaux de MM. Péron et Le Sueur, l'un, médicine naturaliste, correspondant de l'Institut, et l'autre, peintre naturaliste, dessinateur en chef de l'expédition, membre de la Société Phylomatique de Paris, Paris, Imprimerie de A. Belin, 1815.

21130, André Thouin, Secretary of the Administrative Assembly of the Professors of the Muséum national d'histoire naturelle to Péron, 25 thermidor an 12 [13 July 1804].

22002, Rapport fait au gouvernement par l'Institut de France sur le Voyage de Découvertes aux Terres Australes: Extrait du Procès-verbal de la classe des sciences, physiques et mathématiques, séance du lundi 9 juin 1806.

22014–1, 'Copie d'un arrêté du Ministre concernant la publication des résultats zoologiques par souscription' [1805].

22019, 1ère notice sur les travaux que se proposent de publier MM. Péron et Lesueur—Naturalistes de l'expédition de découvertes à la Nouvelle-Hollande [in Péron's hand].

22049, [draft] letter from Péron to the Minister of the Navy, 20 messidor an 12 [9 July 1804].

22052, [draft] letter from Péron to the Professors of the Museum, no date.

22053, [draft] letter from Péron to the Premier Consul Bonaparte, no date.

22054, [draft] letter from Péron to Madame Bonaparte, 25? floréal an 12 [15? May 1804].

22055, [draft] letter from Péron to the Emperor Napoleon, no date.

22059, [draft] letter from Péron to the Emperor Napoleon, no date.

22062–66, [draft] letters from Péron to the Emperor Napoleon, no dates.

22068, Minister of the Interior to Messers Péron and Lesueur, Paris, 9 September 1806.

22071, copy of a letter from Péron to Messers Freycinet frères, commanding the corvettes *Le Phaëton* et *Le Voltigeur* ..., Anvers [Antwerp], annotated 'Paris, Nivôse an 13, 15 janvier [1805]', original in the possession of the Baron de Freycinet, Aubanais, Charente.

22072, copy of a letter from Péron to one of the Freycinet brothers, *c.* 1804, without postal address, original in the possession of the Baron de Freycinet, Aubanais, Charente.

22069–1, Extrait du décret Impérial, rendu au Palais de Saint-Cloud, le 4 août 1806.

23008, draft of a letter from François Péron to 'Monseigneur' [Minister of the Interior, M. Champagny].

23009, [draft response] Péron to M. Degérando, Secretary to the Minister of the Interior, on the subject of corrections to the *Voyage*.

23010, Jean-Marie Degérando to François Péron, 18 Xbre 1806.

23019, Joseph Charles Bailly to François Péron, concerning geological corrections.

24002, invoice (132 F.), Imprimerie Delance et Belin, addressed to Lesueur, dated 10 September 1811, for the printing of 300 copies of the 'Notice historique de F. Péron', by Deleuze.

25003, Laplace, Bougainville, Fleurieu, Lacépède, Cuvier, 'Rapport Fait au Gouvernment par l'Institut de France sur le Voyage de Découvertes aux Terres Australes: Extrait du Procès-Verbal de la Classe des Sciences Physiques et Mathématiques, Séance du lundi 9 juin, 1806'.

35001, Charles-Alexandre Lesueur, sketch of the forest of Tronçais and forges of Rambourg.

35004, Charles-Alexandre Lesueur, sketch *c.* 1810: 'Cérilly où Péron est né et mort'.

35006–1, Charles-Alexandre Lesueur sketch: 'Cérilly étable où est mort mon estimable ami Péron, 14 décembre 1810'.

63020, Charles-Alexandre Lesueur to his father, Jean-Baptiste Lesueur [during his stop at the Ile de France], 24 thermidor an XI de la République [12 August 1803].

63025, Charles-Alexandre Lesueur to his father Jean-Baptiste Lesueur (without address), 19 vendémiaire an XIII [11 October 1804].

63026, letter from Péron to Jean-Baptiste Lesueur [*c.* October 1804].

63027, Charles-Alexandre Lesueur to his father, Jean-Baptiste Lesueur, 19 brumaire an XIII [10 November 1804].

63035, Charles-Alexandre Lesueur to his father, Jean-Baptiste Lesueur, 18 January 1809.

63036, Jean-Baptiste Lesueur to his son Charles-Alexandre Lesueur, Le Havre, 15 February 1809.

63037, Charles-Alexandre Lesueur to members of the Institut, 16 December 1810 [draft, original, Archives nationales, AJ[15] 603, séance du 26 décembre 1810].

63038, letter in Péron's hand: 'Madame …'

63044P, Louis de Freycinet [senior], to his sons, 18 ventôse an 13 [9 March 1805], [transcription by Michel Jangoux, from the Archives Freycinet, carton 9, série 239.

63045P, Elisabeth de Freycinet to her son Henry de Freycinet, capitaine commandant la frégate l'*Elisa* au Havre, Département de Seine inférieure, 17 February 1809, [transcription by Michel Jangoux, from the Archives Freycinet, carton 5, série 239].

63046P, Freycinet senior to Henry de Freycinet, 5 February 1809 [transcription by Michel Jangoux, 1999, from the Archives Freycinet, carton 5; série 239].

63047P, Elisabeth de Freycinet to Henry de Freycinet, 17 February 1809 [transcription by Michel Jangoux, 1999, from the Archives Freycinet, Carton 5; série 239].

63050, Deleuze, Secrétaire de la Société Philomatique to Monsieur Lesueur.

63051, undated letter Duc de Champagny [Minister of External Relations] to Charles-Alexandre Lesueur, at Cérilly, Allier.

63052, Charles-Alexandre Lesueur to an unknown person, Paris, 12 August 1811.

63104, M. Emile de Rochefort to Charles-Alexandre Lesueur, rue St Etienne du Mont no. 16, Paris, 1 January 1839.

63105, M. Emile de Rochefort to Charles-Alexandre Lesueur, rue St Etienne du Mont no. 16, Paris, 12 January 1839.

63106, Rosalie Péron femme Coupery to Charles-Alexandre Lesueur, rue St Etienne du Mont no. 16, Paris, 2 February 1839.

63116, Paul Petitjean, juge de paix du canton de Cérilly, to Charles-Alexandre Lesueur, rue Neuve St Etienne du Mont no. 16, Paris, 29 April 1842.

63202, Charles-Alexandre Lesueur to Madame Laffon, rue Neuve St Etienne du Mont no. 16 à Paris (Seine), 11 June 1842.

65006, carnet, Péron, 'Zoographia Hollandiae-novae marium alluentium illam—No VI—Baie des Chiens—Côtes du Nord-Ouest—Traversée de la N[ouv]elle Hol[lan]de à Timor'.

65007, carnet, Péron, 'Nouvelle-Hollande—Baie du Géographe et Baie des Chiens Marins—No. 2'.

65010, carnet, Péron, 'Zoographiae Hollandiae-novae mariumque alluentium illam–Descriptions zoologiques No. 3—île King—île aux Kanguroos—îles St Pierre et St François—Port du Roi Georges'.

65011, carnet, Péron, 'Zoographiae Hollandiae-novae marium que alluentium illam—Descriptions zoologiques No. 4—îles St Pierre et St François—Port du Roi Georges'.

65012, carnet, Péron, Cap de Bonne-Espérance.

65013, carnet, Péron, 'Zoologie: Animaux observés pendant la traversée de l'île de Timor à la Terre de Diemen du 22 brumaire au 23 Nivôse an X [13 November – 13 January 1802]'.

68261, Péron, 'Histoire du genre Vélelle et des 10 espèces de méduses que nous rapportons à ce genre'.

68308, [Pierre] Marcel de Serres, Montpellier, 7 March 1809, to Péron in Nice.

68309, Péron, 'Histoire du genre Vélelle—Historique'.

68310, fragment of a draft manuscript dealing with five Mediterranean species of velellids, several others from the Atlantic and one from Tasmanian waters.

79058, 'Oiseaux de la Baie du Géographe' [in Lesueur's hand, but thought to be by Péron].

80508, 'Mémoire sur les phoques en général, sur ceux des Régions Australes en particulier et sur les avantages que les Anglais retirent de l'huile et des fourrures de ces derniers. 1ère section: Observations générales sur le genre Phoques'.

Paris

Archives nationales

AJ^{15} 106, Comité du Muséum, Séance du 15 messidor an douze [4 July 1804]; general report drafted by Jussieu, signed by Fourcroy, Vauquelin, Haüy, Desfontaines, Lamarck, Geoffroy Saint-Hilaire, Lacépède, van Spaendonck, Jussieu, Cuvier and Thouin.

AJ^{15} 569, folios 152–3, Antoine-Laurent de Jussieu to the Minister of Marine, 2 thermidor an 6 [20 July 1798].

AJ^{15} 569, folio 335 recto and verso, 'Michaud aux citoyens membres de la Commission nommée pour le voyage scientifique, Paris 24 thermidor an. 6' [11 August 1798].

AJ^{15} 569, pièce 343, undated testimonial (*c.* 1800) on behalf of Pierre Louis Lebrun 'architecte dessinateur', signed by Pierre Joseph Redouté and other artists.

AJ^{15} 569, pièce 367, 'Physiciens et naturalistes nommés pour accompagner le Capitaine Baudin'.

AJ^{16} 6411, 'Registre d'inscription des élèves au cours de l'Ecole de Santé avec table alphabétique pour l'an IV et l'an V'.

AJ^{16} 6412A★, 'Liste d'inscription des élèves qui suivent les cours de l'Ecole de Médecine à Paris, à commencer du 1er nivôse an VI'.

AJ^{16} 6413, 'Registre journalier des élèves inscrits pour suivre les cours des deux semestres de l'an VII; feuillets décadaires des signatures des élèves pour l'an VI et l'an VII'.

AJ^{16} 6415, 'Registre d'inscription des élèves qui suivent les cours de l'Ecole de Médecine (an VIII) …'.

LH 2322/37, Légion d'honneur, dossier Louis Richard [1819].

Marine BB^4 995 [no folio numbers], Baudin to the Minister of Marine, 20 brumaire an 11 [11 November 1802].

Marine BB^4 996, dossier 1, folio 87, Péron to the Minister of Marine in June? 1806.

Marine BB^4 996, dossier 2, folios 37–8 recto and verso, Péron to the Minister of Marine, 4 germinal an 12 [25 March 1804].

Marine BB⁴ 996, dossier 3, folio 59 recto and verso. Jean-Baptiste Chanvalon (Ordonnateur-général, Ile de France) to the Minister of Marine, 21 fructior an 11 [8 September 1803].

Marine BB⁴ 996, dossier 3 [no folio numbers], Antoine Thévenard to the Minister of Marine, correspondence 4–18 germinal an 12 [25 March – 10 April 1804].

Marine BB⁴ 997, dossier 1, folio 44 recto, Péron to the Minister of Marine, 18 germinal an 12 [8 April 1804].

Marine BB⁴ 997, dossier 1, folio 74 recto and verso, Jussieu to the Minister of Marine, 19 thermidor an 8 [7 August 1800].

Marine BB⁴ 997, dossier 3, folio 124 recto, 'Expédition de découvertes: La corvette Le Géographe: Morts à bord ou dans les hôpitaux'.

Marine 5JJ 28–30, Ronsard, journal.

Marine 5JJ 41–2, Hamelin, journal.

Marine 5JJ 46, Bernier, journal.

Marine 5JJ 48, Saint-Cricq, journal.

Marine 5JJ 53. Charles Pierre Boulanger to Nicolas Baudin, 1 ventôse an 11 [20 February 1803].

Marine 5JJ 55, Gicquel, journal.

Bibliothèque nationale

NA Française 9439, Jussieu and Lacépède to the Minister of Marine, 12 thermidor an 6 [30 July 1798].

Estampes Va 260a, Cloître Saint-Benoît.

Bibliothèque centrale du Muséum national d'histoire naturelle

MS 46, Richard, 'Instructions partielles pour les voyageurs naturalistes; instructions sur la minéralogie …'.

MS 1688, Riedlé, journal.

MS 2528, folio 124 (Biographie anonyme de Péron).

MS 100060, Anselm Riedlé to André Thouin, Timor, 6 vendémiare an X [27 September 1801].

Vincennes

Service historique de l'Armée de Terre

16YC 23, 'Contrôle du 2e Bataillon des Gardes nationales volontaires du Département de l'Allier'.

GD/2S 43, pièce 6, 'Mémoire de la vie politique et militaire du Général Laubadère défenseur de Landau' [c. 1803].

GD/2s 43, pièce 52, 'Général Laubadère, Commandant en Chef-Landau—sa justification contre les accusations du représentant du peuple Dentzel'.

Yzeure

Archives départementales de l'Allier

L 54, 'Séances du Département de l'Allier', 1792.

L 60, 'Bureau du detail, 1er Registre des délibérations des Administrateurs du Directoire du Département de l'Allier: 12 août 1791–24 août 1793'.

L 480, folio 46 verso, 'Séance publique du 9 Vendemiaire an 4e'.

L 489, folio 191 recto, 'Lettre au Ministère de l'Intérieur et à la députation du Bourbonnais, au sujet de la gendarmerie', Archives départementales de l'Allier.

2E/44/7, Acte de baptême de Sophie-Anaïs Coupery, 20 octobre 1799.

2E/44/8, Acte de mariage, Marie-Anne [Rosalie] Péron avec Joseph Coupery, 10 Brumaire an sept [31 October 1798]; acte de mariage d'Anne-Sophie Petitjean avec Pierre Raby de la Lande, 16 février 1803.

2E/44/13, Acte de décès d'Anne-Sophie née Petitjean, 30 août 1804.

3E 11549, (actes, notaire Pierre-Lazare Petitjean), 5 mars 1784, 10 juin 1785.

3E 11570, (actes, notaire François Thibault de Beauregard) no. 266, 'Inventaire des effets de la communauté Coupery du 18 juillet 1806'; no. 278, 'Ventes des effets de la succession des effets de Joseph Coupery, des 7, 8, 10 août 1806'; no. 285, 'Liquidation … succession Coupery du 14 août 1806'.

GERMANY
Speyer
Stadtarchiv
Actes de décès, Marie de Dudenhofen, Arrondissement Communal de Spire, 1808, Sterberegister.

MAURITIUS
National Archives
JK 17, folio 207, Testament du C[itoy]en Nicolas Baudin, Capitaine de Vaisseau de la République.

RB 8, folios 171–3, Chief Secretary Barry to the Government of New South Wales, 25 June 1811, enquiring about the existence of Mr de Vernicourt alias Baron Clambe with enclosed copy of a petition by Mrs de Vernicourt.

Theses

Debard, F. S., 'François Péron (1775–1810), Zoologiste du Voyage de découvertes aux Terres Australes: Remarques et observations sur les Pinnipèdes', Thèse pour le Diplôme d'Etat de Docteur vétérinaire, Ecole nationale vétérinaire de Nantes, 1999.

Reeth, B. van, 'Nicolas Baudin et le Voyage aux Terres Australes (1800–1804)', Ecole des Chartes, Paris, 1984.

Published sources
Books

Adams, F. D., *The Birth and Development of the Geological Sciences*, Dover Publications, New York, 1954.

Ambert, J., *Les Illustrations et célébrités du XIXe siècle, 7e série: biographie du général J.-J. Ambert*, Librairie Bloud et Barral, Paris, 1889.

Anon., *Magdeburg als preussiche Festung um 1750: Ein Führer durch das Modell der Festung*, Magdeburger Schriftenreihe, n.d.

Audiat, L., *F. Péron (de Cérilly): sa vie, ses voyages et ses ouvrages*, Enaut, Moulins, 1855.

Audley-Charles, M., *The Geology of Portuguese Timor*, London, Geological Society, 1968.

Baker, S. J., *The Australian Language*, Currawong Publishing, Sydney, 1966.

Barnes, R. W., Duncan, F. and Todd, C. S., *The Native Vegetation of King Island, Bass Strait: A Guide to the Identification, Conservation Status, and Management of the Island's Native Vegetation and Threatened Plants*, Nature Conservation Branch, Department of Primary Industries, Water and Environment, Hobart, 2002.

Barnwell, P. J. and Toussaint, A., *A Short History of Mauritius*, Longmans, Green & Co., London, 1949.

Bassett, M., *The Governor's Lady, Mrs Philip Gidley King: An Australian Historical Narrative*, Oxford University Press, London, 1956.

Bateson, C., *Australian Shipwrecks Including Vessels Wrecked en route to or from Australia, and some Strandings*, vol. 1: 1622–1850, A. H. & A. W. Reed, Frenchs Forest, NSW, 1982.

—— *The Convict Ships 1787–1868*, Library of Australian History, Sydney, 1983.

Baudin, N., *The Journal of Post Captain Nicolas Baudin, Commander-in-Chief of the Corvettes* Géographe *and* Naturaliste, *Assigned by order of the Government to a voyage of Discovery* (trans. C. Cornell), Libraries Board of South Australia, Adelaide, 1974.

Bély, L. (ed.), *Dictionnaire de l'Ancien Régime: Royaume de France, XVIe–XVIIIe siècle*, Presses Universitaires de France, Paris, 1996.

Biernawski, L., *Un département sous la Révolution française, l'Allier de 1789 à l'an III*, L. Grégoire, Moulins, 1909.

Bladen, F. M. (ed.), *Historical Records of New South Wales*, vol. 4, *Hunter and King, 1800, 1801, 1802*, Government Printer, Sydney, 1896 (facsimile edn, Lansdown Slattery, Mona Vale, NSW, 1979).

Blanning, T. C. W., *The French Revolution in Germany: Occupation and Resistance in the Rhineland, 1792–1802*, Clarendon Press, Oxford, 1983.

—— *The Origins of the French Revolutionary Wars*, Longman, London, 1986.

Bodard, G., *Cérilly et les Environs, traditions, documents, légendes*: VI: *Les fêtes de la Révolution et le Citoyen Jean-François Bourgoing*, Imprimerie Etienne Auclaire, Moulins, 1910.

—— *Cérilly et les Environs, la forêt de Tronçais*, Imp. Réunies, Moulins, 1936.

Bonnechose, E. de, *Lazare Hoche*, Hachette, Paris, 1874.

Bonnemains, J., *Exposition du 1er juin au 31 décembre 1997: Œuvres de Nicolas-Martin Petit Artiste du Voyage aux Terres Australes (1800–1804)*, Muséum d'histoire naturelle du Havre, Le Havre, 1997.

Bonnemains, J., Argentin, J.-M. and Marin, M. (eds), *Mon voyage aux Terres Australes: Journal personnel du commandant Baudin*, Éditions Imprimerie Nationale, Paris, 2000.

Bonnemains, J., Forsyth, E. and Smith, B., *Baudin in Australian Waters: The Artwork of the French Voyage of Discovery to the Southern Lands 1800–1804 with a Descriptive Catalogue of Drawings and Paintings of Australian Subjects by C.-A. Lesueur and N.-M. Petit from the Lesueur Collection at the Muséum d'Histoire Naturelle, Le Havre, France*, Oxford University Press, Melbourne, 1988.

Bory de Saint-Vincent, J. B. G. M., *Voyage dans les quatre principales îles des mers d'Afrique, fait par ordre du gouvernement pendant les années neuf et dix de la République, 1801 et 1802, avec l'histoire de la traversée du Capitaine Baudin jusqu'au Port Louis de l'Ile Maurice*, 3 vols and atlas, F. Buisson, Paris, an xiii [1804].

Brown, A. J., *Ill-starred Captains: Flinders and Baudin*, Crawford House, Adelaide, 2000.

Caillé, J., *Un savant Montpelliérain: Le Professeur Auguste Broussonet (1761–1807)*, Editions A. Pedone, Paris, 1972.

Cane, A., *Histoire de Villefranche-sur-Mer et de ses anciens hameaux de Beaulieu et de Saint-Jean*, Editions Un point sait tout, Villefranche-sur-Mer, 1998.

Chaussinand-Nogaret, G., *The French Nobility in the Eighteenth Century: From Feudalism to Enlightenment* (trans. W. Doyle), Cambridge University Press, Cambridge, 1985.

Chimello, S. (ed.), *Avec le Club des Jacobins, la Révolution au quotidien*, Archives municipales de Thionville, Thionville, 1989.

Claymore, S. J. and Markey, A. J., *A Floristic Survey of the Shark Bay World Heritage Area: An Interim Report on Surveys of Peron Peninsula, Edel Land, Bernier Island and Dorre Island*, Department of Conservation and Land Management, Perth, 1999.

Cobban, A., *A History of Modern France*, vol. 1, *Old Régime and Revolution, 1715–1799*, Penguin, Harmondsworth, 1963.

Copans, J. and Jamin, J. (eds), *Aux origines de l'anthropologie française: Les Mémoires de la Société des Observateurs de l'Homme en l'an VIII*, Le Sycomore, Paris, 1978.

Cumpston, J. S., *First Visitors to Bass Strait*, Roebuck, Canberra, 1973.

Cuneo d'Ornano, E., *Hoche, sa vie, sa correspondance*, Librairie Militaire J. Dumaine, L. Baudoin et Cie, Paris, 1892.

Cuvier, G., *Eloge historique de M. Richard*, no imprint details [18 pp; Paris, c. 1821].

—— *Essay on the theory of the earth*, W. Blackwood, Edinburgh, 1822.

—— *Discours sur les révolutions de la surface du globe et sur les changements qu'elles ont produits dans le règne animal*, Dufour et D'Ocagne, Paris, 1825.

—— *Le Règne animal distribué d'après son organisation, pour servir de base à l'histoire naturelle des animaux et d'introduction à l'anatomie comparée*, nouvelle édition [2nd edn], tome ii, Paris, 1829.

Dakin, W. J., *Whalemen Adventurers in Southern Waters: The Story of Whaling in Australian Waters and Other Southern Seas Related Thereto, From the Days of Sails to Recent Times* [1934], Angus & Robertson, Sydney, 1977.

D'Arneville, M.-B., Benoit, J., Chevalier, B., Chiappero, P.-J., Jouanin, C. and Ledoux-Lebard, G. (eds), *L'Impératrice Joséphine et les Sciences naturelles*, Editions de la Réunion des Musées nationaux, Paris, 1997.

Darwin, C., *The Voyage of the Beagle*, Heron, Geneva, (1839), 1968.

—— *The Descent of Man and Selection in Relation to Sex*, London, 1871 [facsimile edition, Random House, New York].

Davies, M., Twidale, C. R., and Tyler, M. J., *Natural History of Kangaroo Island*, Royal Society of South Australia [Adelaide], 2002.

Deacon, G. E. R. (ed.), *Oceans: An Atlas-History of Man's Exploration of the Deep*, Paul Hamlyn, London, 1962.

Deacon, M., *Scientists and the Sea 1650–1900: A Study of Marine Science*, Ashgate, Aldershot, 1997.

Dedieu, J., *Montesquieu et la tradition politique anglaise en France: Les Sources anglaises de l'Esprit des lois*, J. Galbada, Paris, 1909.

Degérando, J. M., *The Observation of Savage Peoples* (ed. and trans. F. C. T. Moore), Routledge & Kegan Paul, London, 1969.

Delaunay, P., *La vie médicale aux XVIe, XVIIe et XVIIIe siècles*, Laboratoires pharmaceutiques Corbière, Paris, 1935.

Desmarest, A. G., *Nouveau dictionnaire d'histoire naturelle appliquée aux arts à l'agriculture, à l'économie rurale et domestique, à la médecine etc.*, rev. edn, Une société de naturalistes et d'agriculteurs, Paris, 1817.

Donovan, E., *An Epitome of the Natural History of the Insects of New Holland, New Zealand, New Guinea, Otaheite, and other islands in the Indian, Southern, and Pacific Oceans, &c.* [vol. 3, *General Illustrations of Entomology*], London, 1805.

Dufour, C. H., *Opuscule sur la statistique proprement dite et l'histoire de l'Art dans le département de l'Allier à partir de 1790*, Enaut, Moulins, 1840.

Dulac, Lt Col., *Les Levées départementales dans l'Allier sous la Révolution (1791–1796)*, 2 vols, Plon-Nourrit et Cie, Paris, 1911.

d'Unienville, R. M., *Histoire politique de l'île de France (1789–1791)*, Mauritius Archives Publication No. 13, Port Louis, 1975.

—— *Histoire politique de l'île de France (1791–1794)*, Mauritius Archives Publication No. 14, Port Louis, 1982.

—— *Histoire politique de l'Isle de France (1795–1803)*, Publications des Archives de Maurice, No. 15, Port Louis, 1989.

Dupaquier, J., *Histoire de la population française*, vol. 3, de 1789 à 1914, PUF, Paris, 1995.

Dupont, M., *Dictionnaire historique des médecins: Dans et hors de la médecine*, Larousse, Paris, 1999.

Duyker, E., *The Dutch in Australia*, AE Press, Melbourne, 1987.

—— *An Officer of the Blue: Marc-Joseph Marion Dufresne 1724–1772, South Sea Explorer*, Miegunyah/Melbourne University Press, Melbourne, 1994.

—— *Nature's Argonaut: Daniel Solander 1733–1782, Naturalist and Voyager with Cook and Banks*, Miegunyah/Melbourne University Press, Melbourne, 1998.

—— *Citizen Labillardière: A Naturalist's Life in Revolution and Exploration (1755–1834)*, Miegunyah/Melbourne University Press, Melbourne, 2003.

Duyker, E. (ed.), *The Discovery of Tasmania: Journal Extracts from the Expeditions of Abel Janszoon Tasman and Marc-Joseph Marion Dufresne 1642 & 1772*, St David's Park Publishing, Hobart, 1992.

Duyker, E. and Duyker, M. (eds, trans.), *Bruny d'Entrecasteaux: Voyage to Australia and the Pacific 1791–1793*, Miegunyah/Melbourne University Press, Melbourne, 1998.

Duyker, E. and Tingbrand, P. (eds, trans.), *Daniel Solander: Collected Correspondence 1753–1782*, Miegunyah/Melbourne University Press, Melbourne, 1995.

Dyer, C., *The French Explorers and the Aboriginal Australians 1772–1839*, University of Queensland Press, St Lucia, Qld, 2005.

Edgar, G. J., *Australian Marine Life: The Plants and Animals of Temperate Waters*, Reed New Holland, Sydney, 2003.

Estensen, M., *The Life of Matthew Flinders*, Allen & Unwin, Sydney, 2002.

Eyer, F., *Wissembourg, Geschichte u. Kunst*, Editions de la Tour Blanche, Wissembourg, 1980.

Fanaud, L., *Lettre de Noblesse de l'Imprimerie moulinoise: Moulins possède-t-il la doyenne des imprimeries françaises?*, Les Imprimeries réunies, Moulins, 1968.

Flinders, M., *A Voyage to Terra Australis: Undertaken for the Purpose of Completing the Discovery of that Vast Country, and Prosecuted in the Years 1801, 1802, and in 1803, in his Majesty's Ship the* Investigator, *and Subsequently in the Armed vessel* Porpoise *and* Cumberland *schooner. With an Account of the Shipwreck of the* Porpoise, *Arrival of the* Cumberland *at Mauritius, and Imprisonment of the Commander during Six Years and a Half in that Island*, G. & W. Nicol, London, 2 vols, atlas, 1814.

Fornasiero, J., Monteath, P. and West-Sooby, J., *Encountering Terra Australis: The Australian Voyages of Nicolas Baudin and Matthew Flinders*, Wakefield Press, Kent Town, SA, 2004.

Forrest, A., *The Soldiers of the French Revolution*, Duke University Press, Durham, NC, 1990.

Forster, C., *France and Botany Bay: The Lure of a Penal Colony*, Melbourne University Press, Melbourne, 1996.

Forster, J. R., *Observations Made During a Voyage Round the World*, ed. N. Thomas, H. Guest and M. Dettelbach with a linguistic approach by K. H. Rensch, University of Hawai'i Press, Honolulu, 1996.

Foucart, A., *Le dernier des Guillemeau, esquisse biographique*, Henri Plon, Paris, 1860.

Fromont, J., 'A Quest for Our Natural Heritage', Winston Churchill Memorial Trust of Australia, Churchill Fellowship Report 2002.

Frost, A., *Convicts and Empire: A Naval Question 1776–1811*, Oxford University Press, Melbourne, 1980.

Gallot, J. G., *Vues générales sur la restauration de l'art de guérir, lues à la séance publique de la Société de médecine, le 31 août 1790 … suivies d'un plan d'hospices ruraux pour le soulagement des campagnes*, Croullebois, Paris, 1790.

George, A. S., *William Dampier in New Holland: Australia's First Natural Historian*, Bloomings Books, Hawthorn, Vic., 1999.

Germain, C., *La Marche et le Bassigny Barrois Mouvant*, Editions du Sapin d'or, Epinal, 1981.

Geyl, P., *Napoleon: For and Against*, trans. O. Renier, Penguin, Harmondsworth, UK, 1965.

Gibson, R., *A Social History of French Catholicism, 1789–1914*, Routledge, London, 1989.

Girard, M., *F. Péron, naturaliste, voyageur aux Terres Australes: Sa vie: appreciation de ses travaux*, J.-B. Baillère, Paris, 1856.

Glacken, C. J., *Traces on the Rhodian Shore: Nature and Culture in Western Thought From Ancient Times to the End of the Eighteenth Century*, University of California Press, Berkeley, 1976.

Gouvion Saint-Cyr, L., *Mémoires sur les campagnes des Armées du Rhin et de Rhin-et-Moselle de 1792 jusqu'à la paix de Campo Formio*, 4 vols, Paris, 1829.

Goy, J., *Les Méduses de François Péron et de Charles-Alexandre Lesueur: Un autre regard sur l'expédition Baudin*, Editions CTHS, Paris, 1995.

Greer, D., *The Incidence of the Terror during the French Revolution: A Statistical Interpretation*, Harvard University Press, Cambridge, Mass., 1935.

Grellet, I. and Kruse, C., *Histoire de la tuberculose: Les fièvres de l'âme 1800–1940*, Editions Ramsay, Paris, 1983.

Guillaumin, E., *François Péron, Enfant du Peuple: Un grand voyage, une œuvre, une vie (1937)*, Les Marmousets, Moulins, 1982.

Hahn, R., *The Anatomy of a Scientific Institution: The Paris Academy of Sciences, 1666–1803*, University of California Press, Berkeley, 1971.

Hamy, T., *Aimé Bonpland, médecin et naturaliste, explorateur de l'Amérique du Sud, sa vie, son œuvre, sa correspondance*, E. Guilmoto, Paris, 1906.

Hennequin, L. A., *La justice et la discipline à l'armée du Rhin et à l'armée de Rhin-et-Moselle (1792–1796), Notes du chef de bataillon du génie Legrand*, Paris, 1909.

Hess, H., *300 Jahre Festung Landau 1688/91–1988/91*, Stadtverwaltung, Landau, 1991.

Historical Records of Australia, *see* Watson, F.

Historical Records of New South Wales, *see* Bladen, F. M.

Hocquet, J.-C., *Le Sel et le pouvoir: de l'an mil à la Révolution française*, A. Michel, Paris, 1984.

Honigman, J., *The Development of Anthropological Ideas*, Dorsey Press, Homewood, Ill., 1976.

Horner, F., *The French Reconnaissance: Baudin in Australia 1801–1803*, Melbourne University Press, Melbourne, 1987.

Huguet, F., *Les professeurs de la faculté de médecine de Paris: Dictionnaire biographique 1794–1939*, Institut national de recherche pédagogique/Centre national de la recherche scientifique, Paris, 1991.

Jennings, J. N., *The Coastal Geomorphology of King Island, Bass Strait, in Relation to Changes in the Relative Level of Land and Sea*, Records of the Queen Victoria Museum Launceston ; new ser., no. 11, 1959.

Kass, T., *Parramatta: A Past Revealed*, Parramatta City Council, Parramatta, NSW, 1996.

Klotz, F., *Ortsgeschichte der gemeinde Dudenhofen/Pfalz*, Herausgeber Gemeindeverwaltung Dudenhofen, Bürgermeister Karl Bettag, Dudenhofen, 1964.

Labillardière, J. J. H. de, *Relation du voyage à la recherche de La Pérouse fait par ordre de l'assemblée constituante, pendant les années 1791, 1792, et pendant la 1ère. et la 2e année de la République Françoise*, 2 vols and atlas, H. J. Jansen, Paris, an VIII [1800].

—— *Novae Hollandiae plantarum specimen …*, 2 vols, Paris, 1804–06.

Lacépède, B. G. E. de, *Histoire naturelle des cétacées*, chez Plassan, Paris, an XII [1804].

Lagarde, G., *Contributions à l'étude des patois bourbonnais: Dictionnaire du parler de la région de Cérilly, préc. de notes sur le parler de la région de Cérilly, suivi d'un lexique français-bourbonnais*, l'auteur, Strasbourg, 1984.

Lamarck, J. P. B. A. de, *Histoire naturelle des animaux sans vertèbres: présentant les caractères généraux et particuliers de ces animaux, leur distribution, leurs classes, leurs familles, leurs genres et la citation des principales espèces qui s'y rapportent: précédée d'une introduction offrant la détermination des caractères essentiels de l'animal, sa distinction du végétal et des autres corps naturels, enfin, l'exposition des principes fondamentaux de la zoologie*, 7 vols, Verdière, Paris, 1815–22.

Laubadère, J.-M. Tenet de, *Mémoire du Citoyen Laubadère, général de division, commandant en chef à Landau, sur la conspiration de cette place*, Imprimerie de Potier, Paris, n.d.

Ledru, P.-A., *Voyage aux îles Ténériffe, la Trinité, Saint-Thomas, Sainte-Croix et Porto Ricco: Exécuté par ordre du gouvernement français, depuis le 30 septembre 1796 jusqu'au 7 juin 1798, sous la direction du capitaine Baudin, pour faire des recherches et des collections relatives à l'histoire naturelle ...*, Arthus Bertrand, Paris, 1810.

Le Garrec, Député J., *Rapport fait au nom de la Commission des Affaires Culturelles, Familiales et Sociales sur la Proposition de loi adoptée par le Sénat, relative à la restitution par la France de la dépouille mortelle de Saartje Baartman à l'Afrique de Sud*, Assemblée nationale, Paris, no. 3563, 2002.

Léon, P., *Les anciennes forges de Tronçais, Syndicat d'initiative Aumance-Tronçais*, [brochure], n.d.

Letouzey, L., *Le Jardin des Plantes a la croisée des chemins avec André Thouin 1747–1824*, Editions du Muséum, Paris, 1989.

Levi, J. S. and Bergman, G. F. J., *Australian Genesis: Jewish Convicts and Settlers 1788–1850*, Rigby, Adelaide, 1974.

Lewinsohn, R., *A History of Sexual Customs*, trans. A. Mayce, Longmans, Green & Co., London, 1958.

Ly-Tio-Fane, M., *Le Géographe et Le Naturaliste à L'Ile-de-France 1801, 1803, Ultime Escale du Captaine Baudin: Deuxième partie, Le voyage de découvertes aux Terres Australes, Collection Lesueur du Muséum d'histoire naturelle du Havre, Dossier 15: Catalogue établi Jacqueline Bonnemains, commenté par Madeleine Ly-Tio-Fane*, MSM Limited, Port Louis, 2003.

McCormick, T., *First Views of Australia 1788–1825: A History of Early Sydney*, David Ell Press/Longueville Publications, Chippendale, NSW, 1987.

Macknight, C. C., *The Voyage to Marege: Macassan Trepangers in Northern Australia*, Melbourne University Press, Melbourne, 1976.

Marchant, L. R., *France Australe: A Study of French Explorations and Attempts to Found a Penal Colony and Strategic Base in South Western Australia 1503–1826*, Artlook, Perth, 1982.

Marvillet, J., Le Caer, J.-P. et al., *Nomenclature officielle des voies publiques et privées*, Mairie de Paris, Paris, 1997.

Mathiez, A., *The French Revolution*, trans. C. A. Phillips, Russell & Russell, New York, 1962.

Meachen, G. N., *History of Tuberculosis*, John Bale, Sons & Danielsson Ltd, London, 1936.

Milbert, J. G., *Voyage pittoresque à l'Ile-de-France, au Cap de Bonne-Espérance, et à l'ile de Ténériffe*, 2 vols, A. Nepveu, Paris, 1812.

Milius, P. B., *Récit du voyage aux Terres Australes par Pierre Bernard Milius, second sur le 'Naturaliste' dans l'expédition Baudin (1800–1804)*, transcribed and ed. J. Bonnemains, Pascale Hauguel, Société havraise d'études diverses, Muséum d'histoire naturelle du Havre, Le Havre, 1987.

Moore, F. C. T. *see* Degérando, J. M.

Moret, J.-J., *Les Ecoles bourbonnaises avant 1789*, Moulins, 1894.

Mortimer, G., *Observations and Remarks made during a Voyage to the Islands of Tenerife, Amsterdam, Maria's Island near Van Diemen's Land, Otaheite, the Sandwich Islands, Owyhee, the Fox Islands, the North-West Coast of America, Tinian, thence to Canton in the brig 'Mercury' commanded by John Henry Cox, Esq.*, T. Cadell, London, 1791.

Nunn, J. M., *This Southern Land: A Social History of Kangaroo Island 1800–1890*, Investigator Press, Hawthorndene, SA, 1989.

Pendleton, E. H., *Brian Pendleton and his Descendants 1599–1910*, privately published, 1910.

Perchet, E., *Histoire de Pesmes* (1896), Res Universis, Paris, 1990.

Péron, F., *Observations sur l'anthropologie, ou l'Histoire naturelle de l'homme, la nécessité de s'occuper de l'avancement de cette science, et l'importance de l'admission sur la Flotte du capitaine Baudin d'un ou de plusieurs Naturalistes, spécialement chargés des Recherches à faire sur cet objet*, Stoupe, Paris, an VIII [1800].

—— *Voyage de découvertes aux Terres Australes, exécuté par ordre de sa Majesté, l'Empereur et Roi, sur les corvettes le* Géographe, *le* Naturaliste *et la goëlette le* Casuarina, *pendant les années 1800, 1801, 1802, 1803 et 1804*, L'Imprimerie Impériale, 3 vols and atlas, Paris, 1807–17; vol. i, Historique, 1807; vol. ii, Historique [completed by L. de Freycinet], 1816; vol. iii, Navigation et géographie [by L. de Freycinet], 1815; Atlas historique [by C. A. Lesueur & N. Petit], 1817.

—— *A Voyage of Discovery to the Southern Hemisphere Performed by Order of the Emperor Napoleon, During the Years 1801, 1802, 1803, and 1804*, printed for Richard Phillips, Bridge Street, Blackfriars, by B. McMillan, Bow Street, Covent Garden, London, 1809.

—— *Entdeckungs-Reise nach den Süd-Ländern ausgefürt auf Befehl Sr. Majestät des Kaisers und Königs, auf den Corvetten dem* Geographen, *dem* Naturalisten *und der Golette dem* Casuarina, *während der Jahre 1800, 1801, 1802, 1803 und 1804* (trans. Ph. W. G. Hausleutner), J. G. Cotta'schen Buchhandlung, Tübingen, 2 vols, 1808–19.

Péron, F. [and de Freycinet, L.], *Voyage de découvertes aux Terres australes, fait par ordre du gouvernement, sur les corvettes le* Géographe, *le* Naturaliste *et la goëlette le* Casuarina, *pendant les années 1800, 1801, 1802, 1803 et 1804*, 4 vols and atlas, Paris, 1824.

—— *Voyage of Discovery to the Southern Lands*, by François Péron, continued by Louis de Freycinet, 2nd edn 1824: Book IV, Comprising Chapters XXII to XXXIV (trans. C. Cornell; introduction by Anthony J. Brown), Friends of the State Library of South Australia, Adelaide, 2003.

Péron, F. A. [and de Freycinet. L.], *Entdeckungsreise nach Australien unternommen auf Befehl Sr. Majestät des Kaisers von Frankreich und Königs von Italien mit den Korvetten der* Geograph *und der* Naturalist, *und der Goelette* Kasuarina *in den Jahren 1800 bis 1804* (trans. T. F. Ehrmann), Verlage des Landes-Industrie-Comptoirs, Weimar, 2 vols, 1808–19.

Péronnet, M. and Varennes, J. C., *La Révolution dans le département de l'Allier: 1789–1799*, Horvath, Le Coteau, 1988.

Piboule, M. and Bertrand, E., *Mémoire des communes Bourbonnaises: Au pays de la forêt: Au long des vieux chemins de Tronçais*, Foyers ruraux de l'Allier, Neuvy, 1995.

Picard, E. (ed.), *Au service de la Nation: Lettres de volontaires (1792–1798)*, Librairie Félix Alcan, Paris, 1914.

Picard, E. and Paulier, V. (eds), *Mémoires et journaux du général Decaen*, Paris, 1910.

Pico, B., Corbella, D. et al., *Viajeros franceses a las Islas Canarias: Repertorio bio-bibliográfico y selección de textos*, Instituto de Estudios Canarios, San Cristóbal de La Laguna, 2000.

Piery, M. and Roshem, J., *Histoire de la tuberculose*, G. Doin & Cie, Paris, 1931.

Pinkerton, J., *Early Australian Voyages: Pelsaert, Tasman, Dampier*, Cassell & Co., London, 1896.

Plomley, B., *The Baudin Expedition and the Tasmanian Aborigines 1802*, Blubber Head Press, Hobart, 1983.

Plomley, N. J. B., *The Tasmanian Aborigines*, Author/Adult Education Division, Launceston, Tas., 1977.

Prentout, H., *L'Ile de France sous Decaen, 1803–1810: Essai sur la politique coloniale du Premier Empire et la rivalité de la France et de l'Angleterre dans les Indes orientales*, Hachette, Paris, 1901.

Quatrefages, A. de, *Hommes fossiles et hommes sauvages: Etude d'anthropologie*, Baillère, Paris, 1884 [facsimile edn, Jean-Michel Place, Paris, 1988].

Raillard, A., *Un coin du Morvan à travers l'histoire*, Civry [Dijon], 1981.

Ramsey, M., *Professional and Popular Medicine in France, 1770–1830: The Social World of Medical Practice*, Cambridge University Press, New York, 1988.

Read, A. L., *Essai sur les effets salutaires du séjour des étables dans la phtisie*, Rivière, Paris, 1767.

Rey, H. J. A. F., *Répertoire bibliographique des travaux des médecins et des pharmaciens de la marine française, 1698–1873, suivi d'une table méthodique des matières, par les docteurs Charles Berger … Henri Rey*, J.-B. Baillière, Paris, 1874.

Rigondet, G., *François Péron, 1775–1810, et l'expédition du Commandant Nicolas Baudin: Les Français à la découverte de l'Australie*, Éditions des Cahiers Bourbonnais, Charroux, 2002.

Rivière, M. S. (ed., trans.), *A Woman of Courage: The Journal of Rose de Freycinet on her Voyage Around the World*, National Library of Australia, Canberra, 1996.

Roth, F. (ed.), *Histoire de Thionvillle*, Gérard Klopp, Thionville, 1995.

Rousseau, J.-J., *On the Origin of Inequality*, trans. G. D. H. Cole, in Hutchins, R. M. (ed.), *Great Books of the Western World*, vol. 38, Encyclopaedia Britannica, Chicago, 1989.

Ruediger, W J., *Border's Land: Kangaroo Island 1802–1836*, Lutheran Publishing House, Morgan, SA, 1980.

Ryan, L., *The Aboriginal Tasmanians*, 2nd edn, Allen & Unwin, 1996.

Saint-Pierre, J.-H. Bernardin de, *Studies of Nature* [*Etudes de la Nature* (1784), trans. H. Hunter], vol. i, London, 1796.

—— *Voyage à l'île de France: Un officier du roi à l'île Maurice 1768–1770*, La Découverte/Maspero, Paris, 1983.

Santana Perez, J. M. and Monzón Perdomo, M. E., *Hospitales de La Laguna durante el Siglo XVIII*, Ayuntamiento de San Christobal de La Laguna, 1995.

Santos, P. E. C., *Apontamentos para o estudo da flora de Macau e de Timor*, Lisbon, 1934.

Scheffer, V. B., *Seals, Sea Lions and Walruses: A Review of the Pinnipedia*, Stanford University Press, Stanford, CA, 1958.

Scott, E., *Terre Napoléon: A History of French Explorations and Projects in Australia*, Methuen & Co., London, 1910.

Serieyx, A., *Wonnerup: The Sacred Dune*, Abrolhos Publishing, Perth, 2001.

Smeaton, W. A., *Fourcroy: Chemist and Revolutionary 1755–1809*, W. Heffer & Sons, Cambridge, 1962.

Smith, S., *Tasmania's French Connections: Report on the Goddard Sapin-Jaloustre Scholarship 2002*, Hobart, December 2003.

Tertian, L., *Orgon*, Cavaillon, Orgon, 1989.

Thomson, J. M., *The French Revolution*, Basil Blackwell, Oxford, 1943.

Toft, K., *The Navigators: Flinders vs Baudin: The Race Between Matthew Flinders and Nicolas Baudin to Discover the Fabled Passage Through the Middle of Australia*, Duffy & Snellgrove, Potts Point, NSW, 2002.

Toussaint, A., *Histoire des îles Mascareignes*, Berger-Levrault, Paris, 1972.

—— *Port Louis: A Tropical City* (trans. W. E. F. Ward), George Allen & Unwin, London, 2nd edn, 1976.

Toussaint, A. (ed.), *Early American Trade with Mauritius*, Mauritius Archives Publication No. 1, Esclapon, Port Louis, 1954.

Tracou, C. and Richard, D., *Villefranche-sur-Mer: La Rade Etincelante*, Editions 2 fab, Villefranche, 1994.

Tulard, J., Fayard, J.-F. and Fierro, A., *Histoire et dictionnaire de la Révolution française 1789–1799*, Robert Laffont, Paris, 1987.

Turbet, P., *The Aborigines of the Sydney District Before 1788*, Kangaroo Press, Kenthurst, NSW, 1989.

Viguerie, J. de, *Histoire et dictionnaire du temps des lumières 1715–1789*, Robert Laffont, Paris, 1995.

Wace, N. and Lovett, B., *Yankee Maritime Activities and the Early History of Australia*, Research School of Pacific Studies, Australian National University, 1973.

Wales, W., *Remarks on Mr Forster's Account of Captain Cook's Last Voyage Round the World in the Years 1772, 1773, 1774, and 1775*, J. Nourse, London, 1778.

Wallace, A. R., *The Malay Archipelago: The Land of the Orang-Utan and the Bird of Paradise, A Narrative of Travel with Studies of Man and Nature*, Macmillan & Co., London, 1869.

Wallace, C., *The Lost Australia of François Péron*, Nottingham Court Press, London, 1984.

Walton, D. W. (ed.), *Zoological Catalogue of Australia*, Bureau of Flora and Fauna/ Australian Government Publishing Service, 37 vols, Canberra, 1983–2002.

Watson, F. (ed.), *Historical Records of Australia*, series 1, *Governors' Despatches to and from England*, vol. 3, 1801–02, Library Committee of the Commonwealth Parliament, Sydney, 1915.

Webb, J. B., *George Caley: 19th Century Naturalist: A Biography*, Surrey Beatty & Sons, Sydney, 1995.

Wells, F. E., Walker, D. I., Kirkman, H., and Lethbridge, R. (eds), *The Marine Flora and Fauna of Albany, Western Australia: Proceedings of the Third International Marine Biological Workshop Organised by Western Australian Branch, Australian Marine Sciences Association*, Western Australian Museum, Perth, *c.* 1991.

White, J., *Journal of a Voyage to New South Wales, with Sixty-Five Plates of Non descript Animals, Birds, Lizards, Serpents, Curious Cones of Trees and other Natural Productions, by John White Esq. Surgeon General to the Settlement*, J. Debrett, Picadilly, London, MDCCXC, [facsimile edition Arno Press & New York Times, New York, 1971].

Articles

Ackerknecht, E. H., 'Paris hospitals around 1800: A new era in medicine', *Symposium Ciba*, vol. 7, no. 3, 1959, pp. 98–105.

Alard, M. J. L., 'Eloge historique de François Péron, Rédacteur du voyage de découvertes aux Terres Australes', *Mémoires de la Société médicale d'émulation*, vol. 7, 1811, pp. i–lxxxii.

Anon. [John Barrow?], 'Art III: *Voyage de Découvertes aux Terres Australes* ... [book review]', *Quarterly Review*, vol. iv, August 1810, pp. 42–60.

Anon., 'Death [Obituary for the Chevalier Vernicourt]', *Sydney Gazette and New South Wales Advertiser*, vol. ii, no. 67, Sunday, 10 June 1804, p. 1.

Anon., 'Depositions Respecting the Ship Union of America', *Sydney Gazette and New South Wales Advertiser*, 28 October 1804, pp. 3–4.

Anon., 'Emile Guillaumin, *François Péron*' [book review], *Bulletin de la Société d'Emulation du Bourbonnais*, tome 39, 1936, p. 112.

Anon., 'Fugitives', *Sydney Gazette and New South Wales Advertiser*, vol. i, no. 1, Saturday, 5 March 1803, p. 3.

Anon., 'Intérieur [report of the presentation of the *Voyage aux Terres Australes* to Napoleon]', *Le Moniteur universel*, no. 13, mercredi, 13 Janvier 1808, p. 1.

Anon., 'Parramatta [auction results]', *Sydney Gazette and New South Wales Advertiser*, vol. ii, no. 58, Sunday, 8 April 1804, p. 3.

Anon., 'To be Sold by Public Auction', *Sydney Gazette and New South Wales Advertiser*, vol. ii, no. 73, Sunday, 22 July 1804, p. 2.

Bailly, J. C., 'Geognotische Bemerkungen über Isle de France', *Zeitschrift fur Miner*, 1825, vol. 19, no. 1, pp. 136–46.

Balouet, J. C. and Jouanin, C., 'Systématique et origine géographique des émús récoltés par l'expédition Baudin', *L'Oiseau et la Revue française d'Ornithologie*, vol. 60, 1990, pp. 314–18.

Bauchot, M.-L. and Bauchot, R., 'Dessins de poissons et de mammifères de la collection du Muséum d'histoire naturelle du Havre', *Bulletin trimestriel de la Société géologique de Normandie et des Amis du Muséum du Havre*, tome 88, fascicules 2, 3 et 4, 2001, 2e, 3e et 4e trimestres, pp. 1–182.

Bauchot, M.-L. and Daget, J., 'Poissons recoltés par C.-A. Lesueur et entrés dans les collections du Muséum national d'histoire naturelle de Paris', *Bulletin trimestriel de la Société géologique de Normandie et des Amis du Muséum du Havre*, tome 66, fascicule 4, année 1979, 4e trimestre, pp. 97–114.

Baudin, N., 'Lettre du capitaine Baudin à Mr Jussieu datée du Port Jackson le 20 brumaire an XI', *Annales du Muséum d'histoire naturelle*, 1803, tome 2, pp. 415–22.

Bertaud, J.-P., 'Du volontariat à la conscription 1789–1815', *Revue historique des armées*, no. 147, 1982, 2e trimestre, pp. 24–33.

Berthoumieu, Abbé and Bourgougnon, C., 'Matériaux pour la flore de l'Allier', *Bulletin de la société d'émulation du Bourbonnais*, 1886, tome xvii, pp. 57–75.

Bodard, G., 'Cahier de la ville et paroisse de Cérilly pour les Etats-Généraux de 1789', *Bulletin de la société d'émulation du Bourbonnais*, année 1910, Décembre, no. 12, pp. 388–95.

—— 'Cérilly sous l'Ancien Régime: Chirurgiens-apothicaires', *Bulletin de la Societe bourbonnaise des études locales*, vol. 1, juillet-août-septembre 1922, pp. 165–9.

Bonnemains, J., 'Biography of Charles-Alexandre Lesueur', in Bonnemains, J., Forsyth, E. and Smith, B., *Baudin in Australian Waters: The Artwork of the French Voyage of Discovery to the Southern Lands 1800–1804 with a Descriptive Catalogue of Drawings and Paintings of Australian Subjects by C.-A. Lesueur and N.-M. Petit from the Lesueur Collection at the Muséum d'Histoire Naturelle, Le Havre, France*, Oxford University Press, Melbourne, 1988, pp. 19–26.

—— 'Charles-Alexandre Lesueur dans le Var en 1809', *Annales du Sud-Est Varois*, tome XIII, 1988, pp. 31–42.

—— 'Les artistes du "Voyage de découvertes aux Terres Australes" (1800–1804): Charles-Alexandre Lesueur et Nicolas-Martin Petit', *Bulletin trimestriel de la Société géologique de Normandie et des Amis du Muséum du Havre*, tome 76, fascicule 1, année 1989, 1er trimestre, pp. 1–55.

—— 'Les illustrations du livre de bord du Capitaine Nicolas Baudin, Expédition de découvertes aux Terres Australes (1800–1804)', *Annales du Muséum du Havre*, no. 26, octobre 1983, no pagination.

—— 'Les illustrations du livre de bord du Capitaine Nicolas Baudin, Expédition de découvertes aux Terres Australes (1800–1804) Répertoire des Documents Retrouvés', *Annales du Muséum du Havre*, no. 33, janvier 1986, pp. 1–20.

—— 'Origine de la Collection "Lesueur" du Muséum d'histoire naturelle du Havre', *Annales du Muséum du Havre*, no. 49, September 1995, pp. 1–23.

—— 'The History of the Lesueur Collection of the Muséum d'Histoire naturelle du Havre', in Bonnemains, J., Forsyth, E. and Smith, B., *Baudin in Australian Waters: The Artwork of the French Voyage of Discovery to the Southern Lands 1800–1804 with a Descriptive Catalogue of Drawings and Paintings of Australian Subjects by C.-A. Lesueur and N.-M. Petit from the Lesueur Collection at the Muséum d'Histoire Naturelle, Le Havre, France*, Oxford University Press, Melbourne, 1988, pp. 65–8.

Bonnemains, J. and Branconnot, J.-C., 'Catalogue des manuscrits et des dessins des cténophores observés par F. Péron et C. A. Lesueur. Collections du Muséum du Havre', *Bulletin trimestriel de la Société géologique de Normandie et des Amis du Muséum du Havre*, tome lxxiii, fascicule 4, année 1986, 4e trimestre, pp. 31–41.

—— 'Les tunciers pélagiques: Salpes et pyrosomes étudiés par François Péron et Charles-Alexandre Lesueur au début du XIXe siècle', *Bulletin trimestriel de la Société géologique de Normandie et des Amis du Muséum du Havre*, tome lxxiii, fascicule 3, année 1986, 3e trimestre, pp. 45–75.

Bonnemains, J. and Breton, G., 'A Propos de l'ouvrage: "Les méduses de Péron et Lesueur, un autre regard sur l'expédition Baudin" par Jacqueline Goy', *Annales du Muséum du Havre*, no. 50, September 1995, pp. 1–8.

Bonnemains, J., Bustaret, C. and Breton, G., 'Etude codicologique des manuscrits et dessins de méduses (1800–1810) de François Péron et Charles-Alexandre Lesueur', *Bulletin trimestriel de la Société géologique de Normandie et des Amis du Muséum du Havre*, tome 82, fascicule 2, année 1995, 2e trimestre, pp. 6–97.

Bonnemains, J. and Carré, C., 'Siphonophores et vélelles observés par F. Péron et C.-A. Lesueur au début du 19e siècle', *Bulletin trimestriel de la Société géologique de Normandie et des Amis du Muséum du Havre*, tome 78, fascicule 2, année 1991, 2e trimestre, pp. 34–82.

Bonnemains, J. and Chappuis, C., 'Les oiseaux de la collection C.-A. Lesueur du Muséum d'histoire Naturelle du Havre', *Bulletin trimestriel de la Société géologique de Normandie et des Amis du Muséum du Havre*, tome lxxiv, fascicules 1 & 2, année 1985, 1er et 2e trimestres, pp. 25–78.

Bonnemains, J. and Jones, D., 'Les crustacés de la collection C.-A. Lesueur (dessins et manuscrits)', *Bulletin trimestriel de la Société géologique de Normandie et des Amis du Muséum du Havre*, tome 77, fascicule 1, Année 1990, 1er trimestre, pp. 28–66.

Bowdler, S., 'Archaeological Research in the Shark Bay Region, Western Australia: An Introductory Account', in Berry, P. F., Bradshaw, S. D. and Wilson, B. R., *Research in Shark Bay: Report of the France-Australe Bicentenary Expedition Committee*, Western Australian Museum, Perth, 1990, pp. 1–12.

Braconnot, J. C. and Bonnemains, J., 'François Péron & Charles-Alexandre Lesueur précurseurs des laboratoires marins de Villefranche: Deux naturalistes havrais en voyage à Nice en 1809', *Mesclun*, 1991, pp. 30–3.

Breton, G., 'Charles-Alexandre Lesueur (1778–1846): L'art au service des sciences naturelles', *Annales du Muséum du Havre*, fascicule no. 8, mai 1977, pp. 1–9.

Brockliss, L., 'L'enseignement médical et la Révolution: Essai de réévaluation', *Histoire de l'éducation*, no. 42, mai 1989, pp. 79–110.

Brown, A., 'The captain and the convict maid: A chapter in the life of Nicolas Baudin', *South Australian Geographical Journal*, vol. 97, 1998, pp. 20–32.

Brugière, J.-B., 'Témoignage' [i], *Bulletin de l'Association François Péron*, no. 13, janvier 2006, pp. 17–22 [part ii, in press].

Buch, L. von, 'Observations sur les volcans d'Auvergne', *Journal des Mines*, vol. 13, 1802–3, p. 249.

——'Einige Bemerkung über die geognostiche constitution von Van Diemens Land', *Mag. Fur die Neu Entdeckungen in der Gesammte Naturkunde*, vol. 6, 1814, pp. 234–40.

Chelin, A., 'Billard, Julien (c. 1781–1846)', *Dictionnaire de biographie mauricienne*, no. 24, octobre 1948, pp. 719–20.

Cleland, J. B., 'Remarkable mistranslations in the English version (1809) of Peron's Voyage of Discovery', *Journal of the Royal Australian Historical Society*, vol. 29, part 4, 1943, pp. 215–16.

Cornillon, J., 'Comment le naturaliste François Péron de Cérilly fit la connaissance de Henri Dufour, artiste à Moulins et devint son ami', *Bulletin des amis de Montluçon*, no. 6, 1927, pp. 15–23.

Crespin, I., 'Middle Miocene Limestones from King Island, Tasmania', *Papers and Proceedings, Royal Society of Tasmania*, 1944, pp. 15–18.

Cuvier, G., 'Mémoire sur l'Onchidie, genre de mollusques nuds, voisins des Limaces, et sur une espèce nouvelle Onchidium peronii', *Annales du Muséum national d'histoire naturelle*, tome 5, 1804, pp. 37–51.

—— 'Mémoire sur les Thalides (Thalia. Brown.), et sur les Biophores (Salpa. Forskaohl.)', *Annales du Muséum national d'histoire naturelle*, tome 4, 1804, pp. 360–82.

—— 'Observations sur l'ostéologie des crocodiles vivans', *Annales du Muséum national d'histoire naturelle*, tome 12, 1808, pp. 1–26, 2 plates [incorrectly labelled 'tome 5, pls 3 and 4'].

—— 'Rapport fait au gouvernement par l'Institut Impérial sur le Voyage de découvertes aux Terres Australes', *Procès-verbaux des séances de l'Académie, Classe des Sciences physiques et mathématiques*, tome iii, séance du lundi 9 juin 1806, pp. 363–67.

D'Emmerez de Charmoy, A., 'Céré, Jean Nicolas de (1737–1810)', *Dictionnaire de Biographie mauricienne*, no. 4, mars 1942, pp. 111–12.

d'Hondt, J.-L., 'Révision des Bryozoaires de Lesueur et Péron conservés dans les collections du Muséum national d'histoire naturelle de Paris', *Bulletin trimestriel de la Société géologique de Normandie et des Amis du Muséum du Havre*, tome lxvi, fascicule 3, 1979, 3e trimestre, pp. 9–24.

Delaunay, O., 'La Révolution française dans l'Allier (août 1792 – septembre 1793), *Notre Bourbonnais*, 10e série, no. 219, 1er trimestre 1982, pp. 2–56.

Deleuze, J. P. F., 'Notice historique sur André Michaux', *Annales du Muséum national d'histoire naturelle*, tome 3, an XII (1804), pp. 191–22.

—— 'Notice historique sur M. Péron', *Annales du Muséum national d'histoire naturelle*, tome 17, 1811, pp. 252–79.

d'Unienville, R., 'Laborde, Léonard Clair (1752–1824)', *Dictionnaire de Biographie mauricienne*, no. 44, janvier 1989, p. 1351.

Ducros, A. and Ducros, J., 'Point d'histoire: nouvelle anthropologie au temps de la Révolution', *Bulletin et mémoires de la Société d'anthropologie de Paris*, vol. 5, no. 4, 1988, pp. 289–92.

Duméril, A. M. C., 'Prodrome général de la classification des serpents', *Mémoires, Academie des Sciences, Institut de France*, vol. 23, 1853, pp. 399–536.

Duméril, A. M. C. and Bibron, G. *Erpétologie Générale ou Histoire Naturelle Complète des Reptiles*, vol. 8, ii, Roret, Paris, 1841.

Dumont, C., 'Lettre à M. Millin, sur le Tablier des Femmes hottentotes', *Magasin encyclopédique*, tome iv, juillet 1805, pp. 84–6.

Duyker, E., 'Charles Alexandre Lesueur (1778–1846)', *Dictionnaire de Biographie mauricienne*, no. 45, avril 1990, pp. 1387–8.

—— 'Petit, Nicolas Martin (1777–1804)', *Dictionnaire de Biographie mauricienne*, no. 46, avril 1991, p. 1427.

—— 'The first French in Australia: The soldiers of the *Batavia*', *Explorations*, no. 13, December 1992, pp. 3–8.

—— 'Josselin and Alexandre Le Corre: Early French voyagers to Van Diemen's Land and New Holland', *Explorations*, no. 13, December 1992, pp. 9–13.

—— 'In search of Madame Kerivel and Baudin's last resting place', *National Library of Australia News*, vol. ix, no. 12, September 1999, pp. 8–10.

—— 'Gicquel Destouches, Pierre-Guillaume (1770–1824)', *Dictionnaire de Biographie mauricienne*, no. 54, Octobre 2000, pp. 1745–8.

—— 'Beckwith, Mary (*c.* 1786–*c.* 1804)', *Dictionnaire de Biographie mauricienne*, no. 55, juillet 2002, pp. 1802–3.

—— 'Bernier, Pierre François (1779–1803)', *Dictionnaire de Biographie mauricienne*, no. 57, juillet 2005, pp. 1958–9.

—— 'Levillain, Stanislas (1774–1801)', *Dictionnaire de Biographie mauricienne*, no. 57, juillet 2005, pp. 1994–5.

—— 'Maugé, René (*c.* 1761–1802)', *Dictionnaire de Biographie mauricienne*, no. 57, juillet 2005, pp. 2003–4.

—— 'Riedlé, Anselm (1768[*sic*]–1801)', *Dictionnaire de Biographie mauricienne*, no. 57, juillet 2005, pp. 2014–16.

—— 'Bailly, Joseph-Charles (1777–1844)'; 'Bellefin, Jérôme Claude (1764–1835)'; 'Cogswell, Nathaniel (1778–1832)'; 'Depuch Monbuton, Louis (c. 1774–1803)'; 'Lalouette de Vernicourt [*dit* De Clambe], Pierre (1754–1804)'; and 'Vasse, Timothée (1774–c. 1801)'; *Dictionnaire de Biographie mauricienne*, in press.

Duyker, E. and d'Unienville, R., 'Faure, Pierre Ange François Xavier (1776–1855)', *Dictionnaire de Biographie mauricienne*, no. 54, octobre 2000, pp. 1744–5.

—— 'Guillemeau, Jean-François (1772–1860)', *Dictionnaire de Biographie mauricienne*, no. 57, juillet 2005, pp. 1983–6.

Edwards, C., 'The history and state of the study of Medusae and Hydroids', *Proceedings of the Royal Society of Edinburgh* (Proceedings of the Second International Congress on the History of Oceanography, Section B. Biology), vol. 73, 1972, pp. 247–57.

Faivre, J.-P., 'La France découvre l'Australie: L'expédition du *Géographe* et du *Naturaliste* (1801–1803), *Australian Journal of French Studies*, vol. ii, 1965, pp. 45–58.

—— 'Les idéologues de l'an VIII et le voyage de Nicolas Baudin en Australie', *Australian Journal of French Studies*, vol. iii, no. 1, 1966, pp. 3–15.

—— 'Une expédition botanique sous le Directoire: Le capitaine Baudin aux "Isles d'Amerique"', *La Revue maritime*, March 1938, pp. 334–56.

Faure, M.-R., 'Sciences naturelles et dessin', *Bulletin trimestriel de la Société géologique de Normandie et des Amis du Muséum du Havre*, tome 81, fascicule 3 & 4, année 1994, 3e & 4e trimestres, pp. 15–33.

Ferguson, W. C., 'Mokaré's domain', in Mulvaney, D. J. and White, J. P., *Australians to 1788*, Fairfax, Syme & Weldon Associates, Sydney, 1987, pp. 121–45.

Flament, P., 'Note sur le 1er bataillon de volontaires de l'Allier (1791–1792)', *Bulletin de la société d'émulation du Bourbonnais*, tome XII, 1904, pp. 217–27.

Fornasiero, J. and West-Sooby, J., 'Baudin's books', *Australian Journal of French Studies*, vol. xxxix, no. 2, 2002, pp. 215–49.

Gelfand, T., 'Empiricism and eighteenth-century French surgery', *Bulletin of the History of Medicine*, vol. xliv, no. 1, 1970, pp. 40–53.

Geoffroy Saint-Hilaire, E., 'Note sur les animaux vivans venus à bord du *Géographe*', *Annales du Muséum national d'histoire naturelle*, Paris, tome 4, 1804, pp. 171–2.

—— 'Note sur les espèces du genre dassyure', *Bulletin des sciences de la Société Philomatique*, [no. xi, 8e année?], tome iii, no. 81, 1803, pp. 158–59 [*sic*; should be 258–9].

—— 'Note sur un nouveau genre de mammifières de l'ordre des rongeurs sous le nom d'hydromys', *Bulletin des sciences de la Société Philomatique* [no. xi, 8e année?], tome iii, no. 93, 1804, pp. 353–4 [as 253–4].

Gérando, J.-M. de, *Considérations sur les diverses méthodes à suivre dans l'observation des peuples sauvages*, Société des Observateurs de l'Homme, an VIII [1800].

Goy, J., 'Histoire des méduses de François Péron et Charles-Alexandre Lesueur, *Bulletin trimestriel de la Société géologique de Normandie et des Amis du Muséum du Havre*, tome 75, fascicule 3, année 1988, 3e trimestre, pp. 41–8.

Goy, J. and Breton, G., 'Les Méduses de François Péron et Charles-Alexandre Lesueur (1775–1810 et 1778–1846) révélées par les vélins de Lesueur', *Bulletin trimestriel de la Société géologique de Normandie et des Amis du Muséum du Havre*, tome lxvii, fascicule 2, 1980, 2e trimestre, pp. 63–76, planches 1–26.

—— 'Les méduses de François Péron et Charles-Alexandre Lesueur (1775–1810 et 1778–1846) révélées par les vélins de Lesueur', *Bulletin trimestriel de la Société géologique de Normandie et des Amis du Muséum du Havre*, tome 75, fascicule 3, année 1988, 3e trimestre, pp. 63–78, planches 1–27.

Goy, J., Bonnemains, J., Breton, G. and Barbiche, J.-P., 'Collections et classification: L'exemple des méduses de Péron et Lesueur', *Actes du colloque REMUS: la Muséologie des Sciences et des Techniques* (12–13 décembre 1991), Palais de la Découverte, Paris, pp. 206–18.

Gray, J. E., 'Catalogue of the slender-tongued saurians, with descriptions of many new genera and species (contd)', *Annals of Natural History*, vol. 1, no. 2, 1838, pp. 287–93.

—— 'Description of some new species and four new genera of reptiles from Western Australia, discovered by John Gould, Esq.', *Annals and Magazine of Natural History*, vol. 7, 1841, pp. 86–91.

Guicheteau, T. 'La vie et la grande aventure du "chirurgien navigan" Jérôme Bellefin', *Bulletin de la Société archéologiquie et historique de Nantes et de Loire-Atlantique*, 183, 1987, pp. 9–22.

Guimera Peraza, M., 'Bernardo Cólogan y Fallon (1772–1814)', *Annuario de Estudios Atlanticos*, 25, 1979, pp. 307–59.

Hamy, E.-T., 'Les collections anthropologiques et ethnologiques du voyage de découvertes aux Terres Australes (1801–1804)', *Comité des Travaux historiques et scientifiques, Bulletin de Géographie historique et descriptive*, année 1906, pp. 24–34.

[Hérault, Curé], 'Texte et documents: La grande peur en Bourbonnais', *Notre Bourbonnais*, 6e série, no. 142, 38e année, 1962, 4e trimestre, pp. 191–2.

Hernandez Suárez, M., 'Breves biographifias actualizadas de personajes Canarios' in Torres, A. M. (ed.), *Historia General de Las Islas Canarias*, tomo vi, Edirca, Las Palmas, 1981, pp. 76–7.

Hervé, G., 'A la recherche d'un manuscrit: Les instructions anthropologiques de G. Cuvier pour le voyage du *Géographe* et du *Naturaliste* aux Terres Australes', *Revue de l'Ecole d'anthropologie de Paris*, 1910, pp. 289–302.

Higgins, L. W., 'The unusual sea-lions of Kangaroo Island', *Australian Natural History*, vol. 24, no. 5, winter 1993, pp. 30–7.

Holthuis, L. B., 'The scyllarid lobsters (Crustacea: Decapoda: Palinuridea) collected by F. Péron and C. A. Lesueur during the 1800–1804 expedition to Australia', *Zoologische Mededelingen* (Leiden), 70, 1996, pp. 261–70.

Huart, P. and Imbault-Huart, M. J., 'L'enseignement libre de la médecine à Paris au XIXe siècle', *Revue d'histoire des Sciences*, tome xxvii, no. 1, 1974, pp. 45–62.

Iredale, T. and Troughton, E., 'Order Pinnipedia', in 'A checklist of the mammals recorded from Australia', *Memoirs of the Australian Museum*, vol. 6, p. 89.

Jamin, J., 'Faibles sauvages … Corps indigènes corps indigents: Le désenchantement de François Péron', in Ville du Havre, *Mers Australes … Terres Australes: l'Expédition Baudin 1800–1804, Exposition 10 décembre 1987–6 janvier 1988*, Bibliothèque municipale du Havre, pp. 25–34.

—— 'Note sur le dynamomètre de Régnier', *Gradhiva*, no. 1, automne 1986, pp. 17–21.

Jangoux, M., 'L'expédition du Capitaine Baudin aux Terres Australes: Les observations zoologiques de François Péron pendant la première campagne (1801–1802)', *Annales du Muséum du Havre*, no. 73, mars 2005, pp. 1–35.

—— 'La première relâche du *Naturaliste* au Port Jackson', *Australian Journal of French Studies*, vol. xli, no. 2, 2004, pp. 126–51.

—— 'Les Astérides (Echinodermes) des Terres Australes ramenés par l'expédition Baudin (1800–1804): Catalogue commenté des dessins inédits de Charles-Alexandre Lesueur conservés au Muséum d'histoire naturelle du Havre', *Bulletin trimestriel de la Société géologique de Normandie et des Amis du Muséum du Havre*, tome lxxi, fascicule 4, 4e trimestre 1984, pp. 25–56.

—— 'Les echinodermes des mers d'Europe observés et figurés par Charles-Alexandre Lesueur', *Bulletin trimestriel de la Société géologique de Normandie et des Amis du Muséum du Havre*, tome lxxii, fascicules 1 & 2, année 1985, 1er & 2e trimestres 1985, pp. 15–23.

—— 'Les zoologistes et botanistes qui accompagnèrent le Capitaine Baudin aux Terres Australes', *Australian Journal of French Studies*, vol. xli, no. 2, 2004, pp. 55–78.

—— 'Vers les Terres Australes', in Morat, P., Aymonin, G. and Jolinon, J.-C. (eds), *L'herbier du monde: Cinq siècles d'aventures et de passions botaniques au Muséum national d'histoire naturelle*, Les Editions du Muséum, Les Arènes/L'iconoclaste, Paris, 2004, pp. 122–9.

Jennings, J. N., 'The coastal geomorphology of King Island, Bass Strait, in relation to the relative level of land and sea', *Records of the Queen Victoria Museum*, Launceston, N.S., no. 11, 1959, p. 4.

Jones, R., 'Images of natural man', in Bonnemains, J., Forsyth, E. and Smith, B. *Baudin in Australian Waters: The Artwork of the French Voyage of Discovery to the Southern Lands 1800–1804 With a Descriptive Catalogue of Drawings and Paintings of Australian Subjects by C.-A. Lesueur and N.-M. Petit from the Lesueur Collection at the Muséum d'Histoire Naturelle, Le Havre, France*, Oxford University Press, Melbourne, 1988, pp. 35–64.

Jouanin, C., 'Joséphine and the natural sciences', *Apollo Magazine*, July 1977, pp. 50–9.

—— 'Les émeus de l'expédition Baudin', *L'Oiseau et la Revue française d'Ornithologie*, no. 29, 1959, pp. 169–203.

—— 'Les premières tentatives d'acclimatation du cygne noir en France', *L'Oiseau et la Revue française d'Ornithologie*, no. 30, 1960, pp. 1–11.

Keraudren, P.-F., 'Nécrologie [François Péron]', *Le Moniteur*, jeudi 24 janvier 1811, p. 93.

Kinscherff, R., 'Die Mühlen am Speyer-und Woogbach', in Kinscherff, R., *Sandhase, Känichskinner, Freischärler: Heimatgeschichten aus der Pfälzischen verbandsgemeinde Dudenhofen*, Hans Lang, Verbandsbürgermeister, Dudenhofen, 1997, pp. 122–3.

Kramp, P. L., 'Synopsis of the Medusae of the world', *Journal of the Marine Biological Association of the United Kingdom*, vol. 40, pp. 1–469.

Kunth, R., 'Richard, Louis Claude Marie', in Michaud, L. G. (ed.), *Biographie universelle*, Paris, 1824, tome xxxvii, pp. 561–70.

Lacépède, E. de, 'Mémoire sur plusieurs animaux de la Nouvelle-Hollande dont la description n'a pas encore été publiée', *Annales du Muséum national d'histoire naturelle*, tome 4, 1804, pp. 184–211.

Laissus, Y., 'Les voyageurs naturalistes du Jardin du roi et du Muséum d'histoire naturelle: Essai de portrait-robot', *Revue d'histoire des sciences*, tome 34, 1981, pp. 259–317.

—— 'Un naturaliste exemplaire, ami de Charles-Alexandre Lesueur: François Péron (1775–1810)', *Annales du Muséum du Havre*, fascicule no. 12, juin 1978, pp. 1–8.

Lamarck, J.-B. de, 'Considérations sur quelques faits applicables à la théorie du globe, observés par M. Péron dans son voyage aux Terres Australes, et sur quelques questions géologiques qui naissent de la connaissance de ces faits', *Annales du Muséum national d'histoire naturelle*, tome 5, 1805, pp. 26–52.

—— 'Sur une nouvelle espèce de Trigonie, et sur une nouvelle huître, découvertes dans le voyage du capitaine Baudin', *Annales du Muséum national d'histoire naturelle*, tome 4, 1804, pp. 351–59, pl. 67.

Lamarck, J.-B. de, and Guyton, L.-B., 'Rapport sur le mémoire de M. Péron sur les observations de la température de la mer', *Procès-verbaux des séances de l'Académie, Classe des Sciences physiques et mathématiques*, tome iii, séance du 11 septembre 1804, pp. 133–8.

Laugier, A., 'Examen chimique des matières salines contenues dans la liqueur que l'on obtient, lorsqu'on fait fondre des Méduses en les abandonnant à une décomposition spontanée', *Annales du Muséum national d'histoire naturelle*, 1810, tome 16, p. 341–9.

Lennier, G., 'Note sur l'expédition française des Terres Australes pendant les années 1802 à 1804', *Bulletin de la Société zoologique de France*, tome 8, 1883, pp. 1–8.

Lentle, R. G. et al., 'Differences in renal and alimentary water conservation account for differences in the distribution of tammar and parma wallabies on Kawau Island, New Zealand', *Australian Journal of Zoology*, vol. 51, issue 4, 10 November 2003, pp. 371–85.

Lentz, T., 'La Révolution à Thionville (1789–1799)', *Le Pays Lorrain*, 87e année, vol. 71, no. 1, janvier–mars 1990, pp. 23–31.

Lesson, R. P., 'Description de quelques reptiles nouveaux ou peu connus' (1829), in Duperrey, L. I. (ed.), *Voyage autour du monde, exécuté par ordre du Roi, sur la corvette de Sa Majesté*, La Coquille, *pendant les années 1822, 1823, 1824 et 1825*, Arthus Bertrand, Paris, 1826–38, tome 2, Zoologie (1), pp. 34–65, pl. 7, fig. 2.

Lesueur, C.-A., 'Mémoire sur quelques nouvelles espèces d'animaux Mollusques et Radiaires, recueillis dans la Méditerranée, près de Nice', *Journal de physique, de chimie, d'histoire naturelle et des arts*, vol. 77, 1813, pp. 119–24 [summarised in *Nouveau bulletin des Sciences, par la Société philomathique*, Paris, Juin 1813, no. 69, pp. 281–5].

Lombard-Jourdan, A., 'François Péron et Charles Lesueur à Timor: Une chasse au crocodile en 1803', *Archipel*, no. 54, 1997, pp. 81–121.

Louis, A. J. B., 'Science—médicine: Mémoires de la Société médicale d'émulation de Paris [Eloge de François Péron]', *Le Moniteur universel*, 7 June 1812, p. 622.

Ly-Tio-Fane, M., 'Contacts between Schönbrunn and the Jardin du Roi at Isle de France (Mauritius) in the 18th century: An episode in the career of Nicolas Thomas Baudin', *Mitteilungen des Österreichischen Staatsarchivs*, vol. 35, 1982, pp. 85–109.

Macmillan, D. S., 'Paterson, William (1755–1810)', in Pike, D. (ed.), *Australian Dictionary of Biography*, vol. 2, pp. 317–19.

Magdeburgische Zeitung [articles on the arrival of prisoners of war], no. 94, 9 August, 1794, p. 1; no. 99, 21 August 1794, p. 1; & no. 122, 14 October 1794, p. 1.

Malte-Brun, C., 'Mémoire sur la découverte de la côte sud-ouest de la Nouvelle-Hollande, ou de la Terre Flinders, de la Terre Napoléon, et de la Terre Grant', *Les Annales des Voyages, de la Géographie et de l'Histoire; ou collection des voyages nouveaux les plus estimés, traduits de toutes les Langues Européennes: des relations originales, inédites, communiquées par des voyageurs Français et Étrangers*, Chez F. Buisson, Paris, tome xxiv, 1814, pp. 273–96.

Masson, F., 'L'impératrice Joséphine et l'acclimatation à Malmaison', *Bulletin de la Société nationale d'acclimatation de France*, soixantième année, 1913, pp. 230–48.

Maury, A., 'Les œuvres mineurs de C.-A. Lesueur, voyageur et peintre naturaliste havrais (1778–1846): du Havre à Nice par la Vallée du Rhône', *Revues des Sociétés Savantes de Haute-Normandie*, no. 4, Octobre 1956, pp. 7–14.

McGeal, C., 'Homeward bound [Saartjie Baartman]', *Guardian Weekly*, 28 February – 6 March 2002, p. 26.

Milne-Edwards, A. and Oustalet, E., 'Note sur l'Emeu noir (*Dromaeus ater* V.) de l'île Decrès (Australie)', *Bulletin du Muséum d'histoire naturelle*, 5, 1899, pp. 206–14.

—— 'Notice sur quelques espèces d'oiseaux actuellement éteintes qui se trouvent représentées dans les collections du Muséum d'histoire naturelle, *Volume commémoratif du Centenaire de la fondation du Muséum d'histoire naturelle*, 1893, pp. 246–52, plate 5.

Mitton, F., 'Généralités sur les églises de la région de Tronçais: Eglise Saint-Martin de Cérilly', *Bulletin de la Société d'Emulation du Bourbonnais*, no. 9–10, September–October 1930, pp. 343–58.

Montaiglon, A. de, 'Description d'un salon peint par François Boucher', *Revue universelle des arts*, tome 4, 1856, pp. 120–2.

Nagapen, A., 'Dr Nils Bergsten érudit mémorialiste et directeur de clinique recherche', *La Gazette des Iles*, juin 1987, pp. 21–3.

Olivier, E., 'Faune de l'Allier', *Bulletin de la Société d'Émulation du Bourbonnais*, 1882, tome XVI, pp. 93–163.

Outram, D., 'The ordeal of vocation: The Paris Academy of Sciences and the Terror, 1793–95', *History of Science*, vol. 21, part 3, no. 53, September 1983, pp. 251–73.

Pelte, S., 'Bory de St Vincent, Geneviève Jean Baptiste (1778–1846)', *Dictionnaire de Biographie mauricienne*, no. 1, février 1941, pp. 5–6.

Perchat, J., 'Où était l'étable de Jean-Gilbert Bonnet?', *Bulletin de l'Association François Péron*, no. 8, juillet 2003, pp. 11–13.

Péron, F., 'Discours préliminaire d'un travail sur les Méduses', *Procès-verbaux des séances de l'Académie, Classe des Sciences physiques et mathématiques*, tome iv, séances du 21 novembre 1808, 28 novembre 1808 et 19 décembre 1808, pp. 136, 140, 147.

—— 'Inventaire général de tous les objets relatifs à l'histoire de l'homme recueillis pendant le cours de l'expédition ou remis à M. Péron, naturaliste zoologiste du Gouvernement dans cette expédition, et présentés par M. Geoffroy et lui à Sa Majesté l'Impératrice Joséphine le 9 prairial an XII [29 May 1804]' in Copans, J. and Jamin, J. (eds), *Aux origines de l'anthropologie française: Les Mémoires de la Société des Observateurs de l'Homme en l'an VIII*, Le Sycomore, Paris, 1978, pp. 195–203.

—— 'Mémoire sur le nouveau genre *Pyrosoma*', *Annales du Muséum national d'Histoire naturelle*, tome 4, an XII (1804), pp. 437–46, planche 72.

—— 'Mémoire sur les établissements anglais à la Nouvelle Hollande, à la Terre de Diemen et dans les archipels du grand océan Pacifique …', présentation, édition et notes de Roger Martin, transcription du manuscrit avec le concours de Jacqueline Bonnemains, préface de Joël Eymeret, *Revue de l'Institut Napoléon*, no. 176, 1998, I, pp. 1–187.

—— 'Mémoire sur quelques faits zoologiques applicables à la théorie du globe, lu à la Classe des Sciences physiques et mathématiques de l'Institut national (Séance du 30 vendémiaire an XIII)', *Journal de physique, de chimie, d'histoire naturelle et des arts*, vol. 59, 1804, pp. 463–80, planches i, ii.

—— 'Notice d'un mémoire sur les animaux observés pendant la traversée de Timor au Cap Sud de la Terre de Van Diemen', *Bulletin des sciences de la Société philomatique*, no. xi, 8e année, tome iii, no. 95, pluviôse an 13 [December 1804 – January 1805], pp. 269–70.

—— 'Notice sur quelques applications utiles des observations météorologiques à l'hygiène navale', *Journal de physique, de chimie, d'histoire naturelle et des arts*, vol. 67, 1808, pp. 29–43.

—— 'Observations sur la dyssenterie des pays chauds et sur l'usage du bétel', *Journal de physique, de chimie, d'histoire naturelle et des arts*, vol. 59, 1804, pp. 290–9.

—— 'Réponse de M. Péron, naturaliste de l'expédition de découvertes aux Terres Australes aux observations critiques de M. Dumont sur le tablier des femmes Hottentotes', *Journal de physique, de chimie et d'histoire naturelle*, tome lxi, 1805, pp. 210–17.

—— 'Sur la température de la mer soit à sa surface, soit à diverses profondeurs', *Annales du Muséum national d'histoire naturelle*, tome 5, an XIII (1804), pp. 123–48 [English translation: 'Fragment from Peron, with notices from other voyagers, on the Temperature of the Sea, at great depths, far from Land', *American Journal of Science*, vol. xvii, 1830, pp. 295–9].

Péron, F. and Lesueur, C.-A., 'Des caractères génériques et spécifiques de toutes les espèces de Méduses connues jusqu'à ce jour', *Annales du Muséum national d'histoire naturelle*, tome 14, 1809, pp. 325–66.

—— 'Histoire de la famille des Molluques Ptéropodes', *Annales du Muséum national d'histoire naturelle*, tome 15, 1810, pp. 57–69, 2 planches.

—— 'Histoire du genre Firole: Firola', *Annales du Muséum national d'histoire naturelle*, tome 15, 1810, pp. 76–82.

—— 'Histoire générale et particulière de tous les animaux qui composent la famille des Méduses', *Annales du Muséum national d'histoire naturelle*, tome 14, 1809, pp. 218–28.

—— 'La conservation des diverses espèces d'animation dans l'alcool', *Journal de physique de chimie, d'histoire naturelle et des arts*, vol. 71, octobre 1810, pp. 265–88.

—— 'Notice sur l'habitation des animaux marins', *Annales du Muséum national d'histoire naturelle*, tome 15, 1810, pp. 287–92.

—— 'Notice sur l'habitation des phoques', *Annales du Muséum national d'histoire naturelle*, tome 15, 1810, pp. 293–300.

—— 'Observations sur le tablier des femmes Hottentotes, avec une note sur l'expédition française aux Terres Australes, et une étude critique sur la stéatopygie et le tablier des femmes Boschimanes, par le Dr Raphaël Blanchard', *Bulletin de la Société zoologique de France*, vol. 8, 1883, pp. 15–33.

—— 'Sur les Méduses du genre Equorée', *Annales du Muséum national d'histoire naturelle*, tome 15, 1810, pp. 41–56.

—— 'Tableau des caractères génériques et spécifiques de toutes les espèces de Méduses connues jusqu'à ce jour', *Annales du Muséum national d'histoire naturelle*, tome 14, 1809 [1810], pp. 325–66.

Peters, E. W., 'Belagern und belagert werdern: Landeshaupstadt Magdeburg: Stadtplanungsamt Magdeburg', in Ulrrich, S. (ed.) *Magdeburger Kasernen*, vol. 81, 2002, pp. 49–50.

Peyerimhoff, M. de, 'Matériaux pour la faune entomologique du Bourbonnais', *Bulletin de la société d'émulation du Bourbonnais*, tome XV, 1879, pp. 293–566.

Pilsudski, J., 'La psychologie du prisonnier', *Revue pénitentiare de Pologne*, vol. iv, no. 1–2, 1929, pp. 3–22 [English translation, pp. 23–41].

Playford, P. E., 'Geology of the Shark Bay area, Western Australia', in Berry, P. F., Bradshaw, S. D. and Wilson, B. R., *Research in Shark Bay: Report of the France-Australe Bicentenary Expedition Committee*, Western Australian Museum, Perth, 1990, pp. 13–31.

Plomley, N. J. B., Cornell, C. and Banks, M., 'François Péron's natural history of Maria Island, Tasmania', *Records of the Queen Victoria Museum* (Launceston), no. 99, 1990, pp. 1–50.

Poole, W. E., Wood, J. T. and Simms, N. G., 'Distribution of the Tammar, *Macropus eugenii*, and the relationships of populations as determined by cranial morphometrics', *Wildlife Research*, no. 18, 1991, pp. 625–39.

Regnard, L. N., 'Stadtmann, Jean Frédéric (1762–1807)', *Dictionnaire de Biographie mauricienne*, no. 21, octobre 1947, pp. 652–3.

Risso, A.(?) 'Résumé des travaux faits par MM. Péron et Lesueur sur les côtes de la Méditerranée', *Nouveau bulletin des Sciences, par la Société philomathique, Paris*, tome iii, 1813, pp. 281–5.

Rousseau, J.-J., 'Considérations sur le Gouvernement de Pologne et sur sa Réformation projetée' (section XII, 'Système militaire'), in J.-J. Rousseau, *Œuvres complètes*, tome iii, Gallimard-Pléiade, Paris, 1964, p. 1014.

Roux, C., 'Les requins des côtes australiennes observés par Péron et Lesueur', *Bulletin trimestriel de la Société géologique de Normandie et des Amis du Muséum du Havre*, tome 78, fascicule 3, année 1991, 3e trimestre, pp. 33–52.

Roux, C. and Bonnemains, J., 'Les poissons du "Voyage de découvertes aux Terres Australes" (1800–1804) étudiés par F. Péron et C.-A. Lesueur: Collection iconographique des dessins de C.-A. Lesueur du Muséum d'histoire naturelle du Havre', *Bulletin trimestriel de la Société géologique de Normandie et des Amis du Muséum du Havre*, tome lxxi, fascicule 1, année 1984, 1er trimestre, pp. 11–90; fascicule 2–3, pp. 31–85; 2e partie, tome lxxi, fascicule 2 & 3, année 1984, 2e et 3e trimestres, pp. 31–85.

Roux-Estève, R., 'Liste des amphibiens et reptiles des collections du Muséum national d'histoire naturelle de Paris, récoltés par Lesueur (1778–1846)', *Bulletin trimestriel de la Société géologique de Normandie et des Amis du Muséum du Havre*, tome lxvi, fascicule 3, année 1979, 3e trimestre, pp. 25–9.

Sankey, M., 'François-Auguste Péron: Le mythe de l'homme sauvage et l'écriture de la science', *Cahiers de sociologie économique et culturelle*, no. 9, juin 1988, pp. 37–46.

Southwood, J. and Simpson, D., 'Baudin's doctors: French medical scientists in Australian waters, 1801–1803', *Australian Journal of French Studies*, vol. xli, no. 2, 2004, pp. 152–64.

Stein, W. A., 'Revolutionäre Schulpolitik und schulische Stabilität im Arrondissement Kaiserslautern' in *Jahrbuch zur Geschichte von Stadt und Landkreis Kaiserslautern*, vol. 16/17, 1978–79, pp. 171–206.

Stocking, G. W., 'French anthropology in 1800', *Isis*, vol. 55, part 2, no. 180, 1964, pp. 134–50.

Topsent, E., 'Eponges de Lamarck conservées au Muséum de Paris', *Archives du Muséum national d'histoire naturelle*, vol. 6, no. 5, 1930, pp. 1–56.

Toussaint, A., 'Bergsten, Nils (1769–1852)', *Dictionnaire de Biographie mauricienne*, no. 19, juin 1946, p. 570.

—— 'Milbert, Jacques Gérard (1766–1840)', *Dictionnaire de Biographie mauricienne*, no. 12, décembre 1943, p. 367.

Trompf, G. W., 'Crocodillians and humans: Mythology, religion, art and literature', in Ross, C. A. and Garnett, S., *Crocodiles and Alligators*, Golden Press, Sydney, 1989, pp. 156–71.

[V., F. C.], 'Rapport sur les Notices sur l'habitation des animaux marins, et notice sur l'habitation des phoques par MM Péron et Lesueur', *Nouveau bulletin des Sciences, par la Société philomathique, Paris*, no. 36, tome ii, 3e année, septembre 1810, pp. 140–1.

Vallance, T. G., 'Origins of Australian geology', *Proceedings of the Linnean Society of New South Wales*, vol. 100, part 1, no. 441, August 1975, pp. 13–43.

Verteuil, J., 'Garnisons moulinoises et régiments bourbonnais', *Société d'Emulation du Bourbonnais*, tome lxix, 1999, 2e trimestre, pp. 435–52.

Vinson, J., 'Garnier, Michel (1753–c. 1820)', *Dictionnaire de Biographie mauricienne*, no. 14, juillet 1944, pp. 428–9.

Wakefield, N. A. and Waterhouse, R. M., 'Some revision in Antechinus (Marsupialia)', *Victorian Naturalist*, vol. 80, 1963, pp. 124–219.

Weiner, D. B., 'French doctors face war 1792–1815', in Warner, C. K. (ed.), *From the Ancien Régime to the Popular Front: Essays in the History of Modern France in Honor of Shepard B. Clough*, Columbia University Press, New York, 1969, pp. 51–73.

Wiehle, M., '1525–2000: Vierhundertfünfundsiebzig Jahre Stadtbibliothek Magdeburg', in Brditschke, I. et al., *Die Stadtbibliothek Magdeburg im Wandel der Zeiten 1525–2000*, Herausgegeben anlässlich des 475 Jubiläums der Stadtbibliothek Magdeburg am 6 November 2000, Magdeburg, 2000, pp. 6–11.

Botanical Index

Includes common, valid scientific, family and manuscript names, and synonyms

Zoological Index

Includes common, valid scientific, family and manuscript names, and synonyms

Acalyptophis peronii, 191
Acanthaluteres peroni, 7
Acasta glans, 159
Actina tenebrosa, 165
Aequorea, 228; *A. pleuronata*, 200; *A. purpurea*, 200
Agama barbata, 143
Aglaura hemistoma, 228
Alabes rufus, 278
Alcyonium, 170, 231; *A. putridosum*, 178
Alectis indicus, 267
Alpheidae, 170
Amphibolurus decresii, 164
Amphipholis squamata, 266
Anapella cycladea, 111
Anas querquedula, 89
Antechinus minimus, 120
Anthothoe abocincta, 165
ants, 81, 172
Arachnids, 239
Arca pistachia, 96, 278; *A. semi-torta*, 269
Archaster angulatus, 86, 96; *A. typicus*, 96
Argia, 56
Argyropelecus olfersi, 261
Arthropoda, 238–9
Asterias obtusangula, 86

Asteroidea, 238–9
Austrelaps superbus, 159
Avicula, 86; *A. virens*, 86

Balistes, 91
Balistoides viridescenes, 164
Balanus roseus, 170
Barbatia pistachia, 96, 278
barnacles, 239; acorn, 159, 170; goose, 77
bêches-de-mer, 193, 239
beetles, 3, 114, 146, 213; blister, 199; fiddler, 142
Berenix thalassina, 200
beroes, 64, 86, 127, 238
birds: albatrosses, 105; Australian raven, 279; black swans, 6, 106, 114; blue wrens, 106, 111; boobies, 89, 106; bronzewing pigeon, 279; Cape rails, 208; cassowaries, xii, 158; cormorants, 89, 106, 172; dodo, 8, 162; doves, 172; eagles, 17; emus, 6, 159, 162–3, 183, 200, 281; fantail, 171; finches, 172; fire-tail, 121; flycatchers, 89, 279; garganey, 89; gulls, 89, 105, 172, 279; magpies, 89; orioles, 17; ostriches, 208; oystercatchers, 279; parakeets, 142; parrots, 106; pelicans, 89, 105, 127, 172, 279; penguin, 172; petrels, 89, 105, 279; rosella, 142; sea eagles, 89, 279; southern boobook, 279; superb fairy wren, 279;

Index

THE MIEGUNYAH PRESS

This book was designed by Sandra Nobes
The text was typeset by Syarikat Seng Teik Sdn. Bhd., Malaysia
The text was set in 11 point Bembo with 14 points of leading
The text is printed on 100 gm Woodfree Stock

This book was edited by Cathryn Game

THE
MIEGUNYAH
PRESS